The People and the Books

THE
PEOPLE
AND THE
BOOKS

18 Classics of
Jewish Literature

A D A M   K I R S C H

W. W. NORTON & COMPANY
Independent Publishers Since 1923
NEW YORK   LONDON

For information about permission to reproduce selections from this book,
write to Permissions, W. W. Norton & Company, Inc.,
500 Fifth Avenue, New York, NY 10110

For information about special discounts for bulk purchases, please contact
W. W. Norton Special Sales at specialsales@wwnorton.com or 800-233-4830

Manufacturing by Quad Graphics Fairfield
Book design by Lovedog Studio
Production manager: Julia Druskin

ISBN 978-0-393-24176-1

W. W. Norton & Company, Inc.
500 Fifth Avenue, New York, N.Y. 10110
www.wwnorton.com

W. W. Norton & Company Ltd.
15 Carlisle Street, London W1D 3BS

1 2 3 4 5 6 7 8 9 0

TO MY TEACHERS

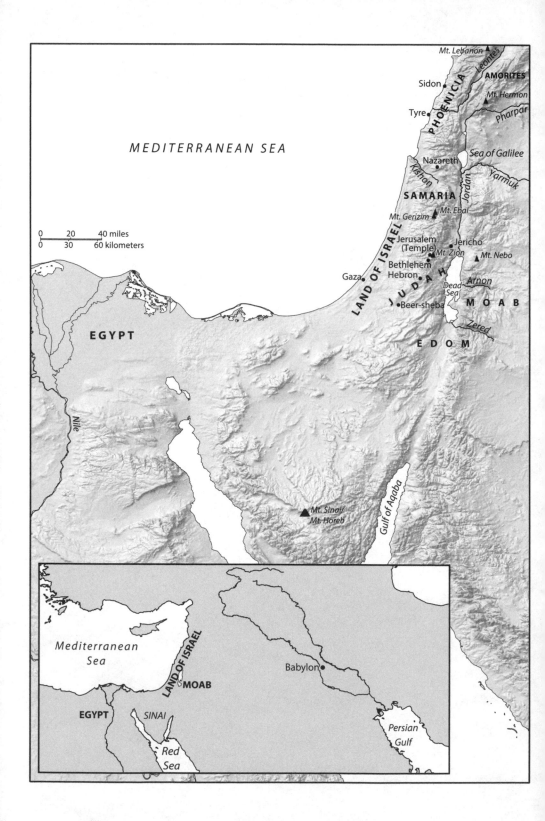

MEDITERRANEAN SEA

Mt. Lebanon

AMORITES

Sidon

PHOENICIA

Mt. Hermon

Tyre

Pharpar

Nazareth

Sea of Galilee

Kishon

Yarmuk

SAMARIA

Jordan

Mt. Gerizim   Mt. Ebal

LAND OF ISRAEL

Jerusalem
(Temple)   Jericho

Mt. Zion   Mt. Nebo

Bethlehem
Hebron

J U D A H

Gaza

Dead
Sea

Arnon

M O A B

Beer-sheba

Zered

E D O M

0   20   40 miles
0   30   60 kilometers

EGYPT

Nile

Gulf of Aqaba

Mt. Sinai/
Mt. Horeb

Mediterranean
Sea

LAND OF ISRAEL

MOAB

Babylon

EGYPT

SINAI

Persian
Gulf

Red
Sea

Contents

Preface

THE PHRASE "PEOPLE OF THE BOOK" DOES NOT ORIG-
inate in Judaism. It is, rather, an Islamic title, used in the Koran to
designate both Jews and Christians—peoples who possess their own
revelations from God in the form of holy scripture. Followers of these
faiths were accorded an intermediate place in Islamic society, not fully
equal to Muslims but better off than outright pagans. Jews, however,
have embraced "the People of the Book" as a peculiarly fitting description, even a title of honor—as though Jewish culture has a special
affinity for books, as though reading and writing are in some sense
constitutive of Jewish identity.

And it is true that for most of Jewish history, books were not just
one element in Jewish culture; they were the core of that culture, the
binding force that sustained a civilization. To study the history of
most peoples is to learn about wars and empires, military heroes and
political reformers, great buildings and beautiful artworks. The Jews,
too, once had their share of these worldly achievements. The Bible is a
record of Israel's generals and kings, and of monuments like the Jerusalem Temple. But in the year 70 CE the Temple was destroyed by a
Roman army, and the country of Judea was abolished. For the next
nineteen centuries, until the founding of the State of Israel in 1948,

the history of Judaism would not be told primarily in political terms. It would be, instead, a history of books.

The canonical books at the heart of Jewish religion are the Bible and the Talmud. These are the texts that have taught many generations of Jews their religious duties and their conception of God. They have also been the foundation of an unbroken tradition of commentary and codification, which is responsible for some of the greatest monuments of Jewish creativity—from the Talmudic commentary of Rashi, the medieval French rabbi, to the *Shulchan Aruch*, the digest of laws that governs Orthodox Jewish practice to this day. In the map of Jewish writing, the law and its commentaries are the central continent. To master them, however, requires a lifelong training available to few people, usually the most devout; and so they appear only incidentally in the pages that follow.

What remains is a literature whose richness and variety testify to the great length and breadth of Jewish history. The books explored in the following pages were written over a span of more than twenty-five hundred years, in Hebrew, Aramaic, Greek, Latin, Arabic, Yiddish, and German. (I have read and cited them in English; the translations I use can be found in the selected bibliographies at the end of each chapter. I've followed these sources for the spelling of proper names, which can often vary in translation.) They include fiction and history, philosophy and memoir, mystical fables and moral aphorisms. Some of them are very famous, familiar to anyone who reads the Bible, while others are known primarily to historians and specialists. Taken together, however, they offer a panoramic portrait of Jewish thought and experience over the centuries. My goal in *The People and the Books* has been to open up these texts to the interested reader—to show what they contain, how and why they were written, and what they can tell us about Judaism and Jewishness.

Perhaps the most striking thing that emerges from reading these books together is the remarkable continuity of Jewish thought, despite all the catastrophes and ruptures of Jewish history. From the biblical book of Deuteronomy in the seventh century BCE to the works of the Yiddish master Sholem Aleichem in the twentieth century CE, a few subjects preoccupy every kind of Jewish writer. They might be reduced to four central elements: God, the Torah, the Land of Israel, and the Jewish people. These subjects have been understood in dramatically different ways at different times, but the questions they raise keep coming back in all possible permutations. Indeed, for Judaism, God, Torah, land, and people are inseparable, so that to ask about one is to ask about the others.

Jewish writers have always wondered, for instance, about what kind of being God is. Is he the personal God who made a covenant with Abraham and Moses, or the impersonal God who created the cosmos and the laws of nature? If he is the latter, then how should we understand the Torah, with its anthropomorphic language and its often arbitrary-seeming laws? These questions have especially troubled Jews who lived at the intersection of Jewish tradition with a broader philosophical culture. That is why Philo, living in Roman Egypt in the first century CE, asked so many of the same questions as Maimonides, who lived in Muslim Egypt in the twelfth century CE. Both of them, as well as Yehuda Halevi in the twelfth century and Spinoza in the seventeenth, wondered about the Jewish rite of circumcision, which seemed so odd to many non-Jews. What was the reason for this commandment? Was it purely arbitrary, or did it encode some medical wisdom or ethical imperative or spiritual truth? And did it need some such meaning to justify its existence?

Similar questions could be asked about many Jewish laws, including those that have specific application to the Land of Israel. In the book of Genesis, God promised that land to Abraham and his descendants forever. Why, then, did God allow the Jews to lose their land and their Temple, where so many crucial rituals were enacted? And what remains of Judaism when these focal points are gone? These questions are already foreshadowed in the book of Deuteronomy in the seventh century BCE. Nearly a thousand years later, after the loss of the Second Temple, a new attempt to answer them led to the creation of rabbinic Judaism, whose ethos is so beautifully captured in *Pirkei Avot*, a collection of aphorisms about Jewish ethical ideals. Eight hundred years after that, the dialogue known as the *Kuzari* asked what the Land meant to the Jews, long after most of them had left it behind. And another eight hundred years after that, Theodor Herzl, an assimilated and secular man who knew very little about Judaism, argued—to momentous effect—that the Land of Israel was still the only salvation for the Jewish people.

For much of Jewish history, however, the Land remained an object of pious longing rather than an actual possibility. Indeed, even before the Jewish War in 66–70 CE, which Josephus writes about with such ambivalent feelings, much of Jewish life was led in Diaspora, which posed its own existential challenges. The book of Esther, which was most likely written in Persia during the fourth century BCE, is perhaps the earliest Jewish book about what it means to live as a minority in a potentially hostile society. It offers perpetually relevant lessons about the importance for Jewish survival of both luck and political skill. The same dynamics reappear five hundred years later in Philo's account of the Jews' precarious position in Alexandria, and fifteen hundred years after that in Glückel of Hameln's offhand observations about the insecurity of the Jews of Hamburg. By the time Sholem Aleichem wrote his Tevye stories around the year 1900, the Jewish heartland of eastern Europe had come to seem like a tightening noose, as the Jews' traditional strategies of survival began to fail.

Still, it is crucial not to read Jewish history merely as a series of persecutions and expulsions. Even as external threats to Jewish security appear in the following pages, so too do remarkable expressions of Jewish creativity and agency. Indeed, the transformation of worldly challenges into imaginative possibilities is one of the great achievements of Jewish mysticism. The *Zohar*, which was written in thirteenth-century Spain (but which most readers attributed to a second-century Palestinian sage), offered a richly inventive worldview that put the individual Jew—his prayers, deeds, and intentions—at the center of a cosmic battle of good against evil. Five hundred years later, in Ukraine, the Hasidic rabbi Nachman of Bratslav used this cosmology as the basis for his own radically inventive fairy tales, parables of the possibility of redemption in a fallen world. Much of the mythology found in such books might appear strange and even heretical today, but for hundreds of years it was an integral part of what Judaism meant.

This is just one example of how reading the Jewish past can help us to escape present-mindedness. In the early twenty-first century, the Jewish world is still primarily shaped by the epochal events of the twentieth: the mass immigration of Jews to America, the founding of the State of Israel, and above all the Holocaust. It can be hard to recognize that the very questions raised by these events—questions about assimilation, nationhood, and providence—are not new in Jewish history but have been part of it from the very beginning. That is why this book concludes around 1914, before those questions took their current, inescapable forms and predetermined polarities. My hope is that readers of *The People and the Books* will find what I have found in writing it: a richer and freer sense of what Judaism has been and can be.

The People and the Books:
A Timeline

This timeline does not include all the major events in Jewish history. Rather, it is intended to provide some essential background for understanding the texts discussed in *The People and the Books*. Many of the dates from the ancient period are speculative; indeed, the existence of figures like Abraham and Moses, and events like the Exodus from Egypt, are known only from the Bible and cannot be independently corroborated. For such events, I have given the estimates of modern scholarship rather than following traditional Jewish authorities, who often give different dates.

CA. 2000–1700 BCE

The patriarchs, Abraham, Isaac, and Jacob, receive covenants from God and settle in the Land of Israel. Famine compels the Children of Israel to go to Egypt, where they are enslaved by Pharaoh.

CA. 1250 BCE

Moses leads the Israelites out of Egypt in the Exodus and receives the Torah from God on Mount Sinai. After forty years of wandering in the desert, the Israelites enter Canaan, their Promised Land. The **book of Deuteronomy** narrates the end of their wanderings, including Moses's death, and sets the terms for the Israelites' possession of the Land.

CA. 1000 BCE

King Solomon builds the first Temple in Jerusalem, as the center of Jewish life and worship.

927–722 BCE

The Israelite kingdom is divided between Israel in the north and Judah in the south. In 722, the Assyrian Empire conquers Israel and deports its people, who thenceforth become known as the Ten Lost Tribes.

622 BCE

During the reign of King Josiah, the **book of Deuteronomy** is discovered in the Temple, leading to a reform of Israelite worship.

597–586 BCE

The Babylonian Empire conquers the Kingdom of Judah and exiles the Jewish ruling class to Babylon. When Jerusalem rebels, the city is conquered a second time and destroyed, along with the Temple.

538 BCE

After the Persian Empire conquers the Babylonians, King Cyrus allows a group of Jewish exiles to return to Jerusalem. They are followed by further waves of Jewish returnees over the next century, although a sizable Jewish community remains in Babylon.

515 BCE

The Second Temple is inaugurated in Jerusalem.

486–465 BCE

Reign of the Persian king Xerxes. The events of the **book of Esther** are set at his court, although the book itself probably dates from the fourth century BCE.

332 BCE

Alexander the Great conquers the Persian Empire and institutes Greek rule in Judea.

167 BCE

Judah Maccabee leads the Hasmonean revolt against Greek rule and restores an independent Jewish state for the first time in more than four hundred years.

63 BCE

The Roman general Pompey intervenes in a Jewish civil war, conquers Jerusalem, and brings Judea under the control of the Roman Empire as a client state.

15 BCE–45 CE

Philo of Alexandria lives in Egypt and writes his *Exposition of the Laws*, a philosophical gloss on the Torah, as well as many other works. He witnesses the massacre of Alexandrian Jews in 38 CE.

66–70 CE

Judea rises in revolt against the Roman Empire, but the rebellion is crushed by Roman armies under the future emperors Vespasian and Titus. The Second Temple is destroyed, never to be rebuilt, marking a permanent change in the nature of Judaism. **Flavius Josephus**, a Jewish general taken prisoner by the Romans, participates in the revolt and then chronicles it in his book *The Jewish War*.

132–135

A second Jewish rebellion, led by Bar Kochba, is put down by the Romans with great bloodshed. The emperor Hadrian erases Judea from the map and renames the country Palestine—the name it would bear for the next eighteen hundred years.

200–500

In a process lasting many generations, the Oral Law is codified as the Mishnah; later legal debates and commentaries are incorporated to create the Talmud. *Pirkei Avot*, a collection of maxims by the Talmudic sages, is compiled around 250 CE.

900–1200

Jewish culture flourishes in Islamic Spain, despite legal barriers and repeated persecutions.

1096

The Jews of the Rhineland are massacred in large numbers by Crusaders.

CA. 1075–1141

The poet **Yehuda Halevi** lives in Spain, departing at the end of his life for Egypt and Palestine. In his last decade he writes the *Kuzari*, a philosophical defense of Judaism.

CA. 1165

Benjamin of Tudela sets out from Spain to tour the Jewish world of the Mediterranean and the Middle East, recording what he finds in his *Itinerary*.

1138–1204

Moses Maimonides is born in Spain and lives most of his adult life in Egypt. After establishing himself as one of the greatest masters of Jewish law, in the 1180s he writes *The Guide of the Perplexed*, in which he attempts to reconcile the Torah with the truths of philosophy.

CA. 1290

The *Zohar*, a mystical exegesis of the Torah and the central work of Kabbalah, begins to circulate in Spain. **Moses de León**, its probable author, claims to be editing a manuscript written by an early Talmudic sage.

1391–1492

A century of persecution and forced conversion of Jews in Spain culminates in the expulsion of Spain's entire Jewish population. Portugal expels its Jews five years later.

CA. 1590

The first publication of the *Tsenerene*, a Yiddish paraphrase of the Bible intended primarily for use by Jewish women.

1632–1677

Baruch Spinoza, a descendant of Portuguese Jews, is born in Amsterdam. Excommunicated from the Jewish congregation in 1656 for his heretical opinions, he works as a lens-grinder and composes radical philosophical works, including the *Theological-Political Treatise* (1670).

1646–1724

Glückel of Hameln lives, works, and raises a family in Germany. She records her life in her Yiddish-language *Memoirs*, the first autobiography by a Jewish woman.

1729–1786

Moses Mendelssohn emerges from a pious Jewish background to become one of the foremost philosophers of the German Enlightenment, testing the limits of Jewish acceptance in Gentile society. His book *Jerusalem* (1783) argues for freedom of religion, while urging Jews to continue to obey Jewish law.

CA. 1740

Hasidism, a charismatic revival movement, begins to spread in eastern Europe under the leadership of the Baal Shem Tov.

CA. 1753–1800

Solomon Maimon is born in Lithuania and raised in a traditional Jewish home. His *Autobiography* (1792–93) records his struggles to escape his background and establish himself as a secular philosopher in Germany.

1772–1810

Nachman of Bratslav, a great-grandson of the Baal Shem Tov, leads a small group of Hasidim in Ukraine. His teachings often take the form of stories, which are published after his death as his *Tales* (1816).

1860–1904

Theodor Herzl, a Viennese playwright and journalist, founds the Zionist movement with the publication of his manifesto *The Jewish State* in 1896. In *Old New Land* (1902), Herzl turns to fiction to imagine the development of a new Jewish society in Palestine.

1859–1916

Sholem Aleichem becomes the most popular Yiddish writer in the world. His stories about **Tevye the Dairyman**, published between 1895 and 1915, depict an archetypal Jewish everyman threatened by the dislocations of the modern age.

1939–1945

During World War II, six million Jews are murdered in the Holocaust.

1948

The State of Israel is founded, restoring Jewish sovereignty to the Land of Israel for the first time in almost nineteen hundred years.

The People and the Books

The Blessing and the Curse

The Book of Deuteronomy

Deuteronomy is the fifth and last book of the Torah—the Five Books of Moses that stand at the heart of Jewish scripture—and it marks a crucial turning point. While earlier biblical books like Genesis and Exodus deal with mythical and miraculous stories—Adam and Eve, the parting of the Red Sea—Deuteronomy is a book devoted to law and history. Above all, it is concerned with the Israelites' relationship to the Land of Israel, which will become a major subject of the later books of the Bible and of Jewish history down to our own day. Most of Deuteronomy records the long speech delivered by Moses to the Israelites as they prepare to cross the river Jordan and take possession of their Promised Land. In the course of this address, Moses institutes some of the most important laws, rituals, and prayers in Judaism. He also sets the terms for the Jews' possession of the Land of Israel, making clear that it is conditional and can be revoked by God as a punishment for sin. The reasons for the laws, the nature of God's justice, and above all, the Jewish longing for a homeland: for millennia to come, Jewish writers and thinkers would wrestle with the problems posed by Deuteronomy.

IN THE YEAR 622 BCE, IN THE EIGHTEENTH YEAR OF the reign of King Josiah, an unexpected discovery was made in the Holy Temple in Jerusalem. The high priest, Hilkiah, discovered something he called "a scroll of the Teaching" in the Temple, and he handed it over to a scribe and royal official named Shaphan. When Josiah read this heretofore-unknown scroll, according to the biblical account in 2 Kings, his reaction was dramatic:

> When the king heard the words of the scroll of the Teaching, he rent his clothes. And the king gave orders to the priest Hilkiah. . . . "Go, inquire of the Lord on my behalf, and on behalf of the people, and on behalf of all Judah, concerning the words of this scroll that has been found. For great indeed must be the wrath of the Lord that has been kindled against us, because our fathers did not obey the words of this scroll to do all that has been prescribed for us."

Josiah then summoned all the inhabitants of Jerusalem to a public reading of the rediscovered book, whereupon the king and the people swore to observe "all the terms of the covenant as inscribed upon this scroll." It is just after this ceremony that the Bible tells us of Josiah's nationwide campaign to burn "all the objects made for Baal and Asherah," the pagan gods worshipped by neighboring peoples, and to centralize all Israelite worship in Jerusalem, putting an end to "the shrines where the priests had been making offerings."

There is something Kafka-like about this scene: Josiah suddenly realizes that throughout his life, and for generations, he and his people have been guilty of breaking laws that they never even knew existed. Evidently, those laws have to do with avoiding idol-worship and praying only in a central location; they are enforced by punishments so dire that Josiah is terrified to read about them; and they are communicated in a scroll called a Teaching, or Torah. All of these facts, as commentators as early as the fifth-century biblical translator Saint Jerome realized, point to one conclusion: that the book found in the Temple during the reign of Josiah was what we now know as the book of Deuteronomy. The king's reforms follow the program of Deuteronomy point for point—so much so that some scholars have suggested that the book was not *found* during his reign but was actually *composed* by his associates, in order to justify his radical centralization of Israelite worship.

Josiah was not the only one to be galvanized, or terrified, by what he had discovered. It was also during his reign that "the word of the Lord came" to the prophet Jeremiah, who spent the rest of his life attacking the people of Judah for breaking faith with the divine covenant, and predicting that punishment was on its way. In particular, Jeremiah, like Josiah, was dismayed by the worship of idols:

> *Like a thief chagrined when he is caught,*
> *So is the House of Israel chagrined—*
> *They, their kings, their officers,*
> *And their priests and prophets.*
> *They said to wood, "You are my father,"*
> *To stone, "You gave birth to me,"*
> *While to Me they turned their backs*
> *And not their faces.*
> *But in their hour of calamity they cry,*
> *"Arise and save us!"*
> *And where are those gods*
> *You made for yourself?*
> *Let them arise and save you, if they can,*
> *In your hour of calamity.*

In his warning against idol-worship and his insistence that Yahweh, the God of Israel, was the one true God, Jeremiah was taking part in a debate that stretched back at least a century. Long before Josiah took the throne, the book of Kings tells us, his great-grandfather Hezekiah undertook a similar anti-idol campaign: "He trusted only in the Lord God of Israel.... He clung to the Lord; he did not turn away from following Him, but kept the commandments that the Lord had given to Moses." Indeed, Hezekiah even exceeded Moses in his zeal against idols. During the forty years of wandering in the desert, Moses had made a bronze serpent; Hezekiah went so far as to destroy this ancient object, "for until that time the Israelites had been offering sacrifices to it."

But Hezekiah's son, Manasseh, seems to have been as treasonous to the God of Israel as his father was faithful: "He rebuilt the shrines that his father Hezekiah had destroyed; he erected altars for Baal and made a sacred post.... He consigned his son to the fire; he practiced soothsaying and divination, and consulted ghosts and familiar spirits; he did much that was displeasing to the Lord, to vex Him." In his worship of Canaanite gods, however, Manasseh was not necessarily in the minority in the Kingdom of Judah. Indeed, to read the books of Joshua, Judges, Samuel, and Kings—the historical books that chronicle the Israelite presence in the Promised Land, from the end of the Exodus to the Babylonian Exile—is to realize that the notion of Judaism as a monotheistic religion was alien, or at least contested, during this period of Israel's history. At this period, in fact, to speak of Judaism at all is an anachronism. The picture the Bible gives is of an Israelite people that freely mingled the worship of pagan gods with the worship of the supreme God, Yahweh. No matter how direly they were chastised by prophets like Jeremiah, the people did not cease to worship these Canaanite gods until after the Babylonian Exile.

If we are looking for the moment that can be called the beginning of Jewish history, then, Josiah's discovery of the book of Deuteronomy can be seen as both a plausible candidate and one of the long series of false bottoms in Jewish history. Does that history begin with Josiah, who discovered Deuteronomy and committed the people to a new, monotheistic faith? Or with David, who received God's promise that his descendants would occupy the throne of Israel forever? Or with Moses, who took the people out of Egypt and received God's law on Mount Sinai? Or with Abraham, who was given the initial promise on which all these later covenants elaborated, as the book of Genesis records:

I will make of you a great nation,
And I will bless you;
I will make your name great,
And you shall be a blessing.
I will bless those who bless you
And curse him that curses you;
And all the families of the earth
Shall bless themselves by you.

Or could the story be taken back even before Abraham? After all, Genesis tells us that it was not Abraham who began the journey to Canaan, the Promised Land; it was his father, Terah, who did not know the Lord, who first "set out . . . from Ur of the Chaldeans for the land of Canaan," though he did not complete the journey. The covenant, the defining concept of Jewish history and identity, turns out to be a process of deferral and renewal, of promises postponed and kept and withdrawn. Abraham, Isaac, and Jacob were promised the Land of Canaan; but at the end of Genesis, their family has been exiled to Egypt, where they will be made slaves and outcasts. Moses is called to lead the Israelites into the Promised Land; but he dies on the eastern side of the river Jordan, condemned to view the land he will never enter. David builds a mighty kingdom, but within two generations it has been split in half.

At the end of this process, with terrible poetic symmetry, we find a small band of Israelite survivors fleeing this conquered land and heading back to Egypt: "all the people, young and old, and the officers of the troops set out and went to Egypt because they were afraid of the Chaldeans" (that is, the Babylonians). Egypt was the land of bondage, which the Israelites had to escape in order for their history to begin; now, at the end of 2 Kings, they find themselves back in Egypt, as if the whole course of their providential history has been reversed, cancelled, withdrawn. That was certainly how it looked to Jeremiah: "They have gone backward, not forward, from the day your fathers left the land of Egypt until today," he told the Israelites in their last days of independence. And it must have looked like a fulfillment of the terrible threat Josiah had discovered in the book of Deuteronomy, which warns what will happen to the Israelites if they do not keep God's commandments:

> The life you face shall be precarious; you shall be in terror, night and day, with no assurance of survival. In the morning you shall say, "If only it were evening!" and in the evening you shall say, "If only it were morning!"—because of what your heart shall dread and your eyes shall see. The Lord will send you back to Egypt in galleys, by a route which I told you you should not see again.

THE DUAL NATURE OF Deuteronomy reflects this dialectic of exile and return. After all, Deuteronomy is both an ending and a beginning: the ending of the Torah and the story of Moses, and the beginning of the history that will occupy the next part of the Bible— that of the occupation of the Promised Land by the Israelites. In the Hebrew Bible, the book is known as *Devarim*, "words," after the phrase that begins it: "These are the words that Moses addressed to all Israel on the other side of the Jordan." Yet the name Deuteronomy gestures appropriately at the book's doubleness: it comes from the Septuagint, the Greek translation of the Hebrew Bible, where it is called *Deuteronomion*, "Second Law" or "Repetition of the Law."

This was the translators' rendering of a common rabbinic name for the book, *Mishneh Torah*, "the repetition of the Torah." The origin of this name seems to have been a kind of misunderstanding: in chapter 17, Moses instructs the future kings of Israel to have a "copy of this Teaching"—"*mishneh Torah*"—made for their personal use.

But it is not untrue to the spirit of Deuteronomy to see it as a "second Torah," as the part that stands for the whole. For one thing, it refers to itself as a Torah, usually translated as "teaching" or "instruction"; only later did the word come to refer to all of the first five books of the Bible. More important, Deuteronomy explicitly takes the form of a summing up of everything that has come before. In his last speeches to the people of Israel before his death, Moses recapitulates the story of the Exodus, restates the Ten Commandments, summarizes and expands on the laws he has given the people, and prophesies their future in the Promised Land. Its last word, and the last word of the Torah as a whole, is "Israel"—suggesting that the whole story of Creation, from the first word of Genesis, has been leading up to its consummation in the delivery of the people of Israel to their homeland.

Because it narrates the death of Moses, Deuteronomy has also long been a source of questions about the traditional Jewish understanding that the entire Torah was written by Moses, at God's dictation. In chapter 31, we read that "Moses wrote down this Teaching and gave it to the priests, sons of Levi, who carried the Ark of the Lord's covenant, and to all the elders of Israel." The Talmud offers two alternative explanations of how this occurred. According to one, each time God dictated a passage of the Torah to Moses, he would write it down on a piece of parchment; at the end of his life, he sewed all these pieces together in a single scroll. According to the other, Moses taught orally during the years in the desert, waiting until the end of his life to write down the whole Torah at once. A different rabbinic source has it that on the last day of his life Moses wrote out the whole Torah thirteen times, giving one scroll to each of the twelve tribes—the political divisions of the people of Israel, named after the sons of Jacob—and putting one in the Ark of the Covenant.

Either way, however, the narration of Deuteronomy continues for another three chapters after we are told that Moses wrote it down; these include Moses's final blessing of the tribes, his ascent of Mount Nebo to view the Promised Land, and his death. How could he have written about things that hadn't yet happened? And if he didn't put them in the Torah, who did? This inconsistency presents no serious challenge to a pious understanding of how the Torah was written: if Moses could part seas and summon plagues with God's help, as he did during the Exodus from Egypt, he could surely write about his death in advance. Still, as often proves to be the case, traditional Jewish commentators took note of an issue that would trouble modern readers, though they offered a different explanation for it. Thus one commentator suggested that the last lines of Deuteronomy, describing Moses's death and the people's mourning, were written down by him, but using tears instead of ink; his successor, Joshua, filled them in after Moses died. It is a symbolic way of acknowledging a different status for the last section of the book.

The ambiguity of Deuteronomy begins with the first line, which sets all the action to follow on "the other side of the Jordan"—a way of referring to the east bank of the river that raises an immediate question. If the east bank—then the Land of Moab, today the Kingdom of Jordan—is "the other side," the writer of Deuteronomy must be located on "this side," that is, in the Land of Canaan—which, according to the book itself, the people of Israel had not yet entered. Historically speaking, this phrasing suggests that Deuteronomy was indeed written much later than the events it describes, during the period when the Kingdoms of Israel and Judah had already been established on the western side of the Jordan. But in a metaphorical sense, this ambiguity appropriately highlights the message of the book of Deuteronomy, which is concerned not just with the conditions for entering the Promised Land but also with the inevitability of leaving it.

Even in translation, it is easy to see that the style of Deuteronomy differs markedly from that of the first four books of the Bible. Where those books move from genre to genre—myth, narrative, law code, architectural plans, genealogy—and often seem to reflect a number of voices, most of Deuteronomy is true to its Hebrew name in seeming like the "words" of a single voice. The book, and especially the sermon and law code that constitute its core, feels like a composition directed by a particular mind at a particular audience—whether or not it was actually spoken, as it claims, by Moses to the assembled people of Israel.

But that dramatic setting only underscores the profound ambivalence of Deuteronomy's tone and message. The moment, after all, should be a joyful one: after forty years in the desert, and centuries in slavery in Egypt before that, God is about to fulfill the promise he made to Abraham so long ago, by bringing the Israelites to their Promised Land. Yet Moses cannot forget the fact that the forty years of wandering already bore witness to what will become a major theme of Deuteronomy: the stubborn refusal of the Israelites to obey their God.

Indeed, the years in the desert can be considered a pre-exile, before there was even a land from which to be exiled. That is because, as Moses explains in the first chapter of Deuteronomy, God had originally planned to lead the Israelites directly from Mount Sinai, where they received his covenant and saw his presence, to the Land of Canaan. But when they first approached the borders of the land, the people insisted on sending scouts to report on its characteristics and inhabitants. And of the twelve scouts, ten brought back a report that the people there, known as Amorites or Canaanites, were so physically intimidating—"we looked like grasshoppers . . . to them"—that the Israelites couldn't possibly defeat them.

Hearing this, the Israelites resumed a complaint they had made many times before: "You sulked in your tents and said, 'It is because the Lord hates us that He brought us out of the land of Egypt, to hand us over to the Amorites to wipe us out.'" This vote of no confidence infuriated God, who declared that he would not deliver the Israelites to Canaan until the whole generation that left Egypt had died out: "your children who do not yet know good from bad, they shall enter it." Whereupon the Israelites turned back to the wilderness and spent thirty-eight years—a period that Deuteronomy passes over in a single sentence—aimlessly wandering, waiting to die.

This lack of faith was a recurrent theme of the Israelite experience in the desert. Rashi, the great medieval commentator on the Torah and the Talmud, made a list of all the moments when the people displayed their lack of trust in God: when they regretted the fleshpots of Egypt, when they were panic-stricken by encountering the Egyptian army at the Red Sea, when the rebel Korach led an uprising against Moses's leadership, and several more; above all, when they made the Golden Calf. Indeed, the episode of the Golden Calf seems to crystallize one of the great mysteries of the Torah, which is the inability of the Children of Israel to remain faithful to God even after receiving the most incontrovertible proofs of his nearness. Just days after God manifested himself on the top of Mount Sinai, with fire and smoke and the sound of horns, and commanded the Israelites not to worship idolatrous images, the people insisted on making and worshipping the Golden Calf, to console themselves while Moses was secluded with God on the mountaintop.

Modern people might question God's existence because of his absence, his silence; but in the Torah, even his indisputable presence does not guarantee faithfulness. This problem is all the more acute because, throughout Deuteronomy, it is precisely the Exodus from Egypt that is meant to validate God's authority, to underwrite all the laws and commandments he lays upon the Israelites. Moses makes this point just before he begins to enumerate God's laws:

But take utmost care and watch yourselves scrupulously, so that you do not forget the things that you saw with your own eyes and so that they do not fade from your mind as long as you live. And make them known to your children and to your children's children: The day you stood before the Lord your God at Horeb, when the Lord said to me, "Gather the people to Me that they may learn to revere Me as long as they live on earth, and may so teach their children."

Here again, Deuteronomy seems to fall prey to an inconsistency that is at the same time a kind of signal. Moses is invoking the unchallengeable proof of God's existence—a kind of proof that only the generation at Sinai (which the Bible also calls Horeb) could receive, of all the generations that ever existed, since only they were privileged to witness God's self-disclosure. Yet just before Moses says this, he has pointed out that the generation that stood at Sinai is no longer living—as we have seen, they were deliberately killed off by God as a punishment, and the people Moses is addressing in Deuteronomy are their children. In other words, Moses is demanding that a generation that did not witness Sinai act as if it did witness Sinai.

Rabbinic commentators, who of course recognized the contradiction in Moses's words, asked why his listeners did not protest. Why didn't they tell Moses that they themselves had not been present at Sinai and were not guilty of the sins of the previous generation? One answer the commentators gave is that the generation about to enter the Land of Israel was so extraordinarily righteous that they willingly accepted the shame of their fathers' sins—and the rebuke along with it.

Another way of putting this insight is that the Israelites who listened to Moses in Deuteronomy were the first generation that had to take God on faith. After all, the Exodus was the moment when God intervened dramatically in human history to display his particular love for the Jewish people. In this sense, Jews must believe in the Exodus in the same way that Christians must believe in the Resurrection: it is the founding miracle, without which nothing else makes sense. And Judaism itself can be seen as a technology for collapsing the distance between the present and the moment of Sinai. This is the meaning of the traditional Jewish belief that the souls of all Jews who will ever live—including the souls of converts to Judaism—were present at Sinai. Or, as Deuteronomy has Moses proclaim, "I make this covenant, with its sanctions, not with you alone, but both with those who are standing here with us this day before the Lord our God and with those who are not with us here this day."

Deuteronomy is thus the first text of Jewish belatedness—as is evident from its obsession with conquering belatedness. Anyone who has attended a Passover Seder, the celebratory meal that commemorates the Exodus, will remember the words of Deuteronomy 26, which were originally a formula to be recited when offering tithes to a priest but which have become the center of the Passover service:

> You shall then recite before the Lord your God: "My father was a fugitive Aramean. He went down to Egypt with meager numbers and sojourned there; but there he became a great and very populous nation. The Egyptians dealt harshly with us and oppressed us; they imposed heavy labor upon us. We cried to the Lord, the God of our fathers, and the Lord heard our plea and saw our plight, our misery, and our oppression. The Lord freed us from Egypt by a mighty hand, by an outstretched arm and awesome power, and by signs and portents."

Most religious creeds are metaphysical, a series of propositions about God and the universe that believers must be accept. Deuteronomy, however, offers a historical creed, a declaration of faith in the truth of a historical event. By repeating this formula, Jews attempt to dissolve all the time that has passed between now and the Exodus, to negate belatedness, to make past and present two faces of a single moment.

The same impulse animates the passage from Deuteronomy that makes up the central Jewish prayer known as the Shema: "Hear O Israel! The Lord is our God, the Lord alone." The lines that follow are all about concrete tools of remembrance:

> You shall love the Lord your God with all your heart and with all your soul and with all your might. Take to heart these instructions with which I charge you this day. Impress them upon your children. Recite them when you stay at home and when you are away, when you lie down and when you get up. Bind them as a sign on your hand and let them serve as a symbol on your forehead; inscribe them on the doorposts of your house and on your gates.

This passage is the basis for the Jewish practices of wearing *tefillin* (phylacteries made of leather straps and boxes) and hanging *mezuzot* (small cases affixed to doorways), objects that contain parchment inscribed with biblical verses. Such objects literally surround the individual with the words of God so that they can never be forgotten. They are the daily, portable versions of the massive memorial that Moses commands the Israelites to construct: "As soon as you have crossed the Jordan into the land that the Lord your God is giving you, you shall set up large stones. Coat them with plaster and inscribe upon them all the words of this Teaching." Moses further tells the Israelites to "read this Teaching aloud in the presence of all Israel," at a festival every seven years, so that "their children, too, who have not had the experience, shall hear and so learn to revere the Lord your God."

It is not hard to see, in Deuteronomy's obsession with remembrance, a deep-seated fear of forgetting. The concern over "Jewish continuity" is not an invention of our era; it goes all the way back to this book. Indeed, by opening with Moses's reproof of the Israelites, Deuteronomy offers a dismal reminder that even the generation that personally witnessed God was not able to keep faith with him. There seems to be something about the presence of God that is hard to bear and about his memory that is almost impossible to sustain. It is no wonder that Josiah, when he read the rediscovered Deuteronomy, was seized with terror: he and his people had fallen into exactly the kind of forgetting that the book itself predicts and warns against.

～ɔɔɤ

AND YET, AS MOSES insists to the Israelites, the laws that he is promulgating in Deuteronomy do not require superhuman strength or dedication to obey. "It is not in the heavens, that you should say, 'Who among us can go up to the heavens and get it for us and impart it to us, that we may observe it?' . . . No, the thing is very close to you, in your mouth and in your heart, to observe it." To a modern reader, indeed, the law code that occupies the heart of Deuteronomy makes much more sense than many of the laws and commandments God issues in earlier books of the Torah. In Exodus, for instance, chapter upon chapter is devoted to the exact specifications for the construction of the Tabernacle, the shrine where the divine presence dwelled. These are some of the first matters God instructs Moses about on Mount Sinai, after delivering the Ten Commandments, yet they have no apparent ethical content. In Deuteronomy, however, it is possible to recognize something like a spirit of social justice.

Partly, this is due to the way that Deuteronomy consistently explains the ethical motive behind its laws. Here, too, it is the Exodus from Egypt, and the generations of slavery that preceded it, that are meant to form the heart of Israelite identity. This emphasis becomes especially clear when Moses repeats the Ten Commandments, which

God originally delivered to the people on Mount Sinai, in the book of Exodus. The fourth commandment is "Observe the sabbath day and keep it holy," and in Exodus this is explained as a recollection of the Creation: "For in six days the Lord made heaven and earth and sea, and all that is in them, and He rested on the seventh day; therefore the Lord blessed the sabbath day and hallowed it." In Deuteronomy, by contrast, the sabbath receives not a cosmic justification but a historical and ethical one: "Remember that you were a slave in the land of Egypt and the Lord your God freed you from there with a mighty hand and an outstretched arm; therefore the Lord your God has commanded you to observe the sabbath day."

The extraordinary ethical discovery of Deuteronomy is that the memory of slavery—which to other peoples would be a great shame, to be forgotten as quickly as possible—can be made the engine of humility and sympathy. "You too must befriend the stranger, for you were strangers in the land of Egypt," Moses instructs; when you free a slave, you must equip him with the tools to make a living, because "you were slaves in the land of Egypt and the Lord your God redeemed you"; "you shall not subvert the rights of the stranger or the fatherless; you shall not take a widow's garment in pawn," for "you were a slave in Egypt." The experience of oppression is meant to make the Israelites forever sensitive to the needs and vulnerabilities of the oppressed.

The same spirit of fairness and compassion is evident in many of Deuteronomy's laws. A poor workman is to be paid his wages every day, before sunset, since "he is needy and urgently depends on it." Bribery of judges is forbidden, for bribes "upset the plea of the just." No one can be convicted of a crime on the testimony of a single witness. Child sacrifice, a Canaanite practice, is strictly forbidden; it is even used as an explanation for why God chose to give the Land of Canaan to the Israelites. Excessive corporal punishment—defined here as more than forty lashes—is forbidden, lest "your brother be degraded before your eyes." Even animals are taken into account: "You shall not plow with an ox and an ass together," because it is unfair to the ass to expect it to keep up with a stronger animal. Similarly, it is forbidden to muzzle an ox as it treads the grain, because it would be cruel to deny the ox a share of the food it is helping to produce.

At the same time, Deuteronomy is capable of unbending harshness toward certain kinds of crimes. Death by stoning is prescribed for idolaters and even for a "wayward and defiant son" whose parents cannot discipline him. Discomfort with such a draconian law is not at all a modern phenomenon. Indeed, Jewish tradition interpreted this statute so narrowly—setting many conditions for the age of the son, the status of the parents, the nature of the defiance, and so forth—that according to one Talmudic opinion it could never be invoked.

In its laws regulating sexual conduct, too, Deuteronomy is often very strict. A married woman who commits adultery, and an unmarried one who is found guilty of fornication, are both sentenced to death. At the same time, in this area too there are suggestions of a movement toward greater equity in terms of the treatment of women. A woman who is proved not to have been a virgin at the time of marriage is condemned to death; but Deuteronomy is concerned that such an allegation could be made falsely by a husband who simply has "taken an aversion" to his wife. A man who makes such a false accusation is to be punished by flogging and a fine, "for the man has defamed a virgin in Israel." Again, if a woman has sex with a man within the confines of a town and does not cry out for help, she is held to have consented and must be stoned to death. But if the act takes place in open country, far away from people who might have heard her cry, she is presumed to be an innocent victim of force, and thus she cannot be punished.

More unexpected, an oddly specific law holds that if a woman intervenes in a fight between two men and grabs the genitals of one of them, "you shall cut off her hand; show no pity." This is the only place in the Bible where a law commands mutilation as a punishment, suggesting the extreme force of the prohibition. Yet it hardly seems that the crime could have been so common as to warrant a special statute.

Later commentators applied themselves to explaining the rationale for this law, arguing that touching a man's genitals was a public humiliation to him, or that it caused pain gratuitously, or that it endangered the man's ability to produce offspring. It also seems possible to connect the prohibition with another Deuteronomic rule, which holds that "no one whose testes are crushed or whose member is cut off shall be admitted into the congregation of the Lord." In addition to prohibiting ritual castration, a feature of other Middle Eastern religions, this rule suggests a concern for bodily integrity that is in keeping with Deuteronomy's general insistence on purity and wholeness.

That insistence seems to underlie certain Deuteronomic edicts that appear to be entirely arbitrary. One famous example is the ban on wearing fabric that mixes linen and wool; this seems to flow more from the law's general dislike of mixtures and impurities than from any practical or ethical principle. Here, too, Jewish tradition struggled to make sense of an apparently senseless law. One canny explanation was that if people knew the rationale behind every law, they would be tempted to reason their way out of obeying it. The ban on mixed fabrics, or the prohibition against eating certain animals, could thus be seen as a reminder that God's ordinances were not to be subjected to the test of human understanding.

Easier to comprehend is the danger to religion posed by false prophets, which Deuteronomy addresses at two different points. The death penalty is prescribed for any "prophet or dream-diviner" who invokes a god other than the Lord—a god "whom you have not experienced," unlike the God of Israel, who showed himself at Sinai. Yet this prohibition does not arise out of a monotheistic certainty that any other god is a false god, unable to work the miracles the seer or prophet might promise. On the contrary, Moses warns against following such figures "even if the sign or portent that he names to you comes true." Powers other than God seem to be efficacious, which is what makes them so dangerous.

Such false prophets are all the more to be feared because Deuteronomy inaugurates the time when God will only communicate with the Israelites through prophets. No more will his voice be directly audible, as it was on Mount Sinai; instead, "I will raise up a prophet for them from among their own people. . . . I will put My words in his mouth and he will speak to them all that I command him; and if anybody fails to heed the words he speaks in My name, I myself will call him to account."

Yet this kind of mediation of God's word creates a need for interpretation and verification. For how can the Israelites be sure that everyone who claims to be God's prophet is really divinely called? Some criterion is necessary to distinguish true prophets from false. The one Deuteronomy offers, however, is almost tauntingly circular: "And should you ask yourselves, 'How can we know that the oracle was not spoken by the Lord?'—if the prophet speaks in the name of the Lord and the oracle does not come true, that oracle was not spoken by the Lord." A true prophecy is a prophecy that comes true. But of course, if you could wait until you knew whether a prophecy was true in order to believe it, you wouldn't need the prophecy in the first place. An oracle about the future is only useful so long as the future is still unknown, as a guide to action whose consequences are not guaranteed. This is the abyss of uncertainty that opens up when God stops speaking in his own voice and withdraws his presence from the world—which is the condition of all subsequent Jewish history.

"JUSTICE, JUSTICE SHALT thou pursue," Deuteronomy exhorts in a famous, stirring phrase. But the second part of the verse is equally important to its vision: "that you may thrive and occupy the land that the Lord your God is giving you." The last section of the Deuteronomic law code makes clear that beyond the ethical and spiritual reasons why the Israelites must live justly and follow God's commands, there are extremely concrete, worldly reasons as well. As the Israelites prepare to enter into the Promised Land, they are being offered a stark choice about the future. Obedience to God's laws will lead to prosperity and independence; disobedience will lead to misery and exile, which Deuteronomy describes in the most harrowing terms.

The starkness of the choice is made manifest in an impressive ceremony that Moses commands the Israelites to perform once they have crossed over the Jordan. They are to go to two facing mountains in the northern part of the country, Mount Gerizim and Mount Ebal, and six tribes are to take up a position on each mountain. Then they must perform a choral recitation: the tribes on Gerizim are to declaim the blessings God offers Israel, while those on Ebal are to respond with the curses he threatens as punishment.

At stake are matters of life and death to an agricultural nation frequently at war with its neighbors. If they obey God, the Israelites will bear many children; rain will come at the right season, so that their crops will grow; their cows and sheep will flourish. They will defeat their enemies in battle and enjoy mastery over their neighbors: "The Lord will make you the head, not the tail; you will always be at the top and never at the bottom." By the same token, if the Israelites do not obey God, they will suffer:

> *Cursed shall you be in the city and cursed shall you be in the country.*
> *Cursed shall be your basket and your kneading bowl.*
> *Cursed shall be the issue of your womb and the produce of your soil, the calving of your herd and the lambing of your flock.*

The list of curses goes on far longer than the list of blessings, gaining in power and specificity until Deuteronomy becomes a nightmare vision of utter catastrophe. God threatens pestilence, fever, drought, crop failure, defeat in battle, madness and blindness, loss of children, exile and dispersion, the desolation of the land, and finally, horribly, cannibalism:

> And when you are shut up in all your towns throughout your land that the Lord your God has assigned to you, you shall eat your own issue, the flesh of your sons and daughters that the Lord your God has assigned to you. . . . And she who is most tender and dainty among you, so tender and dainty that she would never venture to set a foot on the ground, shall begrudge the husband of her bosom, and her son and her daughter, the afterbirth that issues from between her legs and the babies she bears; she shall eat them secretly, because of utter want, in the desperate straits to which your enemy shall reduce you in your towns.

It is hard to not feel that there is a disproportion between the rewards and the punishments that Deuteronomy offers. This is, perhaps, just another way of saying that there is a disproportion between the human capacities for happiness and for suffering. Later commentators tried to capture the wonderful fertility of the Promised Land in exaggerated images—one interpreter has Moses promising wheat kernels the size of a kidney and grapes so big they fill a wine cup each. But the cartoonishness of the image reveals the poverty of our imagination of happiness: you can eat and drink only to satiety, not to blessedness. In contrast, there is no limit to the terror of starvation and war. To balance the extremity of suffering that Deuteronomy promises, it would have to offer an extremity of happiness that goes beyond the physical—it would have to promise a kind of transcendence. Perhaps this is what Moses Maimonides, the great medieval sage and philosopher, meant when he wrote that God gives Israel prosperity, not as a reward for following the commandments, but in order to make it possible for the Israelites to follow more commandments. Only if obedience is its own reward does it become a source of gratification sufficient to balance the terror and misery of disobedience.

What's more, toward the end of Deuteronomy the vision of Israel's future disobedience and punishment seems to become less and less conditional. "When all these things befall you—the blessing and the curse that I have set before you," Moses says at one point, as if the curse has already been earned and is only waiting to be carried out. After all, Moses knows from experience how difficult it is to make the Israelites obey God: "To this day," he complains, "the Lord has not given you a mind to understand or eyes to see or ears to hear."

Deuteronomy claims to be the words of Moses, looking forward to events that have not yet happened. But if the book was actually written much later, as scholars believe—during the reign of Josiah, or perhaps during the Babylonian Exile—then the promise of conquest and exile are not prospective but retrospective, not prophecy but history. By reinscribing their suffering into Deuteronomy, these later writers made it something foretold and therefore providential, explicable, even reasonable: Israel suffered because Israel sinned. By the logic of Deuteronomy, indeed, even the worst historical experiences of the Jewish people cannot be called truly incomprehensible.

No wonder, then, that Jewish tradition and folklore has seized upon the conclusion of Deuteronomy as a chance to push back against divine justice. For the death of Moses, which ends Deuteronomy and with it the Torah, enacts what seems like a terrible disproportion between man's sin and God's punishment. "Never again did there arise in Israel a prophet like Moses—whom the Lord singled out face to face," the book declares. Yet all of Moses's life was devoted to a single goal, that of bringing the Israelites to the Promised Land, and God condemns him to die without setting foot in that land. "I have let you see it with your own eyes, but you shall not cross there," God tells Moses, and it's not clear whether his dying glimpse from Mount Nebo is a consolation or a taunting punishment.

What did Moses do to deserve this? At the beginning of Deuteronomy, Moses himself suggests that it is a punishment for what happened when the Israelites sent scouts to Canaan and were intimidated by their reports: "the Lord was wrathful with me on your account and would not listen to me," he recalls. But it's not clear why Moses should be punished for something that wasn't really his fault. A different and more direct reason is given in the book of Numbers, in the story of Moses striking the rock at Meribah. Having been told by the Lord to bring forth water from a rock for the grumbling Israelites, Moses strikes the rock twice instead—a sin so minor that it is unclear from the biblical text whether it was really contrary to God's instructions at all. But it is enough for God to tell Moses and Aaron, "Because you did not trust Me enough to affirm My sanctity in the sight of the Israelite people, therefore you shall not lead the congregation into the land that I have given them."

The proliferation of legends surrounding Moses's death suggests how much work needed to be done to reconcile the punishment with the crime. These tales speak of the angels refusing to carry out God's command to claim Moses's soul; only when God himself kissed Moses's soul did it leave his body. Other stories have God combing Moses's past for other sins, to add to the sin at Meribah; and Moses calling the elements to witness on his behalf; and Moses causing Heaven and Earth to tremble with the force of his prayers asking to enter the Promised Land. God suggests that if Moses's life were spared, the Israelites might worship him as a god; for the same reason, God hid Moses's burial place so that it could not become a shrine. Finally, God can only console Moses with the promise that he will be the most honored man in Paradise, where he will learn God's secret name.

Perhaps the most ingenious explanation for why Moses was not allowed to enter the Promised Land comes from the Vilna Gaon, a great eighteenth-century sage. If Moses had crossed the Jordan, the Gaon reasoned, he would have built the Temple immediately. A Temple built by Moses would have been so superior in sanctity to the Temple that was later built by Solomon that it could never have been destroyed. Thus when God needed to punish the Israelites, he could not have done so by allowing the Temple to be destroyed, as it was by the Babylonians in 586 BCE. He would have been left with no other choice than to destroy the people themselves. By keeping Moses out of the Land of Israel, then, God ultimately ensured the Israelites' survival. It is a remarkable chain of reasoning, showing how much dexterity would always be needed to reconcile God's justice with his mercy—and to explain the vicissitudes that history had in store for the people of the covenant.

BIBLIOGRAPHY

Ginzberg, Louis. *Legends of the Jews, Vol. III: Moses in the Wilderness.* Philadelphia: Jewish Publication Society, 1911.

Grant, Michael. *The History of Ancient Israel.* New York: Scribner, 1984.

Tigay, Jeffrey. *The JPS Torah Commentary: Deuteronomy.* Philadelphia: Jewish Publication Society, 1996.

Weinstein, Moshe. *The Midrash Says: The Book of Devarim.* Brooklyn, NY: Bnay Yakov Publications, 1985.

2

IN THE KINGDOM OF CHANCE

The Book of Esther

Rembrandt's painting of a scene from the Book of Esther

The book of Esther is one of the most dramatic and popular narratives in the Bible. Jews traditionally read the scroll, or *megillah*, of Esther every year on Purim, the holiday that commemorates the events the book records: the plot against the Jews of Persia by Haman, the royal minister, and their salvation by Mordecai and Esther. It is an occasion for drinking and feasting, for dressing up in costumes and jeering the memory of Haman. Yet to read Esther is to realize that this tale of Jewish salvation is also the archetypal story of Jewish vulnerability. Esther is one of only two books of the Hebrew Bible in which the name of God does not appear, and it can easily seem that luck, rather than providence, is what saves the Jewish people. This makes the book of Esther the classic treatment of themes that would be, and are, central to Jewish history: the precariousness of Jewish life in Diaspora, and the accommodations Jews must make to survive as an often-suspect minority.

WHEN THE ISRAELITES GATHERED BEFORE KING JOSIAH to hear the book of Deuteronomy read aloud, they pledged themselves to follow these rediscovered commandments of God: "And all the people entered into the covenant," we read in 2 Kings. But if they hoped that this collective oath would avert the fate in store for the Kingdom of Judah, they were soon to be disappointed. Already in the 720s BCE, the Kingdom of Israel, Judah's northern neighbor, had been swept away by the armies of the Assyrian Empire. In 597 BCE Judah's turn came, when the Babylonian ruler Nebuchadnezzar II laid siege to Jerusalem and forced the surrender of King Jehoiakim. It was the beginning of the end for Israelite independence, as Judah's ruling classes—"all the able men, to the number of seven thousand"— were deported to Babylon. A puppet king, the twenty-one-year-old Zedekiah, was installed in his place; but soon he rebelled against his overlord, and this time there would be no mercy. In the year 586 BCE, the Babylonians conquered Jerusalem, put out Zedekiah's eyes, and burned down the Temple, the center of Judah's national life and religious practice. To those who lived through the catastrophe, it seemed like the end of the world—and the fulfillment of the terrible curses set forth in the book of Deuteronomy.

But 586 BCE, though it would remain one of the darkest dates in Jewish history—even today, Jews commemorate the Temple's destruction with a fast on that date, the Ninth of Av—was not the end of that history. On the contrary, like so many Jewish endings, it turned out to be simultaneously a new beginning. Half a century later, the Babylonian Empire had itself fallen to the rising power of Persia, and the Persian king, Cyrus, gave permission for the exiles to return to Jerusalem and begin rebuilding the Temple. This proved to be anything but a straightforward task—the books of Ezra and Nehemiah record all the delays and obstructions that the Israelites faced while putting the ruined city back in order. But it meant that for the next six hundred years, the Second Temple would once again provide a focus for Jewish national life, even as the land that was once the Kingdom of Judah metamorphosed from a Persian province to a Greek one, then enjoyed a brief resurrection as an independent state, and finally became part of the Roman Empire.

Just as consequentially, however, the Babylonian Exile marked the birth of a complex new form of Jewish life: Diaspora. Even when some Israelites returned to Judah, many, perhaps most, stayed behind. In Babylon they developed new forms of worship, a canon of sacred texts, and their own ways of thinking about their former homeland. Much of this process is impossible to recover, since the Persian period in Jewish history, from the sixth century to the fourth century BCE, is one of the most scantily documented. What we do have are the stories, some of them written or revised much later, that the Jews told themselves about life in exile—stories that would eventually become some of the last additions to the Hebrew Bible.

Consider the book of Daniel. For various linguistic and cultural reasons, this book is thought to have reached its final form in the second century BCE, when Judea was rebelling against Greek rule. But it is set in the court of Nebuchadnezzar II, just after the Babylonian Exile, and its first six chapters offer a didactic, even propagandistic, image of how Jews in the Diaspora ought to behave. Daniel, we read, was one of the notables deported from Jerusalem along with King

Jehoiakim, and since he was "without blemish, handsome, proficient in all wisdom, knowledgeable and intelligent," he was recruited to serve in the conqueror's imperial bureaucracy. This meant undergoing what is recognizable even today as a process of assimilation. His Jewish name was replaced by a Babylonian one, Belteshazzar; his friends Hananiah, Mishael, and Azariah were renamed Shadrach, Meshach, and Abednego, as if at some early Babylonian version of Ellis Island. He learned to read and speak a new language, Chaldean.

Naturally, assimilation came with its own set of challenges. What about Jewish dietary laws—could they still be practiced in the Diaspora? The first story in Daniel tells how these young Israelites refuse to eat the non-kosher food they are given, surviving instead on legumes and water; with God's help, they manage to stay vigorous and healthy. Then Nebuchadnezzar erects a golden statue and orders the Israelites to bow down to it. When they refuse, mindful of the Ten Commandments' ban on graven images, Shadrach, Meshach, and Abednego are thrown into a fiery furnace; but God performs a miracle, and they emerge unharmed. Later, after the Persian conquest, the new king forbids his people to pray to any god except him. When Daniel is found praying to his own God, he is cast into the lions' den; but once again he is miraculously preserved from harm.

The message of these stories could not be clearer. Jews in the Diaspora are given great opportunities—after all, Daniel rises to become a chief royal counselor—but they are constantly tested by the temptation to renounce their religion, to act more like the people around them. It is a Jewish duty to resist that temptation and remain faithful to Jewish practices, even to the point of martyrdom. God is watching over the Jews and will make sure that any sacrifice for his sake is rewarded.

WHAT MAKES THE BOOK of Esther so powerful—what separates it from almost every other book of the Bible and enables it to speak immediately to the modern reader—is its rejection of each one of these consoling pieties. Esther, too, tells the story of Jews under Persian rule, and of the temptations and challenges they face. Here again are Jews who undergo exile, adopt non-Jewish names, and rise to positions of influence; they are challenged to bow down to their enemies and forsake their ancestral customs. But in Esther, God is not there to intervene and rescue people from the fiery furnace. Instead, it is only very good luck—a series of fortunate coincidences—that allows Esther and her uncle, Mordecai, to prevent a wholesale genocide of the Jews of Persia.

The story of Esther is one of the most popular in the Bible, with the appeal of a melodrama or a novella. Indeed, many scholars today believe that the best way to read the book is as historical fiction—as an imaginary event set at the court of a real king. That king, known in Hebrew as Ahasuerus, is usually identified with Xerxes, the ruler of Persia from 486 to 465 BCE, who is best known in European history as the invader whom the Greeks defeated in the Persian Wars. As we will see, there are several points of similarity between the character of Ahasuerus as described in the book of Esther and Xerxes as we know him from Herodotus's *Histories*. And while the book of Esther has nothing to say about the Greeks, it is very much a story about how Persians relate to other peoples—in this case, the other within, the Jews.

The very name "Jew" is a novelty in the book of Esther. Earlier biblical books speak about twelve tribes of Israel, one of which is Judah; in the book of Kings, to call someone a Judahite is a way of referring to his tribal ancestry. But when the book of Esther introduces its hero, Mordecai, as a Jewish man, *"ish yehudi,"* the sense is different; indeed, the text goes on to specify that Mordecai is not a Judahite but a member of another tribe, a Benjaminite. In the Diaspora, however, such distinctions have melted away, and all the former inhabitants of the Kingdom of Judah are now grouped together simply as Jews.

At first, it is not obvious that Jews are going to play a role in the story that the book of Esther has to tell. The book opens with a

description of the magnificent, six-month-long feast that King Ahasuerus put on in his royal capital at Shushan (or Susa), in the area
known as southwestern Iraq today. "Merry with wine," the king orders
his queen, Vashti, to appear before his guests wearing a royal crown,
"to display her beauty to the peoples." Vashti refuses, for reasons that
are not made clear. Later rabbinical commentators, trying to explain
her behavior, suggest that when Ahasuerus said that she was to appear
wearing a crown, he meant wearing only a crown—in other words,
naked. In any case, something about the request offends Vashti, and
her refusal earns her an instant divorce from Ahasuerus.

This prelude succeeds in giving us a sharp portrait of the king's pet-
ulance and impetuosity—no sooner does he dismiss Vashti than he
seems to regret it—as well as setting the story in motion. Ahasuerus
begins a nationwide search for Vashti's successor, recruiting young
women for his harem. One of the candidates he turns up is Esther,
the niece and ward of Mordecai the Jew, who is evidently some kind
of royal official. (He is said to "sit in the palace gate," which is not just
a location but a position at court.) Esther ends up winning the beauty
pageant and becoming the new queen, even as, following her uncle's
advice, she keeps her Jewish identity a secret.

As it turns out, having a Jew in such a high place will be a significant piece of good luck. For Ahasuerus now appoints as his chief minister Haman, who contracts a ferocious hatred for Mordecai when the
Jew refuses to follow custom and bow down to him. To get revenge,
Haman decides to annihilate all the Jews in the Persian Empire, and
he prevails on the easily swayed king to sign an order to that effect:
"written instructions were dispatched by couriers to all the king's
provinces to destroy, massacre, and exterminate all the Jews, young
and old, children and women, on a single day."

News of the impending catastrophe reaches Mordecai, who urges
Esther to make use of her position to intercede with Ahasuerus:
"Who knows," he says, "perhaps you have attained to royal position
for just such a crisis." (This allusion to fate is the closest that the book

of Esther comes to invoking divine providence; notably, the name of God is not mentioned.) Esther is reluctant at first—there is a rule that no one can enter the king's presence without prior invitation—but she takes her life in her hands, and Ahasuerus pardons her transgression. She invites the king and Haman to a feast, where she plans to plead on behalf of the Jews.

In the meantime, Haman's campaign against Mordecai begins to go awry. Unable to sleep one night, the king asks for the royal chronicles to be read to him, and he learns of a service that Mordecai rendered him earlier in the book: Mordecai overheard two eunuchs plotting against the king and turned them in. Resolved to do something to reward Mordecai, the king (mischievously, perhaps) asks Haman, "What should be done for a man whom the king desires to honor?" Haman, thinking that he himself is the man in question, says that such a man should be dressed in royal garb and led through the streets on the king's horse. Then the trap is sprung: the king commands that this very honor be paid to Mordecai—and that Haman lead the horse.

Haman's personal vendetta against Mordecai having been thwarted, now it remains only to stop his plot against the Jews. This Esther does at the banquet, when she reveals that she herself is a Jew and that Haman's attack on her people would mean taking her own life. Haman, overcome with fear, falls on the queen's couch, leading Ahasuerus to think he is trying to "ravish the queen in my own palace." Instantly, Haman's fate is sealed, and he is hanged from the very gallows he had prepared for Mordecai, who is elevated to chief minister in his place.

By the odd fairy-tale logic of the story, the king is unable simply to countermand his initial order to his people, allowing them to attack and plunder the Jews. Instead, he issues a second order, instructing the Jews to arm themselves and fight back against their enemies. This leads to the book's concluding, celebratory massacre, in which the Jews are said to slay 75,000 of their attackers on a single day. On this troubling note, the book ends, with the Jews enjoying "light and gladness, happiness and honor," and the unusual sensation of striking fear into the hearts of their persecutors: "no one could withstand them, for the fear of them had fallen upon all the peoples."

~ڪڪڪ~

THE HOLIDAY JEWS celebrate to remember this skin-of-the-teeth rescue is Purim. The book of Esther derives this name from the word *pur*, or "lot," because Haman is said to draw lots to determine the date for the massacre of the Jews. Appropriately for a holiday that celebrates a narrow escape from death, it is supposed to be celebrated with wild, carnival-like joy. A famous rabbinical edict says that on Purim, Jews should get so drunk that they can't tell the difference between the words "cursed be Haman" and "blessed be Mordecai." The Vilna Gaon even suggested that Purim was as holy as Yom Kippur, the Day of Atonement, the most important holiday in the Jewish calendar. The Hebrew name "Yom HaKippurim" can be read, in the kind of serious pun so characteristic of Jewish texual interpretation, as meaning "a day like Purim." What Yom Kippur does for the soul, the Vilna Gaon concluded, Purim does for the body. The asceticism of the former finds its complement in the sheer indulgence of the latter.

At the same time, there is some evidence that to the authorities who finalized the Jewish biblical canon in the years 100 BCE to 100 CE, the book of Esther was of doubtful sanctity. Notably, it is the only biblical book not found among the Dead Sea Scrolls, the ancient biblical manuscripts discovered in the twentieth century. This might be an accident, but it is more likely a sign that the Jewish sect that preserved the Scrolls disdained Esther as insufficiently holy. Several authorities quoted in the Talmud seem to share that view. According to one Talmudic story, when a pair of rabbis were repairing the covers of a set of biblical scrolls, they decided that "the Scroll of Esther does not require" a cover. Other rabbis pronounced that Esther is the only biblical book that does not "defile the hands"—that is, does not render the person who handles it ritually impure, as the other canonical books do.

There is one obvious explanation why the book of Esther was singled out in this way: it never mentions God. Still more pointedly, the author of the book—probably a Jew who lived in the Persian Empire during the fourth century BCE—scrupulously avoids showing any of its Jewish characters invoking God's help. And the story of Esther offers plenty of occasions when prayer would have been natural. When Mordecai learns of Haman's genocidal plan, he tears his clothes and puts on sackcloth and ashes, traditional signs of mourning. A little later, Queen Esther, trying to work up the courage to beg a favor from Ahasuerus, decides to fast for three days. Yet neither of them accompanies these gestures with an actual prayer to God. The omission is so notable that when Jewish translators rendered the book of Esther into Greek, they added several passages designed to showcase Esther's and Mordecai's reliance on God, including a long prayer and some heaven-sent dreams. (These passages are included in the biblical Apocrypha under the title "Additions to Esther.")

Today, however, it is this scandalous absence of God that makes the book of Esther seem so contemporary. To secular, assimilated Jews, in particular, the Esther story has an uncanny familiarity, like an old nightmare that has never been entirely forgotten. After all, Mordecai and Esther, like American Jews today, live in a cosmopolitan, pluralist society, where Jews seem defined less by their religious beliefs than by their ethnic loyalties. Just as it is common for American Jews to have first names drawn from Christian or Greco-Roman sources, so these characters are named after Babylonian deities: Mordecai from Marduk, the chief god in Babylon's mythology, and Esther from Ishtar, the goddess of love. (And just as many Jews have a Hebrew name for use in religious contexts, Esther is also known as Hadassah, the Hebrew for "myrtle.") The story is even notably casual about intermarriage. When the king launches his search for a new bride, Mordecai does not forbid Esther to join in, nor does he try to hide her from the king's scouts. Esther is never condemned for eating non-kosher food, or for sleeping with Ahasuerus before marriage, or for marrying a non-Jew—exactly the kind of transgressions that the book of Daniel warns against so vividly.

One way to gauge the surprising worldliness and cosmopolitanism of the book of Esther is by the efforts of traditional Jewish commentators to purge those very qualities from the text. The *midrashim* on the book of Esther—creative interpretations produced over many generations, written down in the Talmud or in the collection called *Esther Rabbah*—are full of attempts to make Esther and Mordecai more Jewishly observant, more concerned with piety and chastity. One midrash says that Mordecai *did* try to conceal Esther from the king's scouts—in fact, he kept her in a cave for four years. But her beauty was so famous that the king insisted on finding her, and he threatened the death penalty for anyone who tried to hide her.

Again, the book of Esther says that while undergoing a year-long makeover to prepare her for the king's bed, Esther was fed with "delicacies"—which would not, of course, have been kosher. Unlike Daniel, Esther is never seen refusing this food; a reader of the Bible would naturally draw the conclusion that Esther was not an observant Jew. So the midrash makes sure to tell us that Esther actually refused to let any of these delicacies touch her lips, insisting on a kosher vegetarian diet. Best of all, later interpreters tried to spare Esther's chastity with a kind of ghostly prophylactic. According to one source, whenever Ahasuerus came to her bed, "God sent down a female spirit in the guise of Esther to take her place with the king. Esther never lived with Ahasuerus as his wife."

Surely the author of the book of Esther, and its original audience, would have found these rabbinical interventions to be puritanical and parochial—just as the contemporary reader does. Here is an example of the way Jewish history has moved, not in a straight line of progress from tradition to modernity, but in hesitant spirals. In some essential ways, Jewish life in twenty-first-century America may resemble the Persia of twenty-five hundred years ago more closely than the Poland of three hundred years ago. Certainly the book of Esther shows that the movement outward into dispersion, exile, and assimilation is no less important in Jewish history than the movement inward into tradition, orthodoxy, and nationhood.

NO WONDER, THEN, that Jews have often seen their history as the continual return of a few basic, archetypal situations and challenges—including the archetype of the persecutor, the enemy intent on exterminating the Jewish people. The book of Esther gives us one of the best known of these enemies in Haman. But Haman himself is described as an Amalekite, a descendant of the tribe that sought to destroy the Israelites during their wandering in the desert. Specifically, Haman is said to be a descendant of Agag, the Amalekite king who was defeated in battle by Saul, the first king of Israel. Since Mordecai is said to be related to Saul—he is called a "son of Kish," and Kish was Saul's father—the contest of Mordecai and Haman can be seen as a replay of the ancient war between Saul and Agag, and the even more ancient war between the Israelites and the Amalekites.

If Haman has ancestors, however, he also has descendants. Reading the book of Esther today, what one finds most striking about Haman's plot is its modern flavor—its resemblance to the distinctly new kind of anti-Semitism that emerged in nineteenth-century Europe. Haman, after all, is not the leader of a rival tribe, like Agag; or a foreign king making war on a Jewish state, like Nebuchadnezzar; or a religious figure demanding that the Jews give up their faith. Rather, he seems most akin to a figure like Hitler, arising seemingly from nowhere to seek the total annihilation of an inoffensive, assimilated Jewish community.

The Persian Empire, after all, was quite accustomed to tolerating cultural difference. The first chapter of the book of Esther makes clear that King Ahasuerus reigns over a diverse assemblage of peoples, "from India to Ethiopia . . . a hundred and twenty-seven provinces." And they enjoy at least cultural autonomy: when the king sends out an edict, he addresses "each province in its own script, and . . . each people in its own language." This Persian pluralism was so benevolent that, as we have seen, it was a Persian ruler who allowed the Jews to resettle in Jerusalem after the Babylonian Exile. Nor did the Jews who remained behind in Mesopotamia suffer from discrimination. Mordecai is some kind of royal official, and he is so loyal to Ahasuerus that he warns the king of a plot against his life.

What makes Haman such a frightening figure, and what justifies the inevitable comparison to Hitler, is the way he reveals the seeming security of the Jewish minority to be a fragile illusion. Persia may sanction difference, even encourage it, but there is something about Jewish difference that is seen to be beyond the pale. In the book of Esther, Haman's hatred is said to be triggered by Mordecai's refusal to bow down to him: "When Haman had seen for himself that Mordecai did not bow down nor prostrate himself before him, he was furious. However, he hated to kill just Mordecai (for they had told him who Mordecai's people were); and so Haman sought to wipe out all the Jews throughout the whole kingdom."

But the leap from personal insult to genocide is as unconvincing, here, as it is when biographers of Hitler speculate that he launched the Holocaust as revenge for the way this or that Jew treated him. And why, for that matter, would Mordecai refuse to bow down to Haman, when he would presumably be called upon to make obeisance to other royal officials, including the king himself?

One explanation, according to some biblical interpreters, lies in the two men's ancestry. Mordecai recognizes Haman as an Amalekite, a descendant of Israel's great enemy, and that is why he will not bow down. His resistance can thus be seen as a form of fidelity to Jewishness and Jewish history, even in the context of Persian pluralism and assimilation. The same principle is expressed in a more pious form in the rabbis' suggestion that Haman wore an idol on his clothes, so that bowing down to him would literally mean bowing down to a strange god. "They say to me: 'Practice idolatry,'" Mordecai says in a midrash. "If I listen to them I am punished, and if I do not listen to them they kill me. [The Jews are] in the position of a wolf which is thirsting for water and finds a net spread over the mouth of a well. It says: 'If I go down to drink, I shall be caught in the net, and if I do not go down, I shall die of thirst.'"

It is this insistence on Jewish difference that strikes Haman as a seditious principle, with the potential to threaten the empire itself. These are the terms in which he presents his plan to Ahasuerus: "There is a certain people scattered, yet unassimilated, among the peoples throughout the provinces of your kingdom whose statutes are different from every other people's. . . . Therefore, it is not appropriate for the king to tolerate them." The rabbis, writing centuries later, had an acute imagination of the grievances Gentiles held against the Jews, and how Jewish particularism might look to a hostile world. Thus the Talmud expands on Haman's indictment: "Their laws are different from all the other nations. For they do not eat from our food and they do not marry our women and they do not marry their women to us. . . . They eat, drink, and mock the throne. For even if a fly falls in a glass of wine of one of them, he casts away the fly and drinks the wine. But if my master, the king, touches a glass of wine of one of them, he throws it to the ground and does not drink it!"

In this way, Mordecai's personal resistance to Haman becomes a symptom of the Jews' fundamental resistance to giving up their particularity, their customs and practices, their sense of peoplehood. Whether in ancient Egypt, in the Christian era, or in the modern world, it is exactly this kind of particularism that has led to charges of Jewish stubbornness and misanthropy. This helps to explain why Haman's hatred of Mordecai instantly encompasses Mordecai's whole people. And the general unpopularity of the Jews is the key to Haman's plans to accomplish their destruction. He will enlist the whole Persian population, encouraging them "to destroy, to kill, and to cause to perish, all Jews, both young and old, little children and women, in one day . . . and to take the spoil of them for a prey." Again, the Holocaust parallel is hard to ignore. As in the countries occupied by the Nazis, Haman counts on the existence of a widespread, barely suppressed hostility toward Jews, only waiting for official encouragement to break into outright violence.

Conspicuously, however, Haman does not name this intolerable people to Ahasuerus. It is as though he had reason to believe that the king would not share his anti-Jewish feeling; and later events prove this to be the case. Ahasuerus does not know that Esther is a Jew when he marries her—she has been instructed to keep the fact quiet by Mordecai, to "pass," a common survival strategy of disliked minorities—but when she reveals the truth, he does not seem at all put off. At the end of the book of Esther, he is happy to put the Jew Mordecai in Haman's high office. And while a technicality of Persian law prevents even the king from revoking his own decrees, he is more than willing to issue a contrary decree authorizing the Jews of Persia to arm themselves in self-defense.

Yet while this royal benevolence is what saves the Jews, the lesson of the whole episode is hardly reassuring: it is possible for a ruler's personal preferences to be overridden all too easily by a hostile politician or popular movement. Indeed, just this would happen again and again in Jewish history, especially in Christian Europe, where the Jews sought refuge from popular hatred in the protection of bishops and kings. Often, however, that protection proved to be unreliable—as when King Edward III, after burdening England's Jews with heavy taxes, finally expelled them from England in 1290; or else impotent—as when German mobs, inflamed by the preaching of the First Crusade in the late eleventh century, defied the nobility and massacred Jewish communities in the Rhineland. In *The Origins of Totalitarianism* (1951), the German Jewish thinker Hannah Arendt traced the fatal weakness of twentieth-century European Jewry back to this ancient habit of seeking high-ranking protectors rather than popular allies.

ONE PURPOSE OF THE Esther story is to explain the origins of the holiday of Purim. Today, scholars believe that the connection between the story and the holiday is more likely to be the other way around—that the author of Esther tailored or invented his story to match pre-existing Purim customs. (The true origins of the holiday are unknown, though scholars have suggested that it may be based on a Babylonian rite or on the Persian New Year.) Similarly, the true source of the name "Purim" is unclear, but the book of Esther provides a clever explanation: Haman decides when to launch his purge of the Jews by casting lots, just as any Roman general consulted auguries before starting a major campaign.

The etymology may not be accurate, but the image of casting lots is thematically perfect for the Esther story, helping to underscore its lesson about Jewish political insecurity. In the absence of real self-determination, the book of Esther shows, chance alone rules Jewish fate in Persia. The figure of Ahasuerus could almost have been invented to illustrate the peril of depending on royal whim. The story begins when, acting on drunken impulse, he summons Queen Vashti to appear before his guests in order to show off her beauty; when she refuses, fearing to transgress against modesty, he just as impetuously divorces her.

Even his graciousness to Queen Esther is essentially whimsical. She knows that she is not supposed to enter the king's presence uninvited, just as Vashti knew she was not supposed to refuse an invitation. But while Vashti's disobedience got her divorced, Esther's disobedience earns her the king's promise to give her anything she wants, "even if it be half the kingdom." After all this, it seems entirely in character for Ahasuerus to casually grant Haman's request to massacre the Jews, in exchange for a payment to the royal coffers: "Well, it's your money, do what you like with the people," the king remarks.

There is no extra-biblical evidence that the Esther story ever actually happened. Yet the way the book of Esther depicts Ahasuerus is remarkably consistent with the way Herodotus, the fifth-century BCE

Greek writer known as the Father of History, describes Xerxes. The last three books of Herodotus's *Histories* deal with the campaigns of Xerxes, including such immortal episodes as the Spartan resistance at Thermopylae in 480 BCE. And the Xerxes who Herodotus gives us is just as impetuous and easily manipulated as the Bible's Ahasuerus. He is shown to vacillate wildly, first planning to invade Greece, then having a bad dream and changing his mind, then having another dream and changing his mind back.

Xerxes's childish willfulness reaches its height when the bridge his army is building across the Hellespont gets washed away in a storm. He responds by ordering his soldiers to give the water three hundred lashes, while declaring: "You bitter water, your lord lays this punishment on you because you have wronged him without cause, having suffered no evil at his hands. Truly, King Xerxes will cross you, whether you like it or not." Herodotus describes these as "barbarous and wicked words," and the scene of Xerxes lashing the water has become a classic symbol of hubris. The failure of the Persian invasion, Herodotus implies, can already be predicted from this demonstration of Xerxes's mad pride, his belief that he can impose his will on the very elements; for it was a fundamental Greek belief that the man who defies fate is certain to be crushed.

Herodotus has occasion to drive this lesson home a little later in the *Histories*. As Xerxes watches his enormous army cross the Hellespont, he weeps, thinking of the brevity of human life: "of all this army, as large as it is, not one man will be alive in a hundred years." His uncle, Artabanus, replies with fatalistic wisdom:

> Short as our life is, there is no man, here among this multitude or elsewhere, who is so happy as not to have felt the wish—not just once, but many times—that he were dead rather than alive. Calamities fall upon us; sicknesses vex and harass us, and make life, short as it is, seem too long. So death, through the wretchedness of our life, is a sweet refuge to mankind: and God, who gives

us the tastes that we enjoy of pleasant times, is seen, in his very gift, to be envious.

The rabbis who wrote *midrashim* on the book of Esther had in all likelihood not read Herodotus. It is all the more remarkable, then, that one midrash should read almost like a direct response to this statement of pagan resignation. The rabbis say that when Haman commanded Mordecai to bow down to him, the Jew responded by pointing out the wretchedness and nullity of even the greatest human being: "Who is man that he should act proudly and arrogantly—man born of woman and few in days? At his birth there is weeping and travailing, in his youth pain and groans, all his days are 'full of trouble,' and in the end he returns unto dust." So far, Mordecai's vision of human life sounds as dark as Artabanus's. But where the Persian sees this as a reason to long for death and complain against God, Mordecai, in language reminiscent of the book of Job, sees human weakness as a proof of God's might: "I bend the knee before God alone, the only living One in heaven, He who is the fire consuming all other fires; who holds the earth in His arms; who stretches out the heavens in His might."

To Herodotus, God is fate; to the rabbis, God is the opposite of and remedy for fate. Chance, the realm of the *pur*, may rule on Earth; but this is all the more reason to place our trust in God, who is above chance just as he is above the Earth. Yet here, as in their treatment of Esther's modesty, the rabbis who interpreted the book of Esther are much more pious and God-fearing than its author was. As the rabbis saw, the whole plot of Esther lends itself to a providential interpretation. Why was Esther plucked from obscurity to become queen, why was Mordecai's good deed remembered by the king, if not so that they would be able to avert Haman's scheme at the last moment? Such intricate plotting suggests a divine plotter at work, as Mordecai hints: "It's possible that you came to the throne for just such a time as this."

Yet the author of the book of Esther never goes further than that bare suggestion. His story takes place in a world where chance is real and redemption is at best hypothetical, where miracles happen in such a way that we cannot be sure they really are miracles, and not just a lucky throw of the dice. Nothing better illustrates this ambiguous realism than the conclusion of the book of Esther. Powerless to revoke his decree authorizing the massacre of the Jews, Ahasuerus issues a second decree, encouraging the Jews of Persia "to organize themselves and to defend themselves, to wipe out, slaughter, and annihilate every armed force of any people or province that was hostile to them, along with their children and women, and to plunder their personal property." The Jews receive this command with "light and joy, rejoicing and honor," and on the appointed day they kill "seventy-five thousand of those who hated them." (The author makes a point of telling us, however, that the Jews did not avail themselves of the chance to plunder their enemies.)

It sounds absurd to say that the king cannot countermand his own orders and has no better recourse than to turn genocide into civil war. But this historically dubious stipulation has a crucial effect on Esther's narrative. Instead of being rescued, the Jews of Persia are compelled to rescue themselves. Self-defense, not royal favor, is shown to be the most reliable protection for Jews.

Yet the book of Esther does not conclude that the only solution to the Jewish predicament is to flee the Diaspora and live in a Jewish country. The idea would not have been unimaginable to the book's author. Thanks to Cyrus, Xerxes's grandfather, Jewish resettlement in the Land of Israel had begun some half a century before the events of Esther take place, though the province was still under Persian suzerainty. Yet not only does Mordecai not abandon Shushan for Jerusalem; he actually takes over Haman's office of prime minister, becoming the chief servant of the same king who had acquiesced in the annihilation of the Jews. The last lines of Esther note that "Mordecai the Jew ranked next to King Xerxes and was influential among the Jews and acceptable to the mass of his own countrymen. He sought the best interests of his people and was concerned for the welfare of his kinsmen."

This is meant to be the story's happy ending. Yet the terms in which

Mordecai is praised sound strangely like a reprise of the very complaint Haman lodged against the Jews in the first place. If Mordecai uses his power as chief minister to look out for "the best interests of his people," doesn't this confirm that the Jews of Persia have different interests from those of the king and the people as a whole—that they have their own "statutes" and their own agenda? As long as Jewish interests are considered different from Persian interests, how could a powerful Jew be immune to the charge of "dual loyalty"?

To use this anachronistic phrase, familiar from contemporary polemics about American Jews' feelings toward Israel, is to show how persistent the dynamics of the book of Esther have been throughout Jewish history. Indeed, the dilemma facing a Jewish servant of non-Jewish power appears in the Bible even earlier than Mordecai. The first and classic example is Joseph, the son of Jacob, who in the book of Genesis is sold into Egyptian slavery by his jealous brothers. Thanks to his skill at interpreting dreams, Joseph rises to become the chief advisor to Pharaoh, just as Mordecai is to Ahasuerus: "Pharaoh further said to Joseph, 'See, I put you in charge of all the land of Egypt.' And removing his signet ring from his hand, Pharaoh put it on Joseph's hand; and he had him dressed in robes of fine linen, and put a gold chain around his neck. . . . Thus he placed him over all the land of Egypt."

Joseph, like Mordecai, uses his power to help the Israelites, inviting his brothers to leave famine-ridden Canaan and settle in Egypt. But this is only possible because the interests of his people and his ruler happen to coincide for the moment. Just a few chapters later in the Bible, at the beginning of the book of Exodus, the equation is reversed: a new pharaoh arises, "who did not know Joseph," and he decides that the prosperity of the Israelites is a potential threat. "And he said to his people, 'Look, the Israelite people are much too numerous for us. Let us deal shrewdly with them, so that they may not increase; otherwise in the event of war they may join our enemies in fighting against us.'"

Just like Haman, this pharaoh sees the Jews as an unassimilable element, a potential fifth column, and he too plans to carry out a genocide against them, by murdering all the Israelites' male children. It is a sign of the profound difference between the worldview of Exodus and the worldview of Esther that in the former book the Jews are rescued in dramatic fashion by the hand of God—with the ten plagues and the parting of the Red Sea—while in the latter God is never mentioned.

What Joseph and Mordecai each demonstrate is the paradox of Jewish power in a condition of Diaspora. When the Jews are powerless, they are prey to the murderousness of their enemies; but if an individual Jew becomes powerful enough to defend his people, the fact of Jewish solidarity can be seen as another proof of dangerous Jewish difference. It is only in the last half-century that this double bind has loosened, thanks to the emergence of two Jewish communities that no longer conceive of themselves as being in Diaspora. In Israel, the Jewish state, serving state interests is usually consistent with serving Jewish interests. In America, in contrast, Jews have assimilated so thoroughly—and have benefited so greatly from the culture of pluralism—that few believe there is a tension between the interests of Jews as Jews and the interests of Jews as Americans. Only if this consensus breaks down will Jews once again know what it means to occupy the dangerously privileged place of Mordecai and Esther.

BIBLIOGRAPHY

Berlin, Adele. *The JPS Bible Commentary: Esther.* Philadelphia: Jewish Publication Society, 2001.

Berquist, Jon L. *Judaism in Persia's Shadow: A Social and Historical Approach.* Minneapolis, MN: Fortress Press, 1995.

The Megillah: The Book of Esther. 35th ed. Translated by Rabbi Meir Zlotowitz. Brooklyn, NY: Mesorah Publications, 2010.

Midrash Rabbah: Esther. 3rd ed. Translated by Maurice Simon. London: Soncino Press, 1983.

3

READING AGAINST THE GRAIN

The Exposition of the Laws by Philo of Alexandria

Philo was a Greek-speaking Jew who lived in Egypt—a one-man example of the cosmopolitanism of the Roman Empire. Yet during his lifetime, from around 15 BCE to around 45 CE, he witnessed a virtual civil war between the Greeks and the Jews of his native Alexandria, demonstrating that the Roman ideal of coexistence had shallow roots. For Philo, a highly educated member of an elite Jewish family, no task was more important than proving that Greek and Jewish culture were, or should be, in harmony. His surviving work takes the form of explanations of biblical stories and verses, which he uses to argue that the wisdom of Judaism and the wisdom of Greek philosophy are one and the same. Philo was among the first Jews, but far from the last, to try to reimagine the Torah as a rational and universal text—not a mere chronicle of Jewish history and legend, but a coded expression of eternal truths about nature and morality. His work remains fascinating as a testimony of how difficult it was, and still is, to reconcile secular thought with the wisdom of Jewish tradition.

THE FESTIVAL OF CHANUKAH, ONCE A MINOR FEA-ture of the Jewish calendar, has become in modern America one of the best-known and most celebrated Jewish holidays. One obvious reason is the fact that it usually falls in December, offering Jews who do not celebrate Christmas a seasonal holiday of their own. But it is ironic that American Jews, who are the most successfully assimilated Jews in history, should have taken Chanukah to their hearts. For the event that it commemorates—the rebellion led by the Maccabees against the Seleucid Greek king Antiochus IV in the mid-second century BCE—was a violent attack on the idea of Jewish assimilation.

This is made very clear in the Second Book of Maccabees, a Greek-language history of the revolt that was excluded from the Jewish biblical canon. At the center of the book is the story familiar from Chanukah. In 167 BCE, Antiochus desecrated the Temple in Jerusalem, installing an image of Zeus and sacrificing pigs on the altar, and prohibited Jews from practicing their religion; women who circumcised their sons were martyred, as were old men who refused to eat pork. But this reign of terror was lifted by Judah Maccabee and his brothers, who led a guerrilla army to victory over the occupiers, rededicated the Temple, and instituted the holiday of Chanukah as a celebration. Eventually, after Judah's death in battle, his brothers would go on to establish an independent kingdom of Judea—the first sovereign Jewish state since the destruction of David's kingdom some four hundred years earlier.

But while Antiochus's persecutions were the climax of the Jews' travails, the author of 2 Maccabees leaves no doubt that the problems began earlier, with the Jews themselves. Foolishly, he writes, the Jews wanted to assimilate to Greek culture—the dominant culture of the Middle East, whose philosophy, athletic contests, and religion all made up a single, highly attractive package. The trouble started when the high priest of the Jerusalem Temple, Jason—whose Greek name bears witness to his own cultural affiliations—introduced Greek customs to the holy city:

> [H]e destroyed lawful ways of living and introduced new customs contrary to the law. For with alacrity he founded a gymnasium underneath the citadel, and he induced the noblest of the young men to wear the Greek hat. There was such an extreme of Hellenization and increase in the adoption of foreign ways because of the surpassing wickedness of Jason, who was ungodly and no high priest, that the priests were no longer intent upon their service at the altar. Despising the sanctuary and neglecting the sacrifices, they hastened to take part in the unlawful proceedings in the wrestling arena after the call to the discus, disdaining the honors prized by their fathers and putting the highest value upon Greek forms of prestige.

To the author of 2 Maccabees, this running after Gentile ways was the original Jewish sin that called forth the punishment of persecution: "For this reason heavy disaster overtook them, and those whose ways of living they admired and wished to imitate completely became their enemies and punished them." The propagandistic message of the book is impossible to miss: piety and traditional worship lead to divine favor, while innovation and Hellenization lead to misery and destruction. "It is God who has saved all his people," 2 Maccabees sums up, "and has returned the inheritance to all."

This message is entirely consistent with the vision of Jewish destiny set forth in the book of Deuteronomy. There Moses offered the Jewish people the choice of life or death, blessing or curse, establishing the principle that it is the Jews' own behavior that is the motive power of their destiny. A neutral reader of the books of Kings, for instance, might conclude that the destruction of the Kingdom of Judah by the

Babylonian Empire was inevitable, a simple matter of power politics—the strong crushing the weak as they have always done. To the author of Kings and the Jewish prophets, however, there was nothing historically determined about it. The fate of Judah was linked to the piety or impiety of its successive rulers and to the people's acceptance or rejection of God's yoke. There is a paradoxical consolation in this view of history, which 2 Maccabees endorses, since it gives the Jews, the smallest and least powerful of peoples, absolute autonomy: their own choices determine their fate. This idea gave the Jews a remarkable power to endure their sufferings. It would also, at the time of the rebellion against Rome, empower some of them to take suicidal risks in the name of God.

But the story of Chanukah was far from the last word on Jewish responses to Greek culture. At the time 2 Maccabees was written, Jews were not living only in Judea; the book opens, in fact, with an epistle from "the Jewish brethren in Judea" to their fellow Jews in Egypt. And Egypt, at this time, was culturally a Hellenic domain, as symbolized by the great city of Alexandria, where Greek arts and letters were cultivated at their highest level. Even in Judea after the Maccabees, there was never the kind of cultural separation between Jew and Greek that the Chanukah story might lead us to expect. Separation was even less possible in Egypt or in the other lands where the Jews could be found. For, as one observer put it in the first century CE:

> No one country can contain the whole Jewish nation, by reason of its populousness; on which account they frequent all the most prosperous and fertile countries of Europe and Asia, whether islands or continents, looking indeed upon the holy city [of Jerusalem] as their metropolis in which is erected the sacred temple of the most high God, but accounting those regions which have been occupied by their fathers, and grandfathers, and great grandfathers, and still more remote ancestors, in which they have been born and brought up, as their country.

So writes Philo of Alexandria, also known as Philo Judaeus ("Philo the Jew"), who lived in Egypt from about 15 BCE to about 45 CE. Already it is possible to see that the simple binary of Jew versus Greek, familiar from the Chanukah story, is totally inadequate to the Jewish experience that Philo knew as a resident of Egypt under the Roman Empire. Philo acknowledges some connection to the Jewish homeland, even as he insists that his own country is the one where he was born and raised. Nowhere in his voluminous writings does he communicate the sense that he is pining for Jerusalem; at one point he mentions having visited the Temple there, but he says very little about the experience.

Of course, Philo's experience of Jewish life was not exactly typical. Little is known about his biography, but we do know that his brother was a leading official in Alexandria and that his nephew, Tiberius Julius Alexander, abandoned Judaism entirely and became a high-ranking governor and general in the Roman Empire. These connections, as well as Philo's very large literary output (his collected works in translation run to some nine hundred closely printed pages), suggest that he was wealthy and well educated, and that he led a leisured, scholarly existence. They also place him in an acculturated Jewish milieu. All of Philo's work was written in Greek, and while much of it takes the form of commentary on the Bible, it does not seem that he was able the read the Bible in Hebrew. He relied, as most Greek-speaking Jews did, on the Septuagint, the Greek-language translation made in Alexandria in the third century BCE.

It says a great deal about Philo's conception of Judaism, and of scripture, that he did not think he was missing out on anything. On the contrary, he believed the Septuagint was just as divinely inspired as the Hebrew original. In his treatise "On the Life of Moses," he repeats the legendary account of how the king of Egypt, "thinking it a scandalous thing that these laws [of Moses] should only be known among one half portion of the human race, namely, among the barbarians, and that the Greek nation should be wholly and entirely ignorant of them," commissioned seventy-two Jewish sages to come to Alexandria and translate the Bible into Greek. (Notice, too, that in this Greek-centered account, the Jews fall into the category of "barbarians," that is, people who were unfortunate enough not to speak Greek.) The translators worked independently, on the island of Pharos in the harbor of Alexandria. Yet when they emerged with their translations, every one of them had used exactly the same words—"as if some unseen prompter had suggested all their language to them."

This could only be regarded as a miracle, as Philo observes: for "who is there who does not know that every language, and the Greek language above all others, is rich in a variety of words?" It was as if, rather than translating words, the sages were all deducing scripture from first principles in the manner of mathematics: "for just as I suppose the things which are proved in geometry and logic do not admit of any variety of explanation, but the proposition which was set forth from the beginning remains unaltered, in like manner I conceive did these men find words precisely and literally corresponding to the things, which words were alone, or in the greatest possible degree, destined to explain with clearness and force the matters which it was desired to reveal."

Cleverly, Philo uses a Greek cultural touchstone—the geometry of Euclid—to lend prestige to the Jewish scriptures, which are said to be every bit as precise and deductive as geometry itself. To his Greek-speaking readers, most of whom must have been Jews like himself, this was an effective way of validating Jewish scripture, which they may have felt to be "barbarian" writings. Once elevated to the dignity of Greek, the Bible could be revered in good conscience. Just as important, a Greek-speaking Jew did not have to feel unequipped to read his own sacred texts, since, as Philo writes, the Septuagint was not derivative of the Hebrew but was its equal: "they would admire and reverence them both as sisters, or rather as one and the same both in their facts and in their language."

YET EVEN AS PHILO LAYS CLAIM to Egypt as his country and Greek as his language, his own work offers evidence that the position of the Jews in Alexandria was just as precarious as that of the Jews of Shushan in the book of Esther (see Chapter 2). In "Against Flaccus," Philo gives an eyewitness account of the terrifying anti-Jewish riots that broke out in his city in the year 38 CE. The man named in the title is Flaccus Avilius, the Roman governor of Alexandria, whom Philo accuses of harboring a Haman-like hostility to the Jews: when he sat as a judge, Philo writes, "whenever any Jew came before him he showed his aversion to him, and departed from his habitual affability in their case."

But though "Against Flaccus" is composed as a prosecutorial attack on the governor, what it really reveals is the widespread popular hostility to the Jews of Alexandria. The Jewish community treasured its communal autonomy, and Philo emphasizes that the Jews had long enjoyed the right to worship and govern themselves as they chose. But the Jews occupied a dangerous middle position in Alexandrian society—less powerful than the Greek-speaking elite that ruled the city, but legally superior to the native, Egyptian-speaking population. This left them exposed to the grievances and envy of both sides, and Philo gives the impression that the city was a powder keg waiting to explode: "the men of Alexandria [were] ready to burst with envy and ill-will . . . [and] at the same time filled with an ancient and what I may in a manner call an innate enmity towards the Jews."

This enmity was ignited into full-fledged violence by a conspicuous display of Jewish pride. In 38 CE, Agrippa, the Roman-appointed king of Judea, was on his way home from Rome, where he had just been confirmed in his title by his friend the emperor Caligula. Agrippa stopped over in Alexandria, where the Jewish community would have welcomed him warmly, perhaps with public demonstrations of support.

(It is even possible that Philo's brother, as a leading citizen, was Agrippa's host in the city—Philo speaks evasively of "the man who was to be his entertainer.") This eager welcome touched off a counterdemonstration by the non-Jewish population. A group of Alexandrians seized on a notorious local madman named Carabbas, a derelict who "spent all his days and nights naked in the roads, minding neither cold nor heat, the sport of idle children and wanton youths." This Carabbas was dressed up as a king and paraded around the streets as a parody of Agrippa, in a spectacle designed to offend the Jewish monarch: they "flattened out a leaf of papyrus and put it on his head instead of a diadem, and clothed the rest of his body with a common door mat instead of a cloak . . . young men bearing sticks on their shoulders stood on each side of him instead of spear-bearers, in imitation of the body-guard of the king."

Flaccus, Philo writes, ought to have put a stop to this public insult to Agrippa, who was, after all, an imperial favorite. But his own anti-Jewish prejudice had been inflamed by his advisers, who told him that the best way to earn the support of the city's population was to advertise his hostility to the Jews. Accordingly, Flaccus "gave complete license and impunity to all those who designed ill, and who were disposed to show their enmity and spite to the king, pretending not to see what he did see, and not to hear what he did hear." Emboldened by this indifference, the Alexandrian mob took their anti-Jewish provocations a fatal step further. They proposed to "erect images in the synagogues"—that is, to repeat in Alexandria the very outrage that had touched off the Maccabean revolt in Judea.

The way Philo describes the Jewish response to this aggression is telling. He does not praise Jewish piety or express horror at the idea of idolatry. Rather, he makes the neutral, almost sociological observation that "contests for natural customs do among all men appear more important than those which are only for the sake of life." This is the wisdom of a man who is used to living in a multicultural society, who knows that communal symbols have a power out of all proportion to their inherent value. Philo goes on to make another, strategically useful point: the synagogues, he writes, were the places where the Jews gathered to offer prayers for the well-being of the emperor. To desecrate the synagogues, then, was to deprive the emperor of his due. In this way, Philo attempts to align the interests of the Jews with those of Caligula in Rome, against the party of Flaccus and the Alexandrians.

The events that followed sound, in Philo's description, like many pogroms and persecutions in later Jewish history. The Jews of Alexandria were driven out of their neighborhoods and "crammed . . . into a very small portion of one." Their businesses were boycotted, so they sank into poverty and starvation. Just as Haman did not personally execute the Jews of Persia but gave the people permission to do so, likewise Flaccus publicly declared the Jews to be "foreigners and aliens," without any legal status, "allowing any one who was inclined to proceed to exterminate the Jews as prisoners of war." The bloodshed, as Philo describes it, was especially brutal, as it always is when neighbors kill neighbors; indeed, the up-close and personal nature of the violence brings to mind accounts of the Rwandan genocide in 1994. Philo writes of Jews being dragged down the street and trampled to death, stoned and beaten with sticks, and burned alive. Worst of all, he writes, was the flippant glee of the attackers: "And those who did these things, mimicked the sufferers, like people employed in the representation of theatrical farces."

Philo's aim in writing "Against Flaccus" was not simply to record the campaign against the Jews, but to show that God would inevitably punish enemies of the Jews. After the riots had run their course, Flaccus was recalled to Rome and sent into exile on a remote island, then killed by Caligula's agents. Too late, Philo writes, he learned his lesson: "O King of gods and men! you are not, then, indifferent to the Jewish nation, nor are the assertions which they relate with respect to your providence false. . . . And I am an evident proof of this; for all the frantic designs which I conceived against the Jews, I now suffer myself," Philo imagines Flaccus crying.

Yet Philo's attempt to cast the Alexandrian riots as a victory for the Jews and the Jewish God can't help but ring hollow. God, after all, did not prevent the massacres or punish their perpetrators. Flaccus's fall from imperial favor seems less like a divine punishment than the common fate of highly placed officials under the impetuous Caligula. And despite what Philo repeatedly implies in "Against Flaccus," Caligula was no reliable ally of the Jews.

That is clear in another treatise, "On the Embassy to Gaius," which forms a kind of sequel to "Against Flaccus." Here, in a rare piece of direct autobiography, Philo writes about how he was chosen to take part in a delegation of Alexandrian Jews that went to seek help from the emperor Caligula after the riots. (He was picked, he writes, because he was "accounted to be of superior prudence, both on account of my age and my education"—a detail that helps historians to estimate Philo's years of birth and death.) When the delegation met him in Italy, however, Caligula treated the Jewish ambassadors with ostentatious disdain. He kept them waiting as he gave orders about the remodeling of some imperial buildings, then asked them jeeringly, "Why is it that you abstain from eating pig's flesh?" Indeed, while Philo had earlier seen Caligula as God's instrument for chastising Flaccus, he now sees the emperor as a determined enemy of the Jews: "he cherished an indescribable hatred against the Jews, so that [the courtiers'] opinion was that no one could do him a more acceptable service than by inflicting every description of injury on the nation which he hated."

What accounts for this extraordinary hostility? The answer Philo gives is simple: Caligula wanted to be worshipped as a god, and he knew that the Jews would never submit to this. To force the issue, the emperor ordered an enormous golden statue of himself to be erected in the Temple at Jerusalem; following in the footsteps of Antiochus, he attacked Jewish piety and pride at their most delicate spot. When Philo and his fellow delegates learned of this plan, they were "struck dumb with astonishment and terror." They recognized that this was exactly the kind of sacrilege that could force a catastrophic confrontation between the Jews and the Roman Empire. "He knew that the Jews would willingly, if it were possible, endure ten thousand deaths instead of one, rather than submit to see any forbidden thing perpetrated with respect to their religion; for all men are eager to preserve their own customs and laws, and the Jewish nation above all others," Philo observes.

Just a quarter-century later, Roman provocations in Jerusalem would in fact lead to the Jewish War that Josephus documents—and to the utter destruction of the Temple, the city, and the Jewish homeland. But Caligula's statue was never built, thanks to the prudence of Petronius, the governor of Syria, who was charged with building it. Rather than force a confrontation with the Jews, Petronius deliberately delayed work on the statue, using as an excuse his desire to have it made as perfectly as possible. Though he incurred the emperor's anger, Petronius managed to put off the issue until Caligula's assassination, in 41 CE, rendered it moot. "On the Embassy to Gaius" does not extend that far: it ends with Philo's promise to tell the story of Caligula's fall in another treatise, which does not survive. It would likely have been a morality tale along the lines of "Against Flaccus," showing how Caligula's offenses against the Jews led to his punishment by God.

Beyond their historical value, these two treatises offer a fascinating portrait of Philo's own mindset as a Jew living in a multicultural city in a multinational empire. He identifies strongly with the Jewish community and makes plain his devotion to the Temple in Jerusalem; he is as horrified as anyone by the thought of its desecration. He is convinced that God is looking out for the Jewish people and will eventually punish its enemies. But his attitude toward Greek and Roman culture is a far cry from the anxious puritanism of 2 Maccabees. A worldly and philosophical man, he knows that Jewish patriotism is not the only patriotism, that every people is equally attached to its own customs. "In all men . . . a love of their country is innate, and an eagerness for their national customs and laws," he writes. "And what belongs to themselves appears beautiful to every one, even if it is not in reality; for they judge of these things not more by reason than by the feelings of affection."

This perspective does not forfeit the Jews' claim to divine favor, but it sets that claim in perspective; it opens up a skeptical, even relativistic space in which to consider the competing claims of different national groups. Notably, when Philo complains about offenses against the Jews and their God, he does so not on religious grounds but on the grounds of the Jews' legal rights, ancient privileges, and loyalty to the Empire. That is, he adopts the kind of arguments he thinks the Romans would be willing to hear, appealing to the consensual values of his society. Philo, one might say, stands both inside and outside Judaism, in a way that perfectly reflects his position as an Alexandrian Jew educated in Greek science and philosophy. And when he comes to interpret the Jewish scriptures, that double consciousness gives him a perspective on Judaism that even today seems powerfully strange.

IT IS HARD TO KNOW just how to categorize Philo as a writer and a thinker. He often addresses metaphysical subjects—the creation of the world, the nature of God—but he is not a philosopher like Plato, whose cosmological ideas he often echoes. He has a well-developed code of ethical behavior, learned from the Greek Stoics, about how to maintain inner freedom in a world ruled by fortune—yet he is not a Stoic teacher like Epictetus, either. In fact, only a few of Philo's numerous works are straightforward philosophical treatises, with titles like "On the Virtues."

The vast majority of Philo's writing takes the form of biblical commentary and paraphrase, focused primarily on the narrative portions of Genesis and Exodus. Though little is known about the date or order of their composition, scholars divide these writings into two series. "The Exposition of the Laws" is, one might say, the beginner's course in Philo's thought. It is a series of essays on major episodes and characters in the Torah, seemingly designed to be read by Jews with little knowledge of Judaism—or perhaps even by non-Jews. From "The Creation of the World" through "On Abraham," "On Joseph," "On the Life of Moses," and "The Decalogue," Philo summarizes some of the best-known Bible stories.

After reading these treatises, the initiate may be ready to proceed to the advanced curriculum of "The Allegory of the Laws." If "The Exposition" is exoteric, meant for a general audience, the treatises that make up "The Allegory" are esoteric: they teach a way of reading the Bible that dismisses its plain sense almost entirely, turning the familiar stories into coded statements of hidden religious and philosophical truths. Where "The Exposition" summarizes, "The Allegory" analyzes, proceeding almost line by line through the first half of the book of Genesis, from the Garden of Eden down to the patriarchs. Philo squeezes the words of the Bible in order to release their hidden essences, until the text almost disappears beneath its own subtexts.

What makes Philo's commentaries unique, and utterly different from the rabbinic commentaries that would define traditional Judaism, is the way they use the Bible to teach ideas and principles that seem more at home in Greek philosophy. The spirit in which he does this is sometimes reminiscent of the way many liberal theologians write about the Bible today. Just as a twenty-first-century reader might focus, for instance, on the humanitarian tendency of some of the laws of Deuteronomy, while ignoring or explaining away the anti-gay laws of Leviticus, so Philo gives us a Bible that conforms precisely to the advanced thinking of his own generation of Greek-speaking Jews.

At the same time, the care he takes to present the Bible as the source of his most cherished convictions suggests his profound loyalty to Judaism. In "On the Life of Moses," he writes scornfully of those— and we can imagine he had his fellow Alexandrian Jews in mind— who give up their ancestral customs: "they overlook their relations and friends, and transgress the laws according to which they were born and brought up; and they overturn their national hereditary customs to which no just blame whatever is attached . . . by reason of their cordial reception of the customs among which they are living, no longer remembering a single one of their ancient usages." Philo is fascinatingly divided between the desire to preserve his Jewish inheritance and his need to make Judaism harmonize with his own "modern" intuitions about God and ethics.

Some of the strategies Philo uses to resolve this tension can be seen in "On the Creation," the treatise that is placed at the beginning of "The Exposition of the Laws." Here Philo faces an acute challenge: to reconcile the cosmology of Genesis, which has the world being created *ex nihilo* by God, with the cosmology of Greek philosophy, which held that the universe was eternal and that God was simply the principle that set matter in motion. (The same problem would be one of the central issues in Moses Maimonides's *The Guide of the Perplexed*, more than a millennium later; see Chapter 7.) As Philo notes early on, "some men, admiring the world itself rather than the Creator of the world, have represented it as existing without any maker, and eternal; and as impiously as falsely have represented God as existing in a state of complete inactivity." Philo, in other words, is acutely aware of the kinds of ideas about the universe that his readers are likely to hold. He knows his audience's mindset because he had the same kind of Greek education they did.

To earn authority for the Bible in this cultural context, it is important to present it as the work not just of a divinely inspired lawgiver, but of a thinker, a philosopher, who has studied the workings of the universe. For Philo, who adheres to the traditional view that Moses personally wrote the five books of the Torah, this means recasting him as one who "had early reached the very summits of philosophy, and who learned from the oracles of God the most numerous and important of the principles of nature."

With these words, Philo skillfully elides the enormous difference between Moses the lawgiver and Moses the philosopher, by suggesting that "the oracles of God" are one and the same as "the principles of nature." In the Bible, it could not be clearer that men come to know God when God decides to reveal himself to them; and the content of his revelations are not the kind of thing that could be deduced from first principles. Much of what God tells Moses on Mount Sinai, for instance, has to do with the exact specifications of the Tabernacle that he wants built in his honor—entirely contingent information, which no amount of philosophy could have discovered.

To Philo, however, God is both a supernatural Creator and at the same time immanent in nature and the laws of nature. This is clear when he discusses the fourth day of Creation, when God made the sun, moon, and stars. In Genesis, God describes his reasons for making these lights in the sky: "Let there be lights in the expanse of the sky to separate day from night; they shall serve as signs for the set times—the days and the years; and they shall serve as lights in the expanse of the sky to shine upon the earth." The heavenly bodies, on this account, are made for practical purposes—to shed light and to divide time.

Philo acknowledges as much: "One of the reasons for His so doing was that they might give light; another was that they might be signs." But the most important reason for the creation of the stars, he believes, is that contemplating them leads men to philosophy:

> [B]eholding . . . the harmonious dances of all these bodies arranged according to the laws of perfect music causes an ineffable joy and delight to the soul. And the soul, feasting on a continuous series of spectacles, for one succeeds another, has an insatiable love for beholding such. Then, as is usually the case, it examines with increased curiosity what is the substance of these things which are visible; and whether they have an existence without having been created, or whether they received their origin by creation, and what is the character of their movement, and what the causes are by which everything is regulated. And it is from inquiries into these things that philosophy has arisen, than which no more perfect good has entered into human life.

The origin of philosophy is wonder, Plato said, and Philo agrees. Stars, on this account, are God's signature, a clue that he leaves in the heavens to start human beings on the path toward understanding him. This seems to imply that the beginnings of divine knowledge are available to all men and nations. The people of Israel may have the most direct and fullest knowledge of God, since they have received the Torah; but there is also a natural path to God, which requires no particular revelation to follow. Indeed, Philo comes close to speaking of a natural law when he writes of a "constitution [that] prevailed in the universal world. And this constitution is the right reason of nature, which in more appropriate language is denominated law, being a divine arrangement."

This sober and rational understanding of a law-governed universe encounters a number of stumbling blocks in Genesis itself, which Philo is careful to smooth away. Consider the biblical account of the creation of human beings. Philo notices that Genesis has God creating man twice. In chapter 1, "God created man in His image, in the image of God He created him; male and female He created them." Then, in chapter 2, comes the famous story of God making man out of earth, breathing life into his nostrils, and extracting a rib to create woman. To modern biblical scholarship, this, like so many other doublings in the Bible, is an artifact of the combination of two different textual traditions.

To Philo, however, there had to be another explanation. First of all, he wants to make clear, the phrase "God created man in His image" is not to be taken literally. "Let no one think that he is able to judge of this likeness from the characters of the body," he warns, "for neither is God a being with the form of a man, nor is the human body like the form of God." Not for Philo, nor for Judaism, the anthropomorphic gods of Greek mythology. No, "the resemblance is spoken of with reference to the most important part of the soul, namely, the mind." Just as the mind is "in some sort the God of that body which carries it about," so God is the mind of the universe, the intellect immanent in nature.

It follows that in this first account of the creation of man, Moses is referring strictly to the creation of the *idea* of man. "Man, made according to the image of God, was an idea, or a genus, or a seal, perceptible only to the intellect, incorporeal, neither male nor female, imperishable by nature." This Platonic notion of a realm of pure idea, superior to ordinary reality and the model for it, will return in much greater detail in "The Allegory of the Laws." For now, in "On the Creation," Philo makes clear that the creation of the idea of man was the first step in the process. Only after the idea was made did God clothe it in flesh and blood. "For . . . the body was created by the Creator taking a lump of clay, and fashioning the human form out of it; but . . . the soul proceeds from no created thing at all, but from the Father and Ruler of all things . . . for this reason, one may properly say that man is on the boundaries of a better and an immortal nature. . . . Mortal as to his body, but immortal as to his intellect." In this way, Philo reads into Genesis a doctrine of the immortal, intellectual soul that is quite foreign to the plain sense of the text.

Philo is quick to explain away other features of the Bible as allegorical and fable-like. He is far from believing, for instance, that there really was a Garden of Eden, with a tree of life and a tree of knowledge growing in it. "For no trees of life or of knowledge have ever at any previous time appeared upon the earth, nor is it likely that any will appear hereafter," he writes almost sarcastically. This is a remarkable statement of the continuity of history. There was not an age of miracles, recorded in the Bible, that is now over; rather, just as the stars have always been tracing their patterns in the sky, so the world has always had the properties it has now. This means that in writing about the trees of Eden, Moses could only have been "speaking in an allegorical spirit." The tree of life is simply a symbol of "the greatest of virtues—namely, piety towards the gods, by means of which the soul is made immortal."

At the end of "On the Creation," Philo summarizes the philosophical doctrines, the "five most beautiful lessons," that he thinks are found in the Genesis story. Each point is formulated as Moses's preemptive strike against a kind of error that is prevalent in Philo's own day. First, "for the sake of convincing the atheists, he teaches us that the Deity has a real being and existence." Second, against "the polytheistic doctrine," Moses "teaches us that God is one." Third, he teaches that "the world was created," thus "refuting those who think that it is uncreated and eternal." Fourth, he shows that "the world is one, since also the Creator is one," against "some persons who believe that there are many worlds." And fifth, "Moses teaches us . . . that God exerts his providence for the benefit of the world"; he is not an Unmoved Mover who merely sets the universe going, but constantly superintends his Creation.

None of these five doctrines is alien to what we now think of as traditional Judaism. But there is a great difference in mood and implication between the Shema—"Hear O Israel! The Lord is our God, the Lord alone"—and Philo's forensic statement that "God is one." The former is a statement of Jewish chosenness; the latter is an intervention into Greek philosophical debates. The tension that pervades Philo's work is that he wants to interpret the particular events and laws of Jewish scripture as abstract truths about the world in general.

THIS TENSION IS ESPECIALLY visible in Philo's two-part treatise "On the Life of Moses." As we have seen, Philo's Moses is not simply the lawgiver of the Jewish people, but a philosopher who teaches universal lessons, often in the form of parable and allegory. Yet there is no way to retell Moses's story without including elements that are far from rational; his was a life full of miracles, from the burning bush to the ten plagues to the parting of the Red Sea and beyond. Philo faithfully records these events, as he must. But he writes about them in a way that acknowledges their strangeness while simultaneously domesticating it into symbolism. Everything that happens to Moses, in Philo's telling, is meant to teach a moral lesson.

Take the episode of the burning bush. In chapter 3 of Exodus, Moses sees "a bush all flame, yet the bush was not consumed" and hears the voice of God calling to him from the bush: "Moses! Moses!" Yet when Philo tells this story in "On the Life of Moses," he insists that Moses did not hear a voice from the bush. On the contrary, he writes, while there was indeed a bush that miraculously burned without being consumed, this took place "in a silence more distinct than any voice by reason of the marvelous sight which was thus exhibited." The meaning of the bush, for Philo, is not audible but visible. It is a symbol that contained, rebus-like, a hidden message about the fate of the enslaved Israelites: "For the burning bush was a symbol of the oppressed people, and the burning fire was a symbol of the oppressors, and the circumstance of the burning bush not being consumed was an emblem of the fact that the people thus oppressed would not be destroyed by those who were attacking them." In this way, Philo does not exactly deny the miraculous nature of the burning bush, but he turns it into a kind of miracle that seems more acceptable to him: a rational message in visual form—that is, an allegory.

Similarly, when Moses ascends Mount Sinai and receives the Ten Commandments—which Philo discusses in another treatise, "The Decalogue"—we are not to think that God physically spoke the words of the law. "Did he then do so, uttering himself some kind of voice? Away! let not such an idea ever enter your mind; for God is not like a man, in need of a mouth, and of a tongue, and of a windpipe." Rather, God miraculously caused "an invisible sound to be created in the air . . . a rational soul filled with clearness and distinctness, which fashioned the air and stretched it out and changed it into a kind of flaming fire." This is no less a miracle than the one the Bible describes, but it is more conformable, Philo feels, with the laws of physics and the dignity of God. Instead of God physically speaking, a "rational soul" communicates God's ideas directly to the intellect.

There are many other moments in "On the Life of Moses" that attempt to reduce the affront to reason in the biblical text. In Exodus, when the Israelites are suffering from thirst, God verbally instructs Moses to strike a rock, and water issues from it. In Philo, Moses is "inspired by God" to strike the rock—not explicitly instructed to do so—and when the water appears, it is for natural reasons: "whether it was that there was a spring previously concealed beneath it, [or] whether water was then for the first time conveyed into it by invisible channels pouring all together and being forced out with violence."

Even so, Philo remains notably defensive about the miracles he has to relate, as is clear from the way he imagines the reader's objections to them. "And if anyone disbelieves these facts," he writes, "he neither knows God nor has he ever sought to know him." All the same, Philo goes on to denigrate the miracles of the Bible as merely "the amusement of God." "The things which are really great and deserving of serious attention," he writes, are "the creation of heaven, and the revolutions of the planets and the fixed stars . . . and the position of earth in the most central spot of the universe": that is, the celestial truths of astronomy, which had traditionally been linked to speculations about the divine in Greek philosophy. When Philo thinks about God, he prefers to think about stars than about burning bushes and water-giving rocks. The former are the respectable manifestations of God's power, while the latter, though undeniable, remain slightly disreputable.

When it comes to Moses himself, Philo prefers to imagine him not as a bearded prophet on a mountaintop, but as a well-educated man, a philosopher—specifically, a Stoic philosopher, who is distinguished by mastery of his passions. Thus we read that the child Moses, having been rescued from the Nile River and raised by Pharaoh's daughter, received a classical education, with teachers imported from Greece (where else?) to teach him "arithmetic, and geometry, and the whole of music." He learned so readily, Philo writes, that "everything in his case appeared to be a recollecting rather than a learning"—a reference to Plato's theory that learning is really a recollection of things known in an earlier life.

But Moses's intellectual achievements are less important to Philo than his ability to put the tenets of Stoicism into practice. Though raised in a royal palace, the young Moses "behaved with temperance and fortitude, as though he had bound [his passions] with reins. . . . And he tamed, and appeased, and brought under due command every one of the other passions which are naturally . . . frantic, and violent, and unmanageable." Moses, in other words, attained the state of rational freedom and equilibrium that was the goal of Stoic discipline. If none of this can be readily deduced from the text of the Bible, that does not worry Philo. He is so certain of the virtues the good man must possess that it is only logical to assume that Moses, who was the best man who ever lived, must have possessed them in abundance.

It follows, for Philo, that the laws Moses taught are not arbitrary, nor do they apply only to one small part of the human race. Rather, the Jewish laws are—if understood properly, that is, allegorically—the most perfect laws ever given to mankind, offering the best way to live for everyone. We are used to contrasting the laws of nature, accessible to human reason alone, with revelation, which can only come from God; but Philo continually blurs this distinction by suggesting that the Laws of Moses are themselves a perfect expression of natural laws. "If any one were inclined to examine with accuracy the powers of each individual and particular law, he will find them all aiming at the harmony of the universe, and corresponding to the law of eternal nature," he insists. That is why Philo can look forward to the day when "every nation, abandoning all their own individual customs, and utterly disregarding their national laws, would change and come over to the honor of [the Jewish] people only; for their laws . . . will obscure all others, just as the rising sun obscures the stars."

It is not hard to make such a universalizing argument for some Jewish laws—say, the Ten Commandments, whose prohibitions on theft, adultery, and murder are shared by all cultures. But as Philo well knew, his view of the naturalness of Jewish law would have sounded highly paradoxical to any non-Jewish reader, and perhaps to some Jewish ones as well. After all, weren't the Jews famous, or infamous, in the ancient world for certain practices that flew in the face of Roman and Greek habits—such as their refusal to eat pork, which the emperor Caligula had openly mocked? And what about the rite of circumcision, which other peoples found so odd? How could such laws be called rational and natural?

Philo takes up this question in his four-part treatise "On the Special Laws," which follows "The Decalogue" and addresses the Mosaic law code in detail. It begins, naturally enough, with the issue of circumcision. Philo is well aware that "the ordinance of circumcision of the parts of generation is ridiculed," and he wants to present a defense of it to the world. For this purpose, it would do no good for Philo to say that Jews circumcise their sons because God commanded them to do so in Genesis: "You shall circumcise the flesh of your foreskin, and that shall be the sign of the covenant between Me and you." This might convince believing Jews, but they are not the ones who need convincing. What Philo needs to show is not that God happened to instruct the Israelites to do something, but that all his instructions are natural and rational.

In fact, Philo argues, there are three good, commonsense reasons for circumcision—not spiritual reasons, but medical ones. First, it prevents painful carbuncles; second, it keeps the penis clean, because no dirt can lodge under the foreskin; third, it increases fertility, allowing "the seminal fluid [to] proceed in its path easily." But Philo takes the argument a step further. Circumcision doesn't just have a pragmatic value; it also has a symbolic value. "First of all," he writes, "it is a symbol of the excision of the pleasures which delude the mind." By "mutilating" the sexual organ, circumcision creates a permanent reminder that sexual pleasure is "superfluous and excessive," a great threat to the kind of self-mastery Philo cherishes. Second, circumcision is "a symbol of man's knowing himself, and discarding that terrible disease, the vain opinion of the soul." His reasoning here is unexpected. Because men and women can have children, Philo argues, they may become "puffed up with arrogance," thinking that they themselves are like gods since they can create life. Marking the reproductive organ is a reminder that man is not a true creator, but an inferior creation.

This kind of symbolic interpretation of the Jewish laws adds to their majesty, but it also has the potential to make actual obedience seem superfluous. After all, if the real meaning of circumcision has to do with continence and humility, can't we simply strive for continence and humility directly, without going to the trouble of being circumcised? Once we understand the meaning of a sign, doesn't the sign itself lose its importance? Philo is acutely aware of this prospect; indeed, he gives the sense that many Jews of his time thought in just this way about the laws. As he writes in the treatise "On the Migration of Abraham," there are some "who, looking upon written laws of symbols of things appreciable by the intellect . . . have treated [them] with neglectful indifference."

But Philo insists that this is an error. "They ought to attend to both classes of things," he continues, "applying themselves both to an accurate investigation of invisible things, and also to an irreproachable observance of [the] laws." Just because "the rite of circumcision is an emblem of the excision of pleasure and all the passions," he writes, taking up the theme of "The Special Laws," it does not follow "that we are to annul the law that has been enacted about circumcision." It is an error to "seek for plain naked truth by itself." Rather, the meaning of the law is inseparable from its form, just as the soul is inseparable from the body:

> But it is right to think that this class of things resembles the
> body, and the other class the soul; therefore, just as we take care

of the body because it is the abode of the soul, so also must we take care of the laws that are enacted in plain terms: for while they are regarded, those other things also will be more clearly understood, of which these laws are the symbols, and in the same way one will escape blame and accusation from men in general.

There is no mistaking the sincerity and passion of Philo's argument; but it is not altogether convincing. He advances two reasons why Jews should continue to obey the Mosaic laws. First, he insists that practice sustains theory: obeying the laws will make us more aware of the meaning of those laws. Second, he warns that publicly disobeying the laws will attract censure. One might think that this censure would come from other, obedient Jews, but Philo says that it comes from "men in general": he seems to think that a law-breaking Jew will be reprehensible even to Gentiles, since even they expect Jews to follow their own ancient traditions.

Neither of these reasons, however, addresses the central point, which is that laws cease to be laws if they are only symbols. To do something because God commanded it is one thing; to do it because other people expect you to do it is quite another. Saint Paul, who was Philo's younger contemporary, can be said to have taken Philo's distinction between the letter and the spirit of the laws and radicalized it. After Jesus, Paul believed, the letter was no longer binding; in fact, it was a positive hindrance to true faith, and following the laws was an example of retrograde "Judaizing." This is one of several ways in which Philo's work shares the intellectual atmosphere of early Christianity, making him a valuable source for scholars interested in the worldview of Paul and the Gospel writers. Indeed, it was the Christians, not the Jews, who preserved Philo's works and transmitted them to posterity. Early Christian writers like Origen and Eusebius cited his works admiringly, while there is not a single reference to him in the rabbinic literature of the period.

IN "THE EXPOSITION OF THE LAWS," Philo strains to keep
the letter of scripture and its inner meaning in balance. In "The Allegory of the Laws," by sharp contrast, the literal sense of biblical stories
is allowed to fall away like a husk, as the secret philosophical meaning
bursts forth in all its grandeur. The Bible, as Philo reads it in these
esoteric treatises, is in fact one giant allegory whose true subject is
not God's calling of the Israelites to be the chosen people, but God's
calling of the individual to live according to virtue. In this way, Philo
gives what might seem to be the parochial scriptures of the Jews a universal status and purpose. The Bible is for the Jews in the first place,
but really it is addressed to everyone. Indeed, at times Philo seems to
suggest that when the Bible says "Israel" or "the Hebrews," it does not
mean the Jewish people, but anyone who is willing to open his mind
to God's message.

The practice of reading allegorically was well established in the
Greek world by the time Philo wrote. The Stoics used allegory to interpret the epic poems of Homer, seeking to turn those often-unedifying
chronicles of divine malfeasance into wisdom literature. Philo uses the
same techniques on the Bible, concentrating on the first half of Genesis, and the boldness of his hermeneutics is astonishing. It's likely that
Philo was not the only Hellenistic Jewish exegete to read the Bible in
this way, but his are the works that have survived, and they present a
radical contrast with our familiar ways of understanding scripture.

Consider his three-part treatise titled "Allegorical Interpretation,"
which is placed at the head of "The Allegory of the Laws." Philo
begins with Genesis 2:1: "The heaven and the earth were finished, and
all their array." This appears to be a statement about cosmology; but
really, Philo declares, it is a statement about the human soul. "Speaking
symbolically, [Moses] calls the mind heaven . . . and sensation he calls
earth," he explains. This dualism, between the mind that is drawn to

celestial truths and the body that is weighed down by material desires, will structure all of Philo's biblical allegories, just as it did so much of Greek philosophy. When we read "heaven and earth," we are meant to think "mind and body"—meant, that is, by Moses himself.

For Philo does not at all acknowledge, or believe, what will occur to any skeptical reader—that his interpretations of the Bible do violence to its plain meaning. On the contrary, he is certain that he is uncovering the true meaning intended by Moses himself. In one of the rare moments of self-revelation in his work, Philo explains that he receives his allegorical insights as divine inspirations, gifts from God:

> Sometimes when I have come to my work empty I have suddenly become full, ideas being, in an invisible manner, showered upon me, and implanted in me from on high; so that, through the influence of divine inspiration, I have become greatly excited, and have known neither the place in which I was nor those who were present, nor myself, nor what I was saying, nor what I was writing; for then I have been conscious of a richness of interpretation, an enjoyment of light, a most penetrating sight . . . having such an effect on my mind as the clearest ocular demonstration would have on the eyes.

This is Philo's intellectual version of a mystic's trance or a poet's inspiration. For him, it takes the form of an epiphany about what Moses really meant. As we have seen in "The Exposition of the Laws," Philo is especially concerned to clear away what might seem like irrational or anthropomorphic descriptions of God. The creation of the world in six days, for example, is to him plainly metaphorical: "It would be a sign of great simplicity to think that the world was created in six days." Today, it might be geology or evolution that would spur a sophisticated Bible reader to interpret the six days of creation allegorically. Since we know from science that the earth is billions of years old, the plain sense of the text is untenable and can only be saved by being considered as metaphor.

Philo comes to the same conclusion by strict logic. Time, he reasons, is "a thing posterior to the world," which can only come into being when there is a world to contain it: "It would be correctly said that the world was not created in time, but that time had its existence in consequence of the world." When Moses says that God created the world in six days, then, he is speaking allegorically, conveying the special status of the number six. In a very characteristic passage of number mysticism, Philo explains that six is "a perfect number," since it is the sum of its factors and also because there are six directions (forward, backward, up, down, right, and left). For these reasons, he feels, six is a fitting emblem of the physical world. Philo is able to perform similar feats of numerical exegesis for every number that comes up in the Bible, including the seventh day of rest and the Ten Commandments.

Philo goes on to offer allegorical interpretations of each feature, sometimes each word, of the Adam and Eve story. He advances a complex metaphysical scheme explaining how God created the world, the relationship of abstract ideas to existing creatures, and the strife between the human soul and the body. At the same time, Philo does away with what strike him as undignified absurdities in the text. Eve, we learn, was not really made from Adam's rib; rather, the rib represents "one of the many powers of the mind, namely, that power which dwells in the outward senses," and woman herself is "the most natural and felicitously given name for the external sense."

Just as heaven and earth became a symbol for mind and body, so here male and female serve the same function. Given Philo's low view of the body and of external sensation, this is hardly flattering to the female. "Hence a man leaves his father and mother and clings to his wife, so that they become one flesh," the Bible reads, in what seems like a strong endorsement of marriage. To Philo, however, this is only a figure, and not a happy one: "On account of the external sensation, the mind, when it has become enslaved to it, shall leave both its father, the God of the universe, and the mother of all things, namely, the virtue and wisdom of God, and cleaves to and becomes united to the external sensation."

Philo applies this same philosophical paradigm to the history of the Israelites. In "On the Migration of Abraham," he turns to the founding event of Jewish history: God's covenant with Abraham in Genesis 12. This too, in Philo's hands, becomes a parable about soul and body. When God tells Abraham, "Go forth from your native land and from your father's house to the land that I will show you," he is not promising Abraham a specific territory, the Land of Israel. Rather, he is instructing Abraham to abandon his body: "for his country is the emblem of the body . . . because the body derives its composition from the earth." The change God wants from Abraham is not geographical but moral: "It is the same as saying, Be alienated from [the senses] in your mind, allowing none of them to cling to you, standing above them all; they are your subjects, use them not as your rulers since you are a king, learn to govern and not to be governed." These are all standard tropes of Stoic ethics, projected onto—or, to Philo, discovered in—the sacred history of the Jews.

The question that arises, then, is whether that history is still actually sacred. Are the Jews a particular group of people with a specific ancestry and homeland, or are they an emblem for a universal condition? Philo's answer seems deliberately ambiguous. In "On the Migration of Abraham," Philo notes that the title of the book of Exodus perfectly describes the central movement of his thought: what he constantly urges is an exodus from the body and the world, to the promised land of intellect and independence. "Egypt, that is to say, the body," he writes, suggesting that every individual's emancipation from the body constitutes a new exodus. "The Hebrews," it follows, are those who "were accustomed to rise up and leave the objects of the outward senses, and to go over to those of the intellect; for the name Hebrew, being interpreted, means 'one who passes over.'"

Does it follow, then, that every emancipated soul is a Hebrew? Philo seems to suggest as much when he discusses a well-known verse from Deuteronomy: "It is not because you are the most numerous of peoples that the Lord set His heart on you and chose you—indeed, you are the smallest of peoples." For Philo, this is an allegory about the soul, which he compares to the population of the earth. In this little world, there are "a great many ranks totally destitute of all order, [such as] pleasures, or appetites or griefs, or again follies and iniquities, and all the other vices which are connected with or akin to them."

But there is only a small and select spiritual population that is "well regulated, that namely which is under the leadership of right reason." When God says that he favors the small nation of Israel, he means that he favors the small number of good instincts in the human soul, and the small number of well-regulated souls, above the disorderly multitude. "In the eye of God a small company that is good is preferred to an infinite number of persons who are unjust," Philo writes, and this small company is the true Israel. It is never quite clear whether he believes that all righteous men are Jews, or that all Jews are—or should be—righteous men, or whether perhaps, at the end of history, the two groups will merge and all humanity will follow the laws of Moses.

Yet Philo has stopped his quotation of Deuteronomy significantly short. He does not quote the next verse, which reads: "but it was because the Lord favored you and kept the oath he made to your fathers that the Lord freed you with a mighty hand and rescued you from the house of bondage, from the power of Pharaoh king of Egypt." Here we return to the traditional understanding of Jewishness as a product of history and covenant, not of individual virtue. By turning the Bible into parable, Philo diminishes—though he never quite dismisses—the contingency and specificity of that history. The pathos of his allegories comes from the way he tries to unite the respect owed to inheritance with the respect owed to reason. Philo of Alexandria was one of the first Jewish intellectuals to feel the pull of these competing demands; he would certainly not be the last.

BIBLIOGRAPHY

Gruen, Erich S. *Heritage and Hellenism: The Reinvention of Jewish Tradition*. Berkeley: University of California Press, 1998.

Kamesar, Adam, ed. *The Cambridge Companion to Philo*. New York: Cambridge University Press, 2009.

Sandmel, Samuel. *Philo of Alexandria: An Introduction*. New York: Oxford University Press, 1979.

The Works of Philo: New Updated Edition. Translated by C. D. Yonge. Peabody, MA: Hendrickson, 1993.

4

CHOOSING
LIFE

The Jewish War
by Flavius Josephus

The Arch of Titus, built to celebrate the Roman victory over Judea

When the Jews of Judea rebelled against the power of the Roman Empire in 66 CE, they started a war that would lead to the destruction of the Temple and the end of Jewish sovereignty in the Land of Israel. It was perhaps the greatest calamity in Jewish history—and also one of the best documented, thanks to one book: *The Jewish War.*

The man who wrote it, Flavius Josephus, was directly involved in the events he describes, having served as a general in the rebel army. After he was captured, he went over to the Roman side, trying to persuade the Jews to lay down their arms. To Josephus, the Jewish rebellion was a suicidal gesture by a small subject people; to the rebels, it was a defiant stand for political and religious freedom. Reading *The Jewish War* means being plunged into this debate, which did so much to determine the shape of Jewish history, and which continues to echo in our own era of religious violence.

ONE DAY ABOUT NOON, LATE IN THE YEAR 5 BCE, anyone who happened to be visiting the Temple in Jerusalem would have been greeted by a strange sight: a group of about forty young men dangling on ropes from the roof, with pick-axes in hand. Herod the Great, the king of Judea, lay dying in his palace, and his people—always restive under his expensive, often-bloody rule—had taken offense at one of his latest acts of civic improvement. On the Great Gate of the Temple, Herod had installed the golden image of an eagle—a sight that would have reminded every Jew passing under it of the power of Rome, whose armies marched under standards adorned with eagles.

Herod could not be accused of underestimating the importance of the Temple to the Jewish people. On the contrary, over the course of his more than thirty years on the throne, he had totally renovated its buildings, adding towers and colonnades and golden roofs, making it one of the most splendid monuments in the Roman Empire. Joseph ben Matthias—the Jewish priest known to posterity as Flavius Josephus, the Latin version of his name—remembered the wonderful sight that Herod's Temple presented to the crowds of Jews who flocked there for the major Jewish holidays:

Viewed from without the Sanctuary had everything that could amaze either mind or eyes. Overlaid all round with stout plates of gold, in the first rays of the sun it reflected so fierce a blaze of fire that those who endeavored to look at it were forced to turn away as if they had looked straight at the sun. To strangers as they approached it seemed in the distance like a mountain covered with snow; for any part not covered with gold was dazzling white.

Herod had given the Temple a physical appearance suited to its importance in Jewish life. Built by Solomon, destroyed by the Babylonians in 586 BCE, rebuilt under the Persian Empire, the Temple was the center of Jewish ritual practice. Animal sacrifices were performed there in a constant stream, especially on the three major holidays—Passover, Shavuot, and Sukkot—when Jews from around Judea, and beyond, flocked to the city to worship. Jews throughout the Roman Empire paid a two-drachma tax for the upkeep of the Temple and its priests.

The Temple was the focus of Jewish pride and aspiration, especially at a time when political sovereignty was elusive. Nominally, Jewish kings had ruled Judea since the second century BCE, when the Maccabee revolt had placed the Hasmonean dynasty on the throne. But no small kingdom in the Middle East could escape the rising power of the Romans, and in 63 BCE Pompey the Great had intervened in a Jewish civil war and brought the country into the Roman sphere of influence. Ever since, Judea's kings had ruled more or less at the sufferance of the emperors in Rome. Herod himself, who was not a Hasmonean or even a Jew but an Idumaean—from a neighboring people that had converted to Judaism—was placed on the throne of Judea by Mark Antony, as a reward for his family's services in Rome's civil wars.

For Herod to put an eagle on the gate to the Temple, then, was a double offense to Jewish sensibilities. Politically, it represented the subjection of Judea to Rome. Religiously, it could be taken to violate the Second Commandment's ban on images. "It was unlawful," Josephus explains in *The Jewish War*, his account of this fateful period in Jewish history, "to have in the Sanctuary images or portrait-busts or the likeness of any living thing."

Two influential rabbis, named Judas and Matthias, began to exhort their pupils that with Herod on his deathbed, the time was ripe to tear down the proud eagle. The rabbis told the young Jews of Jerusalem not to worry about the inevitable punishment: "even if danger was involved, it was a glorious thing to die for the laws of their fathers. For those who came to such an end there was a sure hope of immortality and the eternal enjoyment of blessings, whereas the poor-spirited, knowing nothing of the rabbinical wisdom, through ignorance clung to life and chose death by disease rather than death in a righteous cause."

This message found eager listeners, and soon the rabbis' followers set to work, as Josephus reports:

> At mid-day, when masses of people were walking about the Temple courts, they lowered themselves by stout ropes from the roof and began to cut down the golden eagle with axes. The news quickly reached the king's officer, who hurried to the spot with a large force, seized about forty young men and took them before the king. He began by asking them whether they had dared to cut down the golden eagle. They said they had. Who told them to do it? The law of their fathers. What made them so cheerful when they were about to be executed? The knowledge that they would enjoy greater blessings after death.

The rebels' wish was granted: Herod had the young vandals, and the rabbis who inspired them, burned alive. In itself, this was a minor episode; endless blood had already been spilled in the game of Judean power politics before it happened, and soon afterward Herod's death would be the cue for still more violence. Yet all the Hasmonean and Herodian intrigues were just the prelude to the monumental catastrophe that is Josephus's major subject in *The Jewish War*: the Jewish rebellion against Roman power in 66 CE.

This uprising would last for four years—the last four years of Jewish political independence that the world would see for the next two millennia. In 70 CE, Roman forces led by Titus, the son of the emperor Vespasian, captured Jerusalem and burned the Temple to the ground. Countless Jews died—according to Josephus, the casualties numbered 1,100,000, though as with all ancient historians his figures are not to be taken too literally. A few decades later, after the failure of a second Jewish uprising, the names of Judea and Jerusalem would be wiped from the map. The Temple has not been rebuilt to this day; indeed, Judaism as we now know it, the Judaism of the synagogue, was created as a response to the Temple's absence. Not until 1967, with the Israeli victory in the Six Day War, would the Temple Mount once again fall under Jewish sovereignty.

Compared to this world-historical catastrophe, the vandalism of the year 5 BCE looks like a mere prank. Yet Josephus included the episode of the golden eagle for a reason. Here, in miniature, was the same dynamic that would propel the Jewish War to its terrible ending; and here are the same moral and political questions that the war continues to raise. How should we think about the rabbis and their young followers? Were they patriotic idealists—Judean versions of the American Revolutionary hero Nathan Hale, who regretted that they had only one life to give for their country? Were they religious martyrs, who guaranteed the survival of Judaism by being ready to die for its principles? Or does their language of glorious death and heavenly reward remind us more of the fundamentalist terrorists of our own time—soldiers of faith who are all the more dangerous because they proudly despise life?

Such questions come up again, even more forcefully, when Josephus writes about the Jews' decision to go to war against Rome in 66 CE. Here, if ever, was a doomed struggle: the fight of a small people, and a divided one at that, against the world's greatest empire. Like the young men who vandalized the eagle, the Jews who rose up against Rome—led by a radical party of disaffected priests, known as the Zealots thanks to their zeal for God's honor—were risking death in the name of Jewish independence and religious conviction. Yet this could only be a symbolic sacrifice, for anyone thinking rationally could have foreseen that the Jewish uprising would end in defeat.

Indeed, Josephus, availing himself of the freedom of the ancient historian, puts that very sentiment into the mouth of one of his protagonists—King Agrippa II, a Jewish monarch who ruled over parts of the Middle East as a client of the Romans. In Book II of *The Jewish War*, Agrippa delivers a long speech to the angry Jews in Jerusalem, warning them not to risk a war against Rome: "Will you alone refuse to serve the masters of the whole world? Where are the men, where are the weapons you count on? Where is the fleet that is to sweep the Roman seas? Where are the funds to pay for your expeditions?" Every nation, Agrippa reminds them, has submitted to the Roman yoke: "Are you richer than the Gauls, stronger than the Germans, cleverer than the Greeks, more numerous than all the nations of the world? What gives you confidence to defy the power of Rome?"

Events would show that Agrippa was right: defying Rome was a recipe for disaster. And yet, two thousand years later, the Roman Empire is a subject for historians, while the very city where Agrippa delivered his warning is once more the capital of a Jewish state. In between came two thousand years of statelessness and Diaspora, but also of amazing religious creativity and national endurance—which would not have been possible without the kind of faith displayed by the rebels of 66 CE. Faith, *The Jewish War* shows, is the most powerful of forces, for both destruction and creation. The question Josephus poses is, Who deserves our admiration: the Jews who rushed headlong into glorious death, or the Jews who begged their fellows to see reason and live?

JOSEPHUS DID NOT just write about these issues; he lived them, and he very nearly died from them. Born in Jerusalem in 37 CE, he spent the first half of his life in Judea and the second half in Rome, where he probably died around the year 100. The break in his life came with the Jewish War, in which he was first a general on the Jewish side, then a valued and useful prisoner of the Romans. It was thanks to the war that the Jewish priest Joseph, son of Matthias, became the Roman historian Flavius Josephus. After the fighting ended in a Roman victory, he moved to Rome as part of the imperial entourage and spent the rest of his life trying to explain the Jews to their conquerors.

In *The Jewish War*, completed around the year 75, Josephus set down his views on the causes of the Jewish rebellion and its terrible consequences, while giving a detailed account of his own role in events. Later, in the massive *Jewish Antiquities*, he tried to win the respect of the world for the Jews by retelling all of Jewish history, from Genesis down to his own times. The same goal motivated the short polemical work *Against Apion*, in which Josephus defended his people against various detractors. Finally, his *Life of Flavius Josephus* is the only surviving example of autobiography written in its time; though far from a memoir in the modern sense, it enables us to situate Josephus in his social and political world.

The first thing Josephus tells us about himself in the *Life* is that he comes from the elite of Judean society. One of his ancestors married into the Hasmonean royal family, so that he can claim kingly blood. Just as important, he is a priest, a member of the caste responsible for the rituals and upkeep of the Jerusalem Temple. In fact, he explains, the priesthood is divided into twenty-four ranks, and he belongs to the first and highest. In addition to this family prestige, Josephus claims the personal authority of a learned man in a Jewish culture that already placed a high premium on sacred learning. "When I was a child, and about fourteen years of age," he writes, "I was commended by all for the love I had to learning; on which account the high priests and principal men of the city came then frequently to me together, in order to know my opinion about the accurate understanding of points of the law."

This self-introduction serves an important rhetorical purpose: it places Josephus's Jewish bona fides beyond doubt. This will become important later, when he uneasily describes the conflict between his Jewish and his Roman loyalties. Josephus got his first taste of the world beyond Judea, he writes, at the age of twenty-six, when—like Philo before him—he went to Rome as an ambassador from his Jewish community, hoping to intercede with the emperor Nero on behalf of some fellow-priests who had been unjustly imprisoned. On the way to Rome he survived a shipwreck, and once there he managed to win the emperor's favor thanks to connections in the Jewish community: he befriended a Jewish actor, a certain Aliturius, who was a favorite of Nero. This detail confirms that well before the destruction of the Temple, there was a flourishing Jewish Diaspora throughout the Roman Empire.

It was on his return from this voyage, Josephus writes, that he first got wind of the "hopes of a revolt from the Romans" that were stirring in Jerusalem. In the *Life*, he explains that he immediately opposed the rebels: "I therefore endeavored to put a stop to these tumultuous persons, and persuaded them to change their minds . . . because I foresaw that the end of such a war would be most unfortunate to us. But," he writes regretfully, "I could not persuade them; for the madness of desperate men was quite too hard for me."

In *The Jewish War*, Josephus offers a detailed explanation of how things had come to such a pass. Writing in the aftermath of the Jewish defeat, Josephus begins his story more than two hundred years earlier, with the rebellion of the Maccabees against Antiochus IV (see Chapter 3). This revolt in 167 BCE, which gave us the story of Chanukah, created an independent Jewish state for the first time since the Babylonians conquered David's kingdom four centuries earlier. Yet Josephus wastes no time in establishing his central point: even during this period of Jewish self-rule, the Jews were constantly divided against themselves. "Dissension broke out among the leading Jews," he writes near the beginning of *The Jewish War*, "who competed for supremacy because no prominent person could bear to be subject to his equals." This is the theme of Josephus's dense chronicle of Jewish politics over the next 150 years, as a series of rulers found themselves challenged by their own relatives and other members of the Judean ruling class. Thus the first Hasmonean to claim the title of king, Aristobulus, murdered his brother Antigonus "as the result of slanders invented by unscrupulous courtiers."

In a later generation, another Aristobulus (the tendency of the Hasmoneans to recycle names makes their history especially hard to follow) fought a long-running civil war against his brother Hyrcanus. And it was this internal division that opened up Judea to the power of Rome, when Hyrcanus asked Pompey the Great to intervene to restore him to the throne. Pompey conquered Jerusalem, and to the indignation of the Jews he insisted on entering the sacred precincts of the Temple. "Among the disasters of that time," Josephus writes, "nothing sent such a shudder through the nation as the exposure by aliens of the Holy Place, hitherto screened from all eyes." Pompey even went into the Holy of Holies, the innermost chamber of the Temple, where only the high priest was supposed to enter.

Yet the incorporation of Judea into the Roman Empire was, at first, a pretty mild affair. After his intrusion, Pompey, Josephus notes, treated the Temple with respect: "only one day after the capture he instructed the custodians to purify the Temple and perform the normal sacrifices." The Romans even allowed the Hasmoneans to keep ruling—and fighting one another—for another generation. After all, the Romans were used to ruling over a great variety of peoples, with very different customs and ways of worshipping God. As long as the Jews acknowledged Roman suzerainty, they were mainly left alone to run their affairs as they liked.

Things began to change, Josephus writes, in 40 BCE, when Mark Antony handed the crown of Judea over to Herod, deposing the

Hasmoneans. Antony could give Herod the crown, but he could not give him the country: this Herod had to conquer, in a series of campaigns that took three years. And even once he was in charge of Judea, Herod had to face the fact that the Jews continued to regard him as a usurper. On one occasion, Josephus writes, one of the last surviving Hasmonean princes, Jonathan, was named high priest. But "when he put on the sacred vestments and approached the altar during a feast, the whole crowd had burst into tears," grieving for the fallen dynasty. Herod promptly responded by having Jonathan drowned in a swimming pool.

Herod's own reign, Josephus shows, was just as riven by internal conflict as those that preceded it. The rivalry among his sons, their conspiracies against their father and one another, occupy a long section of *The Jewish War*. At every turn, each claimant to power had to appeal to Rome for support; it became ever clearer that the destiny of Judea was being decided by Roman power. In 6 CE, it became official: the Romans deposed Herod's son Archelaus and decided to administer the province of Judea directly, through an official called a procurator. Even the appearance of Jewish independence was now gone.

By eliminating the Jewish kingship, however, the Romans also eliminated the buffer that insulated them from Jewish grievances. We have already seen, in the episode of Herod's eagle, how sensitive the Jews of Judea were to symbolic violations. But in that case, popular anger had a target in Herod himself. From now on, whenever a Roman official—from the emperor in Rome down to the lowest misbehaving soldier—did something to offend Jewish piety or pride, the Jews' anger would be aimed directly at the Romans.

The next section of *The Jewish War* is a chronicle of such offenses given and taken. The most momentous of these we already saw in the last chapter, when the emperor Caligula decided to erect a giant statue of himself in the Temple. This took place in 40 CE, when Josephus was just a child, but he writes vividly about the episode. When Petronius, the Roman governor, informed the Jews of Caligula's plan, they responded by promising a mass martyrdom: "The Jews replied that for Caesar and the people of Rome they sacrificed twice a day. But if he wished to set up the images in their midst, he must first sacrifice the whole Jewish race; they were ready to offer themselves as victims with their wives and children."

If Caligula had proceeded with his plan, the Jewish revolt might well have broken out in 40, instead of a generation later. The assassination of the emperor removed this threat, but the basic dynamic remained the same: every few years, Josephus shows, the tensions between Jews and Romans would flare up. The Jews took every act of Roman disrespect as both an insult to their religion and a reminder of their powerlessness, so that seemingly trivial episodes threatened to spark riots and worse. On one occasion, Pontius Pilate, the Roman governor from 26 to 36 CE, raised the standards of the Roman legions in Jerusalem. As with Herod's eagle, these Roman symbols infuriated the Jerusalemites, who "do not permit any graven image to be set up in the city." The Jews engaged in an act of mass civil disobedience, falling prone around Pilate's house and remaining there motionless for five days until Pilate, "amazed at the intensity of their religious fervor," gave in and had the standards removed.

Religious holidays were moments of particular tension. On Passover, the holiday that commemorates the Exodus from Egypt, huge crowds of Jews filled Jerusalem to offer sacrifices in the Temple, and the Romans posted armed soldiers to keep the peace. One year, one of these soldiers "pulled up his garment and bent over indecently, turning his backside towards the Jews and making a noise as indecent as his attitude." This insulting gesture spurred some Jews to attack the soldiers with paving stones, and a full-fledged fight ensued, which turned into a deadly stampede; according to Josephus, thirty thousand people were trampled to death. When such a minor provocation could create such a deadly result, it was only a matter of time before the Jews and the Romans were embroiled in full-scale conflict.

The time finally came in the mid-60s, during the rule of the Roman procurator Gessius Florus. Josephus has nothing but abuse for this official, whom he considered greedy, arrogant, and totally unethical: "No one ever had less use for truth or thought out more subtle methods of crime." Josephus even goes so far as to argue that Florus deliberately fomented a Jewish revolt, "his only hope of diverting attention from his own crimes." Whether or not this was the case, it is true that Florus was singularly indifferent to Jewish sensitivities. The Temple's funds, for instance, were supposed to be sacrosanct, having been donated by Jews around the world for its upkeep. But Florus removed a large sum of money from the Temple treasury "on the pretext that Caesar required it." In protest, some Jews began going around the streets with a basket, begging for pennies for the impoverished governor. He responded to this satire by unleashing his soldiers on the city, where they killed thirty-six hundred people.

Things were quickly getting out of hand, and no one was more alarmed than the respectable citizens of Jerusalem—that is, people like Josephus himself. In his depiction of the gathering crisis, Josephus's sympathies are all with this ruling class, which he shows trying its hardest to persuade the masses not to go too far. After the massacre, Josephus writes, the priests publicly displayed the Temple's sacred objects, then "fell down and implored the people . . . not [to] provoke the Romans to plunder the treasures of God." But the tactic didn't work; when a column of soldiers insulted the people of Jerusalem by refusing to return their greetings, another riot broke out.

It was at this point, according to *The Jewish War*, that King Agrippa II made his great oration begging the Jews not to challenge Rome. As we have seen, he reminded the Jerusalemites of the world-conquering power of the Romans and the impossibility of defeating them. Even God, Agrippa argued, must be on the Romans' side, "for without His help so vast an empire could never have been built up." Whether or not Agrippa actually spoke these words, the rhetorical purpose of the speech in Josephus's book is clear. The Jews, Josephus means to show us, were warned: they embarked on revolt in full consciousness of what it would mean. They claimed to be rebelling in the name of God, but even God was plainly not on their side. For whatever came next, Josephus believed, the Jews, not the Romans, would be responsible.

Yet the Jews refused to listen to Agrippa. Indeed, *The Jewish War* repeatedly emphasizes the failure of great oratory to affect the course of history. Agrippa's speech, like several by Josephus himself that follow it, is meant to quiet the crowd and defuse the rebellion; but none of these speeches ever achieves its goal. When religious passion and national pride are at stake, Josephus seems to be telling us, the voice of reason goes unheard.

When war finally came, in 66 CE, the precipitating incident was minor—as minor as the assassination of the Archduke Ferdinand must have seemed in the summer of 1914, before it sparked World War I. A young Temple priest named Eleazar, riding the wave of popular anger, persuaded his fellow priests to stop offering the usual sacrifices on behalf of Rome and the emperor. Here at last was a provocation so direct that everyone involved knew Florus would never tolerate it. The leading citizens, Josephus writes, begged Eleazar's followers to change their minds: "unless they quickly recovered their common sense, restored the sacrifices, and wiped out the insult," the Romans were sure to retaliate.

But the rebels pressed on. They took control of the Temple and surrounded the city's Roman garrison, which negotiated terms of surrender. But when the soldiers came marching out, unarmed, the rebels forgot their promises and massacred the Romans, who "neither resisted nor begged for mercy, but merely appealed loudly to the agreement and the oaths." Josephus means to underscore the point that the Jewish rebellion began with an act of betrayal and dishonor. A fierce opponent of Eleazar's radical party, he paints them in the blackest possible terms.

As fighting between Jews and their non-Jewish neighbors broke out in the Judean countryside, the Roman governor of Syria, Cestius Gallus, marched on Jerusalem with a large, well-trained force. But just

when he had reached the capital and started to besiege it, Cestius inex-
plicably "called off his men, abandoned hope though he had suffered
no reverse, and flying in the face of all reason retired from the City."
Encouraged by this retreat, the Jewish rebels pursued the Romans,
trapped them in a narrow ravine outside Jerusalem, and massacred
the entire legion. It was an enormous, improbable victory for the Jews,
giving them confidence that the power of Rome could be defeated
after all. But for Josephus, who never doubted that the Romans would
ultimately overpower the Jews, each Jewish victory only made matters
worse. He refers to the defeat of Cestius as "disastrous" and expresses
his own feelings, and the feelings of his class, in unmistakable terms:
"After the . . . defeat of Cestius, many prominent Jews fled from the
City like swimmers from a sinking ship."

⁓ᔕᔕᕐ

IT IS NOT HARD to see why Josephus insisted so strongly on his
early opposition to the Jewish revolt. At the time *The Jewish War* was
written, he was living in Rome as a pensioner of the emperor Vespasian. The memory of the Jewish War was still fresh; indeed, Vespasian had become emperor largely on the strength of his success as the
Roman commander in Judea, and his descendants never allowed it
to be forgotten. The Arch of Titus, which still stands in Rome, was
a kind of billboard for the glory of the Flavian dynasty, depicting the
conquered Judeans bearing their sacred objects in tribute to Rome.
Clearly, Josephus had every incentive to minimize his own participation in the rebellion.

But there is no reason to doubt that Jospehus was genuinely dismayed by the news of the revolt. Coming from a highly placed priestly
family, he belonged to the ruling class of Judean society—the very
class that had flourished by making its peace with the Romans and
collaborating with imperial rule. Throughout *The Jewish War*, he
argues that this group did its utmost to avert the rebellion, only to be

persecuted for its efforts by the rebel leaders. For in addition to the religious and patriotic motives, there seems to have been an economic element to the Jewish uprising. One of the first things the rebels did was to burn down the office in Jerusalem that held debt records—a move sure to be popular with the city's poor.

Now comes the first great ambiguity in Josephus's story. Having said that he opposed the war, he has to account for the fact that in short order he agreed to become one of the rebels' chief generals, in charge of defending the northern region of Galilee against the Roman advance. His reason for accepting the appointment, he explains in the *Life*, was that he hoped to serve as a moderating influence in the Jewish camp. Indeed, he claims that he was appointed at first not to fight Rome but to disarm the Jews under his jurisdiction: "being informed that all Galilee had not yet revolted from the Romans . . . they sent me . . . in order to persuade the ill men there to lay down their arms."

But this proved to be a difficult task. Indeed, almost the whole of the *Life* is dedicated to explaining, and justifying, Josephus's conduct as a Jewish general in the Galilee. Not really an autobiography, it is more like a defense brief, meant to show Jews and Romans alike that he had done the best he could in an impossible situation. For while Josephus had been sent as an appointee of what was ostensibly the new government of Judea—the rebels in Jerusalem quickly began minting coins, which bore slogans such as "Freedom of Zion"—what he found in Galilee was a state of anarchy bordering on civil war.

Some cities were eager to take the fight to the Romans, while others refused to join the rebellion. Josephus's own superiors back in Jerusalem schemed against him, with a rival faction trying to get him recalled. Various local warlords controlled parts of the countryside and resisted his authority. One in particular, John of Giscala, became his nemesis and would go on to play a major role in the Jewish War: Josephus describes him as "the most unprincipled trickster that ever won ill fame." And looming over them all was the threat of the approaching Roman legions, which Josephus knew his own troops could never defeat in battle.

The conflicting demands on Josephus the general came to a head when a group of "bold young men" pulled off a daring robbery. The wife of a royal official in the court of Agrippa was making a journey through Galilee when bandits attacked her carriage and made off with a treasure in gold, silver, clothing, and furniture. Agrippa, as we have seen, was a Roman appointee who strongly opposed the Jewish rebellion; by robbing his courtier, then, these young men were also implicitly declaring their anti-Roman sentiments. For Josephus, who still hoped to avert a fight with the Romans, the wisest course of action was to apologize and return the stolen goods. But when the Galileans got wind of his plan, they believed that Josephus had turned into a Roman stooge and was planning to betray the whole country to the enemy. A local leader, Yeshua the son of Sapphias, stirred up a crowd by displaying a Torah scroll and shouting, "O my fellow citizens! If you are not disposed to hate Josephus on your own account, have regard, however, to these laws of your country, which your commander-in-chief is going to betray."

Josephus got out of this scrape, and several others, through what he describes as his own quick thinking and resourcefulness. On one occasion, he writes, he was almost assassinated while giving a speech but escaped by jumping into a boat and sailing away; on another, he outwitted a rebel leader named Clitus and compelled him to cut off his own hand as punishment. Clearly, Josephus had as much to fear from his own side as from the Romans.

For the details of what happened next, we must turn to *The Jewish War*. Once the Roman army arrived in Galilee, under the command of Vespasian and Titus, Josephus had a difficult choice to make. He had done his best to fortify the region's cities against siege, so it would be possible to hold out against the Romans for a little while. Still, his reason told him that the only responsible thing to do was to surrender and beg for mercy: "He saw the inevitable end awaiting the Jews," he writes of himself in *The Jewish War*, "and knew that their one safety lay in a change of heart." Yet his conscience would not allow him to abandon his fellow Jews in their moment of trouble: "He himself, he felt sure, would be pardoned if he went over to the Romans, but he would rather have died over and over again than betray his motherland and flout the trust reposed in him, in order to make himself at home with those he had been sent to fight."

This, then, is how Josephus chose to portray himself in these books written after the Jewish defeat: as the most reluctant of rebels, forced by circumstance and a sense of loyalty into fighting a war in which he never truly believed. Which is not to say that he didn't fight hard. On the contrary, he writes with evident pride about the ingenious strategies he employed when Vespasian's forces, in the summer of 67, laid siege to the Galilean city of Jotapata. Josephus, in command of the city's garrison, knew that Jotapata would soon run out of water. Yet he "ordered numbers of men to soak their outer garments and hang them round the battlements, so that the whole wall suddenly ran with water." This trick disheartened the Romans, who believed that men who could waste water so carelessly must be well supplied for a long siege.

Still, the Romans' military advantage was enormous. They had the most sophisticated artillery, which could launch stones with devastating force: "one of the men standing near Josephus on the rampart got into the line of fire and had his head knocked off by a stone, his skull being flung like a pebble from a sling more than six hundred yards." They had giant metal battering rams, which they used to knock down the defensive walls Josephus had built. The Jews did their best to blunt the attack by using stretched ox-hides to deflect the missiles and blocking the rams with sacks of chaff, "lowered by ropes to the spot where they saw that the next blow was coming."

All this made an impression—the Romans, Josephus writes, "were paralyzed by the Jews' astonishing courage." But even courage, he emphasizes, could not prevail over the Romans' greatest weapon, which was military discipline. In *The Jewish War*, just as he is about to describe the siege of Jotapata, Josephus makes room for a long digression about Roman military organization: what kinds of weapons a Roman legionary carries, how a legion makes its camp, how the soldiers are constantly in training. The Romans value discipline and planning so highly, Josephus writes, that "they regard successes due to luck as less desirable than a planned but unsuccessful stroke, because victories that come of themselves tempt men to leave things to chance."

The contrast with the Jewish rebels could not be clearer. The Jews, Josephus says proudly, have tremendous bravery; without it, they could never have dared to stand up to the Roman Empire. But it is a wild, thoughtless, almost insane kind of bravery that spends itself in ill-considered attacks and last-ditch defenses. "One side was armed with experience as well as prowess," he summarizes, "the other had no weapon but animal courage, no captain but blind fury." In the end, after forty-seven days of heroic resistance, Jotapata fell to Vespasian's army. And "the Romans, remembering what the siege had cost them, showed neither mercy nor pity for anyone. They drove the people down the slope from the citadel and slaughtered them. . . . Many even of Josephus's picked soldiers were driven to suicide; for when they saw that they could not kill a single Roman, they made sure that at least they should not die at Roman hands, and collecting at the far edge of the town they killed themselves."

IF JOSEPHUS HAD JOINED his soldiers in committing suicide, he would have won the praise of the Jews and the respect of the Romans. After all, the idea of meeting death on one's own terms had illustrious precedents in Roman history: legendary figures like Brutus, the assassin of Julius Caesar, had died this way. The Jewish rebellion itself witnessed many acts of suicidal bravery. In *The Jewish War*, for instance, Josephus recounts a scene that took place during the siege of

Jerusalem, when Titus asked for a volunteer for a suicide mission. In a speech, Titus laid out the Roman theory that it is better to die quickly and violently than of natural causes:

> For every good soldier knows that souls set free from the flesh on the battlefield by the sword are given a welcome by the purest element, ether, and set among the stars, and that as friendly spirits and genial heroes they appear to their own descendants; while souls that waste away in sick bodies, even if completely free from spots and stains, vanish into darkness underground and sink deep into oblivion, life, body, and memory too annihilated at one stroke.

Yet if Josephus had chosen this path, his name would now be forgotten and the world would know almost nothing about the Jewish War. His eagerness to live rather than die—and the lengths to which he would go to make sure he survived—cast a stain on his reputation that it is still impossible to ignore. But in choosing life, even at the cost of ignominy, Josephus was remaining true to the logic that had governed his politics from the start. The rabbis who urged their pupils to cut down the golden eagle, and the Zealots who launched a full-fledged war against Rome, either refused to consider the possibility of dying or else saw death as a positive good. Josephus believed that the Jews would be better off living under foreign domination than losing everything in a hopeless quest for independence.

Even during the siege of Jotapata, Josephus admits, he had thought about trying to escape and discussed the idea "with the leading citizens." He tried to convince them that his running away would be to their ultimate benefit, as he writes with startling candor: "Josephus concealed his anxiety for his own safety and declared that it was for their sakes he was arranging to leave. By staying in the town he could give them little help. . . . On the other hand, by escaping from the siege he could send them help from outside on the greatest scale." The Jews, however, were not convinced, and they more or less forced Josephus to remain at his post: "Children, old men, women with infants in their arms wept and fell down before him."

Now, with the Romans in the city and slaughter on every side, he was faced with the same choice; and once again, he chose life. The Romans were desperate to find him, he tells us, because "the war would be virtually over once Josephus was in [their] hands"—a drastic overstatement of his own importance to the Jewish war effort. But, he writes in the third person, "Josephus, helped by some divine providence, had stolen away from the midst of the enemy and jumped into a deep pit connected on one side with a wide cave which could not be seen from above." Along with forty other "persons of importance," he hid out in the cave for two days until the Romans discovered them.

Vespasian sent officers to Josephus offering to guarantee his safety if he surrendered. Clearly, he was inclined to accept the offer, but his fellow captives—who had received no such promise from the Romans—absolutely refused to let him. Death, they reminded him, was better than dishonor: "Are you so in love with life, Josephus, that you can bear to live as a slave?" And so they would compel him to join them in a mass suicide to deprive the Romans of the satisfaction of taking them prisoner. "We will lend you a sword and a hand to wield it," the Jews half-promised, half-threatened. "If you die willingly, you will die as commander-in-chief of the Jews; if unwillingly, as a traitor."

Here Josephus the writer has shown us, in the strongest possible terms, how ignoble it would be for him to surrender. The only way to justify his decision, then, is to introduce an even stronger motive for survival, one so powerful as to trump the claims of honor and loyalty. And the only possible such motive, Josephus realizes, would be a divine command. Thus—very conveniently, the reader might feel—he tells us that he had "dreams in the night by which God had forewarned him both of the calamities coming to the Jews and of the fortunes of the Roman emperors."

God Himself, Josephus implies, had given the victory to the

Romans; indeed, since God was all-powerful, how else could their triumph be explained? And there would be no point in dying for a cause that even God had abandoned. So Josephus makes his decision, with a silent prayer: "Inasmuch as it pleaseth Thee to visit Thy wrath on the Jewish people whom Thou didst create, and all prosperity hath passed to the Romans, and because Thou didst choose my spirit to make known the things to come, I yield myself willingly to the Romans that I may live, but I solemnly declare that I go, not as a traitor, but as Thy servant."

What happens next in *The Jewish War* suggests either that God was watching out for Josephus or that Josephus was very clever about watching out for himself. First, he delivers a long speech to his fellow captives, arguing that suicide, however noble the Romans might think it, is contrary to God's will. "And do you suppose God isn't angry when a man treats His gift with contempt? It is from Him we have received our being, and it is to Him we must leave the right to take it away," he reasons. But just as with Agrippa's speech earlier, this piece of oratory completely fails to move its audience. The Jews "reviled him for cowardice" and seem to be about to carry out the death sentence themselves.

Then Josephus, with typical resourcefulness, comes up with a plan. The Jews will take turns killing one another, drawing lots to determine the order in which they will die. This way, no one will be able to escape: after all, "it would be unfair when the rest were gone if one man changed his mind and saved his life." But when the lots are drawn, Josephus comes out as one of the last two survivors. And what happens? "He used persuasion" on the man who was supposed to kill him; "they made a pact, and both remained alive."

It is impossible to avoid the suspicion that Josephus somehow tampered with the lots so that he would be one of the last survivors, able to do exactly what he said would be "unfair." Certainly, he betrayed his promise to his fellow Jews, all of whom he had just seen killed right before his eyes. Indeed, he himself has just finished making the case that to survive under such circumstances would be utterly ignoble. It is no wonder that ever since, some readers have thought of Josephus as a coward and a traitor—a man who clung to life at too high a price.

But this was not the end of Josephus's stratagems. Having surrendered to the Romans, he was brought before Vespasian, who ordered that he be put in prison. But Josephus "asked to say a word to him in private," and when everyone had withdrawn, the prisoner made an amazing revelation. Inspired by God or by his own ingenuity, Josephus informed Vespasian that the Roman general was destined to become the emperor of Rome. "I come as a messenger of the greatness that awaits you," he promised. "You, Vespasian, are Caesar and Emperor . . . you are master not only of me, Caesar, but of land and sea and all the human race." Only the necessity of giving Vespasian this news, he says, justified his own decision to stay alive: "Had I not been sent by God Himself, I knew the Jewish law and how a general ought to die."

At the time Josephus made this prophecy, in the summer of 67, it must have seemed outlandish. Nero was the emperor in Rome, and Vespasian was just an old soldier, a competent but unglamorous general serving in a provincial campaign. But history turned out to be on Vespasian's side—and Josephus's. The next year, Nero was driven from power and committed suicide, choosing the end that Josephus had so assiduously avoided. In the ensuing power vacuum, a series of Roman generals made their bids to become emperor, each driving out the one before, until the game of musical chairs ended with Vespasian sitting on the throne.

Vespasian, acclaimed as emperor by his troops in Egypt, would have to go to Rome to consolidate his power. But before he left—putting his son Titus in charge of the Judean campaign—he remembered the Jewish prisoner who had predicted his good fortune. "It is shocking," Vespasian said, "that the man who prophesied my rise to power and was the mouth-piece of God should still be treated as a prisoner and endure the lot of a captive." Josephus was released from prison; as a sign of special honor, his chains were not just removed but broken with an axe, "the usual procedure in the case of a man unjustly fettered."

Having earned the Romans' trust, Josephus would remain with

Titus's army as an advisor and translator. When Titus laid siege to Jerusalem, Josephus walked around the city's walls, dodging the arrows and rocks the Jews hurled at him, exhorting his countrymen to give up the fight before it was too late. In one long speech in *The Jewish War*, Josephus tries to convince the Jews of what he himself has already realized: that God has abandoned the cause of his chosen people. This was to strike the Jewish rebels at their most sensitive spot. After all, they had launched the revolt partly in order to defend God's Temple from the insults of the Romans.

But Josephus, looking back on Jewish history, claims that the Jews sinned when they resorted to arms instead of trusting God to protect them. He recounts various episodes from the Bible in which God punished Israel's enemies with plagues: "on no occasion did our fathers succeed by force of arms," he argues, "or fail without them after committing their cause to God." But this was to beg the question; for how would the Jews know whether God was on their side unless they tried to fight? The rebels believed they had indeed committed their cause to God; but as defeat loomed, they resisted the obvious conclusion that Josephus embraced, which was that God had switched sides. "God, who handed dominion over from nation to nation round the world, abode now in Italy," Josephus proclaimed. It was the worst heresy imaginable to those pious Jews who believed that God would always dwell in his Temple in Jerusalem.

FOR JOSEPHUS, TELLING the story of the Jewish War involved a delicate rhetorical balancing act. This was never trickier than in the last part of the book, where he describes the Roman conquest of Jerusalem in 70 CE. On the one hand, he was an unapologetically Jewish writer, who wanted to do justice to the courage of the Jewish rebels and the suffering they had undergone. "The language in which I record the events," he promises at the very beginning of *The Jewish*

War, "will reflect my own feelings and emotions; for I must permit myself to bewail my country's tragedy."

Yet, on the other hand, Josephus was a Jew who had gone over to the Romans, putting his life in Vespasian's hands. At the time he wrote his history, he was living in Rome in Vespasian's own house. What's more, he submitted *The Jewish War* to Vespasian and Titus for their seal of approval. As he says in *Against Apion*, "I was so well assured of the truth of what I related, that I first of all appealed to those that had the supreme command in that war, Vespasian and Titus, as witnesses for me." This was a combination of imperial blurb and prepublication censorship, meant to show that his account of the war could be taken as official.

How, then, could Josephus describe the devastation of Jerusalem— above all, the burning of the Temple, the crowning disaster of the whole war—without seeming to blame the Romans? His solution was to argue that the Jews themselves were to blame for everything that befell them— not the people as a whole, but the rebel leaders, whom he describes as forcing an unwilling people into war. We have already seen how the rebels refused to listen to Agrippa's warning, ignored the priests who begged for compromise, and greeted Josephus's own pleas with arrows.

But the worst excesses of the rebels, he writes, took place in Jerusalem during the siege. The population of the city was swollen with refugees from the countryside and Jews who had come to the Temple to offer sacrifices. Even so, Josephus argues, there would have been enough food to supply the city for a long time, if it were not for the vicious feuds that turned the rebels against one another. There were, in fact, three separate and mutually hostile groups in the city: the Zealots led by Eleazar, a second band led by Josephus's old enemy John of Giscala, and a third commanded by the warlord Simon ben Giora. And Josephus insists that the carnage among these factions had already ruined the city, even before the Romans conquered it.

Thus the famine that accompanied the siege was the fault not of the Romans outside the gates, but of the rebels' infighting: "It was as if to oblige the Romans they were destroying all that the City had laid up against a siege and hamstringing their own powers." This indictment grows all the heavier as Josephus describes how the madness of hunger tore the city apart. Rebel soldiers would torture people suspected of hiding food: "They stuffed bitter vetch up the genital passages of their victims, and drove sharp stakes into their seats." Family members stole food from one another, even mothers from the mouths of their children.

The famine culminates in an episode of cannibalism, which Josephus describes in grotesque detail: a woman named Mary roasted her infant, ate half of it, and offered the other half to the rebels. When the crime became known, Josephus writes, it produced horror in the city: "everyone saw the tragedy before his own eyes and shuddered as if the crime was his." Many of the Jews, too, must have remembered the terrible prophecies laid down in the book of Deuteronomy: "And when you are shut up in all your towns throughout your land that the Lord your God has assigned to you, you shall eat your own issue, the flesh of your sons and daughters that the Lord your God has assigned to you." The suffering of the Jews is never a reason to deny the existence of God, since the word of God has already foretold that such sufferings will come. The curse is as much a part of the covenant as the blessing.

Under these circumstances, Josephus writes, the Roman destruction of the city could actually be seen as a liberation. The people of Jerusalem "suffered nothing worse at Roman hands than they had endured at each other's, and when they had finished there was nothing new left for the City to undergo—she went through greater agony before she fell, and her destroyers accomplished something greater. I mean that her internal divisions destroyed the City, and the Romans destroyed the internal divisions, which were far more firmly established than her walls; and the misery of it all could reasonably be put down to her own people, the justice of it to the Romans."

Even the burning of the Temple, Josephus insists, was not the fault of the Romans—at least, not of the commander, Titus. In Jewish folk tradition, Titus would become one of the great villains, a successor to Haman. Stories tell of how he fornicated with a prostitute inside the Holy of Holies and how God punished him by sending a gnat to roost inside his skull. But Josephus insists that his patron issued specific orders that the Temple should be left alone: "he would not make war on inanimate objects instead of men, or, whatever happened, burn down such a work of art: it was the Romans who would lose thereby, just as their empire would gain an ornament if it was preserved."

It was, instead, an ordinary soldier, acting on the spur of the moment, who threw a lit torch into the Temple and began the conflagration. Seen another way, however, it was God who brought things to this conclusion, to set the seal on his chastisement of the Jews. After all, on the Jewish calendar, the day that the Temple was set on fire was the Ninth of Av—the very same date on which the Babylonians had destroyed the First Temple more than six hundred years before. Surely this was a sign that, as Josephus writes, the Temple "had been condemned to the flames by God long ago; by the turning of time's wheel the fated day had come."

The destruction of the Temple would have been a natural place for Josephus to end *The Jewish War*. But he chose to follow it with what seem like a pair of epilogues, showing how the winners and the losers responded to the outcome of the war. For the Romans, the defeat of the Jewish rebels came at an especially opportune moment. Vespasian was newly installed on the throne in Rome, and his claim to rule came not from birth—he was the first emperor not to belong to the family of Julius Caesar—but from his reputation as a soldier. Now his son Titus could return in glory, having dispatched the latest threat to Roman rule.

As Josephus recounts, the imperial father and son put on a terrific show. In keeping with Roman tradition, a triumphal procession carried them through the streets of Rome, displaying the treasures they had looted from the Temple: a menorah, a golden table, and a Torah scroll. There were traveling stages, several stories high, on which actors portrayed scenes from the war: "Here was to be seen a smiling countryside laid waste, there whole formations of the enemy put to the sword." The

Romans did not deceive themselves about the realities of warfare and conquest. They gloried in what they had done to the Jews, and Josephus saw this as not cruel but natural: "Such were the agonies to which the Jews condemned themselves when they embarked on this war."

But Josephus does not allow the Roman triumph to have the last word in *The Jewish War*. Instead, he switches the scene back to Judea, where Roman troops spent the years after the fall of Jerusalem mopping up the last pockets of resistance in the Judean countryside. Finally, in 73, they reached the forbidding fortress of Masada, where a group of rebels had taken shelter. Despite the steep ravines that made the fortress impregnable, the Romans were able to construct siegeworks that gave them the advantage. Finally, they managed to torch the wall of Masada and spent the night preparing for a final assault the next morning.

At this moment, Josephus inserts the last of the great speeches that punctuate *The Jewish War*. Remarkably, it is a speech that directly contradicts his own understanding of the war, while implicitly rebuking his own actions at the siege of Jotapata. Throughout the book, Josephus has always stood on the side of compromise, reason, and life; he risked dishonor and the hatred of his countrymen in order to cling to life. Now Eleazar, the leader of the Masada rebels, tells his followers in a long and passionate oration that they must embrace death.

This is not just for the usual Roman reason that death is better than captivity and slavery. Instead, Eleazar offers a specifically Jewish case for suicide, based on the realization that Josephus was correct—God has abandoned his chosen people. "Long ago," he says, "God issued this warning to the whole Jewish race together, that life would be taken from us if we misused it." Now that the war is lost, it is clear that "life is the calamity for man, not death." Borrowing a page from Platonic philosophy, Eleazar insists that only death brings real life, while earthly existence is just a living death: "Death gives freedom to our souls ... but while they are confined within a mortal body and share its miseries, in strict truth they are dead."

Throughout *The Jewish War*, we have seen reasonable speech after reasonable speech fall on deaf ears. But now, at last, a speaker manages to persuade his audience, and the Jews in Masada hurry to kill themselves and one another: "as if possessed they rushed off, everyone anxious to be quicker than the next man, and regarding it as proof positive of manliness and wisdom not to be found among the last: so irresistible a desire had seized them to slaughter their wives, their children, and themselves." When only ten are left, they draw lots: one man will kill the other nine, then himself. And unlike Josephus at Jotapata, the men of Masada keep their word.

Here, Josephus seems to say, is where the logic of Jewish rebellion has led: to nearly a thousand corpses piled up in Masada. When a nation makes a fetish of death, it can expect only to die. Yet at the same time, it is impossible to dismiss the nagging feeling that it is Josephus who is the coward, Eleazar the hero. Masada became a symbol of Jewish courage and resistance that continues to inspire, two thousand years later. But a nation of Masadas would soon cease to exist. For the Jewish people, after the catastrophe of the year 70, the challenge would be, rather, to discover a new way to live.

BIBLIOGRAPHY

Goodman, Martin. *Rome and Jerusalem: The Clash of Ancient Civilizations.* New York: Alfred A. Knopf, 2007.

Josephus. *The Jewish War.* Translated by G. A. Williamson, revised by E. Mary Smallwood. New York: Penguin Classics, 1981.

Rajak, Tessa. *Josephus: The Historian and His Society.* Minneapolis, MN: Fortress Press, 1984.

The Works of Josephus. Translated by William Whiston. Peabody, MA: Hendrickson, 1987.

BUILDING FENCES

Pirkei Avot

Pirkei Avot, "The Ethics of the Fathers," is the most popular of rabbinic texts. A collection of sayings and aphorisms committed to writing around the year 250 CE, it records the spiritual and moral wisdom of the great rabbis who lived during the previous centuries. After the destruction of the Temple, and with it the possibility of offering sacrifices to God, it was these rabbis who assumed leadership in Judaism, redefining it as a religion of text and law that could be practiced anywhere in the Diaspora. *Pirkei Avot* sets forth the principles of this new rabbinic Judaism, dwelling on the importance of Torah study, the need for self-restraint, the suspicion of power, and the reality of the world to come, where good deeds will be rewarded and evil punished. The spirit of the Talmud, the massive collection of laws and commentary that defined post-Temple Judaism, is embodied in this short book, one of the world's great documents of religious wisdom.

———

THE JEWISH WAR OF FLAVIUS JOSEPHUS DESCRIBES
Jerusalem under siege as a city equally terrified by the Roman invad-
ers and by its own bloodthirsty, uncompromising leaders. Many Jews,
Josephus tells us, wanted to escape the city and defect to the Romans,
but the Jewish soldiers guarding the gates prevented them from doing
so. This portrait is confirmed by a Talmudic story that became part of
Jewish tradition in the centuries after the fall of Jerusalem—a story
that has fascinating echoes of Josephus's own.

According to this tale, one of the leading dissenters from the Zealots' policy of war at any price was Yochanan ben Zakkai, one of the
most learned rabbis of his generation. "My children," Yochanan asked
the Jewish authorities in Jerusalem, "why do you destroy this city and
why do you seek to burn the Temple?" Better to submit to Vespasian,
he advised, than to see Jerusalem annihilated—exactly the moderate
view that Josephus attributed to the respectable citizens of the capital.
But the Zealots refused to listen, and Yochanan, foreseeing disaster,
also decided to choose life.

He did so by counterfeiting death. Yochanan ben Zakkai asked two
of his disciples to build him a coffin; then he lay down in it and they
smuggled him past the Jewish guards, who knew that corpses could
not remain in the city overnight. Once out of Jerusalem, Yochanan
was brought into the presence of Vespasian, where he emerged from
the coffin and made a single request. "I ask nothing of thee," he said,
"save Yavneh, where I might go and teach my disciples and there establish a prayer house and perform all the commandments." When Vespasian agreed to let Yochanan settle in the town of Yavneh, Yochanan
added a prophecy: just like Josephus before him, the rabbi predicted
that the Roman general was about to become an emperor. Yochanan
was sure of this because according to scripture, "the Temple will not
be surrendered to a commoner, but to a king." And just a few days

later, the story goes, messengers arrived announcing that Vespasian
had been named emperor.

If we are to trust Josephus's chronology, of course, things could not
have happened to Yochanan in just this way: it was Titus, not Vespasian, who was in charge of the siege of Jerusalem. Still, the political
background of the story matches Josephus's account. It is perfectly
plausible that someone like Yochanan would have been opposed to
the Zealots and tried to escape from them. The most important thing
about the story, however, is that it offers a symbolic explanation of
what happened to the Jewish faith after the Temple was destroyed.
When news reached Yochanan ben Zakkai that Jerusalem had been
conquered and the Temple set on fire, "he tore his clothing, and his
disciples tore their clothing, and they wept, crying aloud and mourning." Their sense of desolation must have been overwhelming, literally
cosmic. After all, the Temple was the center of the Jewish universe—
the only place where Jews could offer sacrifices to God as he commanded, and where the high priest could commune with God in the
Holy of Holies. Without the Temple, Jewish faith and practice no longer made any sense.

But what died in Jerusalem, the story tells us, was reborn in Yavneh.
Just as Yochanan underwent a kind of death in order to live, so Judaism, which seemed to die in the Temple's flames, came to life again
under the care of the rabbis. Yavneh, where the sages gathered under
the leadership of Yochanan ben Zakkai, serves as a shorthand for the
transformation of Temple Judaism into rabbinic Judaism. Deprived of
Temple and sacrifice, Judaism would become preeminently a religion
of laws and prayers, practiced at home and in the synagogue. And it
was the rabbis, the custodians of Jewish law, who replaced the priesthood as the leaders of Jewish society.

This transformation of Jewish religious and political life was also a
transformation in the Jewish relationship to texts. In 70 CE, the Jews
lost their Temple. Half a century later, Judea would rise up against the

Romans once again, in the last-ditch effort known as the Bar Kochba revolt; and once again, the Romans would triumph. This time, the emperor Hadrian decided to destroy the city of Jerusalem, replacing it with a Roman colony bearing a new name, Aelia Capitolina. Judea itself was wiped from the map and renamed Palestine, the name it was to bear for the next eighteen hundred years.

With this second catastrophe, one kind of history ended and another began. In *The Jewish War*, Jewish history appears similar to the history of any other nation. It is a chronicle of kings and conquests, a record of power—who won it and what they did with it. But after the first century CE, Jews would not possess that kind of power again until the twentieth century. During that long span of time, then, Jewish history would have to be written in other ways. It would become the story not of power, but of ideas and beliefs. And its most important turning points would not be the winning of wars or the building of monuments, but the writing of books.

In the first five centuries CE, rabbinic Judaism was built on the foundation of two monumental books—or, better, texts, since each runs to many volumes and neither reads like an ordinary book. The first of these was the Mishnah—a digest of the huge body of Jewish law that had been handed down orally over the previous centuries. In the rabbis' view, this Oral Law was every bit as sacred and authoritative as the Written Law found in the Five Books of Moses. Indeed, they believed that the Oral Law was dictated by God to Moses on Mount Sinai and had been transmitted faithfully ever since, teacher to student. The word "Torah," for the rabbis, refers not just to the Five Books of Moses but to this whole body of law and interpretation.

It was not until around 200 CE that this oral tradition was committed to writing in the Mishnah. The impetus to write down what had previously been memorized and recited lay in the dire situation of the Jews after the Bar Kochba revolt. With Jewish life in tatters, the usual networks of face-to-face transmission were no longer dependable; a living tradition had to be consolidated into a text if it was to survive. Yehudah HaNasi—Judah the Prince—was editor of the Mishnah, which collects the legal dicta of the major rabbis of the previous centuries. These sages, known as Tannaim, interpreted the law on a enormous variety of subjects—marriage and divorce, torts and contracts, the sabbath and holidays—arranged in the Mishnah into sixty-three tractates. The Mishnah also contains a great deal of material dedicated to the status of the priesthood and the rituals of the Temple. At the time these laws were written down, of course, the Temple had been gone for over a century. But the rabbis continued to preserve this knowledge in a kind of virtual form, and it remained a focus of Jewish learning even though it could no longer be directly applied.

In the three hundred years after the Mishnah was compiled, Jewish life in Palestine declined under Roman rule, and the center of rabbinic scholarship moved eastward, to Babylonia in the Persian Empire. Babylonia had been home to a Jewish community ever since the First Temple was destroyed and the Jews were exiled to Babylon. Now, as the rise of Christianity in the Roman Empire meant increasing persecution of Jews and Judaism, Jewish learning began to flourish in Persia instead. Rabbis in Babylonia continued to study the Mishnah, ask questions about it, and argue over it. These discussions were themselves remembered and transmitted orally until around 500 CE, when they were codified in the work known as the Babylonian Talmud. (There is also a Jerusalem Talmud, based on the debates of Palestinian rabbis, but it is considered less authoritative.)

The Talmud is made up of the Mishnah and the later commentaries on it, which are called the Gemara ("completion"). The rabbis of the Gemara, known as Amoraim, present themselves in constant dialogue with the Tannaim of the Mishnah. They ask questions about the laws, try to figure out the principles behind them, and apply them to new problems and situations. These discussions were carried on in Aramaic, a Semitic language related to Hebrew that was spoken across the Middle East. As a result, mastery of the Talmud requires knowledge of both Hebrew and Aramaic.

For more than a thousand years—from the writing of the Talmud until the modern age—study of the Talmud was the basis of Jewish education. Even more than the Bible, it was the Talmud that shaped Jewish observance and disciplined generations of Jewish minds (male minds, of course, since Talmud study was confined to men). This training began early: "At five the Bible. At ten the Mishnah.... At fifteen the Talmud," was the curriculum laid down by one early sage. The Talmud was the lingua franca shared by knowledgeable Jews all over the world, and it continues to form the core of education for the very religious today.

The Talmud, then, is more than a book, and it cannot be read in the way that Josephus or even Philo can—after all, the standard edition runs to some six thousand folio pages. What's more, it is a polyvocal text, a record of dozens of rabbis' arguments and insights, in which the process of discussion is just as important as the conclusion eventually reached. In addition to *halakha*, or legal material, it also contains *aggadah*—legends and lore, ranging from miracle stories about famous rabbis to down-to-earth medical and dietary advice. So vast and wide-ranging is it that tradition speaks of "the ocean of Talmud": you can swim in it for a lifetime and never reach the end or the bottom.

FORTUNATELY, THERE IS A BOOK that manages to capture the worldview of the Talmudic sages, their ethical concerns and spiritual priorities. This is the work known as *Pirkei Avot*, usually translated as "The Ethics of the Fathers," though the Hebrew name literally means "The Chapters of the Fathers." *Pirkei Avot* was probably completed around 250 CE, a generation or two after the Mishnah was edited. Instead of laws, it is a collection of aphorisms attributed to great figures in the early period of rabbinic Judaism. In these sayings, we hear about the ideals, the way of life, and the moral dangers that defined Judaism in the post-Temple era.

Much more accessible than the rest of the Mishnah or the Talmud, *Pirkei Avot* is certainly the most popular rabbinic text. It is included in many editions of the Jewish prayerbook, and it is traditionally read on the sabbath between Passover and Shavuot. (Originally, it contained five chapters; a sixth was added later, so there would be one chapter for each sabbath in this period.) Less well known, but crucial for interpreting just what *Pirkei Avot* has to tell us, is the original commentary on the book, "The Fathers according to Rabbi Nathan," which probably originated in the third or fourth century CE.

The story about Yochanan ben Zakkai and Vespasian, for instance, is retold in "The Fathers according to Rabbi Nathan," and it underscores one of the themes of *Pirkei Avot*: the transition from the Judaism of the Temple to the Judaism of the rabbis. The Temple does appear in *Pirkei Avot*, but not nearly as often as one might expect, given the huge role it played in Jewish life for so long. We learn, for instance, that "ten miracles were performed for our ancestors in the Temple." These turn out to be remarkably down-to-earth miracles—not on the order of Moses parting the Red Sea, but more practical signs of divine favor.

The Temple was, among other things, a giant slaughterhouse in which livestock were butchered by the thousands every day. Yet "the odor of the meat never caused a woman to miscarry," *Pirkei Avot* tells us. "That meat never became putrid. No fly was ever seen in the slaughterhouse." Likewise, the Temple was a pilgrimage center where upward of a million Jews would gather for the major festivals. But "although the people were tightly pressed together, there was plenty of room when they prostrated themselves," and "No one ever said, 'There is no room for me to spend the night in Jerusalem.'" These are miracles of amenity, and they seem to express a sort of amazed pride at the smooth running of the Temple: so many people, so many animals, and so few disruptions.

But *Pirkei Avot* does not devote much time to nostalgia for the Temple or to mourning its absence. Instead, it explains, in curt and abstract terms, that the catastrophes that befell the Jews in the then-recent past were not accidents, but divine judgments. "The sword comes into the world," the text says, "because of justice delayed and justice denied, and because of those who misinterpret the Torah." Likewise, "Exile comes into the world because of idolatry, sexual impropriety, bloodshed, and the release of the land." "The release of the land" refers to the biblical law of the sabbatical year, which commands that every seventh year the Land of Israel be left fallow. The Jews' failure to observe this year of rest is thus held responsible for their eventual exile.

Neglecting "the release of the land" might not seem like a sin on the same level as idolatry and bloodshed. The latter, after all, are moral and spiritual crimes, while the former seems at most an offense against ritual protocol. But one of the key lessons of *Pirkei Avot* is that the rabbis did not divide the commandments in this way. Because they believed that all the commandments, or *mitzvot*, were issued by God, all of them had to be observed with equal care. Yehuda HaNasi, a man of such authority that he is known simply as "Rabbi," is quoted in *Pirkei Avot* as saying, "Be as careful in the performance of a minor commandment as a major commandment, since you do not know the reward for the commandments."

Rabbi Eleazar ben Chisma made a similar point with a deliberately counterintuitive saying: "The offering of birds and the onset of menstruation are the main elements of the laws, while astronomy and geometry are but the appetizers of wisdom." The rules for sacrificing birds are some of the most arcane in the Mishnah, and menstruation—which rendered a woman ritually impure and thus cut off from sexual intercourse—might seem like a distasteful or undignified subject. A Torah scholar might be tempted to skip over these areas of law. But even these *mitzvot* are *mitzvot*, which means that they are infinitely more important than merely secular knowledge such as mathematics or astronomy. The fact that Eleazar himself was a noted astronomer only drives the point home: he enjoyed astronomy, but he knew it was unimportant compared to the smallest religious duty.

Their dedication to *mitzvot*, however, meant that the rabbis faced a great dilemma. So many commandments were devoted to Temple matters: sacrificing animals, tithing, priestly purity and impurity. It was possible to follow those laws only in the context of a Temple-based religion. What could the rabbis do to fulfill them, now that the Temple lay in ruins? "The Fathers according to Rabbi Nathan" offers two answers, each of which says something crucial about the worldview of *Pirkei Avot*. The first comes in another story about Yochanan ben Zakkai:

> Once as Yochanan ben Zakkai was coming forth from Jerusalem, Rabbi Joshua followed after him and beheld the Temple in ruins. "Woe unto us!" Rabbi Joshua cried, "that this, the place where the iniquities of Israel were atoned for, is laid waste!" "My son," Rabbi Yochanan said to him, "be not grieved; we have another atonement as effective as this. And what is it? It is acts of loving-kindness, as it is said, 'For I desire mercy and not sacrifice.'"

In rabbinic Judaism, then, piety and ethical living would replace animal sacrifice as the way to please God. Yet this is not to say that rabbinic Judaism would be a religion of the heart alone, dispensing with ritual practice and legal formulas. On the contrary, what is most striking about *Pirkei Avot* is the way it insists on both ethical behavior and absorption in the law, so that these become two sides of the same coin. If many of the Torah's *mitzvot* could not be carried out in the absence of the Temple, rabbis could still remember and transmit those commandments through careful study. Indeed, "The Fathers according to Rabbi Nathan" insists that studying the laws about sacrifices is equivalent to actually offering them. "The study of Torah is more beloved by God than burnt offerings," the text tells us. "Hence, when a sage sits and expounds to the congregation, Scripture accounts it to him as though he had offered up fat and blood on the altar." The rabbi takes the place of the priest, and it is through the study of texts that he worships God.

IT MAKES SENSE that rabbinic Judaism, a religion born out of a terrible rupture, would be highly concerned with establishing continuity. That is why *Pirkei Avot* opens with a genealogy, a list of ancestors stretching back from the present all the way to Moses himself. But unlike the many catalogues of "begats" in the Bible, this is not a biological family tree; rather, it is an intellectual one. Instead of fathers and sons, it records a chain of teachers and disciples, unbroken over the centuries, who were responsible for transmitting the Oral Law.

If there had been no Oral Law, one might say, the rabbis would have had to invent it. After all, the Written Torah, the Five Books of Moses, contains hundreds of commandments that require interpretation if they are to be put into practice. To take a familiar example: in the book of Exodus, God commands the Israelites to do no work on the sabbath, the day of rest. But exactly what activities qualify as work? The Oral Law gave the answers to such questions, showing how the commandments could be carried out in the very different circumstances of later historical periods.

But how could Jews know for certain that these interpretations of the Torah were correct? This could only be assured if the Oral Law were exactly as authoritative and ancient as the Written Law—that is, if the Oral Law, too, had been dictated to Moses on Mount Sinai. By definition, of course, there can be no tangible proof of the antiquity of an oral tradition. Modern scholars believe that most of the laws collected in the Mishnah date back no further than the Hellenistic period of the fourth to the first centuries BCE, at the earliest. But the rabbis of *Pirkei Avot* had no doubt that these laws went back all the way to Moses. The tractate begins by naming the first links in this chain: "At Sinai Moses received the Torah and handed it over to Joshua who handed it over to the elders who handed it over to the prophets who in turn handed it over to the men of the Great Assembly."

The first names in this list are familiar from the Bible: Moses; his successor, Joshua; the elders appointed by Joshua to rule Israel after his death; and finally the prophets, who emerged later in the history of the kingdoms of Israel and Judah. But "the Great Assembly" does not figure in the Bible. It may have been a real institution whose exact function is now lost, or it may have been an invention of the rabbis, designed to bridge the mythic period of Jewish history and the historical period. From here, the genealogy in *Pirkei Avot* turns to named individuals, starting with "Simeon the Just," probably a high priest who lived sometime in the third century BCE. Then come a number of men whose names are otherwise completely unknown and who may also be invented. These in turn hand down the Torah to "the pairs"—a series of sages named by twos, concluding with the famous rabbis Hillel and Shammai, who lived in the late first century BCE. Finally, the list concludes with rabbis familiar from the Mishnah itself, including Yehudah HaNasi, who lived in the second century CE.

In this way, *Pirkei Avot* establishes a chain of authority that dates back more than a thousand years. It is a remarkable claim to continuity, which directly opposes the notion of Jewish history as a series of ruptures and calamities. We hear nothing in this list of the destruction of the First Temple or the Second; nothing about the exile of the Ten Lost Tribes of Israel, or the Babylonian Exile, or the Diaspora following the Jewish War. For these are events in political history, and *Pirkei Avot* is not interested in that way of understanding the past.

Indeed, it is not particularly interested in the whole idea of past and future. What matters is the Torah, and the Torah lives in a perpetual present. It governed the Israelites in the desert, it governs the Jews in the Roman Empire, and it will presumably continue to govern Jewish life until the end of time.

It is especially striking to compare *Pirkei Avot*, and the way it thinks about politics and history, with Josephus, who wrote some two hundred years earlier. In *The Jewish War*, Josephus presents the recent history of the Jews through the lens of pure power politics; it is nothing but a string of court intrigues, family feuds, and aggressive wars. The Zealots themselves took the idea of political sovereignty so seriously that they were willing to die for it in large numbers. *Pirkei Avot*, in contrast, is the work of a powerless and dispossessed people. When it mentions "the government," it means the occupying power of the Romans, and it treats this government with a combination of wary respect and outright fear.

Rabbi Chanina, a priestly official who probably lived through the Jewish War, admits that the government serves a function: "Pray for the welfare of the government, for were it not for the fear of it, people would swallow each other alive." Remembering the desperate civil strife that Josephus records, it is easy to understand Chanina's view: better any government than none at all. But if government is a necessary evil, it is still an evil. Power is never something that a Jew might possess or aspire to; it is always a capricious outside force, whose attention it is dangerous to rouse. "Watch out for the government. They befriend a person to meet their own needs, appearing friendly when it is to their benefit; but they do not stand by a person when that person is in distress," warns Rabban Gamliel, who as a leader of the Jewish community had experience dealing with the Romans. Another sage says succinctly, "Love labor, hate power, and don't try to become the familiar friend of government." "The Fathers according to Rabbi Nathan" expands on this point: "One's name should not come to the attention of the ruling powers," it advises.

"For once his name comes to the attention of the ruling powers, they cast their eye upon him and slay him and take away all his property from him."

For prudential reasons, then, it is best to remain inconspicuous. But one of the most powerful sayings in *Pirkei Avot* seems to go even further. The great rabbi Hillel "once saw a skull floating on the surface of the water. He said to it, 'Because you drowned people, others drowned you. They in turn will be drowned by others.'" This is an enigmatic saying: How did Hillel know that the skull he saw belonged to a murderer? Was he making a point about divine justice, which ensures that a murderer is always punished? Or was he, perhaps, making a more general statement about the world in which he lived? The image of the floating skull seems to suggest that the whole world of action is a scene of pointless slaughter where violence only begets more violence. Better to withdraw from it altogether than to risk taking one's place in the chain of killing.

Still, there is more to the rabbis' distrust of power than fear. One of the roles of a Torah sage was to act as a judge, hearing lawsuits and resolving disputes according to Jewish law. Even this degree of power, however, was shunned by the sages, for two reasons: it was bad for one's character, and it took time away from Torah study, which is what really mattered. According to Rabbi Yishmael, "Whoever restrains oneself from acting as judge removes from oneself enmity, robbery, and perjury. Whoever pompously renders decisions is a wicked and arrogant fool." If one did have to judge, the rabbis advised him to do it without pride or partiality. "When the litigants stand before you, let them appear to you equally culpable," said Yehuda ben Tabbai. "When they leave you, having accepted judgment, let them look equally blameless to you."

"The Fathers according to Rabbi Nathan" adds another point of view, making clear that power, as well as being a burden, can also be a temptation. One leading official ruefully declared: "Whenever someone said to me before I entered into high office, 'Enter it,' I had one wish: to hound him to death! Now that I have come into it, whenever someone tells me to quit it, I have one wish: to upset a kettle of boiling water on him! For to high office it is hard to rise; and even as it is hard to rise up to it, so it is difficult to come down from it." Perhaps the worst danger of all is that a sage might become so accustomed to power that he begins to enjoy it.

The correct attitude, in contrast, was that of Rabbi Nechunya ben Hakanah, who saw public office as a punishment that God inflicted on those who failed to devote themselves to Torah study: "Anyone who will accept the yoke of the Torah, from that one will be removed the yoke of the government and the yoke of worldly care. But anyone who spurns the yoke of the Torah, upon that one will be placed the yoke of the government and the yoke of worldly care." Indeed, one should regard every kind of "worldly care" as a mere distraction, as Rabbi Meir succinctly put it: "Do less business and do more Torah."

BUT WHAT DID THE SAGES mean by "doing Torah"? The answer, it becomes clear in the sayings of *Pirkei Avot*, is something more than simply carrying out the commandments. That was crucial, of course, and much of *Pirkei Avot* is dedicated to describing the ethical ideals of the pious Jew. But Torah was not just a set of practices. It was also a body of knowledge, embodied in the Bible and, even more, in the Mishnah. And since much of this knowledge was transmitted orally, "doing Torah" included the obligation to study, memorize, and teach the Jewish legal tradition. Those who devoted their lives to this study were the rabbis, the sages, and they were to be held in the highest reverence. Indeed, *Pirkei Avot* gives the strong impression that the production of Torah sages is the purpose of Judaism and that the scholar's life is the best one a human being can live.

It was not always possible, of course, for a Jew—and for the rabbis, this always meant a Jewish man—to devote himself full-time to Torah study. One of the recurrent concerns of *Pirkei Avot* is how the scholar should balance scholarship and earning a living. Sometimes the text seems to endorse voluntary poverty for the sake of full-time study: "This is the way of the Torah: you will eat bread with salt. You will drink water by measure, you will endure a life of privation, while you labor in the Torah." But this deprivation is, spiritually speaking, the only true luxury: "Happy shall you be in this world and good will be yours in the world to come. . . . Don't hanker after the tables of kings for your table is greater than theirs."

At the same time, many leading rabbis were landowners and merchants, and Rabban Gamliel says that earning a livelihood is actually a spiritual benefit: "It is good to join the study of Torah to some kind of work, for the effort required by both robs sin of its power. Torah study without work will end up being useless and will cause sin." In any case, for many people, combining work with study was a practical necessity. As Rabbi Eleazar ben Azariah says, realistically, "Where there is no bread, there will be no Torah." At the same time, he completes the phrase by suggesting that those who ignore the Law will never prosper: "Where there is no Torah, there will be no bread."

Wealth aside, *Pirkei Avot* makes clear that in rabbinic Judaism, Torah sages constitute a kind of aristocracy. After the destruction of the Jewish kingdom and the Temple, the old ruling classes—royal officials and priests—no longer had any power. In their place, learned men, the rabbis who could understand and preserve the law, became the elite. They are to be treated with great deference: "Let your house be a meeting place for the wise; sit humbly at their feet; and, with thirst, drink in their words." Yet this was, in part at least, a meritocratic elite. The rich might have an easier path to Torah, but some of the greatest sages came from poor backgrounds, and in principle the study of Torah was open to anyone with the necessary gifts. This made rabbinic Judaism, in a sense, more democratic than the priesthood or the monarchy had ever been: "Since you cannot inherit the Torah," said Rabbi Yose, "you must prepare yourself to study it."

Inevitably, there is a tension between the elite status of the rabbis, which encourages pride, and their piety, which demands humility. *Pirkei Avot* gives the sense that, like scholars in all times and places, the rabbis could be high-handed and short-tempered when dealing with lay people: "Warm yourself by the fire of the sages, but take care that you don't get burned by their coals. Their bite is the bite of a fox; their sting is a scorpion stinging; and their hiss is a viper hiss. Indeed, all their words are like coals of fire."

Recognizing the danger of arrogance, however, *Pirkei Avot* repeatedly warns the learned against glorifying themselves. Yochanan ben Zakkai would say, "If you have learned much Torah, don't take the credit, for it was for that purpose that you were created." Torah study is, after all, a Jew's first duty, and you don't get a special reward for doing your duty. "Don't use [the words of the Torah] as a crown to build yourself up," agreed Rabbi Tzadok, and went even further: "nor as an adze to dig with." That is, the Torah scholar should not attempt to make a living through his knowledge—say, by teaching for a fee. Better to work at a lowly occupation than to make money from the Torah.

Indeed, a Torah scholar is expected to treat the Torah as something more than just a subject that can be learned and taught. It is, as Yochanan says, the very purpose of human existence, and in *Pirkei Avot* it becomes a kind of conscience, a superego that demands constant obedience and attention. Every single moment not spent on Torah study is a moment wasted. "If two sit together and exchange no words of Torah, then they are like an assembly of scoffers," says one sage. "However, when two sit together and do exchange words of Torah, then the Divine Presence dwells with them."

The great Hillel is described in the Talmud as a patient and accommodating teacher, yet even he says, "One who does not study deserves to die." And studying is not enough; the student must retain what he learns, an especially important requirement in a time when Torah was usually learned orally, not from books. To forget a law might mean breaking the chain of transmission forever. For this reason, "one who forgets anything he has learned, Scripture accounts it as if he had sinned against his soul."

Not even the splendor of the natural world—which is, after all, God's creation, no less than the Torah—can be allowed to distract the scholar from his focus on study. One of the most notorious sayings in *Pirkei Avot* drives the point home: according to Rabbi Yaakov, "Were one to be walking on the road while studying and then stop his studies to say, 'How beautiful is this tree!' and 'How nice is that field!' such a person would be considered by the Torah to have sinned against his soul." This does not exactly say that it is wrong to notice the beauty of nature; indeed, Jewish tradition provides specific blessings to recite in the presence of natural wonders. But it makes clear that the Jew's world is supposed to be primarily a textual and intellectual one, not a sensual one. In "The Fathers according to Rabbi Nathan," Rabbi Jacob ben Hananiah takes this commitment to Torah to a graphic extreme: "If one wakes in the night and the first words out of his mouth are not words of Torah, it would have been better for him if the afterbirth in which he lay had been turned over on his face, and he had never been born and beheld the world."

There is a danger, however, that the rabbis' single-minded focus on Torah study could lead the pious Jew into another kind of sin: the sin of divorcing theory from practice. After all, if expounding the law is itself a kind of worship, even a replacement for the Temple sacrifices, then it might seem as if actually following the law were a matter of secondary importance. Intellect and understanding might appear to take precedence over piety and conduct.

That this was indeed a concern for the sages of *Pirkei Avot* is clear from the warnings they issue about it. "I have grown up among the sages all my days," said Simeon ben Gamliel, who was a member of one of the most important rabbinic dynasties. "Yet I have never found

anything better than silence. Study is not the main thing; doing is."
Another rabbi, Chanina ben Dosa, goes even further, suggesting that
knowledge not reinforced by practice is certain to disappear: "One
whose deeds exceed his wisdom, his wisdom will last. One whose wisdom exceeds his deeds, his wisdom will not last." And Rabbi Yishmael
concurs in placing observance of the laws above knowledge of the
laws: "The one who studies in order to teach will be enabled to study
and to teach. The one who studies in order to practice will be enabled
to study and to teach, to observe and to practice."

Even in this hierarchy, however, it is clear that while practice may be
higher than knowledge, knowledge must come before practice. What
makes rabbinic Judaism distinctive is the way it unites intellectual
understanding and ethical behavior into a single way of life—the life
of Torah. In a religion built on a complex system of laws, it is impossible to be fully pious without a good deal of expert knowledge.

Hillel puts the matter succinctly when he says, "The brute will not
fear sin. The ignoramus will not be saintly." The Hebrew term translated here as "ignoramus" is *am ha'aretz*, literally "people of the land"—
in the sense of a peasant or farmer—and it recurs throughout the
Talmud to describe the common Jew, who has little or no knowledge
of Torah. Such a person was often despised by the Talmudic elite, who
did not trust the *am ha'aretz* to follow Jewish law carefully. Certainly,
it is impossible for such a person to become "saintly," since he does not
know exactly what behavior God expects from him. Knowing, for the
rabbis, is a prerequisite of doing: both are necessary for holiness.

And while *Pirkei Avot* is meant to be a resource for every Jew, it
is addressed in the first instance to scholars and sages, and to those
who aspire to join their ranks. The very first maxim in the work sets
the tone. The men of the Great Assembly, we learn, said three things:
"Be deliberate in judgment, raise up many disciples, and make a fence
around the Torah." The judgment in question here is not just personal
judgment about how to live, but the professional judgment involved
in hearing cases under Jewish law. And the same sage who was called

upon to act as a judge would also, naturally, serve as a teacher, responsible for "raising up many disciples."

But what about "making a fence around the Torah"? How did the rabbis understand that evocative phrase? In the first instance, it had a technical legal meaning. To make a fence around a Torah commandment was to enact a new law that made it harder to violate the original commandment. Much rabbinic legislation takes the form of such "fences" around biblical laws. To ensure that Jews did not violate the biblical prohibition against performing labor on the sabbath, for instance, the rabbis evolved a comprehensive theory about what constitutes labor, dividing it into thirty-nine categories and introducing a whole series of rules about what kinds of objects cannot be touched on the sabbath. These wide-ranging prohibitions constituted a fence, marking off whole areas of behavior as potentially dangerous so that a Jew would not inadvertently break the law.

The implications of "making a fence" are clear in "The Fathers according to Rabbi Nathan." Jewish law prohibits husbands and wives from having sexual intercourse during the woman's menstrual period and for a certain period of time afterward, until she has been purified by immersion in a ritual bath. To guard against transgression, "The Fathers" suggests, the law in Leviticus uses very general terms: "Lo, it says, 'Also thou shalt not approach unto a woman . . . as long as she is impure by her uncleanness.'" In other words, the law does not just prohibit sexual intercourse; it prohibits any kind of "approach." "May her husband perhaps embrace her or kiss her or engage in idle chatter? The verse says, 'Thou shalt not approach.' May she perhaps sleep with him in her clothes on the couch? The verse says, 'Thou shalt not approach.'"

The prohibition on "approaching," then, is a fence around the prohibition on sex; it expands the definition of a sin in order to make the sin harder to commit. Just how seriously the rabbis took that prohibition is clear in the following passage, which tells about a pious, learned man who died young. His wife, shocked by the injustice of this, confronted the local rabbis and demanded to know why God would punish a good man with an early death. Finally, a sage got her to confess that even though she and her husband never had sex while she was impure, they did sleep together with their clothes on. "His flesh touched mine but he had no thought of anything," the woman protested. But this was enough to violate the fence around the Torah, and the sage replied sternly: "Blessed be God who killed him." Death was the appropriate punishment, not just for a sin, but for coming too close to a sin.

IN A BROADER SENSE, however, one might say that "making a fence around the Torah" is a good description of the whole ethos of *Pirkei Avot*. Torah, and the way of life it dictates, appear in these sayings as extremely vulnerable, beset on all sides by temptations and distractions. Human beings must fence themselves off not only from the world, which is full of occasions to sin, but also from the sinful parts of their own nature. Indeed, Rabbi Akiva sees the ethical life as the construction of a series of fences: "Tradition is a fence around the Torah. Tithes are a fence around wealth. Vows are a fence around abstinence. And silence is a fence around wisdom."

Pirkei Avot often suggests that only a constant awareness of our propensity to sin can keep us from ethical disaster. An image from "The Fathers according to Rabbi Nathan" captures the atmosphere perfectly: "A parable is told: to what may this be likened? To a thoroughfare which lies between paths, one of flames and the other of snow. If one walks alongside the flames, he will be scorched by flames; and if he walks alongside the snow, he will be frostbitten. What then is he to do? Let him walk between them and take care of himself in order not to be scorched by the flames and not to be frostbitten."

Judaism is not an ascetic religion; the rabbis had no use for celibacy, since they saw marriage and childrearing as religious duties. Indeed, the wariness of the world that *Pirkei Avot* displays is a sign that it is addressed to people living in the world—to Jews who are parents and breadwinners, not monks or hermits. For that very reason, the rabbis preach a severe kind of temperance that entails being in this world and out of it simultaneously. Thus while it is assumed that Jewish men will be married, one of the first maxims tells us: "When a man talks too much to his wife, he causes evil to himself, disregards the words of the Torah, and in the end will inherit Gehinnom [Hell]."

Moses Maimonides interpreted "talking" in this passage as a euphemism for having sexual relations, and he saw the adage as a warning against excessive sensuality, even within marriage. But it is equally possible to take it at face value. A man's conversations with his wife, the sages assume, are not going to be about Torah, but about family or personal matters, and these are always a distraction from the sacred. Even trivial sins, another sage warns, can cost us our lives: "Morning sleep, midday wine, children's talk, and attendance at the meeting places of the ignorant—all will take a person out of this world."

Indeed, to Hillel, everything in the world that human beings strive for is ultimately a cause of misery. He makes the point in a stern catalogue: "The more flesh, the more worms; the more possessions, the more worry; the more wives, the more witchcraft; the more maidservants, the more lewdness; the more menservants, the more theft." What all these things have in common is that they are status symbols in a culture where having many wives and servants was a privilege of the wealthy. (The warning about witchcraft follows from the idea that if a man has many wives, they will compete with one another for his favor, using magic spells if necessary.)

But status symbols mean nothing to a worm-eaten corpse, and Hillel insists that we keep our end constantly before our eyes. Another sage, Akabia ben Mahalel, reminds us that our beginning is just as miserable as our end. "Reflect on three things and you will not come into the grasp of sin: know where you came from; know where you are going; and in whose presence you will have to make an accounting. Where do you come from? From a disgusting drop. Where are you going? To a place of dust, of worms, and of maggots. In whose presence will you have to make an accounting? The most Sovereign of Sovereigns, the Holy One of Blessing."

By the same token, the goods that last beyond the grave should be pursued all the more ardently. Thus the second half of Hillel's catalogue lists the things we should strive for: "the more Torah, the more life; the more schooling, the more wisdom; the more counsel, the more understanding; the more righteous charity, the more peace. One who has acquired a good name has acquired it for himself. One who has acquired the words of Torah has acquired for himself a place in the world to come." Torah knowledge is the only treasure that will not decay, because it alone pleases God and earns us eternal life.

The idea of a world to come, where the pious will be rewarded and the sinful punished, is absolutely central to *Pirkei Avot*. Where the book of Deuteronomy promised blessings and curses in this world— prosperity and good harvests if the Israelites obeyed God, exile and starvation if they disobeyed—the rabbis see the next world as the scene of God's justice. Often they employ commercial metaphors to make the point. Rabbi Akiba imagines God as a storekeeper: "Everything is given on pledge and a net is spread out for all that lives. The shop is open; the shopkeeper extends credit; the ledger is open; and the hand writes." For Rabbi Tarfon, God is a demanding employer: "The day is short, there is much work, the laborers are lazy, the wages are great, and the Householder is insistent."

Such images drive home the point that God is keeping careful records of human deeds and will give every person exactly what he deserves. *Pirkei Avot* is haunted by this sense of divine surveillance: "Think deeply about three things and you will never be gripped by the desire to commit a transgression. Know what is above you: an eye that sees, an ear that hears, and all your deeds are inscribed in a book," says Yehuda HaNasi. Just as we were not consulted about whether we should be born, another sage says, we will not be consulted about our fate in the afterlife: "For against your will were you formed. Against your will were you born. Against your will you live. Against your will you will die. Against your will you will make a reckoning before the Ruler of Rulers, the Holy One of Blessing."

At times, this way of thinking about virtue and reward can sound excessively transactional, as when Rabbi Yaakov says, "This world is like a foyer before the world to come. Prepare yourself in the foyer so that you will be able to enter the banquet hall." But other moments in *Pirkei Avot* suggest a different approach to the *mitzvot*, as when Antigonus of Socho instructs, "Don't be like those who would serve a master on the condition that they would receive a reward. Rather, be like those who would serve without that condition." After all, if Torah is the most precious thing in Creation, no reward for doing Torah could possibly be better than Torah itself. Since carrying out the commandments is the sweetest joy we can know, God can only reward us for following his laws by giving us more laws to follow.

That is why, in the words of Ben Azzai, "The reward of a commandment is a commandment and the reward of a transgression is a transgression." And the same Rabbi Yaakov who spoke about the next world as a banquet hall also says, "An hour spent in penitence and good deeds in this world is better than all of life in the world to come. An hour of contentment in the world to come is better than all of life in this world." The world to come is better than this world, but doing good in this world is better than the world to come. If there is a paradox here, it is the paradox of faith, which finds its greatest satisfaction not in getting a reward but in deserving one.

The endlessness of a Jew's task in this world, then, can be seen as a happy fate. No individual can be perfect or attain perfection in Torah knowledge; but then, it is the striving for perfection that makes a life blessed. As Rabbi Tarfon says in one of the most famous maxims in *Pirkei Avot*: "It is not up to you to finish the work, yet you are not free to avoid it." Today, this is often taken as a comment on humanity's shared responsibility for improving the world, and Tarfon's words can certainly bear that interpretation. But the context makes clear that the "work" that he had in mind was—of course—the work of Torah. "If you have studied much Torah, then you will receive much in wages, for your Employer is dependable to pay the wage for your work," the saying continues.

The same moral urgency animates what is probably the single best-known adage in *Pirkei Avot*, the three-part question of Hillel: "If I am not for myself, who will be for me? And, if I am for myself alone, then what am I? And, if not now, when?" This, too, is a saying that can be interpreted in very different ways. Today, the emphasis often falls on the second question, which is considered an exhortation to universalism and mutual responsibility. The edition of *Pirkei Avot* published by the Reform movement, the most liberal and modernizing of the three major Jewish denominations, annotates it this way: "We also view this statement as an instruction to us not to restrict our concerns for social justice to members of the Jewish community. We are obligated to transcend our particularism and help all in our community who require assistance."

But for most of Jewish history the three questions were read differently, as a statement about the responsibility of the individual before God. That is certainly how Hillel's words are interpreted in "The Fathers according to Rabbi Nathan," which sees them as a reminder about the importance of "laying up merit" in God's eyes. The first question, on this view, tells us that each individual must justify himself before God; the second, that no matter how much we do we can never achieve perfection; and the third, that we must justify ourselves in this lifetime, before it is too late. In the same spirit, Rabbi Eliezer advised, "Repent one day before your death"; and since we never know what day we will die, we must live constantly as if we were on the brink of judgment.

In this way, the rabbis turned the individual Jewish soul into the protagonist of a great moral drama, just at the moment when the Jewish collective had ceased to figure in the drama of politics. In the post-Temple world, *Pirkei Avot* seems to say, the Jews have been deprived of many things, but they cannot be deprived of Torah. And as Ben Bag Bag insists, Torah is everything: "Turn it and turn it, for everything is in it. Reflect on it and grow old and gray with it. Don't turn away from it, for nothing is better than it."

BIBLIOGRAPHY

Akenson, Donald Harman. *Surpassing Wonder: The Invention of the Bible and the Talmuds*. Chicago: University of Chicago Press, 2001.

The Fathers according to Rabbi Nathan. Translated by Judah Goldin. New Haven: Yale University Press, 1955.

Pirkei Avos: Ethics of the Fathers. Edited and translated by Meir Zlotowitz and Nosson Scherman. Brooklyn, NY: Mesorah Publications, 1999.

Pirkei Avot: A Modern Commentary on Jewish Ethics. Edited and translated by Leonard Kravitz and Kerry M. Olitzky. New York: Union for Reform Judaism Press, 1993.

6

THE SCANDAL OF CHOSENNESS

The *Itinerary* of Benjamin of Tudela and the *Kuzari* by Yehuda Halevi

In the twelfth century, Jewish culture thrived in Muslim Spain, even as Jews remained highly vulnerable to persecution and violence. In the book known as his *Itinerary*, the Spanish-born traveler Benjamin of Tudela mixed travelers' tales with statistical evidence to offer a survey of the Jewish world of his time. Though the Diaspora stretched from Spain to Yemen, Benjamin emphasizes that the Jews still longed for the Land of Israel, which was then a backward province ruled by Christian Crusaders. In this condition of exile, the great Spanish-born poet Yehuda Halevi wrote one of the defining works of Jewish thought: the *Kuzari*, a fictional dialogue in which a rabbi convinces a pagan king to convert to Judaism. To make his case, the rabbi advances bold claims for the superiority not just of Judaism as a faith, but of the Jewish people and the Land of Israel over all their rivals. Halevi's vindication of Jewish chosenness defied both the arguments of reason and the actual condition of Jewish powerlessness, making the *Kuzari* the most influential defense of Judaism ever written.

SOMETIME IN THE 1160S, A MAN NAMED BENJAMIN ben Jonah left his native city of Tudela, in northern Spain, and set off to explore the world. Exactly what spurred his long journey—business, piety, sheer curiosity—is not known. But the book he wrote about his travels, known as the *Itinerary* of Benjamin of Tudela, survives as a unique record of Jewish life in the Middle Ages. Everywhere he went, from Spain to Italy to Palestine, Benjamin recorded the size of the local Jewish population, the names of its leading citizens, and whatever notable facts came to his attention. If he couldn't visit a place in person, he allowed travelers' tales and his own imagination to fill in the blank, sometimes to startling effect. He writes, for instance, about the journey to Zin, as he calls China, which involves hitching a ride over a dangerous sea in the claws of "a great bird called the griffin."

For all its obvious inventions, however, the *Itinerary* offers a revealing map of the Jewish world in the twelfth century. For one thing, it makes clear that the overwhelming majority of Jews—as much as 90 percent—lived under Muslim rule, in the zone of Islamic civilization that stretched from Spain in the west to Iraq in the east. When Benjamin visits Christian countries in western Europe, he finds small Jewish communities in even the biggest cities—200 Jews in Arles, 500 in Naples. When he gets to the Middle East, in contrast, the Jewish populations swell dramatically—there are 5,000 Jews in Aleppo, he writes, and 7,000 in Mosul. In Baghdad, the capital of the Islamic caliphate, "there are about 40,000 Jews, and they dwell in security, prosperity, and honor," he reports with pride.

The figures may not be accurate, but the impression they give is unmistakable. Under Muslim rule, Jews thrive; under Christian rule, they languish. This is especially notable in great Christian capitals like

Rome and Constantinople. The two hundred Jews living in Rome include some great scholars, Benjamin reports, but they dwell in a city that even after a thousand years bears witness to the conquest of Judea and the humiliation of the Jews. He notes the palace of Titus, whom the Senate reproved "because he failed to take Jerusalem till after three years, though they had bidden him to capture it within two." In the church of St. John Lateran there are bronze columns purportedly looted from the Jerusalem Temple, "each column being engraved 'Solomon the son of David.'" According to the local Jews, these columns "exude moisture like water" every year on the Ninth of Av, literally weeping over the loss of the Temple.

In Constantinople, which in the twelfth century was still the capital of the much-reduced Byzantine Empire, the Jews are humiliated in a more literal fashion. The city itself fills Benjamin with wonder: "Wealth like that of Constantinople is not to be found in the whole world," he writes. "Here also are men learned in all the books of the Greeks, and they eat and drink, every man under his vine and his fig-tree." All, that is, except the Jews, who are forbidden to live within the city limits. The Jewish quarter by the waterside, with its 2,500 residents, is more like a ghetto:

> No Jew there is allowed to ride on horseback. The one exception is Rabbi Solomon Hamitsri, who is the king's physician, and through whom the Jews enjoy considerable alleviation of their oppression. For their condition is very low, and there is much hatred against them, which is fostered by the tanners, who throw out their dirty water in the streets before the doors of the Jewish houses and defile the Jews' quarter. So the Greeks hate the Jews, good and bad alike, and subject them to great oppression, and beat them in the streets, and in every way treat them with rigor. Yet the Jews are rich and good, kindly and charitable, and bear their lot with cheerfulness.

Not much had changed, it seems, in the eleven hundred years since the Greeks of Alexandria rioted against their Jewish neighbors (see Chapter 3). But things are very different in Baghdad, Benjamin reports. There, the caliph treats Judaism with respect—he even knows Hebrew. The traveler is especially impressed by the status of Daniel ben Hisdai, the exilarch, or official leader of the Jewish community. To Benjamin's dazzled eyes, the exilarch seems little less than a prince himself. While the Jews of Constantinople are forbidden to go on horseback, Daniel ben Hisdai rides in state:

> And every fifth day when he goes to pay a visit to the great Caliph, horsemen, Gentiles as well as Jews, escort him, and heralds proclaim in advance, "Make way before our Lord, the son of David, as is due to him." He is mounted on a horse, and is attired in robes of silk and embroidery, with a large turban on his head, and from the turban is suspended a long white cloth adorned with a chain upon which the cipher of Mohammed is engraved. Then he appears before the Caliph and kisses his hand . . . and all the Mohammedan princes who attend the court of the Caliph rise up before him.

Daniel, in Benjamin's eyes, comes close to being something that the world had not known for a thousand years: a Jewish king. Indeed, "he possesses a book of pedigrees going back as far as David, King of Israel." And as the *Itinerary* shows, images of Jewish power were something Benjamin particularly prized, because so often his travels brought him face to face with Jewish powerlessness.

This was never more striking or humiliating than in the Land of Israel itself. Palestine must have been in some sense the high point of Benjamin's journey, a chance for him to see with his own eyes the places he had been reading about all his life. Biblical stories that we might understand as myths were for Benjamin entirely historical, and he found their traces all over the landscape. In Hebron, he bribed a custodian to take him underground to see the tombs of the patriarchs. Near the Dead Sea, he saw "the Pillar of Salt into which Lot's wife was turned [in the book of Genesis]; the sheep lick it continually, but afterwards it regains its original shape." Post-biblical Judaism, too, left its traces on the land: Benjamin visited the tombs of Hillel and Shammai and other great rabbis.

But when he visited Yavneh, where Yochanan ben Zakkai built his academy after the fall of the Temple, he found no Jews living there. And Jerusalem, where in Josephus's time a million Jews came for the holidays, was now "a small city . . . full of people whom the Mohammedans call Jacobites, Syrians, Greeks, Georgians, and Franks, and people of all tongues." Conspicuously missing from this list are Jews, of whom Benjamin found a total of two hundred, "under the Tower of David in one corner of the city." For Jerusalem at this time was under the rule of Christian Crusaders, who had conquered the city in 1099 and massacred its Jewish population. At the time of Benjamin's visit, around 1170, the signs of Crusader power were everywhere: the building called the palace of Solomon was being used to quarter three hundred Christian knights.

The *Itinerary* gives the sense that Jerusalem, for Benjamin as for many later travelers, was an embarrassing anticlimax. Instead of the wealth of Constantinople and Baghdad, this city, older and more famous than either, offered only ruins: the Western Wall of the Temple, "the pool used by the priests before offering their sacrifices." The only structure still in use by Jews that Benjamin mentions is "a dyeing-house, for which the Jews pay a small rent annually to the king." Even the cemeteries are a witness to Jewish degradation: "the Christians destroyed the sepulchers," Benjamin notes, "employing the stones thereof in building their houses."

After witnessing so much Jewish powerlessness, it is no wonder that Benjamin seized so eagerly on any story, plausible or not, that could be read as an example of Jewish strength. The civilized splendor of Jewish Baghdad is one thing, but what really seems to excite the traveler are Jews, even barbaric ones, who can hold their own in a fight. "The nation called Wallachians," for instance, are little better than bandits, as "they sweep down from the mountains to despoil and ravage the land of Greece." But Benjamin notes with interest that they "give themselves Jewish names. Some people say that they are Jews and, in fact, they call the Jews their brethren, and when they meet with them, though they rob them, they refrain from killing them as they kill the Gentiles. They are altogether lawless," he concludes, not altogether disapprovingly.

Later, Benjamin writes about Yemen, where "the Jews own many large fortified cities. The yoke of the Gentiles is not upon them. They go forth to pillage and to capture booty from distant lands in conjunction with the Arabs, their neighbors and allies. . . . All the neighbors of these Jews go in fear of them," he notes with satisfaction. Yemen, in fact, serves Benjamin as a fantasyland, and he populates it with absurdly huge cities (300,000 Jews in Tanai, 100,000 in Tilmas), using the blank space on the map to project a fantasy of Jewish power.

Another such fantasy appears in his discussion of David Alroy, a real if minor figure from Central Asia who led a failed rebellion against Persian rule. In Benjamin's telling, however, Alroy is a would-be Messiah, promising to lead a Jewish army "to capture Jerusalem and free you from the yoke of the Gentiles." He describes himself as "king of the Jews," like his namesake David, and he has magical powers, including the ability to turn invisible and to walk on water. But Alroy is opposed by the cautious, conservative leaders of Persia's Jewish community, who fear that their government will have them all killed in a reprise of Haman's genocidal conspiracy.

The elders also oppose Alroy's plan to conquer the Land of Israel on theological grounds. "The time of redemption is not yet arrived," they say; "we have not yet seen the signs thereof; for by strength shall no man prevail." This was the standard Jewish response to the Diaspora, which by then had lasted more than a thousand years. It was not for the Jews themselves to return to Palestine; when God had finished punishing them for their sins, he would bring them home in his own fashion. When Alroy persisted in opposing this logic, threatening to take matters into his own hands and march on Jerusalem with a Jewish army, his own father-in-law accepted a bribe and killed him in his sleep.

This whole story—which much later would inspire a novel by another Jewish writer, Benjamin Disraeli—reads like a bitter indictment of Diaspora quietism. And at the end of the *Itinerary*, Benjamin seems torn between his own impatience for the Jews to reclaim their land and his knowledge that the time was not yet right. "If we were not afraid that the appointed time has not yet arrived nor been reached," he writes, "we would have gathered together, but we dare not do so until the time for song has arrived . . . when the messengers will come and say continually, 'The Lord is exalted.'" Jewish life in the Diaspora, the *Itinerary* suggests, can be prosperous and glamorous, or it can be tenuous and oppressive; but it remains a life in hiatus.

AMONG THE ILLUSTRIOUS graves that Benjamin visited in the Land of Israel, one name stands out. In Tiberias, along with the hot springs and the local synagogue, he mentions that "Yochanan ben Zakkai and Yehuda Halevi are buried here." Yochanan is one of many early rabbis whose alleged burial-places Benjamin lists; but Yehuda Halevi is a different story. He was not a Talmudic sage, but a poet, and he died just a few decades before Benjamin's voyage. Many scholars believe that his name is only in the text by accident, since some manuscripts of the *Itinerary* have a different name here—that of an ancient rabbi who would fit more naturally alongside Yochanan ben Zakkai.

Still, if Yehuda Halevi's grave did lie in Tiberias, it would be conclusive proof that he died as he had hoped, in the Land of Israel. For the last years of Halevi's life were entirely directed toward the idea of the land—not just as the conventional object of prayers for redemption, but as a living possibility, a place where a Jew might actually go to be closer to God. Some of his most famous and moving Hebrew poems are expressions of this longing, at once spiritual and highly concrete, to be united with the land:

> *My heart in the East, and I in the West,*
> *as far in the West as west can be!*
> *How can I enjoy my food?*
> *What flavor can it have for me?*
> *How can I fulfill my vows*
> *or do the things I've sworn to do,*
> *while Zion is in Christian hands*
> *and I am trapped in Arab lands?*

In these lines, translated from the Hebrew by Raymond Scheindlin, it's possible to read the basic facts about Halevi's own life and the geopolitics of his age. The date of his birth is uncertain—estimates range from 1070 to 1085—and even the place is unclear: he was either from Tudela, like Benjamin the traveler, or from the similarly named Toledo. But in either case, it is certain that he lived "as far in the West as west can be," in Spain, at a time when the peninsula was divided between Christian rulers in the north and Muslim rulers in the south. During this period, the Jews participated in what is now regarded as a cultural golden age—an era when Spain's sophisticated Islamic civilization made it one of the most enviable places in the world. It was one of the rare moments in Jewish history when Jews assimilated culturally, if not socially, into their surrounding milieu: they spoke and wrote Arabic, lived in the same fashion as their Muslim neighbors, and participated in a lively exchange of philosophical ideas and poetic styles.

As a minority caught between Christian and Muslim communities, the Jews sometimes benefited from their marginal status, and individual Jews rose to amazing heights in the service of some Muslim rulers. Shmuel HaNagid, "Samuel the Prince," who died just two decades before Yehuda Halevi was born, became the vizier of Grenada, the highest-ranking official in the state. He also wrote Hebrew poetry; this was, among other things, a golden age for Hebrew literature, perhaps its greatest flourishing between ancient times and the twentieth century.

It is easy, however, to romanticize this era. The truth is that the position of the Jews in Spain remained fragile, vulnerable to both popular hostility and sudden changes of government. This became clear in 1090, when as a young man Halevi would have heard about the conquest of Grenada by the Almoravids. This fervently Islamic sect from North Africa conducted a purge of the city's Jewish population, putting an end to the fabled culture of tolerance. Later in the same decade, the global powerlessness of the Jews was underscored once again, when the First Crusade devastated German Jewish communities on the way to its conquest of Jerusalem. Halevi commented on this state of affairs in a poem:

> *Between the Christian and Muslim troops,*
> *my own troops perish,*
> *for they go out to battle each other,*
> *and in their defeat, it is we who fall—*
> *so it has always been for Israel.*

In many ways, Yehuda Halevi followed the established pattern for cultivated Andalusian Jews. In addition to being a poet, he was a practicing physician and a community leader in Toledo and Cordoba, the cities where he spent his adult life. But toward the end of his life, Halevi departed from that pattern in a dramatic and significant fashion. At a time when Spain was the peak of civilization and Palestine, as Benjamin of Tudela showed, was a war-torn and deserted backwater, Halevi conceived the idea that he must make a pilgrimage to the Land of Israel. He elaborated this dream in fervent poems, and despite what must have been the deep skepticism of friends and family, he finally decided to put it into practice. In the year 1140, when he was probably in his mid-sixties, Halevi embarked on the dangerous journey across the Mediterranean, landing first in Egypt, where he spent much of the next year. In the spring of 1141, he set sail for Palestine.

The months Halevi spent in Egypt are by far the best documented of his life. This is because of one of the most amazing discoveries in the history of scholarship: the unearthing of the archive known as the Cairo Geniza, by Solomon Schechter, in 1896. This midden of discarded paper, accumulated over the ages in the attic of a synagogue, turned out to contain manuscripts and letters dating back a thousand years—including letters from and about Yehuda Halevi. As a result, it's possible to trace his activities in the nine months he spent in Egypt in great detail, and to know the exact date he boarded ship for Palestine: May 7, 1141.

From the Geniza, too, comes a letter written later that year which refers to Halevi as dead. If he did get to Palestine, then, he could only have spent a few months there before he died, and the exact manner of his death remains unknown. A medieval tradition, written down centuries later, holds that Halevi was killed by an Arab horseman at the gates of Jerusalem while he was reciting one of his passionate poems of Zion. Such a symbolic martyrdom seems unlikely, however, and it's possible that the aging poet simply died of natural causes after an arduous journey. If Benjamin is to be trusted, his tomb was in Tiberias and was on display for pilgrims some thirty years later.

In time, Halevi's poetic achievement faded into obscurity. Though some poems were preserved in the Jewish liturgy, most of his verses had been all but forgotten by the time a medieval manuscript collection surfaced and was published in the nineteenth century, returning Halevi's name to the front rank of Jewish literature. But another work of Halevi's did keep his name alive down the centuries. This was not a poem but a prose dialogue, the *Kuzari*. It would become one of the most influential treatises ever written about the Jewish religion—and a monument to Halevi's romance with the Land of Israel.

To understand the strange and sometimes disturbing forms that Halevi's vision of Judaism takes, it's crucial to note the full Arabic title of the *Kuzari*: "The Book of the Khazars: The Book of Proof and Demonstration in Defense of the Despised Faith." At the time Halevi was writing (the first mention of the *Kuzari* dates from 1129, but it was revised and rewritten up until 1140), Judaism was indeed a "despised faith" in the eyes of the world. While Muslims and Christians battled for control of Spain and the Holy Land, Jews were left to suffer the consequences. It was against this background of inferiority that Halevi advanced his radical claims for the superiority of Judaism over all other faiths.

The form Halevi chose for the *Kuzari* offers a clue to his aspirations. Just as Benjamin of Tudela had eagerly written down half-imaginary stories of Jewish kingdoms and bandits, so Halevi seized on a rare example of Jewish sovereignty: the kingdom of the Khazars, located in Asia between the Black Sea and the Caspian Sea. News of the Khazars, whose king and ruling class had converted to Judaism sometime in the eighth century CE, reached the Jews of Spain in the form of rumors and semi-fictional correspondence. Because little was actually known about the Khazars, they proved an ideal screen on which to project fantasies of Jewish power.

Halevi's book is cast as an account of the Khazar king's conversion to Judaism, and it seeks to explain why such a ruler would choose to throw in his lot with the "despised faith." Why not convert to Islam or Christianity, which were so much bigger and more powerful? Or why not embrace the ecumenical approach of the philosophers, who see all religions as metaphorical and think that God can be known through intellect alone? Indeed, when the dialogue begins, the king is willing to listen to representatives of each of these ways of thinking, but he doesn't think it necessary to talk to a Jew: "As regards the Jews, I am satisfied that they are of low station, few in number, and generally despised," he observes.

To overcome this reluctance, Halevi shows the king in extensive dialogue with a rabbi, who lays down the reasons why Judaism is the one true faith and argues that only as a Jew can the king truly serve God. Eventually the king is convinced; he converts to Judaism, undergoes circumcision, and begins to spread the faith among his people. But that is far from the end of the story. Once the king has converted, the rabbi goes on to instruct him in the principles and practices of Judaism, defending along the way many things that might strike the outsider as odd or illogical. And all the time, the rabbi seeks to bolster the king's convictions against the temptations of philosophy—which proves, much more than Islam or Christianity, to be Judaism's most dangerous rival. The whole dialogue's purpose, Halevi says at the outset, is "to state what arguments and replies I could bring to bear against the attacks of philosophers and followers of other religions": the philosophers, notably, come first.

The *Kuzari* begins with a description of the king's crisis of religious conscience. He is a pious man, "zealous in the performance of the Khazar religion"; but one night he dreams that an angel appears to him, telling him that the Khazar faith is not the correct one: "Thy way of thinking is indeed pleasing to the Creator, but not thy way of acting." This angelic message establishes on the first page what is perhaps the most basic distinction in the *Kuzari*: the difference between thinking and acting, between holding right opinions about God and doing what God commands. If all that mattered were good intentions, then the angel would not have had to appear to the king in the first place. The angel's message makes clear that God requires something more than "thinking": he wants human beings to worship him in a particular fashion, to perform the specific actions that please him most.

By framing the discussion in this way, Halevi manages to disqual-ify from the start the whole approach to religion typical of the people he calls "the philosophers." Halevi's original readers would have iden-tified this term with classic Muslim thinkers like Al-Farabi and Avi-cenna; but even without any knowledge of the intricacies of medieval Arabic thought, it's possible to understand the basics of what Halevi means by "philosophy." Indeed, the very first person the king turns to in his religious quandary is a philosopher, who gives a brief sketch of how he thinks about God and faith.

To be a philosopher is to understand God in a very different way than he appears in the revealed religions. To a Jew, Christian, or Mus-lim, God is a Creator who intervenes in history in decisive ways— revealing his will to certain chosen prophets, performing miracles, even taking on human form. It makes sense to pray to such a God, because he has demonstrated that he takes a great interest in human affairs and is willing and able to change the course of events. The phi-losopher, in contrast, rejects this way of thinking about God. The first words he speaks to the king make this clear: "There is no favor or dis-like in God, because He is above desire and intention."

The philosopher, it becomes clear, is not a skeptic or an atheist; he does not doubt the existence of God. Rather, he understands God in the way that Aristotle understood him, as "the Cause of causes in the creation of all creatures." God is the First Cause, the being who sets the universe in motion, without whom nothing else could exist. He alone is perfect, while everything else is imperfect. But as the philos-opher points out, the idea of a perfect being excludes the possibility that God might desire anything. For we only desire something if we lack it, and if God lacked anything, he would not be perfect.

It follows that God cannot be imagined as acting in history to bring about particular results. Indeed, God is not the kind of being that knows what happens to humanity on a day-to-day basis. Our world is subject to change, but God, as the perfect being, cannot change, which means that his knowledge, too, cannot change. "He, therefore, does not know thee," the philosopher tells the king, "much less thy thoughts and actions, nor does He listen to thy prayers, or see thy movements." This God is a principle, not a personality; as the philosopher puts it, he acts not as a "Will" but as an "Emanation," a self-propagating force. In some ways, he could be thought of as simply a law of nature, and it makes no sense to pray to a law of nature.

What the philosopher can do, instead of praying to God, is to contemplate God. When a human being is sufficiently gifted and undergoes the right training, he can understand the nature of God and the universe so perfectly that his mind is, effectively, united with the divine intellect. Such a man "has grasped the inward truths of all branches of science," the philosopher explains, and "has thus become equal to an angel." He has left humanity behind, if not physically, then mentally and spiritually, and so he is no longer worried about bodily sickness or death: "Thus the soul of the perfect man and that Intellect become One, without concern for the decay of his body or his organs, because he becomes united to the other." In this state, the philosopher comes to know the same truths that the great thinkers of the past knew, and so he is united with them: "His soul is cheerful while he is alive, because it enjoys the company of . . . Plato and Aristotle."

Anyone who knows God in this rational, contemplative way will have no use or need for organized religion. The philosopher speaks about religion with a kind of contempt, advising the king that it doesn't matter which faith he adopts, since all of them are equally illusory. The king should simply pick whatever religion he likes, "for the management of thy temperament, thy house and country, if they agree to it"; that is, he should choose his faith based on political expediency. Naturally, no one deciding on that basis would ever pick the "despised faith" of Judaism.

The king's response to the philosopher's opening speech is tellingly ambivalent: "Thy words are convincing, yet they do not correspond to what I wish to find." He is clearly drawn to the idea of the Aristotelian

God, but his own religious experience prevents him from accepting it. He continues to believe that his dream was a message from God, and nothing could be clearer than that the philosophers' God does not send people messages. In fact, what the philosopher tells the king is the exact reverse of what the angel said in his dream: where the philosopher says that understanding God correctly matters more than ritual, the angel told him that pure understanding was not enough. "I know already that my soul is pure and that my actions are calculated to gain the favor of God," the king explains. If something is nonetheless lacking in his observance, it must mean that God does care about human actions after all: "There must no doubt be a way of acting, pleasing by its very nature, but not through the medium of intentions."

The king decides, then, to explore the claims of revealed religion, and he begins with the most obvious candidates: "I will ask the Christians and Moslems, since one of these persuasions is, no doubt, the God-pleasing one." First, he summons a Christian "scholastic" or theologian, who explains that his belief is in every respect the opposite of the philosopher's. A Christian is sure that "God takes care of the created beings, and keeps in touch with man; that He shows wrath, pleasure, and compassion; that He speaks, appears, and reveals Himself to his prophets and favored ones."

This is a God worth praying to. So far, however, the scholastic could be a believer in any monotheistic faith. What defines a Christian more particularly is belief in the truth of certain doctrines, which he lists: that Jesus is the son of God, that he was incarnated in "the semblance of a human being," that he is part of the Trinity along with God the Father and the Holy Spirit, and that he was crucified for the redemption of mankind.

Yet even as the scholastic explains these doctrines, he keeps insisting on the close dependence of Christianity on Judaism. Christians, he points out, believe in "all that is written in the Torah and the records of the Children of Israel," which they revere as the Old Testament. Indeed, they glory in calling themselves the new Children of

Israel, "although we are not of Israelitish descent," because they took over God's blessing that was originally bestowed on the Jews. Jesus himself was a Jew, Halevi emphasizes, and he followed the Jewish law: "It is also stated in the New Testament, I came not to destroy one of the laws of Moses, but I came to confirm and enlarge it."

The king does not exactly reject what the Christian tells him, but neither can he embrace it, for "logic rejects most of what thou sayest," he protests. The idea of God becoming man, of a woman giving birth to God, may seem natural to someone raised as a Christian; but to the king, hearing these ideas for the first time, they seem too strange to believe: "I cannot accept these things, because they have come upon me suddenly, not having grown up in them." Significantly, the king is not closing the door on miracles and supernatural revelations; he is willing to believe, but he feels the need of some "semblance of logic," an argument that will convince his reason, not just his heart.

When the "doctor of Islam" takes his turn before the king, he too starts by listing the central doctrines of his faith. The Koran is the word of God, and its perfection testifies to its divine origin; Muhammad is "the seal of the prophets," and the faith he founded supersedes Christianity and Judaism; all nations are invited to convert to Islam; and believers will be rewarded in paradise. But once again, the king remains skeptical. The Koran "may be a miracle," he allows, but since he cannot read Arabic, there is no way for him to test its perfection. "Even if it were read to me," he notes, "I could not distinguish between it and any other book written in the Arabic language."

Hearing this, the doctor shifts his ground. Not only is the Koran miraculous, he argues, but Muhammad performed miracles, which testify to the truth of Islam. But the king is left to register the same skepticism he expressed about Christianity. It is true, he grants, that God can perform miracles: "the human mind cannot believe that God has intercourse with man, except by a miracle which changes the nature of things." But how is he to believe that the specific miracles claimed by Islam really happened? For a miracle to be credible, the king says, it must meet certain standards of evidence: for instance, "it must . . . have taken place in the presence of great multitudes, who saw it distinctly, and did not learn it from reports and traditions."

Now the Muslim doctor walks directly into the trap that Halevi has laid for him. Islam does believe in certain miracles that were performed publicly, before a great number of people, he protests: "Is not our Book full of the stories of Moses and the Children of Israel? No one can deny what He did to Pharaoh, how He divided the seas. . . . His speaking to Moses on the mount," and all the other things God did when he brought the Children of Israel out of Egypt. Surely no one could doubt the truth of these stories: "is this not so well known that no suspicion of deceit and imagination is possible?"

But of course, long before these stories were part of the Koran, they were part of the book of Exodus. Halevi has cleverly constructed his dialogue so that both the Christian and the Muslim end up identifying Judaism as the proof and ground of their own faith. To believe that Christians possess God's new covenant, one must first believe in the covenant that God made with the Jews; to believe that Islam's miracles are true, one must first believe that God performed miracles for the Jews. The king, then, is left with no choice but to turn to the religion he first dismissed as too insignificant to bother with. "I see myself compelled to ask the Jews," he says. "For I see that they constitute in themselves the evidence for the divine law on earth."

NOW ENTERS THE RABBI, who will go on to be the king's interlocutor and instructor during the rest of the *Kuzari*. The king starts out treating the rabbi with open contempt: "I had not intended to ask any Jew," he says, "because I am aware of their reduced condition and narrow-minded views, as their misery left them with nothing commendable." Halevi knows that people are influenced in their judgment by worldly considerations of prosperity and power, and that the world holds the Jews' low status against them as a proof of their error. This may be true even of Jews themselves, who must sometimes have looked at the distribution of power in the world and been ashamed of their helplessness. After all, the *Kuzari*, though formulated as a defense of Judaism against its enemies, was written for a Jewish audience, and it is meant to assuage Jewish fears and concerns.

The rabbi, undaunted, begins by declaring the principles of his faith. From the start, it is clear that he is taking a different approach from those of the philosopher, the Christian, and the Muslim. Judaism, according to the rabbi, is not defined by any particular dogma about the nature of God, the Creation of the world, Heaven and Hell, or any other strictly theological question. Its creed is entirely historical, demanding belief that certain things really happened to the Jewish people:

> I believe in the God of Abraham, Isaac, and Israel, who led the children of Israel out of Egypt with signs and miracles; who fed them in the desert and gave them the land, after having made them traverse the sea and the Jordan in a miraculous way; who sent Moses with His law, and subsequently thousands of prophets, who confirmed His law by promises to the observant, and threats to the disobedient. Our belief is comprised in the Torah—a very large domain.

There is almost a warning note in that last sentence: the rabbi is not going out of his way to depict Judaism as an easy or accessible faith. On the contrary, unlike the Christian and the Muslim, his declaration of belief makes no mention of conversion, no promise of reward for anyone who accepts his religion. Judaism, the rabbi implies, is for Jews—Abraham and his descendants, who were given the Torah as a special possession.

The king's first reaction to this speech is to blame the rabbi for his parochialism. Why, he asks, did he not speak about God as "the Creator of the world, its Governor and Guide"—universal attributes that all peoples could worship? But the rabbi replies that these aspects of God are too abstract to inspire concrete faith. As he will do at other moments in the dialogue, Halevi offers a parable to make the matter clear. Suppose, the rabbi asks the king, that he were told that the king of India—then a distant, barely known land—was the most just and admirable of monarchs. Would he feel bound to revere that king, based solely on his reputation? Of course not, the king of the Khazars says: mere hearsay is not enough to convince him. But what if, the rabbi returns, the king of India sent a messenger "bearing presents which thou knowest to be only procurable in India, and in the royal palace, accompanied by a letter in which it is distinctly stated from whom it comes?" In that case, the king acknowledges, things would be different: now he would have tangible "proof of his power and dominion."

It is just so, the rabbi says, with God. Any philosopher, or the follower of any faith, can make claims about the power and majesty of God. But the Jews do not worship God in the abstract; they worship "the God of Abraham, Isaac, and Jacob," the God who made himself known through specific actions in history. God, the rabbi points out, when giving the Israelites the Ten Commandments, did not identify himself as "the Creator of the World" but as "the God who has led you out of the land of Egypt." The Jews know God not through Genesis, but through Exodus; not as the universal creator, but as their particular lawgiver.

Now the rabbi, like the Christian and the Muslim before him, is making an appeal to miracles. But unlike their miracles, Halevi means us to understand, the supernatural events of Jewish history are evidence-based and indisputable. The Exodus from Egypt involved six hundred thousand Israelites, all of whom witnessed the parting of the Red Sea and the appearance of God on Mount Sinai, all of whom wandered in the desert. How could six hundred thousand people all be deluded or untruthful? "This is irrefutable, a thing which occurred to six hundred thousand people for forty years," the king agrees. At last, he has found a miracle so public that its veracity cannot be doubted.

What Halevi does not consider, of course, is the possibility that the six hundred thousand people are just as fictitious as the parting of the waters. After all, both are known to us only through the Bible. What we have is not many individual testimonies to a miracle but a single testimony, which could very well be invented. But modern skepticism about the Bible stems from a conviction about the unlikeliness of miracles that Halevi doesn't share. To him, the idea that the Exodus was invented out of whole cloth is less likely than the idea that it really happened. The former would have required a conspiracy; the latter only an act of God. If we think differently today, it is because we find fraud easier to imagine than miracles.

The king, then, does not raise any objections to the historical veracity of the Bible; and once that is granted, the case for Judaism as the one true religion becomes strong. One thing, however, continues to trouble the king—the very thing that the rabbi proudly insisted on. Why would God reveal himself only to the Jews, rather than to the whole world? "The perfection of [Moses's] work," the king argues, "was marred by the fact that his book was written in Hebrew, which made it unintelligible to the peoples of Sind, India, and Khazar. . . . Would it not have been better or more commensurate with divine wisdom, if all mankind had been guided in the true path?"

Here Halevi reaches the core issue of the *Kuzari*, and one of the central, perpetual problems for Judaism. In Deuteronomy, there is no doubt or unease about the fact that God has made his covenant with the Israelites and them alone. That is the unquestioned premise of Moses's catalogue of curses and rewards. But for Yehuda Halevi, living in a multicultural society and inheriting the universalism of Greek philosophy, the chosenness of the Jewish people becomes a serious problem. Why, indeed, did God reveal himself in Hebrew and not in other languages? Why is God the God of Abraham and not simply the Creator of the world?

These questions pose an existential challenge to Judaism, and Halevi responds to them with a simple, radical answer. God chose the Jews because they are qualitatively superior to all other peoples, and the reason they are superior is that God chose them. If this is a scandal to reason, so be it; it is a scandal the *Kuzari* embraces and even flaunts. "The Law was given to us," the rabbi explains, "because He led us out of Egypt, and remained attached to us, because we are the pick of mankind."

To explain this superiority, Halevi develops a theory of spiritual inheritance that sounds almost genetic. Adam, the first man, was entirely perfect, since he was made directly by God. This meant that he enjoyed "connection with beings divine and spiritual." He passed on this "divine influence" like a chromosome to his son Seth, and so on down to Noah and then Abraham. In each generation, there was one man who inherited the blessing—not an implausible reading of the book of Genesis, which indeed seems to single out one person at a time as the special focus of God's (and the narrative's) attention. From Abraham, the divine essence—what the Bible calls the blessing and the birthright—passed to Isaac and then to Jacob, whose name was changed to Israel. It may not seem fair that Isaac's brother Ishmael and Jacob's brother Esau were denied their share in this divine legacy, but fairness, Halevi insists, has nothing to do with it.

After Israel, the blessing did not remain with one son but multiplied and spread to encompass all the Israelites. "This is the first instance of the divine influence descending on a number of people, whereas it had previously only been vouchsafed to isolated individuals," the rabbi notes. And Halevi is consistent in drawing out the implications of this genetic metaphor. If holiness is heritable, then all Jews have it; a bad Jew may have only a small amount of the "divine essence," but it is enough for him to transmit it to his children. If there is any doubt that Halevi is talking about an innate characteristic rather than a product of Jewish belief, the rabbi removes it when he informs the king about the status of converts. "Any Gentile who joins us unconditionally shares our good fortune," he says, "without, however, being quite equal to us."

The proof of the Jews' divine essence, of their membership in an "angelic caste," is that only this people is capable of producing prophets. (Converts, the rabbi explains later, can "become pious and learned, but never prophets.") Prophets, in Halevi's scheme, stand in the same relationship to ordinary human beings as humans do to animals. They are capable of supernatural feats: walking through fire, seeing the future, never getting sick or growing old, and other miracles recounted in the Bible. These are proofs of divine favor that no philosopher, however wise and virtuous, has ever enjoyed, because even the greatest human intellect is inferior to the divine essence. In another parable, the rabbi likens the philosopher to an ignorant person who walks into a doctor's office and starts dispensing medicines at random, "knowing nothing of the contents, nor how much should be given to each person." The biblical prophets, in contrast, are like expert physicians who can help mankind because they know the exact formulas needed to gain God's favor.

Naturally, this is music to the king's ears. What has he been looking for, from the beginning of the *Kuzari*, if not the correct practices that his dream told him he was lacking? "The theory I had formed, and the opinion of what I saw in my dream thou now confirmest," he tells the rabbi, "that man can only merit divine influence by acting according to God's commands." Still, he is troubled by the stark contrast between the rabbi's high claims for the Jews and their low condition in the world. Aren't the Jews in exile, the prey of every people?

The rabbi can't deny it, but he manages to turn even exile into a paradoxical proof of chosenness. Other nations thrive or suffer for natural or historical causes, he explains, but the Jews' "affairs are not managed by simple laws of nature, but by the divine Will. You . . . see that drought, death, and wild beasts pursue [us] as a result of disobedience, although the whole world lives in peace. This shows you that [our] concerns are arranged by a higher power than mere nature." Just as Deuteronomy promised, the Jews had life and death set before them, the blessing and the curse; if they were cursed, it is because they chose wrongly by defying God. This punishment will last until it has achieved its purpose of making the Jews repent: "If the majority of us ... would learn humility towards God and His law from our low station, Providence would not have forced us to bear it for such a long period." But the rabbi remains confident that at the end of this period of testing, the Jews will be restored to their rightful place at the head of mankind. "If we bear our exile and degradation for God's sake ... we shall be the pride of the generation which will come with the Messiah," he tells the king.

At last, the king is convinced. Judaism triumphs over its rivals, in the *Kuzari*, not because the king has an epiphany or a conversion experience, but because of the force of the rabbi's argument. The king of the Khazars can never fully share the Jewish essence, but he accepts that this faith comes closer than any other to pleasing God. So he took his vizier, Halevi writes, and "arrived one night at the cave in which some Jews used to celebrate the Sabbath. They disclosed their identity to them, embraced their religion, were circumcised in the cave, and then returned to their country, eager to learn the Jewish law."

IN THE FIRST PART of the *Kuzari*, the king speaks to the rabbi challengingly, at times even contemptuously. It is up to the Jew to prove to the king that his religion, so unimpressive in worldly terms, is actually the best avenue to God. But in the next four sections, as the rabbi continues to answer the king's questions about Judaism in theory and practice, the tone changes. Now that the king has converted, he stands in a different relation to the rabbi. No longer a master but a supplicant and pupil, he acknowledges the rabbi's authority and turns to him for help in understanding his new faith.

Many subjects are addressed in the course of this lesson, including the sabbath, the liturgy, the Talmud, and asceticism (Judaism, the rabbi stresses, is opposed to ascetic withdrawal from the world), as well as Hebrew grammar, mystical traditions, and Jewish sectarian divisions. Throughout, Halevi acknowledges that Judaism has no shortage of practices and beliefs that are difficult for human reason to accept. In fact, it is striking that some of the questions the king asks the rabbi are the very same ones that Philo tried to address in his biblical commentaries more than a thousand years earlier (see Chapter 3)—and that still perplex Jews today.

Consider the ritual of circumcision. Many Jewish laws, the rabbi insists, are "social and rational," and these are shared by every kind of society—for instance, the Ten Commandments' prohibition of theft and murder. But circumcision does not fall into this category. It is a gratuitous act, hard to justify on any rational basis: "Consider how little circumcision has to do with philosophy," Halevi writes. For the rabbi, however, this inexplicability is what makes circumcision particularly precious. We cannot understand the reason for it, but we know that God does nothing without a reason, and so we must have faith that it fulfills some integral part of the divine plan. Returning to the metaphor of the physician, the rabbi likens circumcision to a medicine prescribed by a doctor to a sick patient. The patient may not understand how or why the cure works, but he must still follow the doctor's orders. "Reason must rather obey," the rabbi says, "just as a sick person must obey the physician in applying his medicine and advice."

The same holds true of other seemingly irrational Jewish practices, such as the animal sacrifices conducted at the Temple before its destruction. To Halevi, who lived more than a thousand years after animal sacrifice had ceased, this practice seemed alien and a little repellent: "Thou slaughterest a lamb and smearest thyself with its blood, in skinning it, cleaning its entrails, washing, dismembering it

and sprinkling its blood. . . . If this were not done in consequence of
a divine command, thou wouldst think little of all these actions and
believe that they estrange thee from God rather than bring thee near
to Him." But again, sacrifice is a practice commanded by God, and so
it is efficacious: "As soon as the whole is properly accomplished, thou
seest the divine fire, or dost notice in thyself a new spirit, unknown
before, or seest true visions and great apparitions."

In Judaism, then, some actions must be performed not because
we understand them, but simply because they were commanded. We
must have faith that following the established steps will lead to the
expected result, which is closeness to God. In this sense, "religious
deeds are . . . like nature," the rabbi argues; they are processes that
work, that have certain actual effects, whether or not we understand
the exact reason why. (And of course, in the twelfth century, few natural processes were correctly understood.) The rabbi uses the example of sexual intercourse. To the first human beings, he argues, there
would have appeared to be no connection between sex and childbirth.
In itself, sex might have appeared "vain" and "absurd," much as the
Temple sacrifices now appear. Only with time did people learn that
sex is actually the means of continuing the human race. Just so with
God's commands: "Being ignorant of their designs one thinks it is but
play till the result becomes apparent."

Once again, it is clear that Halevi is emphasizing the *Kuzari*'s original distinction between intentions and actions. Reason and logic,
the philosophers' tools, are not sufficient to make sense of a divinely
revealed faith. Yet Halevi is himself partly a rationalist, a man familiar
with the philosophy of his time, and the appeal of reason keeps haunt-
ing the *Kuzari* like a ghost that cannot be laid to rest. In the book's
fifth section, in particular, the king asks the rabbi to expound Judaism
in terms of Aristotelian philosophy in order to satisfy his questioning
intellect: "Tradition in itself is a good thing if it satisfies the soul, but a
perturbed soul prefers research," that is, scientific knowledge.

The rabbi agrees to satisfy the king's request. "I will give thee a clear standpoint, which will assist thee to acquire clear notions of matter and form, elements, nature, soul, intellect, and metaphysics in general," he promises. In fact, he does this so successfully that he ends up making secular philosophy a little too attractive to the king. The rabbi has to insist that reason can never give as satisfying or complete an account of the nature of the universe as the Torah does. The philosopher speaks of the world as the product of combinations of the four elements, but "according to the Torah, it was God who created the world, together with animals and plants. There is no need to presuppose intermediaries or combinations." At a certain point, the religious believer must simply learn to accept things on faith: "If thou wouldst endeavor to confirm or refute these views logically, life would be spent in vain."

The difference between a philosophical and a Jewish understanding of the world can be summed up in a point of language. In the Torah, God is called by two different names: Elohim, which is a plural noun, and YHWH—the name, traditionally unpronounced by Jews, that is often rendered as Jehovah or Yahweh. According to modern biblical scholarship, this is because the Torah as we know it is the fusion of several different textual sources. Halevi, of course, had no such notion of the human authorship of the Torah, and for him the double name is meant to impart a lesson. "Elohim," the rabbi says, "is a term signifying the ruler or governor of the world," and it is plural because the early "gentile idolaters" conceived of each force in nature as a separate god. "These deities," the rabbi explains, "were as numerous as are the forces which sway the human body and the universe."

In a more philosophical sense, "Elohim" is God understood as the sum of the forces that set the world in motion. This is the kind of God that can be known intellectually, by speculating on the nature of things. But such a God, like the God that the philosopher described at the beginning of the *Kuzari*, is "too far removed and exalted to have any knowledge of us, much less to care about us." In today's terminology, we would no more give our love and devotion to God-as-Elohim than we would love the second law of thermody-namics or the Big Bang.

That is why God revealed, to the Jews and them alone, the name YHWH. This is God's "proper name," the rabbi explains, like "Reuben or Simeon" for a human being. It is the name we use to call him and speak to him. YHWH is the God who hears prayers and inter-venes in history, who created Adam and took the Jews out of Egypt. In Book Four of the *Kuzari*, Halevi sums up the difference between YHWH and Elohim: "The meaning of Elohim can be grasped by way of speculation, because a Guide and Manager of the world is a pos-tulate of Reason.... The meaning of YHWH, however, cannot be grasped by speculation, but only by ... intuition and prophetic vision." The king immediately understands this distinction, which mirrors his original distinction between intentions and actions. "Man yearns for YHWH as a matter of love, taste, and conviction," he observes, "while attachment to Elohim is the result of speculation."

Judaism, then, represents a living refutation of the pretensions of philosophy. Jewish history, Halevi insists, cannot be understood in purely secular terms. Rather, "heavenly dictated events mostly came to pass in the holy land, and among the privileged Israelite people.... For this reason, the Israelites serve ... as evidence against the heretics who followed the view of the Greek Epicurus, that all things are the out-come of accidents."

IF THE PEOPLE OF ISRAEL are uniquely privileged in their rela-tionship with God, it makes sense that the Land of Israel should be similarly singled out. After all, prophecy, according to the rabbi, is the highest form of divine knowledge, vouchsafed to the Israelites alone; and "whoever prophesied did so either in the Land, or concerning it." To the king, the idea that God might take a special interest in one particular territory seems even stranger than the idea that he might restrict his revelation to just one people. But the rabbi explains that the Land of Israel's spiritual endowment is analogous to the physical resources of other lands. "There are places in which particular plants, metals, or animals are found," he points out. And the Holy Land's chief export, one might say, is God.

The Torah proves that God has always made himself known in the Land. Indeed, the rabbi argues that Palestine is "where the calendar began after the six days of creation," so that the beginning of the day should be calculated from there and not, as it might seem, from China, where the sun rises in the east. The Garden of Eden, the rabbi asserts, was actually located in Palestine. This is the land of Mount Sinai, where God gave the commandments to Moses, and of Mount Moriah, where Isaac was bound for sacrifice by his father Abraham and then was miraculously spared when God sent a ram to be killed in his place. Jewish history begins with God's summoning of Abraham to leave Ur and settle in the Land of Israel, which Halevi likens to the process of planting: "Thus the agriculturer finds the root of a good tree in a desert place. He transplants it into properly tilled ground, to improve it and make it grow."

The crop that Abraham produced was prophecy, which was the common possession of the Israelites "as long as they remained in the land and fulfilled the required conditions." Prophets, throughout the *Kuzari*, are considered superior to philosophers; what philosophers can only speculate about, prophets know with certainty. Yet at the time Halevi was writing, prophecy had long since disappeared from the world, and the Land of Israel was in the possession of Christian Crusaders, who prohibited the Jews from entering it. "All nations make pilgrimages to it," the rabbi says bitterly, "excepting we ourselves, because we are punished and in disgrace."

The question naturally arises, then, whether the Land of Israel is still a Holy Land. Now that the Temple is gone and the Jews are dispersed, isn't Palestine simply just another country—and a poor and desolate one at that? ("I have never heard," the king tells the rabbi skeptically, "that the inhabitants of Palestine were better than other people.") In practice, certainly, Jews who thrived in Spain and Egypt and Mesopotamia displayed little interest in living in Palestine or even visiting it. The Land remained an object of prayer and pious hope—as we have seen with Benjamin of Tudela, who longed for the day when it would be redeemed—but the idea of actually settling there remained outside the realm of possibility.

But in the *Kuzari*, Halevi strongly insists that even in its fallen state, the Land of Israel remains uniquely blessed. There is an obvious analogy to be drawn between the Land and the people themselves. Just as the Jews remain God's chosen people even in exile, so the Land remains his favorite territory even in its abandonment. God's preferences are inexplicable but irrevocable. Halevi quotes a series of rabbinic sayings about the importance of the Land and the blessings that accrue to those who live there: "It is better to dwell in the Holy Land, even in a town mostly inhabited by heathens, than abroad in a town chiefly populated by Israelites," and "he who walks four yards in the Land is assured of happiness in the world to come."

It follows that the Jews of the Diaspora are remiss in not even trying to return to the Land of Israel. The king is not slow to make this point: "If this be so, thou fallest short of the duty laid down in thy law, by not endeavoring to reach that place, and making it thy abode in life and death." And the rabbi, who has a ready response to most of the king's doubts and questions, can do nothing but agree with him. The Jews are indeed culpable in their indifference to the Land of Israel.

Still, Halevi is not calling for any kind of mass return to the Land, much less a political movement to regain sovereignty, of the kind that Benjamin of Tudela's legendary king David Alroy dreamed about— and that Theodor Herzl, the founder of modern Zionism, would actually initiate almost eight hundred years later (see Chapter 13). In the historical circumstances of the twelfth century, the idea that the Jews might reclaim Palestine as their homeland was simply unimaginable. If Halevi blames his fellow Jews, it is not for political quietism but for a lack of pious ardor. The reason that God has not yet restored the Jews to Palestine, the rabbi explains, is simply that the Jews do not want it sincerely enough. "Were we prepared to meet the God of our forefathers with a pure mind," he says, "we should find the same salvation as our fathers did in Egypt." As long as the Jews fail in this wholehearted devotion, all their prayers about Zion are "but as the chattering of the starling and the nightingale."

So the rabbi says in the second part of the *Kuzari*; and at the end of the whole book, it turns out that he really means it. It might be impossible for all the Jews to return to Palestine without divine assistance, but one solitary pilgrim could at least make the journey, and that is what the rabbi decides to do. The king tries to dissuade him: after all, he points out, the divine presence is no longer to be found in Palestine, while "with a pure mind and desire, one can approach God in any place." The king recognizes that the rabbi's actions represent a serious existential challenge to Diaspora Judaism. If God can only be found in one particular place, what does that mean for the devotions of all the Jews who will never reach that place?

The rabbi is quick to disavow any such idea. It is not necessary to go to the Land of Israel to be in touch with God, since the divine spirit is "with every born Israelite of virtuous life, pure heart, and upright mind." Yet the implications of the rabbi's pilgrimage are impossible to ignore, since it brings up once again the central distinction in the *Kuzari*: the difference between intentions and actions. The Jew in Diaspora, one might say, is relying on his good intentions, his piety and devotion to God, and assuming that these will be enough. That is the position that the king urges in the last pages of the book: "If thou believest in all that thou sayest, God knows thy mind." There is no need to actually go to Palestine, as long as God knows that you really want to go.

But if there is one thing the rabbi has taught the king, and the reader, during the course of the dialogue, it is that God is not satisfied with intentions. If he were, there would be no need for the king to have converted to Judaism in the first place; the Khazar religion, whatever it entails, would have pleased God just as much as any other. No, Halevi has driven home the point that God gave the Jews specific laws that must be carried out in the correct ways if they are to be effective, just like natural processes.

The question that arises in the last pages of the *Kuzari*, then, is whether making *aliyah*—going to the Land of Israel—is one of these indispensable laws; and the answer Halevi gives is ambiguous. As we have seen, the rabbi admits that pious Jews in the Diaspora are connected to God. But he also says that piety is enough only "when action is impossible"; otherwise, "actions must be perfect to claim reward." And in his case, going to Jerusalem is not impossible. It is only difficult and dangerous, and that is not enough to dissuade him from making the attempt. He is an old man, the rabbi points out, and he does not have much to lose. Even if a pilgrim to Palestine dies, "he has obtained the divine favor, and may be confident that he has atoned for most of his sins by his death. In my opinion this is better than to seek the dangers of war in order to gain fame and spoil by courage and bravery." It is only by the extraordinary devotion of individual Jews, Halevi implies in the book's last lines, that the Jewish homeland will ever be restored: "Jerusalem can only be rebuilt when Israel yearns for it to such an extent that they embrace her stones and dust."

With these words, the rabbi takes leave of his pupil the king, who wishes him God's protection on his journey. For Yehuda Halevi, of course, this conclusion was more than literary. After he finished the *Kuzari*, he himself undertook the same pilgrimage as the rabbi; and just as he had anticipated, it cost him his life. The choice facing Halevi, in a sense, was an echo of the one that faced Josephus more than a thousand years earlier: to escape the Land of Israel and live, or to embrace the Land and die.

Halevi took the second course, whereas Josephus had taken the first. This is a testimony to the power of the religious imagination, which is more powerful than political reality. For while Josephus was the product of a living Jewish kingdom, for Halevi the Land of Israel existed only in biblical images and theological ideas. In the *Kuzari*, the holiness of the Land becomes a corollary of the holiness of the Jewish people. To believe in either, the rabbi argues, is to defy reason and to trust in the authority of prophecy, tradition, and miracle. The *Kuzari* is a monument to that defiance, which is why, in our age of reason, it still has the power to provoke.

BIBLIOGRAPHY

Halevi, Yehuda. *The Kuzari*. Translated by Hartwig Hirschfeld, introduction by Henry Slonimsky. New York: Schocken, 1964.

Halkin, Hillel. *Yehuda Halevi*. New York: Nextbook/Schocken, 2010.

The Itinerary of Benjamin of Tudela: Travels in the Middle Ages. Cold Spring, NY: NightinGale Resources, 2010.

Scheindlin, Raymond P. *The Song of the Distant Dove: Yehuda Halevi's Pilgrimage*. New York: Oxford University Press, 2008.

7

THINKING TOWARD GOD

The Guide of the Perplexed by Moses Maimonides

*A 1986 Israeli banknote featuring a 1744
imagined portrait of Maimonides*

Many Jewish thinkers, ancient and modern, have confronted the troubling opposition between the conclusions of reason and the dictates of faith. Writing in Egypt in the late twelfth century, Moses Maimonides, the supreme Jewish thinker and legal commentator, set out to eliminate that "perplexity" once and for all. In his treatise *The Guide of the Perplexed*, Maimonides argues that reason and faith are not contradictory, as they

might appear. Rather, through a close analysis of biblical text, he demonstrates that everything in scripture
that sounds contrary to reason—from the existence of
angels to the ritual of circumcision—should be understood as teaching a rational truth. Properly understood,
God does not have a body or any desires, but is rather an
utterly transcendent power whom we can come to know
only through rigorous thinking. To reconcile this austere philosophical creed with Jewish text and tradition
required a monumental effort of intellect, making the
Guide the central work of Jewish philosophy.

REASON, THE *KUZARI* INSISTS, CAN TAKE US ONLY
part of the way toward God. Through the intellect, we can come to know
Elohim, the God who governs the universe through natural forces; but we
can never reach YHWH, the personal God who chose the Jewish people.
The former is the God we speculate about, but the latter is the God we love.
Just around the time Yehuda Halevi was writing, however, an even greater
Jewish thinker was born—one who would go on to challenge this bina-
rism. To love God, Moses Maimonides argued, means nothing more or less
than to think about him, passionately and perpetually. Indeed, the whole
purpose of human intellect is to come to a correct understanding of God.
Those who have the ability, training, and character required to achieve this
kind of understanding are the truly blessed. Everyone else, including the
majority of people who think simplistically and over-literally about God,
doesn't really know him at all.

Maimonides set himself the task of teaching Jews the proper way
to think about God. This meant overturning what he saw as common
misconceptions—for instance, the ideas that God has a body and that
angels are humanoid figures with wings. There is no doubt that a plain
reading of the Bible encourages such errors, however, so Maimonides
also had to teach Jews a new way of reading scripture—one that care-

fully distinguished between the surface meaning and the hidden truth. And as a product of the philosophically advanced culture of Muslim Spain, Maimonides needed to reconcile the Bible's worldview with what he regarded as the irrefutable scientific truths taught by Aristotle and other secular philosophers. If there is only one truth, then reason and religion cannot be in conflict; if they seem to be, it is only because we don't correctly understand what religion has to teach us.

All of this amounted to a revolution in Jewish thought. If Maimonides was a revolutionary, however, he was one who worked within Jewish tradition, not against it. The same man who formulated such daring reinterpretations of Jewish doctrine was also one of the greatest masters of Jewish law who ever lived. Before he wrote *The Guide of the Perplexed*, his major philosophical treatise, Maimonides completed an even more monumental work, a comprehensive digest of Jewish law called the *Mishneh Torah*. This work, he claimed, incorporated the definitive teachings of Judaism on every conceivable subject; it reduced the tangled and ambiguous legal debates of the Talmud to a clear, usable code. To write such a book, Maimonides had to digest centuries' worth of legal literature. Just as important, he had to have immense confidence in his own powers of judgment, since he was effectively saying that the *Mishneh Torah* superseded the central texts of Jewish tradition. No wonder that Jews came to say, "From Moses to Moses, there was none like Moses": Moses Maimonides, like the original Moses, was a lawgiver to the Jewish people.

Moshe ben Maimon, to use his Hebrew name, was born in Cordova in 1138, a product of the same Muslim Spanish milieu that fostered Yehuda Halevi and many other Jewish luminaries. But he arrived just as this golden age of Jewish history was coming to an end. When he was around ten years old, the Almohads, a puritanical Muslim sect, emerged from North Africa to conquer the cities of southern Spain. According to contemporary reports, some Jewish communities under Almohad rule were given the choice of converting to Islam or facing death; others were subject to discrimination and persecution.

Maimonides's family was long established in Spain, boasting many generations of Jewish scholars and judges, but the catastrophe forced them to flee—first to Fez in North Africa, and then, around the year 1166, to Egypt, where they settled in the capital, Fustat. From then until his death in 1204, Maimonides would be a leading figure in the Egyptian Jewish community. Jews there and around the world read his books and sought his opinions on legal issues. Like other illustrious Spanish Jews, Maimonides made his living as a medical doctor, and in this field too he rose to the heights. He wrote a number of works on medicine, and his patients included high-ranking Muslim officials in the court of Saladin.

By the time Maimonides began to write *The Guide of the Perplexed* in the 1180s, his major works of Jewish law—the *Mishneh Torah* and the earlier *Commentary on the Mishnah*—were behind him. He was firmly established as the age's leading Jewish jurist. A new philosophical work from his pen was sure to attract attention from both his friends and his detractors, of whom there were many. Yet unlike most authors, Maimonides did not want his work to reach a large audience. On the contrary, as he makes clear in the introduction to the *Guide*, he originally had in mind just a single reader: his student Joseph ben Judah, who had left Egypt for Syria before his studies were complete.

As Maimonides explains, Joseph was at a perilous stage in his education. He had gone through the preliminary subjects of mathematics, logic, and astronomy—the basics of medieval higher education—and had just begun learning what Maimonides calls "divine matters" and "the secrets of the prophetic books." A student at this juncture was especially prone to the spiritual and intellectual malaise that Maimonides calls "perplexity": "you were perplexed, as stupefaction had come over you." In this condition, Maimonides writes, a man—and in his time and place, only men could receive this kind of advanced education—cannot reconcile what he has learned about scientific matters with what he reads in the Bible. He is experiencing what might be called a crisis of faith:

The human intellect having drawn him on and led him to dwell within its province, he must have felt distressed by the externals of the Law. . . . Hence he would remain in a state of perplexity and confusion as to whether he should follow his intellect, renounce what he knew concerning the terms in question, and consequently consider that he has renounced the foundations of the Law. Or he should hold fast to his understanding of these terms and not let himself be drawn on together with his intellect, rather turning his back on it and moving away from it, while at the same time perceiving that he had brought loss to himself and harm to his religion.

In this condition of "heartache and great perplexity," Maimonides writes, a man will be tempted to make one of two sacrifices. Either he will sacrifice his belief in the Torah, which seems so full of scientific errors and absurdities, or else he will sacrifice his intellect, which seems to be turning him against the faith of his fathers. In Maimonides's view, however, either sacrifice would be a mistake, for a human being needs both reason and the Law in order to reach God. His goal in writing the *Guide*, then, is to show Joseph ben Judah—and all readers similarly afflicted—that the choice they seem to be facing is a false one. And the method he will use to solve this problem is to show that the Bible is not to be taken literally. Rather, it is full of "very obscure parables," metaphoric ways of speaking and thinking, which if properly understood will turn out to be entirely consistent with the truths of reason. "If we explain these parables to him or if we draw his attention to their being parables," Maimonides promises, "he will take the right road and be delivered from this perplexity. That is why I have called this treatise *The Guide of the Perplexed*."

It is crucial for Maimonides's purposes, however, that the teaching he is about to impart is not intended for just any reader who happens to pick up the book. He is fully aware that for most people reading the Bible means reading it literally, so that to destroy their belief in the surface meaning of the text would be equivalent to destroying their faith itself. Such an author might well appear, in the eyes of an ordinary reader, to be a heretic; and indeed, Maimonides and the *Guide* were regularly subjected to attacks by the pious in later years. In the early thirteenth century, for instance, Jews in France had copies of the *Guide* publicly burned by the Christian authorities, claiming that it was offensive to religion.

That is why Maimonides identifies himself with what he sees as an ancient tradition of Jewish esotericism—a way of discussing important subjects indirectly and privately, in such a way that the initiated will be enlightened while the public won't be troubled. The Talmud, for instance, says that there are two subjects that should not be taught publicly: the "Account of the Beginning," the description of the creation of the world in Genesis, and the "Account of the Chariot," the lurid vision of the prophet Ezekiel. Both of these played a central role in Jewish mysticism and lent themselves to extreme kinds of metaphysical speculation. As a result, the rabbis warned against sharing them too widely: "The Account of the Chariot ought not to be taught even to one man, except if he be wise and able to understand by himself, in which case only the chapter headings may be transmitted to him."

Maimonides quotes these words and applies them to his own work in the *Guide*. "For my purpose," he warns the reader, "is that the truths be glimpsed and then again be concealed, so as not to oppose that divine purpose which one cannot possibly oppose and which has concealed from the vulgar among the people those truths especially requisite for His apprehension." This is, then, a frankly elitist approach to religious truth. There are matters that the majority of people are simply unequipped to understand, so that full knowledge will always be the preserve of a small group.

It is significant, however, that Maimonides's approach to the "Account of the Beginning" and the "Account of the Chariot" is not at all mystical. He has no interest in numerology, incantations, or magic formulas, with which other speculators tried to decipher these biblical enigmas. Rather, he states with assurance that these two accounts originally meant nothing more or less than "natural science" (the Beginning) and "divine science" (the Chariot). The mystery of these subjects is that there is no mystery. They were simply the names that Jewish tradition gave to the rational study of the world and the deity, the same topics that the philosophers treated in their books.

In fact, Maimonides insists that Judaism had possession of this knowledge before the Greek philosophers came along. As he will argue in detail in the *Guide*, even the most seemingly visionary descriptions in the Bible—for instance, the image of God standing on "a pavement of sapphire," which Moses sees at Mount Sinai—can only be understood as parables teaching truths about nature. If the Jews of his own time find such notions shocking, Maimonides writes, it is because, over the centuries of their exile, they have forgotten how to read these parables.

What this means is that Maimonides sees himself, and wants readers to see him, not as a revolutionary but as a restorer. "Know," he writes later in the *Guide*, "that the many sciences devoted to establishing the truth regarding these matters that have existed in our religious community have perished because of the length of time that has passed, because of our being dominated by the pagan nations, and because . . . it is not permitted to divulge these matters to all people." All that remained of this ancient knowledge in the Talmud and other rabbinic books were "a few grains belonging to the core, which are overlaid with many layers of rind." Because the Jews had forgotten how to read correctly, taking the surface meaning to be the only meaning, it is as if "people were occupied with these layers of rind and thought that beneath them there was no core whatever."

Maimonides presents himself forthrightly as a rationalist. Yet in the context of religion, he knows, reason can be as scandalous as the most exotic mysticism, or even more so. That is why, despite his rational interpretation of the accounts of Creation and of the Chariot, he still follows the rabbinic principle that these things should be taught only to a few, and then only in hints and flashes. "It is incumbent upon us, the community of those adhering to Law, not to state explicitly a matter that is either remote from the understanding of the multitude or the truth of which as it appears to the imagination of these people is different from what is intended by us," he warns. Only a student who, like Joseph ben Judah, is of good character, well trained in Jewish law, and knowledgeable about the sciences will be able to hear Maimonides's message without being frightened by it. To spring "divine science" on an unprepared mind, he writes in one of his characteristically vivid similes, would be like giving an infant "wheaten bread and meat and giving him wine to drink. [This] would undoubtedly kill him, not because these aliments are bad or unnatural for man, but because the child that receives them is too weak to digest them."

Such reticence, however, creates a problem for Maimonides the author. Oral instruction can be confined to a small audience, handed down in private from teacher to student over the generations. But once you put your teachings into a book, they become available to everyone who knows how to read. "How then," Maimonides asks himself, "can I now innovate and set them down?" To this question he gives two answers. The first is that he owes it to posterity not to let his discoveries die with him. "If I had omitted setting down something of that which has appeared to me as clear, so that that knowledge would perish when I perish . . . I should have considered that conduct as extremely cowardly," he writes. In particular, it would have been a betrayal of "everyone who is perplexed," who could benefit spiritually from Maimonides's insights: "It would have been, as it were, robbing one who deserves the truth of the truth."

But elsewhere in the *Guide*, when he is not writing specifically about this issue, Maimonides suggests another explanation for his own daring. While he denies having received any divine revelation, in a deeper sense Maimonides believes that all thoughts, all insights, are a gift from God. He uses the metaphor of overflow: it is an overflow of the divine essence, a self-giving of God, that stimulates our rational and imaginative faculties into action. When a man's rational faculty receives this overflow, Maimonides explains, "it makes him into a man who inquires and is endowed with understanding, who knows and discerns." And if he receives enough of this divine intellectual stimulus, his own mind begins to overflow, and the thoughts God has given him demand to be shared with other minds. "Were it not for this additional perfection," Maimonides writes, "sciences would not be set forth in books and prophets would not call upon the people to obtain knowledge of the truth."

FOR A BOOK that intends to take on the largest metaphysical questions, the *Guide* begins modestly, with a series of chapters that read like an extended lesson in Hebrew vocabulary. That is because Maimonides believes the source of "perplexity" is a failure to read the Bible properly—in particular, a failure to understand when the Bible is using words metaphorically and symbolically. Consider the account of the creation of human beings in Genesis: "And God said, 'Let us make man in our image, after our likeness.'" We know what human beings look like; so it seems to follow that if men are made in the image and likeness of God, we know what God looks like as well. God must have a body.

Certainly, that is the impression a casual reader of the Bible would have to come away with. After all, the Bible speaks of God walking in the Garden of Eden, sitting on a throne, showing Moses his back, and enjoying the smell of sacrificial meat. Mentally and emotionally, too, God seems to be like us. He gets angry, he can be disappointed, he rewards the people he loves and punishes the people he hates. Of course, God can't be just like us; he is infinitely powerful, which makes him in some basic sense unknowable. But the points of similarity are clear enough for us to feel that in praying to God we are talking to someone who will understand us.

To Maimonides, this way of thinking about God—the idea that God has a body and a mind, needs and desires—is the number one error that he sets out to eradicate. Perhaps because the belief in God's corporeality was so widespread, Maimonides assails it in passionate terms: "Know accordingly . . . that when you believe in the doctrine of the corporeality of God or believe that one of the states of the body belongs to Him, you provoke His jealousy and anger, kindle the fire of His wrath, and are a hater, an enemy and an adversary of God, much more so than an idolater." A person who believes that God has a body is actually, for Maimonides, an infidel, an unbeliever.

It says a great deal about Maimonides's understanding of religion that he places such an extreme emphasis on holding the right idea about God. Judaism can be defined in many ways—as a community of believers, a chosen people, a system of laws, a religious tradition. What it was not, until Maimonides, was a creed, a set of propositions that the believer must accept. It was Maimonides who first drew up, in his *Commentary on the Mishnah*, a list of thirteen principles of faith in which every Jew was supposed to believe—one of which is the incorporeality of God.

For this reason, the *Guide* opens by defining the words "image" and "likeness," or rather by correcting the popular, erroneous definition of those words. "People have thought," Maimonides writes, "that in the Hebrew language *image* denotes the shape and configuration of a thing. This supposition led them to the pure doctrine of the corporeality of God. . . . For they thought that God has a man's form, I mean his shape and configuration," if perhaps "bigger and more resplendent." In fact, Maimonides insists, this kind of physical likeness is denoted in Hebrew by an entirely different word. The word the Bible uses, *tselem*, is applied not to physical appearance but to essence—"the notion in virtue of which a thing . . . becomes what it is." The same is true of the word "likeness." After all, in Psalms, the poet writes "I am like a pelican in the wilderness"; but this is a way of expressing sadness and clearly does not mean "that its author resembled the pelican with regard to its wings and feathers."

To understand what about humanity makes us the image and likeness of God, then, we have to ask what it is that constitutes humanity's essence, the quality that separates us from every other created being. The answer, for Maimonides as for Philo long before him, is clear: "Now man possesses . . . something in him that is very strange as it is not found in anything else under the sphere of the moon, namely, intellectual apprehension." Just as the Greeks taught, man is a rational animal, and it is "because of the divine intellect conjoined with man" that we are created in God's likeness. But the intellect, Maimonides insists, is a completely bodiless phenomenon: "no sense, no part of the body, none of the extremities are used" when we think.

Maimonides exalts the intellect as the essence of man: "This capacity," he writes, "is the noblest of the characteristics existing in us." That is because it is only through the intellect that we can achieve real knowledge of and closeness to God. When Maimonides assembled a list of beliefs that every Jew is supposed to hold, he did not mean only that a Jew must publicly affirm them as a way of identifying his membership in a community. He meant that the principles must be genuinely believed; and it is impossible to believe something that you do not understand. "The belief is not the notion that is uttered," he writes later in the *Guide*, "but the notion that is represented in the soul."

It follows that, for Maimonides, a person who thinks wrongly about God is not actually thinking about God at all. Say, for instance, that a man knew the word "elephant," but when you asked him what an elephant was, he replied "that it is an animal possessing one leg and three wings, inhabiting the depths of the sea, having a transparent body and a broad face like that of a man in its form and shape, talking like a man, and sometimes flying in the air, while at other times swimming like a fish." It's easy to imagine such a creature making an appearance in a medieval bestiary. But could you say, Maimonides asks, that a man who described an elephant this way was actually talking about an elephant, merely getting some of the details wrong? No, you would have to conclude that "the thing he has imagined as having these attributes is merely an invention and is false and that there is nothing in existence like that." To think wrongly about an elephant is to think about something other than an elephant. And the same applies to God. If a man says that he knows God but then goes on to say that God has a body, then what he knows is not God but a fictional being he has invented and given the same name.

Maimonides grants that the Bible makes it easy to fall into such an error. That is because, according to an old rabbinic saying he repeatedly invokes, "The Torah speaks in the language of the sons of men." The "multitude," the mass of people whose understanding is necessarily inferior, "perceive nothing other than bodies as having a firmly established existence and as being indubitably true." In common speech, to say that something "is" means that it occupies a space—that is, that it exists physically. And if God is supreme perfection, then the only way human beings can express that perfection is by attributing to him all the qualities that we consider perfect in ourselves. If a man couldn't move, for example, we would consider him seriously disabled. Thus the Bible attributes to God the ability to move—not because he actually has a body that is capable of motion, but in order to convey the idea that he is in no way deficient. The same is true even of the notion of life itself. It is inaccurate to say that God is "alive" in the same way that human beings are alive. After all, our life implies the inevitability of death, whereas God can never die. Yet we speak of God as living, because in human terms being alive is superior to being dead.

These are necessary fictions, which begin to give the common people some notion of God's existence. Without them, most people would reach the end of their lives "without having known whether there is a deity for the world, or whether there is not." The time comes, however, when the rare person of true understanding—"the few solitary individuals that are 'the remnant whom the Lord calls'"—is able to dispense with these metaphors and parables, "to put an end to the fantasies . . . from the age of infancy." In his list of biblical vocabulary, then, Maimonides systematically dismisses every anthropomorphic implication. God does not go out or come in, he is not high above us in the sky, he does not stand up or sit down.

But it is not just a body that we must not attribute to God. If God is one—and that is another of Maimonides's thirteen principles, as well as being the message of the Shema prayer—then there can be no predicates or adjectives of any kind applied to him. It is not hard to understand, Maimonides writes, that God does not really have "an eye, an ear, a hand, a mouth, a tongue." These are figurative descriptions, meant to suggest that God sees and hears. Harder to grasp is the idea that in God's case, even seeing and hearing are figurative expressions. In truth, God does not perceive what goes on in the world the way human beings do. "He does not possess any faculty," Maimonides insists; "there does not exist in Him anything other than His essence in virtue of which object He might act, know, or will."

Yehuda Halevi, in the *Kuzari*, rebelled against the belief of the "philosophers," who held that God was so perfect as to be entirely removed from the human world, taking no notice of what happens here below. In certain passages of the *Guide*, Maimonides seems to come close to exactly that position. For if God is utterly transcendent, then "there is no relation between God, may He be exalted, and time and place." As a logical proposition, "there is . . . no relation in any respect between Him and any of His creatures." That is because relation implies some kind of similarity, while there can be absolutely no point of contact between the divine and the material. "For instance," Maimonides says in another concrete metaphor, "there is no relation between a hundred cubits and the heat that is in pepper." The former is a quantity, the latter a quality, and there is no way to compare them. A hundred cubits can't be longer than the taste of pepper; the taste of pepper can't be stronger than a hundred cubits. "How then could there subsist a relation between Him . . . and any of the things created by Him," Maimonides asks, "given the immense difference between them with regard to the true reality of their existence, than which there is no greater difference?"

If there is no way to speak of God in human terms, if "the language of men" is merely a beginner's attempt to describe the indescribable, it follows that the most fitting description of God is to say nothing. And that is, in fact, Maimonides's austere conclusion. In keeping with the medieval philosophical tradition of the *via negativa*, he believes that "the description of God . . . by means of negations is the correct description." Anytime you attribute a quality to God, no matter how pious your intention—even if you call God good, merciful, or just— you violate his essential unity. Once you understand that no word or concept available to human beings truly applies to God, then you can gain knowledge of God only by understanding the way in which each word fails to describe him. "You come nearer to the apprehension of Him, may He be exalted, with every increase in the negations regarding Him," Maimonides writes.

Another simile helps Maimonides to clarify how this process works. Say that a group of people have heard the word "ship" but have no idea what a ship is. Eventually it becomes clear to one person that a ship is not a mineral. Then another person realizes it is not an animal; a third, that it is not a perfect shape like a rectangle; a fourth, that it is not solid but hollow in the middle. With each negation, they come closer to an accurate picture of what a ship is; and if enough false possibilities are ruled out, they will eventually have an accurate mental image. We should think about God in the same way, by stripping away false descriptions until what is left over is something like the truth. "For on every occasion on which it becomes clear to you that a thing . . . should be negated with reference to Him, you undoubtedly come nearer to Him by one degree."

To follow this path is to run up against the very limits of language, which are the limits of thought. "For the bounds of expression in all languages are very narrow indeed," Maimonides observes, "so that we cannot represent this notion to ourselves except through a certain looseness of expression. Thus when we wish to indicate that the deity is not many, the one who makes the statement cannot say anything but that He is one, even though 'one' and 'many' are some of the sub-divisions of quantity," and God is not subject to quantification. At the very least, Maimonides holds, we should not make the mistake of thinking we are honoring God when we multiply adjectives for him. Long prayers and elaborate sermons do the very opposite of what they intend: instead of bringing us closer to God, they drive us further away from him. For anyone "who affirms that God . . . has positive attributes," he concludes severely, "has abolished his belief in the exis-tence of the deity without being aware of it."

THE EARLY CHAPTERS of *The Guide of the Perplexed* are devoted to clearing away errors and establishing the correct view of God. Yet once we have learned to understand God as Maimonides wants us to, we are left with a new problem: How could this God be the Jewish God? As Halevi argued in the *Kuzari*, the basic fact about the Jewish God is that he intervenes in history. He called Abraham and gave the Torah to Moses, he picked individuals to become his prophets, and he performed miracles to demonstrate his favor. How could Maimon-ides's God, who has no attributes and no relationship to the world, do any of these things?

To answer this challenge, Maimonides embarks on a far-reaching reinterpretation of Judaism. This involves challenging conventional Jewish views about Creation, prophecy, and the commandments, all of which the *Guide* thinks about in radical new ways. Yet Maimon-ides's philosophical and rationalist view of God, he maintains, is con-sistent with everything in the Bible—if only we are able to read the Bible properly, to access the core instead of the rind. Once again, the revolutionary presents himself as simply restoring a wisdom that used to be the common property of the Jewish sages. Some of the things he says about God may appear "foreign to our Law," Maimonides acknowledges; "however, matters are not like this." "All these views,"

he insists, "do not contradict anything said by our prophets and sus-
tainers of our Law."

The first item on the *Guide*'s agenda is the creation of the world,
where Maimonides immediately encounters a serious inconsistency
between the teachings of science and the teachings of Judaism. Maimonides was not announcing a new theory but simply reiterating the
standard medieval view when he declared that the universe is composed of "many spheres, one contained within the other, with no hol-
lows between them. . . . For they are perfectly spherical and cling to
each other, all of them moving in a circular uniform motion." At the
center of these concentric spheres lies our planet, which is the home
of mutability, since the four elements are constantly changing their
combinations. But each sphere above the earth contains only stars and
planets, which are made of a different material and are not subject to
change. Because these spheres are in motion, they must in some sense
be alive, since inanimate things do not move themselves. Indeed, Maimonides writes that the spheres are "living and rational," that they
possess intellects and souls.

To complete this world picture, Aristotle, in the fourth century
BCE, proved that it was necessary to postulate the existence of God.
The argument is simple. The spheres are constantly in motion, and
everything that moves has to have a mover. Outside the highest sphere,
then, was a force that imparted movement to the spheres, and this was
the First Mover, itself unmoved, which is identical with God. For various reasons, which Maimonides explains, Aristotle believed that the
universe was eternal: God always has and always will put the spheres
into motion, and there was never a moment when they emerged out
of nothingness. To believe otherwise involved certain seeming contradictions. For instance, the definition of God is that he is unmoved; he
is the cause of other things, but nothing causes him. But if the universe was created in time, then there must have been some cause that
prompted God to change from not creating it to creating it. In Maimonides's words, "there indubitably must have been in His case some-

thing that caused Him to pass over from potentiality into actuality." And that cause would be prior to God, which is impossible.

Maimonides admits that "this is a great difficulty" for the Jewish understanding of God and Creation. For the account of Creation in Genesis seems to say that God created the universe out of nothing at a certain moment. "In the beginning, God created the heavens and the earth": for this to happen, it must have been the case that at some time God existed and the heavens and earth did not. Indeed, Maimonides zeroes in on this question as the heart of the conflict between philosophy and Judaism. If the universe existed eternally, then it is bound by eternal, unchanging rules, and there is no room for God to enter into history. If the universe was created by divine fiat, however, then God's will is effective, and he could choose to intervene in his Creation at key moments—for instance, when he appeared to Moses and the Israelites on Mount Sinai and gave them the Torah.

Everything depends, then, upon this seemingly abstract cosmological question. "Know that with a belief in the creation of the world in time," Maimonides writes, "all the miracles become possible and the Law becomes possible." After all, the story the Bible tells raises a number of questions that cannot be answered without resort to divine volition. "Why did God give prophetic revelation to this one and not to that? Why did God give this Law to this particular nation, and why did He not legislate to others? . . . What was God's aim in giving this Law?" The Jewish answer to such questions, and the one Yehuda Halevi gave in the *Kuzari*, is "He wanted it this way; or His wisdom required it this way." But if we accept the Aristotelian worldview, "there would be no way" to answer those questions except by "giving the lie to, and the annulment of, all the external meanings of the Law."

This is one of the moments in *The Guide of the Perplexed* that, from the time it was written down to our own day, has made readers wonder what exactly Maimonides is trying to tell us. Does he, in fact, reject the Aristotelian view, as he claims to? Or is he trying to say—esoterically, using the kind of hints and flashes he promised to employ at the beginning of the *Guide*—that he actually agrees with Aristotle? After all, "giving the lie to . . . the external meanings of the Law" is a pretty good description of what Maimonides himself does in the *Guide*. It is conceivable that in his heart of hearts, Maimonides was philosopher enough to go all the way with Aristotle despite the damage this would do to Judaism. If he conceals his true beliefs, it may be because, as he has said so often, the truth is not something to be casually paraded before the common people in a book. Certainly, Maimonides is fond of ambiguous remarks that leave the reader pondering his true intention. When he describes the Aristotelian argument for the eternity of the universe, for instance, he writes: "This also is a great difficulty. Every intelligent man ought to reflect concerning its solution and the disclosing of its secret." But no unlocking of the "secret" follows, and the remark leaves the reader wondering just what conclusion the "intelligent man" is supposed to reach.

What is clear is that Maimonides finally asserts that the problem of the creation of the universe cannot be solved by human reason. Either of the proposed solutions—eternity or creation *ex nihilo*, Aristotle or Genesis—leaves us with unanswerable questions. We are left to choose the least bad option, and as Maimonides writes, "a certain disgrace attaches to us because of the belief in creation in time," but "an even greater disgrace attaches to the belief in eternity." That is because in a situation like this, where unaided reason is helpless, it is incumbent on a Jew to trust in the wisdom of the Bible and the prophets. "Prophecy . . . explains things to which it is not the power of speculation to accede."

Once again, Maimonides clarifies things with a metaphor or fable. Imagine that a boy is born on a deserted island and his mother dies. He grows up knowing only his father, never seeing a woman or a female of any species. Then, one day, he asks the same kind of question Maimonides is asking: "How did we come to exist, and in what way were we generated?" The father explains that a baby is generated in its mother's womb, grows there until it reaches a certain size, and then emerges through an opening "in the lower part of the body." But the child immediately objects. Every living thing he has ever seen needs to breathe, eat, and excrete; does a fetus in the womb breathe, eat, and excrete? The father answers no, not having the benefit of modern biology, and the boy is convinced that the story must be a lie. He is unable to conceive that the state of a human being before it is born could be so different from when it is fully grown.

So too, Maimonides concludes, with us, when we speculate about the creation of the universe. Aristotelians assume that we can reason backward from the way things are now to the way they used to be and always have been. Believing Jews, in contrast, argue that the state of the universe "in the beginning" was so different from what it is today—as different as a fetus from a full-grown man—that we can have no accurate knowledge about it. "A being's state of perfection and completion furnishes no indication of the state of that being preceding its perfection," Maimonides writes. With this principle, he announces, he has defeated the Aristotelian challenge to the Bible once and for all: "For it is a great wall that I have built around the Law, a wall that surrounds it warding off the stones of all those who project missiles against it."

ONCE HE HAS ESTABLISHED that God can intervene in Creation, however, Maimonides is by no means eager to exploit the principle. On the contrary, the *Guide* consistently interprets the Bible in such a way as to limit the active participation of God in history. As far as possible, Maimonides wants to convert the miracle-ridden narrative of sacred history into a rule-bound, naturalistic, and rational account. This is in keeping with his basic understanding of God as a being with no body, no personality, and no desires—a philosophical God who does not act in an impetuous or unpredictable fashion.

This vision of God is, he well knows, at odds with the surface meaning of the biblical text, where God often seems to behave in exactly those ways. Just as he reinterpreted individual words in the first part of the *Guide*, then, Maimonides goes on to explain the supernatural phenomena of the Bible in ways that make them less of a scandal to reason. Angels, for instance, appear at various key moments in the biblical story, and in most of these cases they are said to have the appearance of human beings. In Genesis, for instance, two angels spend the night in Lot's house in Sodom.

To Maimonides, however, angels can no more be imagined as having human forms than God himself. On the contrary, what Judaism calls angels, he asserts, are nothing more or less than what philosophy calls the intelligences of the celestial spheres. And these intelligences govern the Earth, not in the way of capricious rulers, but in the way of physical laws. Angels are more or less what we would now call natural forces—the powers that work, regularly and predictably, to make our world what it is. To say that God sends angels to Earth, then, is simply a metaphorical way of saying that God rules the world through natural forces. "For you never find," Maimonides writes, "that . . . an act was performed by God otherwise than through an angel."

In this way, Maimonides ingeniously reverses the whole implication of angelology. Rather than divine messengers who appear at God's whim, like the courtiers of an earthly king, angels become forces like gravity that express God's will in their very reliability and permanence. To some, Maimonides knows, this will seem like a debunking; an angel that appears on fiery wings seems a more impressive proof of God's existence than a natural law. But to think this way is a sign of mental immaturity. "If you told a man . . . that the deity sends an angel, who enters the womb and forms the fetus there," Maimonides writes, "he would be pleased with this assertion and would accept it and would regard it as a manifestation of greatness and power on the part of the deity." If, however, "you tell him that God has placed in the sperm a formative force shaping the limbs and giving them their configuration, and that this force is an angel . . . the man would shrink from this opinion." But it is such natural phenomena, not gaudy miracles, that truly attest to the power and wisdom of God.

If this is the case, then why does the Bible often speak of angels appearing in human form? How can a natural force take on such a shape? Maimonides's answer represents another step in his rationalizing program. "Every vision of an angel," he writes, "occurs only in a vision of prophecy and according to the state of him who apprehends." A vision of prophecy is a kind of controlled hallucination in which the prophet sees things that do not really exist; it is a moment when metaphors turn into perceptions. If we read the Bible carefully, Maimonides insists, we will find that anytime an angel enters the scene, the text signals that we are reading about a subjective vision, not an objective description of something that really happened.

When Maimonides says, then, that "to every prophet except Moses our Master prophetic revelation comes through an angel," he is not saying that an angel stood at the prophet's shoulder telling him what to say. Just the opposite: "through an angel" means through a natural process. This entails another major revision of traditional Jewish understanding. For Yehuda Halevi, the proof of Jewish superiority was that only the Jews are able to produce prophets, who are a species of supermen able to work miracles and receive words from God. For Maimonides, in contrast, a prophet is something more like an extremely intelligent and insightful person, whose faculties are so well developed and perfectly balanced that he is able to say exactly the right words for any occasion.

This account does not leave God out of the picture entirely, since for Maimonides all intellectual activity ultimately comes from God. But this happens in an indirect fashion, as the divine essence "overflows" downward through each of the spheres and then finally down to human beings on Earth. Most of the time, this overflow reaches just one of our mental faculties: either the reason, in which case the recipient becomes a "man of science," or the imagination, which produces "soothsayers, augurs," and "all those who do extraordinary things by means of strange devices and secret arts." It is only when both these faculties are stimulated to their height and beyond that a person becomes a prophet, able to see "visions of prophecy" and speak inspired words.

One thing that defines a prophet is that he is supposed to be able to see the future; in Deuteronomy, the test of a true prophet is that his predictions came to pass. For Maimonides, however, this too is not a miraculous power, but simply the refinement of a skill everyone possesses. "The faculty of divination exists in all people," he writes, "but varies in degree." Everyone is able, to some extent, to predict what will happen in the future based on what is happening now. But only very gifted people can predict accurately and precisely, and only a prophet is able to do it instantaneously. In such cases it may seem that the prophet is not thinking at all, but actually seeing the future. What is really happening, however, is that "the mind goes over all [the] premises and draws from them conclusions in the shortest time, so that it is thought to happen in no time at all."

If prophecy is defined in this way, it follows that not just anybody is able to become a prophet. God does not choose fools or wicked people and transform them into prophets: "it is not possible that an ignoramus should turn into a prophet; nor can a man not be a prophet on a certain evening and be a prophet on the following morning, as though he had made some find." But this view, that "prophecy is a certain perfection in the nature of man," raises an obvious question. Surely non-Jews can achieve mental perfection as readily as Jews; why is it, then, that only Jews have ever been true prophets? To answer this objection, Maimonides inserts a caveat. Everyone "who according to his natural disposition is fit for prophecy" can become a prophet, but God sometimes intervenes to prevent people from prophesying, so that only his chosen ones can actually succeed. Divine intervention, in this case, proves to be solely a veto power.

Maimonides's naturalistic understanding of prophecy is able to cover, with some stretching, almost all of the examples in the Bible.

A great lover of lists, he draws up a list of eleven degrees of prophecy, showing how the various prophets' experiences were more or less complete. Samuel, who heard a voice in a dream, was inferior to Isaiah, who saw God in a dream; while Abraham, who heard a voice in a waking vision, was better than either.

But there is one example of prophecy that does not fall into this schema—one prophet of whom the Bible makes very clear that he spoke to God not in a dream or a vision, but directly and in front of a multitude of witnesses. That is Moses, who received the Law from God on Mount Sinai. If Judaism is to have any supernatural sanction, if the Law that Maimonides spent his life studying is to be more than just well-thought-out human legislation, then Moses has to be different from other prophets. Indeed, he has to be different from all men who ever lived, and the revelation at Sinai must be a unique moment in the history of the universe—the one time when God, who has no voice and no body, showed himself and spoke.

Maimonides has no choice but to affirm this, and so he does—though here, too, some readers have wondered about his sincerity. "To every prophet except Moses our Master prophetic revelation came through an angel," he writes—that is, through the mediation of a natural process. But Moses's "miracles do not belong to the class of the miracles of the other prophets," and "his apprehension is different from that of all those who came after him in Israel." The intellect, Maimonides has already written, is incapable of penetrating the Creation and has no choice but to take it on faith; the same is true of Sinai, the other hinge moment in cosmic history. Moses's "is a rank that we are incapable of grasping in its true reality." In these two cases, we are forced to believe that God broke with his usual abstraction, the impersonality that defines him, and made his will known in a spectacularly concrete fashion. But Maimonides is entirely certain that there will be no third moment like this. We cannot hope that in some messianic future God will reveal himself again as He did on Sinai: "It is a fundamental principle of our Law that there will never be another

Law." Any religion that claims to be based on a second revelation—such as Islam, under whose reign Maimonides lived all his life—is therefore an illusion.

HERE AGAIN, HOWEVER, Maimonides has asserted the possibility of the miraculous only to drastically limit its scope. God could presumably have commanded the Israelites to do anything he wanted, simply because he wanted it. But just as the cosmos, in Maimonides's view, is governed rationally and not whimsically, so Jewish law is a rational construct, every part of which can be shown to be purposeful and useful. If there is something in the commandments whose purpose we fail to grasp, the failure is ours: "all the Laws have a cause, though we ignore the causes of some of them and we do not know the manner in which they conform to wisdom."

But those exceptions are few, since Maimonides believes that a rational case can be made for just about all the laws, even the oddest. The laws given in the Torah—both the Written Torah and the Oral Torah, which is handed down over the generations and interpreted by sages—can be divided into two types. The first type, which Maimonides follows tradition in calling "judgments," are those in which "it is clear to us in what way they are useful." These are the kinds of laws that any human community would make for itself, regardless of whether it benefited from divine inspiration, such as "the prohibition of killing and stealing." Other laws, however, are distinctively Jewish, and these are the ones that seem arbitrary and inexplicable. Why does the Torah forbid Jews to plant a field with different kinds of seeds? Why does it forbid wearing a garment made of mixed linen and wool? The supreme example of this type of commandment, which we have already seen troubling Philo and Yehuda Halevi, is circumcision. How can anyone possibly make a rational case for cutting off a boy's foreskin on the eighth day of his life?

This distinction, between obviously useful laws and seemingly pointless ones, turns out to parallel another distinction that Maimonides makes a little later in the *Guide*. Jewish law, he writes, has two goals: "the welfare of the soul and the welfare of the body." To serve the body, the Law prevents crime and disorder, warding off dangers to our well-being and peace of mind. The Law encourages us to become good people—fair, just, kind, generous—because these moral qualities enable us to live together in peace and prosperity. But moral perfection is not an end in itself; being a good person is necessary but not sufficient. The goal of human life, the reason why we cultivate goodness in the first place, is intellectual perfection. Thinking correctly about God and the universe is the supreme human activity, and the "ultimate perfection" for human beings is to hold "opinions toward which speculation has led and that investigation has rendered compulsory."

Before we can become intellectually perfect, however, we must deal with the standing challenge to the mind posed by the fact that we have bodies. To Maimonides, mind and body are complementary opposites, like form and matter. A human being is made up of both, but it is the mind that makes us distinctively human, while the material body is constantly pulling us toward vice. "All man's acts of disobedience and sins," Maimonides writes, "are consequent upon his matter and not upon his form, whereas all his virtues are consequent upon his form." When we are governed by matter, we engage in "eating and drinking and copulation"; when our form is in charge, we "control . . . desire and anger" and gain a true apprehension of God.

Jewish law, then, does everything it can to restrain and chastise the body. This does not lead to the point of asceticism: Judaism frowns on chastity and commands every Jew to marry and have children. (Maimonides himself spent the first part of his life devoted to study, but then he got married and started a family in his late forties.) Rather, Maimonides describes the pious Jew's attitude toward his bodily appetites in a striking metaphor. Imagine a man who has been tasked by his king with transporting dung from one place to another. A dignified and free man who had to perform this unpleasant task would do it secretly, a little bit at a time, so he would not be seen by others or get himself dirty. A slave, in contrast, would "throw himself with his whole body into this dung and filth, soil his face and hands, and carry the dung in public, laughing the while and rejoicing and clapping his hands."

So, too, with our sexual and other appetites. Wise people attend to them in private and as little as possible; fools make them the center of their lives and spend their days wallowing in them. And the Law is designed to humble and reduce our appetites, making it easier for us to be wise. It is for this reason, Maimonides writes, that the Torah prohibits homosexuality and bestiality—not because there is anything intrinsically wrong with these acts, but because they represent a multiplication of the varieties of sexual temptation. Sex that leads to procreation is bad enough, but sex that can't even justify itself by producing children is a sheer vice. "For the thing that is natural should be abhorred except for necessity, all the more should deviations from the natural way and the quest for pleasure alone be eschewed."

The same principle explains the commandment of circumcision. According to Maimonides, circumcision brings about "a decrease in sexual intercourse and a weakening of the organ in question, so that [sexual] activity be diminished and the organ be in as quiet a state as possible." Today, parents who have their children circumcised prefer to minimize the pain involved and the possible reduction in sensitivity, but to Maimonides the pain is the whole point: "The bodily pain caused to that member is the real purpose of circumcision."

Jewish law, then, is designed to foster a certain human type, which for centuries was the Jewish ideal: "man should not be hard and rough, but responsive, obedient, acquiescent, and docile." But as we have seen, the law is also meant to train human beings in the correct way of thinking about God. And it is here that the "statutes," the seemingly irrational commandments, come into play. To rescue these laws from the suspicion of arbitrariness, Maimonides performs a wonderful feat of historical imagination. In the twelfth century, the main rivals to

Judaism were the other monotheistic religions descended from it, Christianity and Islam. But at the time the Torah was given, Maimonides reminds the reader, most people were idolaters and pagans who worshipped nature with magic rites. The Israelites had to be taught to abandon such practices and cleave to the one true God.

Whenever a law commands or prohibits something for obscure reasons, then, Maimonides explains that the original intention was to counter a specific idolatrous belief or practice. Why are Jews forbidden to wear garments made of linen and wool mingled together? Because the priests of the "Sabians," as Maimonides calls the Middle Eastern pagans, "put together in their garments vegetal and animal substances," and the Jews are being discouraged from following Sabian practices. Why is it forbidden to eat the fruit of any tree during its first three years? Because the Sabians would offer the first fruits of their sacred trees to their gods in "an idolatrous temple" and believed that failure to do this would result in the death of the tree. Why do Jews not eat milk and meat together? Maimonides isn't entirely sure, but "it is in my opinion not improbable that—in addition to this being very gross food . . . idolatry had something to do with it. Perhaps such food was eaten at one of the ceremonies of their cult or at one of their festivals."

In this way, Maimonides turns the "statutes" from a scandal to reason into a clever instrument of policy. They serve the second of the Law's two aims, the inculcation of correct ways of thinking about God. But there is, as he recognizes, something unsettling about the implications of this way of interpreting the Law. After all, the Torah doesn't just forbid idolatrous sacrifices. It establishes a very detailed system of its own sacrifices, spending many chapters on the design of the altar and the procedure for the slaughter. But it is hard to imagine that Maimonides's God could take any pleasure in such offerings. How could the First Cause enjoy the smell of incense?

Maimonides concludes that the Temple, with all its paraphernalia and rituals, was actually intended by God as a "gracious ruse." Sacrifices meant nothing to God for their own sake, but they were such an accustomed part of religion, at that time and place, that simply abolishing them would have shocked the Israelites too deeply. Instead, the Torah chose to centralize, limit, and regularize sacrifices. In this way, the occasions for magical thinking would be reduced, while the Israelites would be able to accept the Law as something recognizably sacred. Maimonides explains this in one of the boldest passages in the whole *Guide*:

> His wisdom, may He be exalted, and His gracious ruse, which is manifest in regard to all His creatures, did not require that He give us a Law prescribing the rejection, abandonment, and abolition of all these kinds of worship. For one could not then conceive the acceptance of [such a Law], considering the nature of man, which always likes that to which it is accustomed. At that time this would have been similar to the appearance of a prophet in these times who, calling upon the people to worship God, would say: "God has given you a Law forbidding you to pray to Him, to fast, to call upon Him for help in misfortune. Your worship should consist solely in meditation without any works at all."

Maimonides is saying that God doesn't want prayers, or answer them, any more than he wants or responds to animal sacrifices. The right way to approach God, as Maimonides has said again and again, is to think about him; any "works," even pious ones like praying and fasting, bring us no closer to God. But this is too much truth for the Jews of the Middle Ages to handle. Once again, the elitism and esotericism of Maimonides's approach is evident. When he wrote the Torah, Moses allowed the Israelites to cling to their rituals like a child to its security blanket, even though they were inherently worthless. If another Moses were to come along in the twelfth century—like, for instance, Moses Maimonides—he too would have to make concessions. He could not deprive the Jews of prayer, no matter how otiose prayer might be in itself.

It was one thing to deny the need for sacrifices; after all, the Temple had been in ruins for over a thousand years when the *Guide* was written, and Judaism had long since adapted to its absence. But here Maimonides seems to deny the possibility of any kind of mutual relationship between God and man. We can think about him, but we cannot speak to him, and he certainly does not speak to us. This denial has serious moral implications, since it seems to rule out the possibility of divine reward and punishment. God, it seems, does not take notice of our actions, so how can he judge us for them?

Here, too, Maimonides candidly follows his logic to its necessary conclusion. All the passages in the Torah that promise reward for obedience and punishment for disobedience are also part of God's "ruse": "For this too is a ruse used by Him with regard to us in order to achieve His first intention with respect to us." Maimonides can't even endorse such an elemental religious principle as the idea that God punishes the wicked. This belief is "necessary for the abolition of reciprocal wrongdoing," he writes, and so the Torah fosters it for utilitarian purposes. But it does not correspond to any reality.

Or does it? Here again, Maimonides's answers become highly ambiguous, and what he says at one point in the *Guide* is hard to reconcile with his views at other points. Reward and punishment, he writes, are a ruse. Yet he also affirms that it is "a fundamental principle of the Law . . . that all the calamities that befall men and the good things that come to men, be it a single individual or a group, are all of them determined according to the deserts of the men concerned." This appears to be an ironclad guarantee that divine providence is real. But then, a few pages later, Maimonides inserts what sounds like a disclaimer: "In this belief . . . I am not relying upon the conclusion to which demonstration has led me, but upon what has clearly appeared as the intention of the book of God and of the books of our prophets." This seems to imply that reason and revelation give contradictory answers. Yet Maimonides has consistently argued that reason must come first and that religion must be brought into harmony with it.

It might be possible to achieve such a harmony, however, if we think carefully about what providence actually means. As we have already seen, Maimonides does not define closeness to God in moral terms. It is the intellect, not ethical behavior, that defines the individual's relationship to God. It makes sense, then, that providence is "consequent upon the intellect." The more intellectually perfect a human being is, the better he will understand God; and the better he understands God, the more God will take care of him. Maimonides follows his elitism to its ultimate conclusion: "Divine providence does not watch in an equal manner over all the individuals of the human species, but providence is graded as their human perfection is graded."

Taken in its plain sense, this appears either outrageous or absurd. It shocks the conscience to believe that God cares more for intelligent people than for unintelligent ones; and it is obviously untrue that intelligent people are immune to evil and misfortune. It's necessary to ask, then, just what Maimonides means by God "watching over" individual human beings. The whole tendency of the *Guide* has been to reinterpret anthropomorphic views of God in naturalistic terms. Could the same thing be done with the concept of "watching over"?

That seems to be what Maimonides implies when he turns to the classic text on providence and theodicy, the book of Job. Job is a good and pious man who is afflicted with horrible punishments for no apparent reason. At first he complains about his misfortune, but he is silenced when God appears in a whirlwind and overawes him with declarations of his own overwhelming power: "Where were you when I laid the earth's foundations? Speak if you have understanding." To Maimonides, this speech reaffirms the basic principle of his own philosophical faith, which is that God is completely beyond human comprehension, and therefore human judgment. No word used by human beings can be applied to God, and that includes words like "providence" and "justice." "The notion of His providence," Maimonides writes, "is not the same as the notion of our providence; nor is the notion of His governance of the things created by Him the same as the notion of our governance of the things which we govern."

It takes a philosopher, a person of perfected intellect, to truly understand and accept this fact with all its implications. But once it is understood, human suffering will no longer pose an obstacle to the intellectual love of God. "If man knows this," Maimonides writes, "every misfortune will be borne lightly by him. And misfortunes will not add to his doubts regarding the deity and whether He does or does not know and whether He manifests neglect, but will, on the contrary, add to his love." This, perhaps, is what Maimonides means by "providence is consequent upon the intellect": not that understanding God renders man immune to misfortune, but that it enables him to bear misfortune with equanimity. This would be an entirely rational and non-miraculous interpretation of providence, in keeping with Maimonides's earlier interpretations of prophecy and angels.

Near the end of *The Guide of the Perplexed*, Maimonides offers one last parable, which captures his understanding of the relationship between God and human beings. "The ruler is in his palace," he writes, "and all his subjects are partly within the city and partly outside the city." The ruler, of course, is God, and we are all his subjects; but not all of us are equally close to him. Those outside the city "have no doctrinal belief" but are pagans and barbarians with no conception of God; in Maimonides's view, "they do not have the rank of men." Next come those inside the city who have turned their backs on the ruler's palace: these are people "who have adopted incorrect opinions" about God, either because of their own errors or because they were brought up with false beliefs. Such heretics are dangerous, Maimonides writes, because they have the capacity to lead a person away from the true faith.

One step higher on the ladder are those "who seek to reach the ruler's habitation and to enter it," but who don't know the right way to get there. These, for Maimonides, are law-abiding Jews, who observe the commandments but remain ignorant of their true meaning. (Note that the situation of such people—which would include the vast majority of Jews who have ever lived—is only a little better than those of non-believers.) Then come those who reach the palace and walk around it but never enter it. These are the Jewish sages, who spend their lives studying the Law and master its intricacies but fail to think philosophically about God.

The supreme rank, the one that every human being should strive to attain, is that of the people who sit with the ruler inside his palace. These are the ones who speculate about divine science and have come to know, "to the extent that that is possible, everything that may be ascertained" about God. Maimonides himself presumably occupies this rank, or aspires to. Yet even the man who is closest to God remains fundamentally ignorant about him. He has merely "come close to certainty in those matters in which one can only come close to it." Absolute knowledge about God is, as Job learned, impossible for a human being. The *Guide* is the attempt of the greatest Jewish thinker to state the truth about a subject that in the end can only be adequately expressed by silence. For as Maimonides writes, citing the book of Psalms, "silence with regard to You is praise."

BIBLIOGRAPHY

Davidson, Herbert. *Moses Maimonides: The Man and His Works*. New York: Oxford University Press, 2005.

Halbertal, Moshe. *Maimonides: Life and Thought*. Princeton: Princeton University Press, 2014.

Lewis, Bernard. *The Jews of Islam*. Princeton: Princeton University Press, 1987.

Maimonides. *The Guide of the Perplexed*. Translated by Shlomo Pines. 2 vols. Chicago: University of Chicago Press, 1963.

8

THE SECRET LIFE OF GOD

The *Zohar*

Kabbalah, the tradition of Jewish mysticism, goes far beyond the stories of the Torah and the laws of the Talmud in its attempt to achieve knowledge of God. Kabbalah's mystical explanations of Jewish practices, its picture of a universe moved by divine and satanic forces, its promise of magical powers to the initiated—all present a vision of Judaism very different from the one most Jews learn today. The book at the center of Kabbalah is the *Zohar*, a mystical scripture that was first disseminated in Spain in the thirteenth century. Its teeming pages tell the story of a group of ancient rabbis who discovered in the verses of the Torah secret truths about the nature of the Godhead and the creation of the world. Reading the *Zohar* means plunging into a world of divine metaphor in which every human act from sex to prayer turns out to have supernatural repercussions. For its students throughout Jewish history, the *Zohar* promised the individual Jew a crucial role in the cosmos and a new kind of knowledge of God.

IN THE LAST YEARS OF THE THIRTEENTH CENTURY, A mysterious book began to circulate among the Jews of Spain. For a thousand years, the texts at the center of Judaism had been the Bible and the Talmud: the former told the sacred history of how the Jews were chosen by God, while the latter set forth the detailed laws by which God expected his people to live. Now, however, a group of mystics living in Castile began to talk and write about a third crucial source, one that was actually older than the Talmud itself but had only recently been rediscovered. This was the work that would, over centuries of editing, take shape as the *Zohar*—in its final form, a 2,400-page compendium in which scholars discern some twenty discrete sections or textual layers.

The Hebrew word *zohar* means "splendor" or "brightness," and the book's title comes from a verse in the book of Daniel, where Daniel prophesies what will happen at the Last Judgment: "Many of those that sleep in the dust of the earth will awake, some to eternal life, others to reproaches, to everlasting abhorrence. And the knowledgeable will be radiant like brightness [*zohar*] of the sky, and those who lead the many to righteousness will be like the stars forever and ever." Knowledge, the verse tells us, is the key to redemption; only those who know will get the chance to become like the stars. But what is it that the righteous need to know?

The traditional answer is the Torah itself, the law that God gave to the Jewish people, which has always been at the heart of Judaism. And the *Zohar* agrees that to become radiant we must learn the Torah. But what the author of the *Zohar* finds in the Torah is very different from what earlier readers found there. "Woe to the man who says that the Torah intended simply to relate stories and the words of commoners," the *Zohar* instructs, "for, if this were the case, we ourselves at the present time could make a Torah from the words of commoners and do even better." This blasphemous-sounding statement seems to fly in the face of the very idea that the Torah is a divine document, perfectly designed by God to tell the Jewish people what they needed to know. Indeed, the *Zohar* goes on to suggest that "if the intention [of the Torah] was to deal with the affairs of this world, then the books in the world"—that is, the profane wisdom books of the philosophers and the Gentiles—"contain better things. Shall we then follow them, and make a Torah out of them?"

Of course, the *Zohar* has no such thing in mind: "But all the words of the Torah are exalted and are supernal mysteries," it concludes. The point of these shocking statements is simply to drive home the message that the Torah contains much more than its surface meanings. Superficially, there is much in the Torah that might seem inconsequential or irrational—a problem that thinkers from Philo to Maimonides tried to address in their philosophical works. The very idea that God would stoop to recording the words of men—including a fair number of sinners and wrongdoers—seems counter-intuitive, insulting to the divine dignity. "Come and see," the *Zohar* explains. "A mortal king considers it below his dignity to converse with a commoner, let alone write down a commoner's words." Why, then, should the King of Kings "collect the words of commoners, such as those of Esau, Hagar, Laban's to Jacob," and those of other non-Israelite characters in the Bible? How could such profane talk make up a divine book?

The answer the *Zohar* gives is that the Torah is an even deeper and more mysterious book than we might have supposed. "Every single word is there to demonstrate supernal matters"; that is, to reveal cosmic mysteries about the true nature of God. "The narratives of the Torah are the garments of the Torah," and it is crucial not to mistake the mere coverings for the thing itself: "If a man thinks that the garment is the actual Torah itself, and not something quite other, may his spirit depart, and may he have no portion in the world to come." Fortunately, the *Zohar* would unfold the secret mysteries that the Torah concealed. To read the *Zohar* was to attain the brightness of the knowledgeable; it was to be admitted into the tradition of Jewish mysticism known as Kabbalah.

Kabbalah, with its daring new interpretations of Judaism and its intricate mystical symbolism, had developed in Jewish Provence, Catalonia, and Castile over the course of the twelfth and thirteenth centuries. By the time the *Zohar* appeared, it could draw on a richly elaborated mystical tradition, and in the following centuries it would become the kabbalistic book *par excellence*, the central work of Jewish mysticism. Indeed, for many Jews in the late Middle Ages and the Renaissance, the *Zohar* joined the Bible and the Talmud as the third canonical Jewish text that had to be mastered if one was to be a knowledgeable Jew. By the eighteenth century, the Hasidic master Pinchas of Koretz could go so far as to say that "the Zohar has helped me to remain a Jew." For him, and for generations of readers like him, Judaism without the mystical dimension revealed in the *Zohar* would have been a feeble shadow of religion.

Yet how could it be that readers of the thireenth century suddenly understood the Torah better than the great sages of Jewish antiquity? If the *Zohar* contained the essence of Judaism, how could that essence have been concealed for so long? The *Zohar* itself solves this conundrum in a simple and daring fashion: it does not present itself as a new work, nor did its first readers approach it as such. Instead, it claims to record the teachings and conversations of a group of rabbis who lived in the second century CE, whose leader was the great Talmudic sage Simeon ben Yochai. Simeon appears in the Talmud as a rabbi of a special kind: he is not merely a wise man and an interpreter of the law, but a holy martyr possessed of magical powers. He is exactly the kind of figure who would be credible as a teacher of mystical secrets.

The Talmudic story goes that Simeon was in conversation with some other rabbis when he made a highly disparaging remark about the Romans, who at that time were the occupying power in Palestine. When one of the rabbis present ventured to praise Roman achievements, remarking that they were at least excellent at building roads, bridges, and baths, Simeon retorted sharply: "All that they made they made for themselves; they built market-places, to set harlots in them; baths, to rejuvenate themselves; bridges, to levy tolls for them." When word of this seditious remark reached the Roman authorities, who were already wary of any signs of Jewish resistance, they issued an order for Simeon's execution.

It is at this point that Simeon's story moves from political intrigue to outright legend. At first, Rabbi Simeon and his son, the almost equally wise Rabbi Eleazar, went and hid in the house of study, surviving on bread and water smuggled in by Simeon's wife. But eventually Simeon worried that his wife would be tortured and reveal their location, so he took Eleazar with him to hide in a cave. There they sat, up to their necks in sand, for twelve years, eating and drinking from a carob tree and a well that had miraculously sprung up near them. Throughout the twelve years, Simeon and his son did nothing but study Torah.

But when the Roman emperor died, causing his decree against Simeon to lapse, and the father and son emerged from their cave, it turned out that such a superhuman degree of holiness left them unable to deal with the ordinary, fallen world. The first thing they saw upon rejoining society was a man plowing a field on the sabbath, a major sin, and when they cast their eyes upon the sinner he was burned up. One might think that God had sent Simeon to be a righteous avenger, chastising the Jewish people for their laxity. But the Talmudic story suggests that the rabbinic authorities were none too eager to hold the Jews to this kind of fanatical standard. Indeed, as Simeon and Eleazar went about the countryside burning up sinners, a voice from Heaven intervened to stop them: "Have you emerged to destroy my world? Go back to your cave!" Not until they had spent another year in the cave learning the value of moderation and compassion were the pair freed a second time; now, whenever the anger of Eleazar would burn someone up, the gaze of Simeon would heal them. "My son," Simeon concluded, "you and I are sufficient for the world." The two of them were as holy and as knowledgeable as all the rest of the Jewish people put together.

It is this mysterious and ambiguous figure to whom the *Zohar* ascribes its doctrines. Many readers, in fact, knew the book simply as "the teachings of Rabbi Simeon." And the form of the book seemed to support the attribution. It was not written in Hebrew, which was the standard language of scholarly and religious discourse among medieval Jews; nor did it use Arabic, like the treatises of Yehuda Halevi and Maimonides, products of an advanced Jewish-Arabic culture. Rather, the *Zohar* was written in Aramaic, the language that had been the lingua franca of the Middle East around the time the Babylonian Talmud was written, in the third to fifth centuries CE. To any reader of the Talmud, who was used to associating Aramaic with Jewish antiquity, the language of the *Zohar* would have bolstered its claim to be an ancient text. And the landscape of the *Zohar* was the landscape of Palestine, where Simeon ben Yochai lived. Often it recounts conversations that are supposed to have taken place during journeys to and from various Palestinian cities, whose names were familiar to Spanish Jews from the Talmud.

Yet if the *Zohar* was so ancient, why didn't it turn up until the late thirteenth century—and why did only one person seem to have a copy of it? For it was a single man, Rabbi Moses de León, who was responsible for distributing the *Zohar*, section by section, to its first avid readers. So closely associated was Moses de León with this new book—which he also quoted extensively in Hebrew writings issued under his own name—that it was natural for his contemporaries to wonder whether Moses, rather than Simeon, was the true author of the *Zohar*. Indeed, this very accusation was leveled in the only piece of contemporary historical evidence we have about the *Zohar*. This is a fragment of a memoir by Rabbi Isaac of Acre, a Palestinian Jew who came to Spain in the 1290s specifically in order to find out the truth about this amazing text.

According to Rabbi Isaac's diary—which itself survives only in the form of quotations, preserved in a book of much later date—he "went to Spain to find out how the book of the Zohar, which Rabbi Simeon and his son Rabbi Eleazar composed in the cave, came to exist in his time." Isaac did not doubt that the *Zohar* was a divine book—"I saw that its words were wonderful, drawn from the celestial source, the fountain that pours forth without being itself replenished." Yet when he asked various Spanish kabbalists "whence had come these wonderful mysteries that had been transmitted orally and not written down, and that were now plain to all who could read," the answers he received were unconvincing: "Some said one thing and some said another."

One of the theories Rabbi Isaac heard was that, in fact, Moses de León was not just the disseminator of the *Zohar* but its author. Accordingly, Isaac tracked down Moses in the city of Valladolid and asked him for the truth; and Moses assured him that indeed, he had in his house in Avila an ancient book written by Rabbi Simeon ben Yochai, "and when you come to see me there I shall show it to you." Unfortunately, however, Moses de León died shortly after this meeting and never got the chance to show Isaac the original manuscript of the *Zohar*. And as he pursued his inquiries, Isaac ended up hearing a very different story about how the *Zohar* came to be. According to this version, after Moses's death a Spanish kabbalist approached his widow, trying to acquire the manuscript of the *Zohar*—"a book . . . whose value surpasses both crystal and gold." But Moses's wife, who should have known if anyone did, said outright that no such manuscript ever existed:

> May God do so to me and more also if my husband ever possessed such a book. But he wrote what he did out of his own head and heart, and knowledge and mind. And when I saw him writing without any material before him I used to say to him: Why do you tell everybody that you are copying from a book when you have no book, and you write out of your own head? Would it not be better for you to say that the work was your own brainchild, because then you would get more credit? And he would reply: If I told them my secret and that what I wrote was my own invention, they would pay no heed to my words, and would not give me a

penny for them, because they would say that I had made it all up. But, as it is, when they hear that I am copying extracts from the *Zohar* that was written under the influence of the Holy Spirit by Rabbi Simeon ben Yochai, they pay a lot of money for them, as you can see yourself.

This damning evidence seems to prove that the *Zohar* was a work of pseudepigraphy—that is, an original work attributed to a famous earlier author in order to give it greater authority. Yet the idea that Moses could have invented the *Zohar* as a money-making scheme seems impossible to credit—the book is too vast, complex, profound, and passionately sincere to be dismissed as a scam. Indeed, Rabbi Isaac himself was sure that even if the *Zohar* was Moses de León's own creation, nevertheless "he was a master of the Holy Name, and whatever he wrote in this book he wrote through its power." Like Joseph Smith, the founder of Mormonism, who claimed to transcribe the Book of Mormon from golden plates that he was never able to produce, Moses de León—who modern scholars believe, on both circumstantial and internal evidence, must have written at least the core of the *Zohar*—was a religious genius who preferred to call his masterwork a discovery rather than an invention.

THE MAIN BODY of the *Zohar* takes the form of a verse-by-verse commentary on the Torah, with the bulk of the text dealing with the books of Genesis and Exodus. This is interrupted by a number of separate sections with their own titles, which present dramatic episodes such as the death of Rabbi Simeon, or document visionary journeys among the heavens, or explicate the meaning of the letters in the name of God. What the *Zohar* does not even attempt to do is systematically expound a set of doctrines or ideas in a way that might be useful for the novice reader. Instead, it rests on a highly developed system of mystical concepts that are not so much explained as taken for granted and expanded on, often in what seems like random order. To open the *Zohar* and begin reading, then, is to be plunged instantly into a murky ocean of symbols and allusions that is just about impossible to penetrate unaided.

In addition to being a commentary, however, the *Zohar* is also a dramatic work—Gershom Scholem, the great twentieth-century scholar of Jewish mysticism, described it as a "mystical novel"—whose "plot" is the ongoing discussions of Rabbi Simeon ben Yochai and his disciples. Often their sayings are given with no preface at all, or merely a curt "Rabbi Eleazar commenced his discourse thus," or "Said Rabbi Yudai." But in other passages their discourses are set into a narrative framework that emphasizes the intimacy of the mystic companions and their passionate love of Torah. Sometimes, a pair of rabbis will meet a mysterious stranger or a precocious child on their journeys who reveals unexpected secrets to them. Often a speech is concluded by the listeners weeping for joy or prostrating themselves in gratitude: "If we had come into the world only to hear this we should have been content," the rabbis are wont to exclaim after learning a new Torah secret.

In one section, known as "The Greater Assembly," three of Rabbi Simeon's listeners die in ecstasy after hearing him teach, then are carried up to heaven by angels: "Blessed is their portion, for they have ascended in complete perfection," he pronounces. In another, "The Lesser Assembly," Simeon himself dies, like Socrates, after a night of teaching his disciples; unlike Socrates, his bier flies into the air and shoots fire. Throughout, Simeon is portrayed as the miracle-worker he is in the Talmud, a unique human being who knows more about God and Torah than anyone else who has ever lived.

The effect of this scene-setting is to heighten the emotional stakes for the reader. Unlike the Talmud, where the discussion of Torah matters is lucid and focused on logical concepts, the *Zohar* never forgets that it is revealing mystic secrets to a select audience. It offers an almost conspiratorial allure: "Whatever the companions have revealed among themselves is good and proper, but not to the rest of mankind," Rabbi Simeon says at one point. In another passage, the *Zohar* uses an erotic image to explain the relationship between the Torah and the initiates who learn its secrets:

> What can be compared to this? It is like a girl, beautiful and gracious, and much loved, and she is kept closely confined in her palace. She has a special lover, unrecognized by anyone and concealed. . . .What does she do? She opens a tiny door in the secret palace where she lives and shows her face to her love. Then she withdraws at once and is gone. None of those in her lover's vicinity sees or understands, but her lover alone knows. . . . So it is with the Torah. She reveals herself only to her lover.

At the same time, the *Zohar* emphasizes that the study of Torah—of the true, hidden meanings of Torah—is an activity with cosmic repercussions. More than an act of piety or an intellectual exercise, Torah interpretation is a way of sharing God's power: "For the Holy One, blessed be He, is attentive to the voice of those who occupy themselves with the Torah, and through each fresh discovery made by them in the Torah a new heaven is created."

This audacious suggestion, that men can become through study God's partners and helpers, points to the central reason for the *Zohar*'s appeal. Medieval Jewish philosophy had evolved an understanding of God that allowed for almost no contact between the divine and the human spheres. Maimonides's *Guide of the Perplexed*, which was certainly known to Moses de León (records show that a copy was in his library), insisted that human beings could know God only negatively, by perpetually paring away the metaphors and images with which we try to understand his total otherness. Jewish practices, Maimonides explained, could mostly be explained as historical responses to idolatry, or as instruments of moral and political education. Sacrifices and even prayer meant nothing to God, who by definition could take no interest in human affairs. The relationship between God and man, in the Maimonidean system, was highly intellectual and basically one-directional: men reached God by thinking about him. He did not think about them.

The *Zohar* boldly reverses every one of these Maimonidean claims. It is not true, the *Zohar* insists on every page, that we cannot know anything about God's interiority. On the contrary, the Torah, read properly, reveals that God is not a negative abstraction but a complex and dynamic system, full of movement and possibility, which it is possible to understand in great detail. Furthermore, it is not true that mankind's role in the universe is essentially passive, a matter of directing the mind toward God. The *Zohar* teaches that this world is actually a vast battleground, full of angels and devils, in which the forces of evil are constantly attempting to interfere with God's unity. Human actions, as the *Zohar* sees it, are a matter of the utmost urgency, because God needs us as much as we need God. "He created man upon the earth," Rabbi Eleazar teaches, "who is like a model of the upper glory, in order to restore this glory and to complete it on all sides."

In drawing this picture of God and the world, the *Zohar* was directly defying the tradition of the *via negativa*, the idea that God could only be understood negatively, by naming what he was not. For once you allow yourself to believe that this world is God's mirror, rather than just his product, then the religious imagination is licensed and even compelled to express itself in images and symbols. The world itself becomes an encyclopedia of metaphors, in which everything we see and do bears some occult likeness to the divine. And it is the sheer proliferation of symbols that gives the *Zohar* its atmosphere of teeming, chaotic creativity. Everything, in the *Zohar*, is related to everything else. The vowel-points of Hebrew letters, the way a flame rises from a wick, the colors of the rainbow, the form of the human body, sexual intercourse, rivers and fountains, seeds with their husks and kernels, even the hairs of a beard—all exist in order to teach us esoteric truths about the nature of God. And of course, the elements of Judaism, too, must be reinterpreted according to this vision. The patriarchs, Moses, the commandments, the Temple, the sabbath and festivals: all encode profound secrets about God and man. Ultimately, nothing less than the fate of the universe depends on the deeds of the Jewish people.

EVERY MONOTHEISTIC RELIGION must eventually confront the problem of how to relate God's infinity to the finitude of human life. If God, by definition, is utterly beyond human understanding, then how can we enter into a relationship with him? There seems to be an absolute gulf between God and Creation, and it is difficult to understand how it could ever be bridged. To this problem, the kabbalistic tradition that reaches full flowering in the *Zohar* gives a highly imaginative answer. God, the *Zohar* grants, is in the ultimate sense unknowable. This is the aspect of God that it refers to as *En Sof*, "without end," the Infinite. *En Sof*, like the Maimonidean God, is completely beyond the power of the human mind to understand or express. "*En Sof* cannot be known," the *Zohar* explains, "and does not produce end or beginning... there are no end, no wills, no lights, no luminaries in *En Sof*. All these luminaries and lights depend on it for their existence, but they are not in a position to perceive."

At another point, the *Zohar* compares *En Sof* to the ocean: "the waters that come from the sea cannot be grasped, nor do they have form." Yet even the ocean does take on a certain form, since it is delimited by the land; the earth defines the sea by providing a container for it. "When the waters of the sea spread themselves over a vessel, which is the earth, an image is formed, and we can then make a calculation," the *Zohar* explains. But what is the vessel that allows us to make an image of God? What could possibly contain the Infinite?

The answer the *Zohar* gives is that God is contained in the *sefirot*. The word *sefirot*—singular *sefirah*—is difficult to translate; originally it comes from the Hebrew word for counting, and it is used in Kabbalah to enumerate the ten stages, or attributes, or aspects of God's self-disclosure. These can be seen as the successive phases by which God transitions from the unknowability of *En Sof* to the God we recognize and worship in this world. They are, in the *Zohar*'s image, the vessels that enclose God's being so that we can come to recognize it.

Each *sefirah* is given a Hebrew name that points to its role in the divine process. In descending order, they are Keter (Crown), Hokhmah (Wisdom), Binah (Understanding), Hesed (Love), Din or Gevurah (Judgment/Power), Tiferet (Beauty), Netsach (Endurance), Hod (Splendor), Yesod (Foundation), and Malkhut (Kingdom). These names are only loosely suggestive, however, and some *sefirot* are also known by alternative titles. (What's more, in the *Zohar* itself, the word *sefirah* seldom appears—usually they are referred to metaphorically, as "powers" or "levels" or "sides"—and their titles are often exchanged for different, metaphorical or allusive labels.) The traditional diagram of the system helps to illuminate the relationships among the *sefirot*:

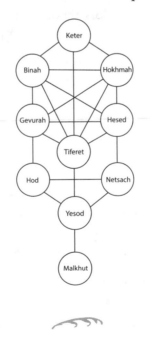

IN THIS COMPLEX of forces, a few areas are particularly significant. At the top of the diagram, we find the *Zohar*'s answer to the problem of Creation—how something finite came from the Infinite. The answer is that this did not happen all at once, but through a kind of divine chain reaction in which each stage moves closer to perceptible reality. God as *En Sof* is beyond the scope of the *sefirot*, since nothing at all determinate can be said about it. But Keter, the first *sefirah*, represents the divine will that first manifests itself as a drive toward Creation; it is almost as indescribable as *En Sof,* but it initiates the process of emanation that will lead to our world. The *Zohar* describes this beginning in a poetic rhapsody:

> At the very beginning the king made engravings in the supernal purity. A spark of blackness emerged in the sealed within the sealed, from the mystery of En Sof, a mist within matter, implanted in a ring, no white, no black, no red, no yellow, no color at all. . . . Within the spark, in the innermost part, emerged a source, from which the colors are painted below, and it is sealed among the sealed things of the mystery of En Sof. It penetrated, but did not penetrate, its air; it was not known at all, until from the pressure of its penetration a single point shone, sealed, supernal. Beyond this point nothing is known, and so it is called "beginning": the first word of all.

This is the mystic language of paradox, which cancels itself out in the attempt to grasp the ungraspable. The revelation of the Infinite in material form takes the form of a black spark, a colorless color, that penetrates and does not penetrate. The point made by this spark is the second *sefirah*—Hokhmah, the divine Thought—which is then unfolded into Binah, the source from which the universe flows. In another metaphor, Binah is the womb that is fertilized by Hokhmah in order to give birth to Creation. If the process the *Zohar* describes here is hard to visualize, if the distinctions among the *sefirot* seem elusive, that is because it is trying to describe the very thing that Maimonides said was indescribable: the transition between God's ultimate otherness and knowable reality. (No wonder the *Zohar*'s language of points and sparks seems to anticipate our own current favorite metaphor for Creation, the Big Bang.) In the attempt to capture this process, the *Zohar* often becomes exotically florid, multiplying numbers and images in an attempt to bring form to the formless:

> It is taught: Hokhmah broke out along its paths and brought a wind to the sea, and the waters were gathered into one place, and the fifty gates of Binah were opened. From these paths ten crowns emerged with shining rays, and twenty-two paths remained. The wind burst out down these paths, and the fifty gates of Binah were opened, and twenty-two [letters] were engraved on the fifty gates of the Jubilee, and were crowned with the seventy-two letters of the holy name.

Despite all these esoteric images, however, the top of the sefirotic tree, the unfolding of Keter into Hokhmah and then Binah, lies essentially beyond the scope of human knowledge. It is with the next stage of the *sefirot*—the sixfold figure with Tiferet at its center—that we reach the aspect of God with whom we have some kind of relationship, the God of the Bible to whom we pray. (Another name for Tiferet is "the Blessed Holy One.") And here a second polarity comes into play: the top-down movement of Creation is cut across by the right-left opposition between Hesed, the force of God's love, and Din, the force of his judgment.

Din, which is also known as Gevurah (Power), is the face of God that deals harshly with humanity, issuing laws and punishing misdeeds; it is the opposite of Love, which is God as pure benevolence. Both of these powers must exist if the world is to be governed, which is why Din and Hesed find their balance in Tiferet, which is also known as Rachamim (Mercy). To use one of the many biblical analogies in the *Zohar,* Hesed is Abraham, the first man to love God, and Din is Isaac, who feared God when he was offered up as a sacrifice; but

Tiferet is Jacob, the perfect man, the synthesis in which opposites are transcended.

And here we encounter the first fracture in the sefirotic system. Judgment, which is represented as God's left hand or left side, is not always content to stay under the guidance of Mercy. It yearns to break loose, to manifest itself as terrifying, uncontrolled, violent power. When this happens, Judgment becomes what the *Zohar* calls "the other side," the force of evil in the world, from which demons and wicked spirits take their strength. In this way, the *Zohar* proposes its own theodicy—an explanation for how a good God could allow evil to exist in the world. Evil, in this view, is what happens when one of God's attributes runs wild; it is not an entity or force in its own right, but the product of an internal imbalance among God's powers. "One came out of the other," the *Zohar* says, "for from goodness evil emerged, and from Mercy Judgment emerged, and one was entirely contained in the other."

The metaphorical imagination that is so fertile throughout the *Zohar* is especially vivid when it comes to creating myths and images to describe "the other side." If asked, most Jews today would probably say that Judaism does not believe in Hell or in demons or devils—that these mythical entities can find no place in a monotheistic religion. But the *Zohar*, which helped shape the religious lives of Jews for centuries, definitely does not share this view. It speaks vividly about Samael and Lilith, the king and queen of the demons, who roam the world preying on human souls. Lilith, in particular, is cast as a temptress who uses sex to lure men into sin: "This is the finery that she uses to seduce mankind: her hair is long, red like a lily; her face is white and pink; six pendants hang at her ears; her bed is made of Egyptian flax; all the ornaments of the East encircle her neck." But after a man has given in to Lilith and had sex with her, she reveals her true appearance as "a fierce warrior, facing him in a garment of flaming fire, a vision of dread, terrifying both body and soul, full of horrific eyes, a sharpened sword in his hand with drops of poison suspended from it."

A less dramatic, but still more important, kabbalistic image for the evil forces in the world is the *kelipot*, the "shells" or "husks." The shells are the obstructions that enclose and hide the kernel of divinity in the universe; they are synonymous with the powers of "the other side." At times, the *Zohar* speaks of the shells as if they, like Judgment, have a necessary place in the divine economy: "It was necessary for the Holy One, blessed be He, to create everything in the world, and to order the world therewith. All consists of an inner kernel, with several shells covering the kernel.... Everything is constructed according to this pattern here below, so that mortal man is in this image in this world: kernel and shell, spirit and body, and all is for the well-ordering of the world." But if the shells protect the divine, they also conceal it and obstruct our access to it. In another passage, the shells are identified with the four terrible forces seen by the prophet Ezekiel in his vision, "a stormy wind ... a great cloud, with flashing fire, and brightness around it."

The universe the *Zohar* describes is one in which evil is constantly threatening to break loose, making the moral life of mankind a dramatic confrontation with demonic powers. This dualism is mapped in complex ways onto Jewish rituals, laws, and institutions, which are deeply concerned with separation between the holy and the profane, the permitted and the forbidden. The Land of Israel, to take one example, is metaphysically separated from the rest of the planet, in a way Yehuda Halevi would have approved, because it alone is exempt from the rule of the husks, the evil powers that dominate most of the Earth.

"In the Holy Land everything is arranged in a different manner," the *Zohar* explains, "for the hard shell is broken in that place and has no dominion over it at all." Even with the Jewish people in exile, the shells still cannot control the Holy Land, because God covered it with "a holy covering, a thin curtain, to protect that place, so that the hard shell should not seal it." This "thin curtain" serves a double function, according to the *Zohar*. On the one hand, it prevents the sacred influence from raining down on the Land of Israel as it did when the

Temple stood. At the same time, however, it is a permeable membrane, which the souls of Jews who die in the Land are able to pass through on their way to Heaven. Dying in the Holy Land therefore offers an immediate route to God, whereas Jews who die in the rest of the world—where the hard shell reigns supreme—are condemned to see their souls "journey and wander and transmigrate."

The distinction between the sabbath and the days of the week is equally loaded with metaphysical meaning. Weekdays are the domain of strict judgment, Din, while on the sabbath "all judgments are suppressed, and pleasure and joy abound everywhere." Celebrating the day with three rich meals is not simply a treat after a long work week, but a divine commandment whose neglect causes a direct injury to God: "It is through these meals that Israel are recognized as sons of the King. . . . If a man impairs just one meal he causes a defect to appear in the world above." This feasting is also a way of providing sustenance for the extra soul with which all Jews are endowed on the sabbath: "because of the additional soul they forget all pain and anger and there is nothing but joy in both the upper and the lower worlds." No wonder the *Zohar* holds the sabbath alone to be equal in worth to the whole Torah.

THE OPPOSITION BETWEEN right and left, the holy and "the other side," Love and Judgment, is one of the primary fractures in our world. The other polarity that the sefirotic tree helps to illustrate is the one between Tiferet, the most important divine attribute, and Malkhut, the lowest *sefirah*. These two *sefirot* are aligned along the central axis of the tree and are connected by Yesod, which comes between them. When the divine realm is in proper harmony, God's influence descends to the world through this chain until it reaches Malkhut, which in turn passes on the divine blessing to our world. In this aspect, Malkhut is known as the Shekhinah, the divine presence that dwells with the people of Israel and protects them in their journey through history; one synonym for the Shekhinah is "the assembly of Israel." The Shekhinah is the key mediator between the *sefirot* as a whole and the world below, which is our world. (Although, to be precise, the *Zohar* posits several layers of reality between the *sefirot* and our world, filled with angels and other supernatural beings.)

The *Zohar* offers many metaphors for the descent of God's influence through the *sefirot*. It is figured as rain pouring down, as the distribution of food, as a river watering a garden: "Just as a fountain or a water source fills a mighty stream, and from thence sources of rivers extend and flow on every side, so here . . . these are the holy, supernal rivers of pure balsam." One important image sees Keter, the first *sefirah*, as the head of "the Ancient Holy One," a white-haired old man whose beard drips sacred oil: "The oil flows in the head of the king, and from his head to the splendor of the sacred beard, and from there it flows into all the precious garments with which the king clothes himself." Elsewhere, the *Zohar* scrutinizes the natural world for a sign of the relationship between Tiferet and Malkhut and finds it in the image of a candle's flame: "In the rising flame there are two lights: one is a radiant white light, and one is a light that contains black or blue. The white light is above, and ascends in a direct line, and beneath it is the blue or black light, which is a throne for white, and the white light rests upon it." In this simile, the white light represents Tiferet, which rests upon the black light, Malkhut.

But the most important metaphor of all is the most unexpected: sexual intercourse. The union of Tiferet, the male principle in the Godhead, with Malkhut, the female principle, takes place by means of Yesod, which descends from Tiferet in the manner of a phallus. Indeed, the whole upper nine *sefirot* can be seen, in the classic diagram, as a sketch of the human body, with the three top *sefirot* as the head, Din and Hesed as the left and right arms, and Yesod as the penis. In this configuration, the *sefirot* represent the primal man, known as *Adam Kadmon*, and so human beings can be said quite literally to have been created in the image of God. Again, the contrast between the *Zohar* and Maimonides is explicit: the kabbalists affirm the physical likeness of man and his Creator, which the *Guide of the Perplexed* goes to such lengths to deny.

According to this way of looking at the *sefirot*, the divine essence is transmitted from Tiferet to Malkhut in the same way that semen is transmitted from the male to the womb of the female. Such kabbalistic eroticism is absolutely pervasive in the *Zohar*, and it depends on elevating the Shekhinah into a kind of female God or divine principle. (Some scholars speculate that the introduction of a feminine divinity into Judaism was influenced by the cult of the Virgin Mary, which the Jews of Provence and Christian Spain would have encountered on every side.) To Scholem, it was this feminization of the divine that accounted for the tremendous popular success of Kabbalah among the Jews: "The introduction of this idea was one of the most important and lasting innovations of kabbalism. The fact that it obtained recognition in spite of the obvious difficulty of reconciling it with the conception of the absolute unity of God, and that no other element of kabbalism won such a degree of popular approval, is proof that it responded to a deep-seated religious need."

When Tiferet and Malkhut are joined as man and wife, then the sefirotic sphere is in harmony and the world is blessed: "And when he is aroused by her, how many are they that stand on every side in order to be refreshed and blessed from there. . . . Then she ascends into the mystery of mysteries, as is fitting, and receives pleasure from her husband, as is proper. . . . And after she has received pleasure from her husband they are all refreshed and nourished." But unfortunately for mankind, this union is not continual. When Adam ate the fruit of the Tree of Knowledge, he separated the Shekhinah from Tiferet; the destruction of the Temple compounded this rupture. In the *Zohar*, the Shekhinah is compared to the moon, which receives illumination from the sun, Tiferet. But just as the moon goes through phases of darkness, so the Shekhinah is sometimes severed from the source of radiance: "But once the Temple was destroyed the light darkened, and the moon was not illuminated by the sun." And when the holy spouses are divorced in this manner, the Earth is plunged into darkness, Israel goes into exile, and the powers of "the other side" rule. In one passage, the disorder of the universe is traced directly to a dysfunctional sexual relationship between the two aspects of God:

> Come and see. When the Holy One, blessed be He, is with the Assembly of Israel [that is, the Shekhinah], on those occasions when He is with her, and she arouses delight in Him first and draws Him to her with great love and desire, then she is filled from the right side [the side of Hesed], and there exist large crowds on the right side. But when the Holy One, blessed be He, arouses love and delight first, and she is aroused afterward, and not at the same time that He is aroused, then all is on the female side, and the left is aroused [the side of Din], and large crowds exist and are aroused on the left side throughout all the worlds.

So far, it might seem as if the fate of the world is subject to an arbitrary and almost mythological process. In Greek mythology, feuds between the gods are occasions for disasters to mankind; are Tiferet and the Shekhinah no more than the equivalent of Jupiter and Hera, quarreling spouses who inflict collateral damage on our world? There is, undoubtedly, a strong element of mythology in the *Zohar* that verges at times on polytheism. The very idea of a God made up of ten *sefirot* seems hard to reconcile with the traditional Jewish insistence on the unity of God.

Yet the *Zohar* insists that it is possible to unify the *sefirot* into a single whole, to restore the intimacy between Tiferet and Malkhut. Indeed, nothing less than this is the mission of the Jewish people on earth. Judaism, properly understood, is not just an arbitrary set of commandments and prohibitions, but a technology for bringing God into harmony with himself. The *Zohar* brought to Judaism something that the austere philosophy of the Middle Ages lacked: the sense that God needs man as much as man needs God. Why, Rabbi Eleazar asks at one point, are souls sent down to be born in this world, when God knows that human beings are inevitably going to die? "What need has He of them?" The answer is that only human goodness allows the divine influence to flow through the *sefirot* into the world:

> A cistern is a place where water does not flow of its own accord. When then does the water flow? When the soul is perfected in this world, when it ascends to the place to which it is linked, then it is perfect on all sides, both above and below. And when the soul ascends, the desire of the female is aroused for the male, and then water flows upward from below, and the cistern becomes a well of living water.

Perhaps the most important religious teaching of the *Zohar*, reiterated again and again, is that the upper world, with all its esoteric activity, is an image of the lower world, and vice versa: "When the Holy One, blessed be He, created the world He constructed the lower world on the pattern of the upper world. One parallels the other in everything, and this is His glory both above and below." We have already seen that the human form parallels *Adam Kadmon*, the flow of rivers and the flame of a candle parallel the sefirotic relationships, and human sexual intercourse parallels the divine union. The left side of God is the female and the right side is the male; night is the realm of "the other side," day the realm of life. Even the Milky Way, the *Zohar* says, is actually "the snake of the firmament," set there to remind us of "the supernal, primordial snake by whom Adam was seduced" in the Garden of Eden. The world of the *Zohar* is full and overfull of meaning, a vast dictionary of symbols in which we read the truth about God. Indeed, the world was created for no other purpose than man's enlightenment: "everything that the Holy One, blessed be He, made on earth was made with the mystery of wisdom, and it is all to demonstrate supernal wisdom to mankind, so that they might learn the mysteries of wisdom from what is made."

It is because Creation is so intimately linked to God, "the lower world" to "the upper world," that what happens below can affect what happens above: "When a man provides this stimulus below, it is as if he makes the holy name in complete perfection. Whatever he does below stimulates the world above." Consider the central Zoharic mystery of sex. The union of man and woman in lawful sexual intercourse is a cosmic duty, since erotic union on earth stimulates erotic union within the Godhead: "Whoever refuses to procreate diminishes, as it were, the image that comprises all images, stops the waters of the river from flowing, and damages the holy covenant on all sides." It is especially meritorious for a Torah scholar—one of the mystic initiates the *Zohar* calls "the companions"—to have sex with his wife on the sabbath, because this is the time when Tiferet and Malkhut are united in the sefirotic realm: "Because of this the companions have intercourse only when men cease from their work, and the Holy One, blessed be He, begins His work. And what is His work? Intercourse with the consort, in order to produce holy souls for the world, and therefore on this night the companions sanctify themselves with the sanctity of their Creator and direct their minds and fine children are produced."

In this sense, one might say that the *Zohar* is the most remarkably sex-positive document Judaism ever produced. Certainly it is far from Maimonides's notion that sex is like transporting dung, something undignified that should be taken care of in secret. Yet at the same time, precisely because sex is so important, the *Zohar* insists that it be done the right way: "One should not act licentiously or obscenely, or with whorish intention like animals." This means that a man—and of course, all the *Zohar*'s imagined readers are men—must not think about another woman while having sex with his wife: "If a man defiles himself by evil thoughts when he comes to have intercourse with his wife, and sets his thoughts and desire upon another woman, and emits semen with these evil thoughts, then he exchanges the exalted levels of the world above, the level of holiness, for the level of uncleanness." Moreover, a man must attend to his wife's sexual satisfaction: "When he is with her he should give her joy for two reasons. First, because the joy of intercourse is the joy of [fulfilling] a commandment, and the joy of a commandment is the joy of the Shekhinah."

These principles are designed to foster conjugal intimacy. In contrast, the *Zohar* treats sex outside the permitted boundaries as an extremely grave sin. "There are three acts that drive the Shekhinah away from the world and prevent the Holy One, blessed be He, from dwelling in the world," and all of them are related to sex. The first is having sex with a woman while she is menstruating, a traditional Jewish taboo that the *Zohar* emphasizes: "there is no defilement in the world greater than that of menstruation." The second is for a Jewish man to have sex with a Gentile woman. Because the circumcised penis is related to the *sefirah* Yesod, it has a sacred status—the *Zohar* calls it "the holy covenant" and "the covenant of the holy name"—and it must not be "introduced . . . into a foreign domain." (The *Zohar*'s need to emphasize this prohibition makes one wonder about the prevalence of such "mixed" relationships in medieval Spain.) Finally, the *Zohar* is extremely opposed to abortion. Because it understands birth as summoning a pre-existent soul into a newly created body, the *Zohar* sees abortion as not just murder, but the destruction of God's handiwork: "Such a man destroys the work and skill of the Holy One, blessed be He."

Sex, however, is just one of the realms of Jewish life with which the *Zohar* is concerned. Equally important is prayer, an activity that the *Zohar* endows with urgent metaphysical purpose. Here again, the contrast with Maimonides is stark: while the philosopher saw prayer as more or less a sop thrown to human weakness, the kabbalists saw it as a tool for rectifying the imbalance in the divine sphere. Here the *Zohar* introduces the important concept of *kavanah*, intention or concentration in prayer. When recited with the correct mystical intention, Jewish prayers effect a repair, or *tikkun*, in the sefirotic system. (This mystic purpose is far from the present-day meaning of the phrase *tikkun olam*, "repair of the world," which American Jews often use to refer to working for social justice.)

"In the benedictions with which man blesses the Holy One, blessed be He, his purpose is to draw out life from the source of life for the holy name of the Holy One, blessed be He, and to cause some of the supernal oil to pour over it," the *Zohar* explains, using one of its favorite metaphors for the divine influence. "These blessings are drawn out by man, through words, from the supernal source, and all the levels and sources are blessed." This does not mean that Jews should pray spontaneously from the heart, ignoring the fixed forms of the prayerbook; but it does mean that the traditional blessings should be recited with deliberate mystic purpose. God's presence, in another Zoharic image, is like a gazelle that threatens to run away from the worshipper: "Consequently we need to take hold of the Holy One, blessed be He, and restrain Him . . . so that man should not be forsaken by Him even for an hour." The idea that prayer can coerce God—not to grant favors, but to remain in the worshipper's presence—is a striking testimony to the active agency that the *Zohar* allows to the individual Jew.

Similar mystical justifications are provided for many Jewish practices. As we have seen, many Jewish thinkers had expressed their bafflement or discomfort with the more arbitrary commandments by trying to find some reasonable explanation for them. The *Zohar* inverts this procedure: it too has justifications for the *mitzvot*, but these are not rational explanations, they are mystical explanations. Take circumcision, which for Philo and Maimonides had the symbolic purpose of chastening the sexual appetites. In the *Zohar*, by contrast, it is explained as a kind of sympathetic magic that has the power to save the universe: "The blood that comes from the child is preserved before the Holy One, blessed be He. And when judgments are aroused in the world, the Holy One, blessed be He, looks at the blood, and saves the world. . . . It is because of this blood that the world is perfumed with Love and all the worlds survive."

It is not only the world above that benefits from pious Jewish practice, however. The human soul, too, is one of the mysteries that the book seeks to explain, and it teaches that this soul benefits from righteousness, prayer, and Torah study. Every human being, the *Zohar* teaches, is actually composed of three souls, each of which is given a different Hebrew name. The *nefesh*, the animal spirit that every living thing possesses, enters the human being at birth and is destroyed at death. But the higher souls—the *ruach* and the crowning spirit, *neshamah*—have to be earned through merit: "Whoever studies my Torah and observes it will receive from me the *neshamah* that is hewn from My Throne and that gives life to those who possess it." It follows from this principle that only Jews, who follow God's commandments, are able to earn a *neshamah*; other peoples must be content with a mere *nefesh*. In this way, the *Zohar* endows the Jews, the most powerless of nations in a worldly sense, with a metaphysical guarantee of their significance.

Indeed, every individual soul, in the *Zohar*'s interpretation, has a role to play in the cosmos: "The souls of all mankind ... before they came down into the world, were engraved before Him in the firmament, in the precise form that they were to assume in this world." God's throne is a vast storehouse of souls in which the spirit of everyone who will ever be born resides, waiting to be called and put into a body. The souls themselves are created by the divine intercourse of Tiferet and Malkhut, and the labor pains of Malkhut, the Shekhinah, are described in the *Zohar* in bizarrely mythological terms. Taking inspiration from an image from Psalms, the Shekhinah is described as a hart, and when it is time for her to deliver a soul, she is bitten on the genitals by a snake, which creates an opening and allows the soul to emerge.

Once the soul is prepared to descend into a body, the *Zohar* imagines it taking an oath before God, promising to "study the Torah, to gain a knowledge of Him and the mystery of faith. For whoever lives in this world and does not strive to gain a knowledge of Him," the *Zohar* warns, "it were better for him not to have been created." This imperative, to gain knowledge of God, had always been at the heart of Judaism. What distinguishes the different tendencies of Jewish thought, and the books that represent them, is the very different ways they define that knowledge. For the rabbis of *Pirkei Avot*, ethical behavior and Torah study were the route to God; for the rebels Josephus wrote about, it was armed struggle for God's sovereignty; for Maimonides, it was intellectual contemplation. The *Zohar*, however, outdoes them all in the radical strangeness and urgency of its prescriptions. It enchants the universe like no other Jewish book, plunging the Jew into the middle of a supernatural drama in which his own actions and intentions influence the fate of the universe. For Spanish Jews whose brilliant culture was soon to go into eclipse, leading finally to their expulsion from their homeland, this assurance of their cosmic centrality was perhaps the most important lesson of the *Zohar*.

BIBLIOGRAPHY

Green, Arthur. *A Guide to the Zohar*. Palo Alto, CA: Stanford University Press, 2004.

Scholem, Gershom. *Major Trends in Jewish Mysticism*. New York: Schocken, 1946.

Tishby, Isaiah, ed. *The Wisdom of the Zohar*. Translated by David Goldstein. 3 vols. Portland, OR: Littman Library of Jewish Civilization, 1989.

The Zohar. Translated by Harry Sperling and Maurice Simon. 5 vols. London: Soncino Press, 1984.

9

DAUGHTERS OF ZION

The *Tsenerene* and the *Memoirs*
of Glückel of Hameln

*Bertha Pappenheim, the descendant
and translator of Glückel of Hameln,
dressed as Glückel for a portrait*

Though women have always played a central role in the practice of Judaism, their voices are almost never heard in classic Jewish literature. Scholarly and philosophical writing was, until the twentieth century, the exclusive province of a male elite; even the Bible was unavailable to most women, since they did not learn Hebrew. For eastern European Jewish women, the book that gave them access to Judaism's foundational stories was the *Tsenerene*, a Yiddish retelling of the Torah. Incorporating traditional commentaries, myths, worldly advice, and lessons in female virtue, the *Tsenerene* was for centuries the book that did most to shape Jewish women's lives. One such woman, Glückel of Hameln, lived in Germany in the seventeenth century, where she raised a large family and ran a business. Her *Memoirs*, originally written for her children, are the best record we have of what it meant to be a Jewish woman in her time and place.

THE *ZOHAR* BUILT ITS THEOLOGY ON THE IDEA THAT God was feminine as well as masculine. Yet its own readership—like that of most classic Jewish texts—remained strictly limited to men. Indeed, only married men past the age of forty were supposed to be initiated into the *Zohar*'s mysteries, since they would presumably be pious and settled enough not to be shocked into heresy by its secrets. In any case, to read the *Zohar* or to study the Talmud—the text at the heart of traditional Jewish education—required a knowledge of Aramaic, which only some men and almost no women possessed. Even Hebrew, the language of the Bible, was not part of a Jewish woman's education. Women played a central role in the practice of Judaism, since they were responsible for observing all the laws of the home, from keeping the sabbath to cooking kosher food to obeying the rules of *niddah*, sexual purity related to the menstrual cycle. But how could they participate in Judaism's textual heritage, which did so much to define men's experience of their religion?

For Jewish women living in Germany and eastern Europe, the answer had to involve Yiddish. Yiddish emerged along with the earliest Jewish settlement in western Germany and eastern France, around the tenth century CE, fusing German with Hebrew to create a new, distinctively Jewish language. As Ashkenazi Jews—whose name comes from the traditional Hebrew name for Germany, *Ashkenaz*—migrated to eastern Europe, they took Yiddish with them. Hebrew remained the Jews' holy tongue, which boys learned at school so they could read the Bible, and it remained the language of international scholarly discourse. But Yiddish was the *mama-loshn*, the mother tongue, which all Jews learned growing up and in which the business of ordinary life was conducted. This meant that if a text was to reach women—and a large proportion of men, too, who were not educated enough to read Hebrew on their own—it had to be written in Yiddish.

The spread of the printing press in the sixteenth century transformed Jewish book culture no less than its Christian counterpart. A new market for Yiddish books opened up, composed largely of female readers, which publishers hurried to satisfy—often by publishing translations of secular romances. But the book that did most to connect Jewish women to Judaism's traditional sources was the *Tsenerene*, which became such a standard text that it is sometimes referred to as "the Yiddish Women's Bible." First published in the 1590s, the *Tsenerene* would go through more than two hundred editions, making it one of the most popular Yiddish books of all time. Few Ashkenazi Jewish households were without a copy.

The book's title gives a hint as to its intended female audience. *Tsenerene* is the Yiddishized pronunciation of the Hebrew words *Tz'enah ur'enah*, "Come out and see," which are quoted from a verse in the Song of Songs: "Come out and see King Solomon, O daughters of Zion." In choosing this phrase, the book's author—Joseph ben Isaac

Ashkenazi, from Janov in Poland—signaled that he was writing primarily for women. Yet the title page of the 1622 edition states that the *Tsenerene* was written "in order to enable men and women to find a balm for their souls, and to understand the words of the Living God in simple language." Any Jew who could not read the Bible in Hebrew could approach it through the humble Yiddish of the *Tsenerene*, and many Jewish children would have first absorbed the Bible's stories through their mothers' reading aloud from its pages.

The *Tsenerene*, however, is not simply a translation of the Bible; if it were, it might never have become so popular. What Joseph ben Isaac Ashkenazi produced, instead, was a free paraphrase and interpretation of the Five Books of Moses, drawing on a wide range of sources to give the reader a sense of how Jewish tradition understood the text. The *Tsenerene* is divided into the weekly Torah portions read aloud in the synagogue, with the accompanying readings from other parts of the Bible known as the *haftorah*. This allowed the reader to keep up with the community's Torah reading, which otherwise she might not be able to understand. For each portion, the *Tsenerene* offers a verse-by-verse commentary and interpretation of the kind known as midrash—an imaginative expansion on the biblical text. The book regularly quotes the Talmud, other classic rabbinic sources, and later commentators like Rashi and Nachmanides—the kind of authorities that young men would learn as part of their advanced education. Reading it, we are hearing not just the ideas of Jacob ben Isaac Ashkenazi, but the accumulated wisdom of the sages dating back more than a thousand years. By translating all of this into Yiddish, the *Tsenerene* opens up the world of textual interpretation to the common reader, male and female. Today, when traditional Jewish ways of reading the Bible are completely unknown to many Jews, the *Tsenerene*—still in print after four hundred years, under the English title *The Weekly Midrash*—continues to be an ideal introduction.

THE BIBLE IS A BOOK of stories, not a book of moral lessons, and it is not shy about presenting even the most venerable figures in an ambiguous light. When Abraham pretends that Sarah is his sister, encouraging Pharaoh to try to seduce her, or when Jacob tricks his brother Esau out of his birthright, they do not exactly seem like role models. This willingness to portray the patriarchs and matriarchs of Judaism realistically, with their own weaknesses and failures, is one reason why the Bible stories remain so vital and pertinent after thousands of years.

The *Tsenerene,* however, has no use for this kind of narrative ambiguity. It is a didactic book whose goal is to draw useful moral lessons from the biblical text. Indeed, like *Pirkei Avot,* it advances a whole ethical worldview, presenting definite views about what makes a good person and a good Jew. But where *Pirkei Avot* is devoted to rabbis and Torah scholars, and places Torah study at the center of its vision of the ideal Jewish life, the practical ethics of the *Tsenerene* are meant for a wider audience. In its pages, the Bible is harvested for maxims that will prove useful to husbands and wives, fathers and mothers, businessmen and homemakers. It makes the connection, which often seems elusive, between the characters in the Bible and the needs of the common Jewish reader.

In keeping with its intended audience, the *Tsenerene* is especially interested in using the Bible's female characters to model feminine virtues. The lives of the matriarchs and of figures like Eve and Miriam demonstrate the qualities that Jewish tradition honors and seeks to inculcate in women: piety and charity, humility and obedience. At the same time, however, the *Tsenerene* acknowledges that the Bible's treatment of its female characters is often sternly judgmental. We are meant to learn not just from the matriarchs' virtues but also from their faults and failures. This presents the *Tsenerene* with a rhetorical problem: how to write about women, for women, while still acknowledging the many moments in which the Bible seems to hold women in low regard.

This dilemma is never more acute than right at the beginning of Genesis, with the story of Adam and Eve. God created woman by putting Adam to sleep and taking a rib from his side, which was then fashioned into Eve. What is this episode supposed to teach us about the proper relationship between man and woman? We might suppose that it says something about the primacy of man, relegating woman to a secondary, even servile position. But that is not the way the *Tsenerene* reads the story. Rather, the first moral lesson it derives from the creation of Eve is one binding on husbands: "God made Adam sleep to teach us that a man should not constantly fight with his wife. If he sees that she does something which displeases him, he should pretend that he does not see it and 'sleep' through it." The sleeping Adam becomes the model husband, one who does not monitor his wife's behavior too closely but knows when to shut his eyes.

The *Tsenerene* takes seriously God's rationale for creating woman: to be a helpmate for man. But here, too, it manages to interpret the text in a way that does not relegate the wife to being merely her husband's assistant. Rather, a wife's moral character is seen as determining her husband's character and thereby his fate; the woman sets the moral direction for her family. As it frequently does, the *Tsenerene* makes its point with a fable: "There is a story of a righteous man who had a wife who was a very good woman. They had no children, so they divorced. She then married an evil man and made him righteous, and he married an evil woman who turned him evil."

In this story, men are the raw material, morally speaking, and their wives have the power to shape them for good or ill. This means that men need marriage more than women do. "A man seeks a wife: a woman does not seek a husband," the book continues. This is not because men are active and women passive, or because women must preserve their chastity at all costs. Rather, it is because women are more self-sufficient than men: "Woman was taken from man, and so he searches for her. But the woman has not lost anything and therefore need not search." A similar lesson can be drawn from the fact that Adam was created from the dust of the earth, while Eve was created from Adam's rib: "A woman is strong by nature because she was created from a bone, and a man is weak for he was created from the earth, and dissolves quickly." Likewise, "women have sweet voices, because they were created from a bone. Strike one bone against another and it tinkles and echoes, but if you strike earth against earth it makes no such sound."

When it comes to the story of Eve and the serpent, the *Tsenerene* faces a bigger hurdle. Here, at the start of the Jewish tradition, is a story that seems to blame woman for the introduction of sin and death into the world. How can women's honor be redeemed in a way that still remains faithful to the text of Genesis? What explanation can we find for Eve's violation of God's simple command not to eat the fruit of the Tree of Knowledge? In fact, the *Tsenerene* can find several. Perhaps "according to her understanding, the woman did not lie: she simply misunderstood." Eve thought that the fruit of the Tree was forbidden only when it was still on the branch "in the center of the garden," as God had described it, but that fallen fruit was permitted to eat. Or perhaps her mistake was thinking that God had forbidden her from even touching the fruit, so that when she touched a piece and nothing bad happened, she assumed that the ban was an empty threat.

Still, the *Tsenerene* cannot gainsay the fact that Eve sinned. Does it follow, however, that she was more to blame for eating the fruit than Adam was? The Bible story puts the blame on the woman for giving the man the fruit to eat: "God asked Adam why he had eaten from the fruit, and Adam answered that his wife had given it to him." To which the *Tsenerene* adds, impatiently, "What kind of answer is that? If his wife had given it to him, did that make him guiltless? God Himself had forbidden the fruit to him. . . . Was Adam so stupid that he listened to his wife after God had forbidden him to eat?" At least let Adam bear his own sin, rather than forcing Eve to be responsible for both of them.

And perhaps Eve had some reason for making Adam share her sin, other than simple wickedness. After all, God created Eve to be Adam's wife and commanded them to be fruitful and multiply. But this would be impossible if they had no sexual desires, and it was not until eating the fruit of the Tree of Knowledge that desire appeared. "My wife," Adam explains, "therefore gave me the fruit so that I would desire her." In a roundabout way, Eve was simply trying to follow God's command, to create the necessary conditions for the human race to exist. Alternatively, the *Tsenerene* ventures, once she had eaten the fruit and knew she would die, she gave Adam the fruit because she couldn't bear the thought of him outliving her: "She thought to herself that if she would die, let her husband die too and not take another woman as a wife." On this explanation, it was love, rather than wickedness, that made Eve ensnare Adam.

Even if you grant that Eve sinned, however, there is something unfair and excessive about the idea that all women should share her punishment. "Not all men suffer from the curse of Adam," the *Tsenerene* observes: not every man has to sweat for his bread, since some are rich and live at leisure. But "all women, rich or poor, are cursed" to give birth in pain, and in fact, "rich women suffer more in childbirth and pregnancy" because their bodies are weaker and unused to travail. This represents a kind of divine mercy toward the poor and hardworking: "Women who are forced to work have easier pregnancies because God pities them."

But is it fair that all women should suffer, to the end of time, because of Eve's mistake? "If Eve had not eaten from the Tree every woman would have given birth easily, much like a hen, which lays its eggs painlessly." The *Tsenerene* offers the formula for a prayer that protests this injustice: "Master of the Universe, because Eve ate of the Tree of Knowledge, must we women all give birth in deathly pain? If I had been there I would have had no enjoyment from the fruit." In this way, a Jewish woman disclaims the notion of original sin and demands to be judged on her own actions and merits. She refuses to share responsibility for Eve's misdeed, which she is able to recognize as wrong.

By the time the *Tsenerene* finishes its extensive interpretation of the Adam and Eve story, the implications of that story have become significantly more friendly to women. The primacy of husbands over their wives is, of course, upheld, but in a complex way that allows for mutuality, equal dignity, and affection. "Another kindness which God shows is that although woman is cursed in that she must obey her husband as a servant obeys his master, still she does not dislike him. God has made her love her husband, despite the fact that he rules over her," the book concludes. Marriage is not an equal relationship, but it is one informed by love, and that lessens the sting of subordination. Still, subordination is a curse, and the *Tsenerene*'s willingness to say so may explain why women readers placed so much trust in it as a guide to scripture and to life.

The next woman to emerge into the spotlight of the biblical narrative is Sarah, the wife of Abraham. In chapter 12, we read of the highly irregular episode in which Abraham, traveling with Sarah in Egypt, tells her to pretend to be his sister, lest Pharaoh have him killed so that he can lay claim to her. To justify himself, Abraham says, "Behold now, I know you are a beautiful woman to look upon"—that is why she is at risk of attracting Pharaoh's attention. The midrashic method of interpretation, however, does not always read the biblical text in its narrative context. Rather, it isolates individual words and uses them to anchor new chains of interpretation. This results in readings that sometimes feel strained or sheerly invented to the modern reader. But if you assume that God placed each word in the Bible for a specific reason, then this focus on the implications of every word begins to make more sense.

Thus the *Tsenerene* seizes on the word "now" in Abraham's speech. Why does he say, "Behold now, you are a beautiful woman"? The reason, we learn, is that only "now" has he realized what Sarah looks like: "Abram and Sarai were modest, and Abram had never seen Sarai's skin uncovered. But as they traveled over water, Sarai was forced to lift the hem of her dress. Abram then said, 'Now I know that you are beautiful.'" This interpretation is really an imaginative extension of the Bible story, adding new details and episodes that are nowhere to be found in the text; but this midrashic technique is seen as revealing the full truth of the text rather than embellishing it. In this case, it is used to draw a lesson about feminine modesty. If Sarah kept her entire body covered at all times, even in front of her husband, then the ordinary Jewish woman can learn from her to practice modesty in dress.

Later, we are told that Sarah's virtue was rewarded by various miracles that go unmentioned in the biblical text. "Our Sages say that during Sarah's lifetime her candles burned from one Shabbat eve to the next; the dough she kneaded was blessed; and a cloud hovered over her tent." These signs bring the matriarch close to the latter-day Jewish woman reader, whose ritual responsibilities were the same—lighting candles on Friday evening and preparing the dough for bread. Further, though she lived to be one hundred and twenty-seven years old, "Sarah had no need of cosmetics. She was as lovely at twenty years as a young girl of seven." The greatest blessing in Sarah's life, however, was becoming a mother to Isaac, when she was already so old that childbearing seemed impossible. This is one of the major themes of the Genesis story, but the *Tsenerene* underscores it by quoting a rabbinic interpretation that depends on *gematria*—the assigning of numerical values to Hebrew letters and words. The word for "was" in the verse "The life of Sarah was one hundred and twenty-seven years" has the numerical value of thirty-seven; from this we learn that "Sarah actually lived a real life for only thirty-seven years, from the time of Isaac's birth until the sacrifice, when he was thirty-seven years old. The years before his birth were not considered true life, for a person who is childless is compared to the dead."

If motherhood is the defining achievement of a woman's life, the *Tsenerene* suggests, matchmaking—finding a mate for herself and, later, for her children—is its central drama. Thus the book makes much of the story of Eliezer, Abraham's servant, who goes to find a wife for Isaac and meets the virtuous Rebecca. The retelling of this episode is full of practical advice about matchmaking, using the Bible story to state Jewish folk wisdom on the subject. For instance, when Abraham insists on finding his son a wife from his own family back in Mesopotamia, rather than from among the "daughters of Canaan," the *Tsenerene* says this has less to do with avoiding idol-worshippers than with domestic harmony: "When a man takes a wife from his own family there is peace between them for one cannot taunt the other with a lack of family prestige."

When Eliezer arrives in Mesopotamia, he declares that he will wait by a well for a woman to approach; if she charitably offers to water his camels, he will know she is a fitting match for Isaac. Meeting a young girl on her own to assess her suitability, however, struck the author of the *Tsenerene* as a violation of etiquette. Ordinarily, girls would be met by prospective grooms or matchmakers only in the company of their parents: "Why [did] Eliezer want to meet the young girl at the well to see if she was kind? He could have met her at her father's house and seen whether she was pious and clever." The book offers a canny explanation: "The reason is that at a parent's house one cannot really discern if a child is bright. The child may be stupid, but parents show a child how to present himself in his best light in front of a guest. Eliezer therefore wanted to see her at the well, when she was by herself, to see if she would act properly of her own accord." This explanation speaks volumes about the jockeying for position and the self-advertising that was involved in arranging a traditional Jewish match. Still, the reader is reassured that just as God sent Rebecca to the well so she would meet Eliezer and marry Isaac, so "all matches are from God. Indeed, the Sages say that forty days before a person is born an announcement is made in heaven that he shall marry so-and-so's daughter."

In the next generation, the story of Jacob—who worked for Laban for seven years in order to marry Rachel but was tricked into marrying Leah instead—offers more opportunities for the *Tsenerene* to discuss the relations between men and women. When Jacob agreed to the long period of service, the Bible says that the days seemed to pass quickly

because he loved Rachel so much. But to the *Tsenerene*, "this is a difficult statement to understand. As a rule when one loves a woman then
each hour, each day, is long, until they can be together. Why does it say
here that it seemed like a few days?" Here the book is troubled by what
seems like psychological inaccuracy, just as at other moments it tries to
resolve problems with biblical chronology. It responds by offering an
alternative interpretation that accords better with the reader's instinctive sense of how a man in love is supposed to behave: "The answer is
that once the seven years were through, it then seemed to Jacob that he
had only worked a few days, because of his great love for her."

The *Tsenerene* is equally troubled by what seems like Jacob's crudeness when he asks Laban "Bring me my wife . . . so that I may go to
her"—a seemingly explicit statement of sexual desire. Surely a patriarch should not speak so indecorously about his wife-to-be? "Even the
most boorish man would not say such a thing," the book exclaims. But
we are assured that Jacob was not motivated by lust, only by a pious
desire to start bearing children for the sake of God. "The answer is
that he said, 'I am already eighty-four years old, and I am destined to
have twelve children. It is time for me to take a wife.' His thoughts
were only for his children."

As the story goes on, the *Tsenerene* works hard to smooth over the
sharp edges, the naked emotions, that the Bible is comfortable displaying. The Bible explicitly says, for instance, that when Leah had children
and Rachel could not, Rachel was jealous. But how could an ethical
paragon be so ungenerous? "Rashi writes that she did not envy Leah
her many children," the book reassures us. "This would be incomprehensible behavior on the part of such a righteous woman. Rather, she
envied her good deeds, thinking that Leah must be very righteous to
deserve a greater portion. And this it is permissible to envy."

A greater problem arises when it comes to the story of Jacob's flight
from his father-in-law, Laban. When Rachel joined Jacob in running
away, we read in the Bible, she stole her father's *teraphim,* his idols or
household gods. It looks very much as though Rachel, despite hav-

ing married into God's chosen people, was still attached to the idols she had grown up worshipping, and she couldn't bear to be separated from them. Of course, this idea was totally anathema to the traditional Jewish interpreters whose views we read in the *Tsenerene*. The book prefers Rashi's view that "she stole them in order to put an end to his idol worship": Rachel was actually serving God by making it harder for Laban to pray to idols. Alternatively, she stole them "so that people would see that they had allowed themselves to be stolen, and were not divine."

In the next generation, that of Jacob's children, comes the terrible story of the rape of Dinah by Shechem, which Dinah's brothers avenged by slaughtering the entire male population of the rapist's city. The *Tsenerene* seizes on this story to inculcate some lessons about female modesty. Why does the Bible describe Dinah as "Leah's daughter," rather than naming her father as we might expect? This is no idle decision—for traditional Jewish exegesis, nothing in the Bible is there by accident—but a way of hinting that Dinah was "a forward girl, just like her mother, who had gone out to meet Jacob and had told him to come to her tent." Just so, Dinah's rape was the result of her failure to stay modestly at home, and so essentially her own fault. The *Tsenerene* drives the point home relentlessly: "The *Midrash* states that a woman whose home is always kept warm by her presence atones for the sins of her entire household. . . . Just like the vine which grows within the house and sends its branches outside, so too should your wife grace her home from within, sending her children out into the world to study Torah." One wonders if this insistence on what amounts to a Jewish form of purdah was so extreme precisely because actual Jewish women did *not* stay modestly at home, as they were supposed to. If the *Tsenerene* is so anxious to police the conduct of Jewish women, that may be because they remained, like the matriarchs themselves, too human to fit any pious ideal.

THE *TSENERENE*'S FOCUS on women, its consciousness that it is speaking to women readers, is evident throughout the book. "One should not hold women in low esteem," it emphasizes when discussing the song that Miriam, Moses's sister, sang at the Red Sea. "They are just as worthy as righteous men. . . . One must hold women in high esteem, for when a woman is righteous, her goodness is boundless." Yet as this suggests, female honor is conditional on strict observance of the constraints of modesty. Indeed, the book goes on to say that even while Miriam was singing her song, she took care to beat a drum to drown out her own voice, because "it is sinful for a man to listen to a woman's singing."

Similarly, when it comes to the story of the Golden Calf in the book of Exodus, women are acquitted of that sin because the "women had refused to give their jewelry for making the Calf," while they willingly donated their gold and jewels to build the holy Tabernacle. "There was no woman among the worshippers of the Golden Calf," the *Tsenerene* assures us. Yet just a few pages earlier, it relays the unflattering Talmudic dictum that "ten portions of speech were given to the world; women took nine portions, leaving one for the rest of the world." Women are said to be especially prone to talking too much in synagogue: "The Torah tells us not to work with fire [on Shabbat], to teach women—who attend synagogue especially on Shabbat—not to discuss their cooking while there, as they are wont to do . . . for in the synagogue . . . one is forbidden to indulge in idle talk."

This unstable mixture of attitudes toward women—admiration and suspicion, reverence and reproof—makes the *Tsenerene* a revealing document of traditional Jewish views about the sexes. The book's didactic purpose, however, extends beyond specifically female behavior to embrace all Jewish readers. It sets out a classically Jewish ideal of ethics and behavior, using the biblical stories to drive home messages about how Jews should act in all areas of life.

Like *Pirkei Avot* more than a thousand years earlier, this ideal places Torah study at the center of Jewish spirituality. "Let your speech be principally of Torah, and not of passing matters," the *Tsenerene* advises in interpreting a verse from Deuteronomy. Indeed, so central is the Torah to the *Tsenerene*'s worldview that it portrays the major personages of the Bible studying Torah long before the Torah itself had been given to Moses. Early in the book of Exodus, for instance, we learn that the tribe of Levi was not forced into slave labor like the other Israelite tribes. This was because "Pharaoh had commanded that the tribe of Levi be left free to study the Torah, so that they could teach the people the commandments." Yet at this point in Jewish history there was no Torah to teach; Mount Sinai and its revelation still lay in the future.

Even earlier, in Genesis, the *Tsenerene* offers a description of Sarah kneading dough "the day before Pesach"—although Pesach, the holiday of the Jewish deliverance from Egypt, would not be instituted for hundreds of years. It is as though the Jewish interpreters whose views are incorporated in the *Tsenerene* projected the Judaism they knew, with its rituals, holidays, and Torah study, back into the time of the patriarchs regardless of the anachronism. They simply could not envision Jewish life otherwise.

In general, the *Tsenerene* likes to imagine a high degree of continuity in Jewish history, at times using mythical means. In Exodus, when Moses returns to Egypt after receiving God's commands from the burning bush, the Bible says that he "took his wife and sons and set them upon a donkey." The *Tsenerene* immediately connects this donkey with other biblical donkeys, insisting that they are one and the same: "Moses . . . placed them on the same donkey upon which Abraham had placed Isaac when going to sacrifice him. And on that same donkey the Messiah will ride upon his arrival." This miraculously long-lived donkey becomes a witness to the preordained patterns of Jewish history: each of these journeys becomes a version of the others, using the self-same animal. Similarly, the *Tsenerene* says that the ram's horn that the Israelites blew at Mount Sinai came from the ram that was sacrificed in Isaac's place many generations earlier. And the oxen that pulled the wagons carrying the Tabernacle during the Israelites' wandering in the desert were the same ones that King Solomon sacrificed when he built the Temple centuries later.

The *Tsenerene*'s ethical advice extends beyond exhortations to Torah study. "The study of Torah itself is not the most important thing: rather, to do good deeds," the book explains, a message that would be especially pleasing to an audience of Yiddish-speaking laypeople. In fact, one of the *Tsenerene*'s constant concerns is the proper attitude toward wealth and worldly success, matters that concern the businessman more than the scholar. Wealth is not to be despised: "Wealth can be a crown to the wise," enabling a person "to do a host of *mitzvot*, including the giving of charity." By the same token, however, wealth presents a variety of temptations that can turn it into a curse. "In the hands of the wicked wealth becomes foolishness and is his downfall," the book warns. "He gives no charity and thinks very highly of himself, refusing to speak with others. People begin to hate him and avoid him, and despise him for not wanting to do favors.... He gives himself a bad reputation and everyone talks about him."

The key to enjoying wealth wisely, the *Tsenerene* says again and again, is to recognize that it was not earned through one's own merits, but is strictly a gift from God. "When God gives a person wealth, he must realize that God, in His goodness, has granted it to him. He should not feel that he himself earned the wealth, or that God gave it to him because of his good deeds; rather, it was simply God's act of mercy." The words in Deuteronomy that are part of the Shema prayer, "You shall love the Lord your God ... with all your might," the *Tsenerene* interprets to mean "with all your resources": "You should love God with your money. Your money should not be more beloved to you than a *mitzvah*." It goes on to tell the story of a rabbi who paid the exorbitant sum of 1,000 gulden for an *etrog*, the fruit used in the Sukkot rituals; there can be no better use of wealth than to carry out God's commandments.

There is no area of life, however modest, that cannot benefit from moral lessons drawn from the Five Books of Moses. "God gave His commandments in connection with every one of a person's actions," the *Tsenerene* says, and it takes any opportunity to apply those commandments to everyday situations. "Do not take vengeance and do not bear a grudge," the Torah says, and the *Tsenerene* offers a humble illustration: "If a neighbor comes to borrow a utensil, do not be vengeful and say: 'You didn't want to lend me your ax, so I won't lend you my sieve.' This you may not do." From the biblical description of the garments of the priests, we learn "that when a person prays or fulfills a commandment he should dress neatly and be scrupulously clean." God will bless the desert for hosting the Israelites during their wanderings; "how much more will He repay a landlord who has a scholar stay with him in his house, and gives him food honorably." After the description, in Leviticus, of how to deal with cases of leprosy, the *Tsenerene* notes that the spirit too suffers from certain illnesses, above all "the 'illness' of speaking ill of others. . . . For this reason, a person should not get used to talking too much."

Still, if the *Tsenerene* were nothing but a collection of maxims and advice, it probably would not have become such a popular book. Much of its fascination derives, rather, from the way it adorns the biblical stories with imaginative details, bringing them to more vivid life by piling new myths and miracles on the old ones. Take the story of Aaron's rod, in the book of Numbers, which is made to blossom and grow almonds as a sign that Aaron is God's anointed priest. This seems marvelous enough, but the midrash adds to it:

> Another miracle is that there were two almonds upon the stick, one on the right side and one on the left side. The one on the right side was sweet, and the one on the left side was bitter. When Israel sinned the almond on the right side lost its color, and became pale and thin, and the one on the left side became beautiful in color and plump. When the people were pious, though, the almond on the right side became beautiful in color and the nut on the left

side thinned out and was pale. Thus through the stick it could be
seen when Israel was pious or wicked.

Elsewhere the reader learns about the *shamir*, the magic worm that
was used to engrave the gemstones on the high priest's breastplate,
and about Abraham's magic sword engraved with God's name, which
Jacob sold to Esau in exchange for the birthright. None of these details
can be found in the Bible itself; they are all midrashic additions, ways
of elaborating the text in accordance with later commentators' sense
of what was meaningful and appropriate.

Other kinds of lore reveal the secrets of what happens before birth
and after death. When the Torah speaks of the ritual purity laws per-
taining to a woman who has given birth, the *Tsenerene* quotes a midrash
about how a child in the womb is taught the entire Torah by an angel:
"When the time comes for the child to go out into the world the angel
hits him on the mouth and he forgets all. For this reason the child wails
as soon as it is born." When Korach, the rebel against Moses's authority,
is swallowed by the earth, we learn about the Dante-like punishments
in Hell, *Gehinnom,* which is "half fire and half hail and snow. The
wicked jump from the fire to the hail, and from the hail to the fire, and
are utterly exhausted, but never achieve rest."

Often the *Tsenerene*'s mythic tales take the form of just-so stories.
Why do old men have gray beards? "Before Abraham's time, one could
not recognize who was the father and who was the son; no one had
beards or signs of age. Came Abraham and prayed that men should
grow beards, and old men should have gray hairs, so that it would be
recognized who was the father, and who the son. Abraham was the
first to have a gray beard, a feature that beautifies an elderly man."
Similarly, before Jacob, old people did not get sick before they died;
"they would simply sneeze and fall down dead, even on the street or
on a journey." Sickness, which we might regard as a curse, was actually
a blessing, given in response to Jacob's prayer: "Jacob prayed that he

should become weak before death, so that he should know when to leave his children his last will and testament."

Throughout, the book instructs the reader in what might be called practical magic, or else just superstition: "One who drops bread crumbs on the ground brings poverty upon himself." One must stay away from wicked people because "when the Angel of Death is given permission to kill, he kills whomever he encounters," and he might slay an innocent person who is too close to the guilty one. Later, in Deuteronomy, we learn that "out of any hundred people, one dies another death, and the remainder through the evil eye."

The *Tsenerene*'s power comes from the way it manages to make the biblical stories at once more exotic, by emphasizing or inventing supernatural details, and more domestic, by extracting useful advice about ethics and conduct. A reader could marvel at the miracles God performed for Abraham and Moses, and yet recognize something of her own life in the details about motherhood and matchmaking and moneymaking. Most important, perhaps, the generations of Jews, men and women alike, who relied on this book for their knowledge of Judaism's holiest texts were taught not just a collection of tales, but a way of reading—one that delved below the surface of the Torah to discover additional meanings in its stories, its words, even its individual letters. In this way, the *Tsenerene* initiated common readers into the classic Jewish approach to texts, so that even if they never read a page of Talmud—much less a philosophical treatise by Maimonides—they would have some sense of what it means to read as a Jew.

～⁕～

IN ITS COMMENTARY on the book of Numbers, the *Tsenerene* offers a parable to explain the value of God's commandments to human beings. "There is a parable told of a person who falls overboard from a ship into the sea. The captain of the ship then throws him a long rope, and tells him to hold onto it, for it will save him. So did man's soul fall overboard from beneath the Holy Throne, into this world. And thus did God tell us: 'Hold tightly to My commandments and you will stay alive, in this world and in the World to Come.'"

In 1690, a Jewish woman named Glückel, in mourning for her beloved husband, began to write an account of her life. And she started it with a recollection of this story from the *Tsenerene*, which she must have read over and over during her long lifetime. Her book would "be no book of morals," she wrote, half regretfully, half proudly. "Such I could not write, and our sages have already written many. Moreover, we have our holy Torah in which we may find and learn all that we need for our journey through this world to the world to come. It is like a rope which the great and gracious God has thrown to us as we drown in the stormy sea of life, that we may seize hold of it and be saved."

This allusion suggests how deeply the *Tsenerene* penetrated into the consciousness of Jewish women readers. For in many ways Glückel was a representative Jewish woman of her time and place. Born in Hamburg in 1646, she devoted her life not to philosophical speculation or Talmudic analysis, like the men whose works make up so much of the Jewish tradition, but to the ordinary business of life: making money, raising a family, surviving dangers, and grasping opportunities. Certainly, Glückel does not hold herself out as any kind of Jewish exemplar: "Not that I wish to put on airs or pose as a good and pious woman. No, dear children, I am a sinner," she writes at the beginning of her book. "Alas, the care of providing for my orphaned children, and the ways of the world, have kept me far from that state."

But, of course, it is precisely her "ordinariness" that makes her, in the Jewish literary tradition, so unique. Copies of the manuscript of the *Memoirs* of Glückel of Hameln, written originally for the edification of her own children, survived for generations after her death in 1724. It was not until 1896 that the book was first published, in the original Yiddish, and not until the twentieth century that it was translated into German and eventually English. By then, it was recognized as an indispensable document of the experience of Jewish women in Ashkenazi society—an experience that finds virtually no representation in classic Jewish literature. (No wonder one of its translators was the pioneering Austrian Jewish feminist Bertha Pappenheim, who also happened to be one of Glückel's descendants.) No Jewish women (and for that matter, few Jewish men) are so vividly themselves on the page.

One constant in Glückel's life, the *Memoirs* reveal, was insecurity. When she was not yet three years old, the Jews of Hamburg were expelled by the burghers who ran the city. The Jews settled in nearby Altona, which was under the more tolerant rule of the king of Denmark. But since their business remained in Hamburg, the men were forced to smuggle themselves back into the city: "Naturally, many a poor and needy wretch would try to slip into the city without a pass. If the officials caught him, he was thrust into prison, and then it cost all of us money and trouble to get him out again. . . . Coming home, our poor folks often took their life in their hands because of the hatred for the Jews rife among the dockhands, soldiers, and others of the meaner classes. The good wife, sitting home, often thanked God when her husband turned up safe and sound." Much of Glückel's adult life would be spent in Hamburg, but the Jews remained there only on sufferance, which could be revoked at any time: "from time to time we enjoyed peace, and again were hunted forth; and so it has been to this day and, I fear, will continue in like fashion as long as the burghers rule Hamburg."

Yet this insecurity—which sometimes erupts, in the *Memoirs*, into stories of outright persecution and murder—does not at all seem to define the tenor of Glückel's life. It remained a kind of background noise, which she, like Jews in so many times and places, had no choice but to tune out. What absorbs her, rather, are the two enterprises to which she devoted her life: the business of making a living, and the equally demanding business of making good matches for her children. These were inextricably linked in Glückel's society, just as they were for the marriageable girls in Jane Austen's novels. Money and marriages were the ways Glückel could measure the success of her family and the respect that her community afforded her.

The longing for such respect is one of the most notable features of Glückel's character, as we come to know it in the *Memoirs*. Late in life, after losing two husbands and most of her money, Glückel barely manages to survive on her own. Yet when one of her sons-in-law invites her to live with him, she refuses, having "many reasons for wishing never to live with my children." The main reason, she makes clear, is fear of being treated disrespectfully, of not being given the recognition and privileges she deserves. "My children's bread... seemed bitterer than the bread of strangers, for my children, God forbid, might have cast it in my teeth, and the thought of this was worse than death." We can gauge her anxiety by how relieved she is when her son-in-law and daughter turn out to treat her well: "Shall I write you of how they treated me? There would be too much to tell. May the Father of goodness reward them! They paid me all the honors in the world. The best of everything was placed on my plate, more than I wanted or deserved." The examples of good treatment she gives are touchingly modest: if she were not at home at lunchtime, Glückel writes, her daughter would save her portion of the meal, so that "I always found my dinner awaiting me, three or four of the most tasty dishes." Plainly, it is not the food that matters, but the deference and respect that it represents.

So, too, with the money Glückel often has occasion to discuss. Hardly a man is introduced in the pages of the *Memoirs* without an estimate of his net worth, and she has a remarkable memory for the details of business transactions—the deals that succeeded and the ones that ended in disastrous losses. (One of the torments of her later life was the incompetence of her son Loeb, who made a botch of his career as a merchant and ended up in debt.) Yet Glückel, as a good reader of the *Tsenerene* and other edifying Yiddish books, knew that it was a sin to desire money for its own sake. She regularly punctuates her story with admonitions to her children not to care too much about money, using her first husband, Chaim, as an example. "The whole day he ran about upon his business, still he never failed to set aside a fixed time to study his daily portion of the Torah," Glückel writes. She brings up one occasion when Chaim refused to interrupt his prayers to entertain a business proposal: "He once missed a bargain in this way, to the loss of several hundred thalers. He never regarded these things, but served God faithfully and called upon Him with diligence; and He repaid him for all, two and threefold over." Just as the *Tsenerene* teaches, money is a gift from God, and Glückel quotes that book almost verbatim when she writes, "It is not enough to serve God with all our soul; the commandment adds, 'and with all thy might,' meaning with all our possessions."

Chaim was a trader in jewels and precious metals, and we see in the *Memoirs* how Jewish businessmen thrived thanks to their international network of relatives and acquaintances. In a business that was so speculative and relied so heavily on trust and credit, these kinds of personal connections were the oil that made the machine work. But Chaim was unusual, it seems, in relying on his wife's business judgment, allowing Glückel to play an active role in her family's fortunes. "Not that I mean to boast," she writes proudly, "but my husband took advice from no one else, and did nothing without our talking it over together." After his death, Glückel was compelled to go into business for herself, and she assures us that she made a success of it: "My credit grew by leaps and bounds. If I had wanted 20,000 Reichsthalers ... during a session of the Bourse, it would have been mine."

If she had been born centuries later, perhaps Glückel would have had her own career in business or finance. But as a woman in seventeenth-century Germany, inevitably the main occupation of her life was bearing and raising children, no fewer than twelve of whom survived. Childbearing began in her teens and continued until middle age; on one occasion, Glückel and one of her grown daughters were both in labor at the same time. "Every two years I had a baby, I was tormented with worries as everyone is with a little house full of children," she writes. "I thought myself more heavily burdened than anyone else in the world and that no one suffered from their children as much as I." Not until later, when she lost Chaim, did she come to look on this life as a happy one: "Little I knew, poor fool, how fortunate I was when I seated my children 'like olive plants round about my table,'" she reflects, quoting the Psalms.

When Chaim lay dying, Glückel writes, he was reluctant to call a doctor because he didn't want the world to know that he was sick: "He clung to the foolish fancy that it might do his children harm; people would say that the weakness was in the blood. For he never had thought of else than his children." This is a telling example of the overwhelming concern for children, for the status and prospects of the next generation, that determined so much in Glückel's life. Money was valuable to her not so much for what it could buy as for what it represented; and what it represented above all was security for her children.

For this reason, negotiations over marriages were highly unsentimental affairs in which the parties quickly got down to brass tacks. One of Glückel's daughters is offered a match with a young man who possessed "5,000 Reichsthalers cash, besides half a house worth another 1,500 Reichsthalers, and silver Torah decorations and other things." At first she agrees to the match, then hesitates when her investigations discover that the boy in fact only has 3,500 thalers to his name: "I wanted to break the match, since it did not fulfill the promises made in the wedding contract." The negotiations stretched on for more than a year, until "I was, God be my judge, dragged into it by the hair of my head and forced to take my daughter to Berlin and marry her forthwith." Another episode in the *Memoirs* concerns a proposed match between one of Glückel's daughters and Moses Krumbach, "son of the rich Abraham Krumbach of Metz." The match nearly unravels when Glückel receives "letters from several hands, warning me not to conclude the match, for the lad had many, many failings." For the Jewish bourgeoisie, marriage was like a business deal—highly speculative, based on imperfect information, and capable of causing ruin if it went wrong. Loeb's business failure, for instance, is blamed largely on his father-in-law, who "far from keeping a steady eye on him, let him run like a loose sheep."

It makes sense, then, that successful weddings are the most exciting and significant events in the *Memoirs*. Every detail of the etiquette surrounding a wedding—where it was held, what was served, the cost of the presents—sent signals regarding the family's status and wealth. When she herself was married as a young teenager, Glückel recalls, there was a contretemps when her groom-to-be's family sent peasant carts, rather than fine carriages, to pick up the bridal party: "Despite her anger, my mother could do nothing about it." Far different was the wedding of her own daughter Zipporah, a splendid affair that was honored by the presence of the prince of Cleves: "Never a Jew received such high honor in a hundred years," Glückel writes with satisfaction.

Ironically, for a woman who devoted so much care to arranging her children's matches, it was her own decision to take a second husband that led to Glückel's downfall. For fourteen years after Chaim's death, she refused to get remarried out of loyalty to his memory—"I could never find a second Chaim Hameln"—and, perhaps, because she enjoyed the social and financial independence of widowhood. But eventually money troubles overwhelmed her, and at age fifty-four she decided to accept one of the many offers with which, she assures us, she was showered. Hirz Levy of Metz was an appropriate-seeming match: a widower himself, he had the reputation of being a wealthy man, and during the wedding festivities he made all the right moves, impressing Glückel by giving her expensive treats like "lemons and Portugal oranges," as well as "a gold chain with a gold trinket."

Glückel had low expectations of her second marriage: all she wanted was material comfort enough to "live out my days in peace, and do somewhat too for the good of my soul." Her children, too, were part of her calculus: "I believed I was marrying a man who with his means and distinguished station could have aided my children and put them in the way of great wealth." But it was not to be; "the Most High God laughed at my plans and proposals." Instead of assuring her security,

Hirz Levy ended up going bankrupt, plunging her into the disgrace she feared more than anything else. Glückel writes about him with great bitterness, even seeing his death as a kind of betrayal: "He went to eternal peace, and left me sitting with my cares and woes."

This sad end to her prosperous career gives Glückel ample opportunity to remind her children, her intended readers, of the evanescence of wealth and the inscrutable wisdom of providence: "I thank my Creator for showing me more mercy and grace in my heavy punishment than I, unworthy sinner, merit or deserve, and teaching me patience with all my sorrows." Just as she promised at the beginning of the *Memoirs*, Glückel is not a saint. The world, not Heaven or Torah, is what fills her thoughts. Like most of us, she is more concerned with respectability and success than with the fate of her eternal soul. But when it comes to ultimate values, she continually upholds what she learned from the *Tsenerene* and books like it. She knows that wealth is meaningless, that God is watching over the universe, that the best Jewish life is one of prayer and study. Her achievement, like that of generations of Jews, was to be able to hold in productive tension the real and the ideal, the world she lived in and the world as God wanted it to be. As she told her children: "Put aside a fixed time for the study of Torah, as best you know how. Then diligently go about your business, for providing your wife and children a decent livelihood is likewise a *mitzvah*—the command of God and the duty of man."

BIBLIOGRAPHY

Kriwaczek, Paul. *Yiddish Civilization: The Rise and Fall of a Forgotten Nation.* New York: Knopf, 2005.

The Memoirs of Glückel of Hameln. Translated by Marvin Lowenthal. New York: Schocken, 1977.

The Weekly Midrash: Tz'enah Ur'enah. Translated by Miriam Stark Zakon. 2 vols. Brooklyn, NY: Mesorah Publications, 1994.

10

HERESY AND FREEDOM

Theological-Political Treatise by Baruch Spinoza

Baruch Spinoza is the most famous heretic in Jewish history. Expelled from the Jewish congregation of Amsterdam in 1656, he spent the rest of his short life developing a radically new understanding of God, nature, politics, and ethics. The *Theological-Political Treatise*, one of Spinoza's two major works, stands at the intersection of Jewish tradition with modern secular thought. While addressing some of the same theological issues that had concerned Jewish thinkers since Philo, Spinoza gave these problems totally new answers, arguing that the Bible could be interpreted by reason alone and that Jewish chosenness was a fiction. His arguments for religious toleration and political democracy made him a thinker for the modern world, and his book raises the momentous question of what place such a world might hold for Jews and Judaism.

BARUCH SPINOZA, BORN IN AMSTERDAM IN 1632, lived at the same time as Glückel of Hameln, and not very far away; in fact, Amsterdam was one of the cities where Glückel's family did business. Yet the difference in their intellectual and spiritual worlds was enormous. Glückel's life and beliefs would have been familiar to a Jew of a hundred or five hundred years before. While she was no scholar, she imbibed the traditional beliefs and customs of Ashkenazi Jewry. But the Sephardic Jews of Amsterdam—descendants of the Jews of Spain; in Hebrew, *Sepharad*—were just emerging from a century of disruption, which had left them all but cut off from the knowledge and practice of Judaism.

The golden age of Jewish life in Spain was never all that golden. As we have seen, the Jews of Iberia were always subject to violence from their Muslim and Christian neighbors. But it was at least a period of relative toleration and flourishing cultural exchange, and it came to a dramatic end. In 1391, an outbreak of anti-Jewish hatred led to the massacre of thousands of Jews across Spain and forced many more to convert to Christianity to save their lives. Over the next century, repeated waves of forced conversion created a new population of *conversos*, or New Christians—sometimes insultingly referred to as *marranos*, "swine."

This persecution culminated in 1492, when King Ferdinand and Queen Isabella ordered the expulsion of all Jews from their Spanish domains. The majority of the Jewish exiles took refuge in neighboring Portugal; but five years later, Portugal too ordered its Jews to convert or leave. The result was the creation of a large population of Portuguese-speaking *conversos*, many of whom tried to retain some parts of their Jewish identity even as they outwardly practiced Catholicism. Around the year 1600—more than a century after they were forced to go underground—some of these *conversos* began to settle in Amsterdam, where they enjoyed an unprecedented degree of toleration from Dutch society. Soon these Portuguese Jews, most of them merchants and traders, were able to return openly to Judaism, and they established synagogues under the leadership of rabbis imported from elsewhere in the Jewish world. This was a community of Jews who approached Judaism from a unique perspective of blended loyalty and alienation—Jews who had to relearn what it meant to be Jewish.

It makes sense, then, that seventeenth-century Amsterdam would produce the most famous freethinker in Jewish history: Baruch Spinoza, who was excommunicated from the synagogue in a public ceremony in 1656. The Spinoza family was one of the hundreds of Portuguese Jewish clans that made their way to Amsterdam in the early seventeenth century. They were merchants, not especially wealthy or outstandingly successful, though Spinoza's father was a solid enough citizen to serve on the governing board of the Beth Jacob synagogue. Baruch, as he was known in Jewish contexts—at home, where Portuguese was spoken, he was called Bento, and once he entered Gentile society he went by the Latin Benedictus, all versions of the word "blessed"—went to a Jewish school, where he learned Hebrew and the Bible. In the higher grades, before he left school to work in the family business, Spinoza would have been exposed to some Talmud study and Jewish philosophy—above all, to Maimonides, whose *Guide of the Perplexed* had an enormous influence on his own thought.

But somewhere along the way, Spinoza's thinking about religion wandered drastically from the conventional Jewish path. The Dutch Republic of his time was the most liberal and tolerant society in Europe, a place where cutting-edge ideas about science and philosophy could be openly espoused. Thinkers who could not teach their theories in their native countries moved to Holland or published their works there—such as the French-born René Descartes, the leading philosopher of the age. And unlike in Glückel's Hamburg, where Jews and Gentiles kept a wary distance, Spinoza's Amsterdam allowed for free commercial and intellectual exchange between people of different faiths. A curious young man like Spinoza could easily discover ideas about religion that the average Dutch Jew, or Christian, would find blasphemous.

Just what Spinoza was saying in his early twenties to so anger the Jewish authorities is not known for certain. One story in an early biography has it that two of his friends, having heard about his unorthodox religious views, asked him leading questions in the hope of drawing forth some blasphemy. "Does God have a body? Is the soul immortal?" they asked, and Spinoza supposedly answered in the negative to both questions. Of course, the idea that God has no body wouldn't have appeared blasphemous to Maimonides, who spent so much of the *Guide* arguing exactly that point; and Maimonides's conception of what happens to the soul after death is far from what we ordinarily think of as immortality. But then, Maimonides had always been a controversial thinker, whose rationalism challenged the way most Jews experienced their faith.

Even if Spinoza had invoked this illustrious example, then, it might not have helped in his defense. His friends, scandalized by his views, spread the word that Spinoza "had nothing but hatred and contempt for the Law of Moses." The story continues that the rabbi who had taught the young man begged him to reconsider and even offered him a bribe to at least pay lip service to Jewish beliefs. But Spinoza refused and calmly accepted the sentence of excommunication, or *cherem*, that the leaders of the Jewish community pronounced on him, saying: "All the better; they do not force me to do anything that I would not have done of my own accord if I did not dread scandal."

It was a remarkable display of composure, considering the extremity of the language used against Spinoza in the public proclamation of the *cherem*. This text invoked the curses that Moses sets out in Deuteronomy as punishment for those who disobey God: "Cursed be he by day and cursed be he by night.... Cursed be he when he goes out and cursed be he when he comes in." But more than disgrace or even damnation was at stake. The excommunication forbade all Jews— including his own family—from having anything to do with Spinoza: "no one should communicate with him, neither in writing, nor accord him any favor nor stay with him under the same roof nor come within four cubits of his vicinity." Jews had been excommunicated in the city before, but the document condemning Spinoza was the most extreme *cherem* ever issued by the synagogue of Amsterdam.

Cut off from the Jewish community, Spinoza was deprived of family, friends, and livelihood. For the rest of his life he would live on his own, supporting himself modestly as a grinder of lenses—an occupation that put him in touch with some of the leading scientists of his day, who were interested in the burgeoning field of optics. Yet the *cherem* also left Spinoza in a uniquely privileged position as a philosopher. No longer part of the Jewish community, yet not a member of the Dutch Reformed Church either, he was one of the few people in Europe who could claim to live a truly secular life, unbound by any kind of religious discipline. He was free to pursue his thoughts wherever they led, and even, with some caution, to publicize them, thanks to Holland's liberal intellectual climate. Although his magnum opus, a summary of his metaphysical and moral thought called the *Ethics*, remained in manuscript until after his death, his ideas began to percolate through the international republic of letters. He soon gained a reputation as a daring and unorthodox thinker, whose views on the philosophical issues of the day were sought after by a small but influential group of like-minded men—and loathed by the conventionally pious, who learned to associate Spinoza's name with the unspeakable crime of atheism.

It was not until 1670, however, when he was thirty-seven years old, that Spinoza felt compelled to set down his ideas in print. He was driven, in part, by the scandal that had recently erupted concerning his friend Adriaan Koerbagh, a lawyer and physician who had published a book that went too far even for the lenient Dutch. In the guise of a learned treatise on the foreign origin of various Dutch words, Koerbagh ridiculed all organized religion as mere superstition and denied the divinity of Jesus. Crucial to his offense was that he published these dissident views not in Latin, the language of scholars and philosophers, but in Dutch, so that the common people could read them. To the religious and political leaders of Amsterdam, this constituted a serious attack not just on faith but on public morals, and they responded by sentencing Koerbagh to ten years in jail—though he died after just a year of incarceration.

In the aftermath of this affair, which showed that there were limits to what a philosopher could safely say even in Holland, Spinoza decided to publish the book that he had been working on for several years. The *Tractatus Theologico-Politicus*, or *Theological-Political Treatise,* was designed—in the words of its subtitle—to "demonstrate that freedom to philosophize may not only be allowed without danger to piety and the stability of the republic, but cannot be refused without destroying the peace of the republic and piety itself." While it was not a full exposition of Spinoza's philosophy, the *Treatise* delved deeply into his views of God, the nature of scripture, and the proper role of religion in society. Spinoza knew that what he had to say on these subjects was challenging and even dangerous. When the book appeared at the beginning of 1670, its title page omitted the author's name and claimed that it had been printed in Hamburg by a fictitious publisher, in order to shield the actual, Amsterdam-based publisher from prosecution. But Spinoza hoped that the book would help to convince his countrymen of the need to separate religion from philosophy and to grant individuals the utmost freedom to believe and think what they wished.

At the end of the *Treatise*, Spinoza humbly announces that "I have written nothing in it that I would not very willingly submit to the examination and judgment of the sovereign authorities of my own country. If they judge that anything I have said here conflicts with the laws of the land or is prejudicial to the common good, I wish it unsaid. I know that I am human and may have erred." Still, he insists that "whatever I have written should be entirely consistent with . . . piety, and with morality." His readers, however, didn't see it that way—including the authorities whose judgment he invited. Instead, the *Treatise* was immediately assailed as a dangerous attempt to undermine belief in God—in the words of one critic, it "seems to have the principal goal of destroying all religions and particularly the Jewish and Christian ones, and of introducing atheism, libertinage, and the freedom of all religions." By 1674, sale of the book had been banned throughout Holland, and Spinoza—whose identity as author didn't remain secret for long—found himself under attack even from liberal thinkers whom he expected to be his allies. The experience was so discouraging that Spinoza resolved not to publish his *Ethics* until after his death—which came at the age of just forty-four, in 1677.

BY THE TIME SPINOZA published the *Treatise*, he had not been a member of Amsterdam's Jewish community for fourteen years. While it's not clear exactly how strictly the *cherem* was enforced—there are reports of Spinoza being in the company of some fellow Jews even after he was excommunicated—it's certain that he no longer made his life among Jews. He moved out of Amsterdam, and his closest friends and intellectual partners were now freethinking liberal Christians like Koerbagh. Unlike the philosophical works of Maimonides or Yehuda Halevi, then, Spinoza was not writing for a specifically Jewish audience, and the *Treatise* cannot, like the *Guide* or the *Kuzari*, be called a work of Jewish philosophy. It was addressed in the first instance to the international society of the learned, who could read its Latin prose, and especially to Dutch intellectuals, who were the target of Spinoza's calls for *libertas philosophandi*, "freedom of thought."

Yet to read the *Treatise* is to see Spinoza address, one by one, the very topics that had concerned earlier Jewish thinkers, especially Maimonides. What is the status of scripture, and what kind of truth is it able to reveal? What did the prophets really know about God? What is the validity of Jewish law, and why was it given in the first place? How can we reconcile our intellectual and scientific knowledge about the universe with our religious beliefs? Like Philo, the Greek-speaking Jew of Alexandria, and Maimonides, the Arabic-speaking Jew from Spain, Spinoza stood at the intersection of Judaism with a wider, more powerful, and more seductive intellectual world. He was asking the question that Jews in such a position always asked: How much of Judaism could, and should, be preserved in the face of other ways of thinking—above all, the rationalism of the philosophers?

The key difference between Spinoza and his predecessors is that whereas they lived in worlds dominated by religion and could hardly imagine human life without it, he was living at the dawn of the modern age, in one of the first times and places where a truly secular life seemed possible. In the preface to the *Treatise*, Spinoza observes that in the Amsterdam he knows, religious differences are only skin-deep: "It has been the case for a long time that one can hardly know whether anyone is a Christian, Turk, Jew or Gentile, other than that he has a certain appearance and dresses in a certain way or attends one or another church and upholds a certain belief or pays allegiance to one magistrate rather than another. Otherwise their lives are identical in each case." This was a fact he was uniquely well placed to know, as one of the few men of his era who had lived intimately among both Jews and Christians, yet shared the beliefs of neither.

Further, the philosophy that Spinoza learned at university and through his own extensive reading offered a wholly different perspective on the universe from the Aristotelean thinking known to Maimonides. Spinoza was a contemporary of Descartes and Newton, and he studied the new science, which offered comprehensively materialist explanations for why the world was as it was. Instead of invoking divine will to explain, say, the motion of objects, it was now possible to see everything that exists as simply bodies in space, obeying nothing but the laws of physics. What's more, the scientific method could be applied to religion itself, used to analyze its truth claims and to separate the facts of the Bible from its myths.

This is not to say that Spinoza discarded religious language entirely. On the contrary, the *Treatise* continually makes reference to God and encourages the love of God. But just as Maimonides, in the *Guide*, defined God in a way that bore little relationship to the way ordinary Jews thought of him, so Spinoza substituted his own vision of God for the traditional God of the Bible. Where Maimonides's God was wholly transcendent—so far above human experience as to be beyond language and understanding—Spinoza's God was wholly immanent, identified with the totality of what exists. In the *Ethics*, Spinoza famously refers to *Deus sive Natura*, "God or Nature"; for him, these were one and the same thing. Or, as he puts it in the *Treatise*, "because the power of nature is nothing other than the power of God itself, it is certain that we fail to understand the power of God to the extent that we are ignorant of natural causes."

If God is nature—in the sense of "everything that is," from stars to thoughts—then his attributes take on a new meaning. For Spinoza, as for all previous thinkers, God is perfect; but this doesn't mean perfectly just, kind, or wise. Rather, it means that God or nature can exist in no other way than it does. Everything that happens is totally determined, and there is no sense in which human beings have freedom of action. We are not independent entities, but "modes" of God's existence; and the activity of the human and natural worlds is just the necessary, law-bound unfolding of these modes. To love God, then, is not to feel the kind of gratitude or awe we might feel toward a father or judge. It is to affirm the absolute necessity of everything that exists, in the same intuitive way that we affirm the truths of mathematics. Indeed, this kind of acceptance is, for Spinoza, the key to human happiness and the goal of his philosophical teaching. That is why he indignantly rejected the accusation of atheism: in his own view, he was not denying God, but teaching humanity to understand God correctly.

Spinoza's totally immanent God turns out to have much in common with Maimonides's totally transcendent one. Neither God can hear prayers, intervene in human affairs, or feel emotions of any kind. Both must be approached strictly through the intellect, by trying to understand as much of the universe as is possible for human minds. And both present very serious challenges to any straightforward reading of the Bible, which anthropomorphizes God both physically and psychologically. To connect such a God with Judaism as it had been practiced for thousands of years—whether it is the esoteric Judaism of the *Zohar* or the pious folk religion of Glückel of Hameln—required a revolution in language and thought. That is why Spinoza follows in Maimonides's footsteps by warning that the *Treatise* is a book for the philosophical elite only: "As for others, I am not particularly eager to recommend this treatise to them, for I have no reason to expect that it could please them in any way."

The great difference between Spinoza and Maimonides, which marks one as a medieval Jewish thinker and the other as a modern secular thinker of Jewish origins, lies in their ways of responding to this challenge. Maimonides begins from the premise that the Bible is true, which means that nothing in it can contradict the equally secure truths we discover through reason. If the Bible seems to teach something that reason rejects—such as that God sat on a throne or walked in the Garden of Eden—then we have to interpret biblical language allegorically, so that it conforms with rational truth. This is how Maimonides promises to cure the reader's "perplexity," by showing that the contradictions between faith and philosophy are merely apparent, not real. Maimonides's rationalism, then, remains securely within Judaism—as is evident from his own life, which was spent in the study of Jewish law.

In the *Treatise*, Spinoza attacks Maimonides on precisely this point. "Maimonides' view," Spinoza writes, was that if the literal sense of any biblical passage "is found to conflict with reason, no matter how evident that may seem in itself, he insists that it should then be construed differently." What this means, Spinoza argues, is that "according to Maimonides, [the Bible's] true sense cannot be established from itself and should not be sought from the Bible itself." You can only know what the Bible is trying to say if you know, independently through reason, what it must be trying to say; otherwise, you would fall into the trap of taking it too literally. But as Spinoza points out, this means that the interpreter has basically unlimited power to impose meaning on the biblical text: "we are permitted to

explain and distort the words of Scripture according to our own pre-
conceived opinions, and to reject the literal sense, even when it is perfectly lucid and explicit."

Spinoza dissents strongly from this Maimonidean way of reading,
and he proposes instead what we now recognize as a critical and historical method. We cannot approach scripture with the presupposition
that it is "true," in the sense of conformable with reason, since that is
the very thing a reading of scripture must prove. His own approach
is described with a simplicity that would have been shocking to the
first readers of the *Treatise*: "I hold that the method of interpreting
Scripture does not differ from the method of interpreting nature, but
rather is wholly consonant with it." The Bible does not require some
special inspiration or divine guidance, but simply the same kind of
attention to evidence, logic, and deduction that we apply to a scientific
experiment.

This is the approach Spinoza describes as "interpreting Scripture . . . from Scripture itself." To know what scripture means, we have
to learn as much as we possibly can about what scripture is: when it
was written, in what language, by what authors, and for what purpose.
In other words, Spinoza wants to apply to the Bible the same kinds of
historical tests one would use for secular literature. The first corollary
of this principle is that no one can really understand what scripture is
saying without a good knowledge of Hebrew, such as Spinoza himself
possessed. ("All the writers of both the Old and the New Testament
were Hebrews," he reminds the reader, perhaps with a little pride.)

Next, "it is important to know the life, character and concerns
of each writer" who contributed to the Bible, because "we are more
readily able to explain someone's words the better we know his mind
and personality." Implicitly, Spinoza is discounting the idea of divine
inspiration. When we read the books of the Bible, we are not hearing God's voice, but the voices of the actual human beings who wrote
them. Finally, there is the question of the reliability of the text itself:
Spinoza sets aside the traditional view of the inerrancy of scripture,

treating it like any other human document that can be corrupted by transmission and copying.

Spinoza is by no means certain, however, that we are able to attain sufficient knowledge about any of these matters to really understand the Bible. Accurate knowledge of biblical Hebrew, he believes, has been lost over the long course of Jewish history: "The Jewish people have lost all their cultural and artistic accomplishments—no wonder, after suffering so many massacres and persecutions—and have held on to nothing but a few fragments of their language and a few books.... Thus the meaning of many nouns and verbs occurring in the Bible is either completely unknown or disputed." Spinoza capitalizes on his insider's knowledge of Hebrew—something the average Gentile reader did not share—to point out several reasons why the text is hard to interpret: the absence of vowels, the tendency of certain letters to be used interchangeably.

We don't know for certain who wrote the Bible, when, or why. And without this knowledge, Spinoza reasons, "our efforts to get at its true sense will be fruitless." He drives home the point by audaciously comparing the Bible to outright works of fiction by Ariosto and Ovid. The deeds of Samson in the book of Judges are no more credible than those we read about in Greek myth or Italian poetry; yet "we persuade ourselves" that the writer of the Samson story was a true historian of sacred matters, while Ovid "intended to write only fables." How do we know, Spinoza implicitly asks, that Samson wasn't intended as just another fictional character, whom we now piously take to be real? Without knowing who wrote the book of Judges and for what purpose, we can never be certain how it should be read.

READING THE BIBLE in this scientific spirit does not mean, however, that Spinoza simply dismisses it as a collection of antique fictions. On the contrary, the *Theological-Political Treatise* devotes a good deal of thought to the question of what remains of the Bible's authority once we stop reading it as a divinely dictated record of true events. Is there any sense in which scripture can still be understood as the word of God, as almost everyone in Europe in Spinoza's time agreed that it was? If we conduct, in Spinoza's words, "a fresh examination of Scripture with a free and unprejudiced mind," what does it tell us?

For Spinoza, the answer depends on first establishing what God really is and how he teaches human beings. In the Bible, the standard way for God to communicate truths to men is "prophecy or revelation," which Spinoza defines as "certain knowledge about something revealed to men by God." Yet if God is nature, the totality of what exists, then there is another way besides revelation to gain certain knowledge about him. There is also scientific reasoning, the kind of thinking that gives us access to the eternal and indubitable truths of mathematics. We know with the most absolute kind of certainty that one plus one equals two; and this is, to Spinoza, a piece of knowledge about reality, which means about God. "It follows," he concludes, "that the word 'prophecy' could be applied to natural knowledge. For what we know by the natural light of reason depends on knowledge of God and his eternal decrees alone." If God is nature and a law of nature is his "decree"—a decree made not whimsically, but necessarily—then science is the true revelation.

This way of speaking allows Spinoza to keep up the appearance of piety, even as he advances ideas that are radically at odds with Christian and Jewish teaching. The same technique can be seen in the *Treatise*'s discussion of miracles, which appear in the Bible as interruptions of the course of nature. The common people's understanding of miracles, Spinoza writes contemptuously, envisions the existence of "two powers, distinct from each other, the power of God and the power of natural things . . . they imagine the power of God to be like the authority of royal majesty, and the power of nature to be like a force and impetus." When the divine will overrides the force of nature, a miracle results—for instance, in the book of Judges, when God prevents the sun from setting so that Joshua can win a battle.

But this way of thinking about miracles is obviously incoherent, once you accept Spinoza's premise that God and nature are identical. "The universal laws of nature," he writes, "are simply God's decrees and follow from the necessity and perfection of the divine nature." God, one might say, is the law of gravity, so he cannot possibly suspend the law of gravity without a contradiction in his nature, which is impossible. If we want to see divine power in action, we have to look not at miracles but at the regular course of events.

If prophecy and miracles are inconsistent with a true, philosophical understanding of God, however, why does scripture speak of them so often? A strongly skeptical answer might be that it is because the Bible, like Ovid's *Metamorphoses*, is a work of fiction, a retelling of legends that never had any historical reality. But Spinoza prefers to give a more moderately skeptical answer, one that preserves the possibility of the Bible transmitting some kind of truth. When we read about supernatural events in scripture, he holds, we have to remember to distinguish what really happened from the explanations of those events given by the Bible's authors. A miracle is simply something that those writers could not explain with their limited understanding of how the world works; "the term 'miracles' can be understood only with respect to human beliefs."

Consider the story of Joshua's battle, in which he commands the sun to stop moving in the sky: "And the sun stood still, and the moon stayed, until the nation had avenged themselves of their enemies." This story became hugely problematic for Bible-readers in the seventeenth century because it clearly depends on the idea that the sun revolves around the Earth—an idea that Copernicus had proved false. How could the Bible, which was the word of God, contain such a blatant error about how the universe operates? Spinoza's way of reading scripture, however, removes the difficulty. He does not deny that something happened during the battle to make the light last longer, but he does dismiss the explanation of that phenomenon offered by the

Bible's human author, who was writing out of the limited astronomical knowledge of his time. "Nothing in the Bible is clearer than that Joshua, and perhaps the author who wrote his history, thought that the sun moves round the earth and the earth is at rest and the sun stood still for a period of time," Spinoza observes. This was simply a human error, and what appeared to Joshua as a miracle must have had some other, purely natural cause. For instance, earlier in the same story we hear of large hailstones raining down on the Israelites' enemies: perhaps "the large amount of ice which was in the air . . . [caused] a greater refraction than normal," causing the light to linger.

Spinoza takes a similar approach to the question of prophecy. Whenever the prophets tell us about seeing God in various human and nonhuman forms, we know rationally that they could not actually have been seeing God, because God has no shape. But we do not therefore have to conclude that the prophets were lying or making things up. Rather, Spinoza urges us to see the prophets as intensely imaginative individuals who really believed they were seeing visions. They did not have special insight into the nature of reality in the way that philosophers do, but they had the power of embodying their teachings in memorable images and words. "The prophets," Spinoza argues, "were not endowed with more perfect minds than others but only a more vivid power of imagination." This explains why different prophets saw God in different forms and used different words to represent his voice. Each saw the God that his particular mind and character predisposed him to see: "If the prophet was cheerful, his revelations were of victories and peace and other things that conduce to happiness . . . if on the other hand he was gloomy, his revelations concerned wars, torments and everything bad."

If prophets were not philosophers, it follows that we do not have to listen to what they purport to tell us about the nature of God or reality. But Spinoza maintains that once these visionary errors are stripped away, the prophets still communicate an important and valid message—one that has to do not with philosophy but with morality. The whole moral teaching of the Bible can be reduced to a single sentence: "that there exists a supreme being who loves justice and charity, and that, to be saved, all people must obey and venerate Him by practicing justice and charity towards their neighbor." Spinoza knows perfectly well that the way he interprets these formulas and the way the average believer will interpret them are quite different. He doesn't believe that people are "saved" in the sense of being sent to Heaven rather than Hell, and he doesn't think we have a choice about "obeying" God, given that the course of nature is determined by necessity. But he deliberately uses language that can be interpreted in different ways by the philosophical elite and the common believer:

> It has nothing to do with faith whether one believes that God is everywhere in essence or in potential, whether He governs all things from liberty or from the necessity of nature, whether He issues edicts like a prince or teaches them as eternal truths, whether man obeys God of his own free will or by the necessity of the divine decree, or whether the reward of the good and punishment of wrongdoers takes place naturally or supernaturally. . . . Indeed everyone . . . must adapt these doctrines of faith to his own understanding and interpret them for himself in whatever way seems to make them easier for him to accept unreservedly and with full mental assent.

What Spinoza is arguing, then, is that true knowledge of God is not necessary for piety. Most people will believe erroneous things about God because they lack the intelligence to attain real philosophical knowledge. To a conventionally religious person, of course, such ignorance would be disastrous: since the Reformation, Europe had been wracked by wars between Catholics and Protestants, each determined to impose their own, "correct" understanding of God on the other. And of course, for many centuries Christians had oppressed and done violence to Jews because of their rejection of the "correct" way of knowing God.

But Spinoza declares modern man liberated from this kind of dogmatic strife. All that matters is whether people behave well to one another, acting with justice and charity; everything else is strictly a matter of private conscience. "Faith therefore allows every person the greatest liberty to think," he concludes, "so that they may think whatever they wish about any question whatever without doing wrong. It only condemns as heretics and schismatics those who put forward beliefs for the purpose of promoting disobedience, hatred, conflict and anger." For Spinoza the heretic, this was the ultimate retort to the Jewish authorities who had excommunicated him: judge people not by their thoughts but by their deeds.

To complete his analysis of the Bible, Spinoza also had to complete his reckoning with Judaism. At the center of Judaism lies the claim that God chose the Jewish people to enter into a unique relationship with him, to receive his laws and live under his rule. This idea is every bit as scandalous to reason as the Bible's miracles and prophecies, and it too had troubled earlier Jewish thinkers. Spinoza, however, had a freedom in dealing with the question that his predecessors lacked. As a Jew who openly rejected Judaism, he was under no compulsion to vindicate the idea of Jewish chosenness. He was free to explain it, as he had miracles and prophecies, in rational and secular terms.

In fact, the third chapter of the *Treatise* begins with a sharp rebuke to the whole idea of chosenness, which Spinoza sees as a kind of childish vanity. "Anyone who thinks that he is happy because his situation is better than other people's, or because he is happier and more fortunate than they, knows nothing of true happiness and joy, and the pleasure he derives from his attitude is either plain silly or spiteful and malicious." God, as Spinoza understands him, is not the kind of being that singles out individuals or groups. Blessedness properly understood means "wisdom and knowledge of truth," full intellectual assent to the idea of God and everything it implies, and not divine special treatment.

Still, Spinoza does not altogether deny that the Israelites enjoyed divine favor. Rather, he characteristically redefines what divine favor means. The most important kinds of blessings are intellectual and internal, and they "were never peculiar to any one nation but were always common to the entire human race." To enjoy those internal blessings, however, requires a certain degree of cooperation from external circumstances, what can be called "gifts of fortune": plenty, peace, security, good health. These are the kinds of goods that human beings try to preserve by organizing themselves into political bodies. Accordingly, an unusually successful and long-lived commonwealth can be said to enjoy "God's external assistance," by which Spinoza means simply worldly prosperity and well-being.

It is in this sense, and this sense alone, that the Israelites of biblical times were chosen by God: "Their election and vocation therefore lay only in the success and the prosperity at that time of their commonwealth." And this success was owed to the system of government bestowed on the Israelites by Moses, the first lawgiver. The many, highly specific laws contained in the Torah do not have any intrinsic value, nor does their performance please God. Rather, they were designed to accustom the people to obedience in every aspect of their lives. And the Israelites needed this kind of thoroughgoing indoctrination because they were a servile people, newly liberated from slavery, who lacked the intellectual and moral sophistication to know what is right and to do it for its own sake. Moses's teaching was highly effective: it forged the Israelites into a nation that remained sovereign over its territory for hundreds of years. This was partly due to the very idea of chosenness, which encouraged the people to hold themselves aloof from their neighbors and see them as inferiors and enemies: "the love of the Hebrews for their country was not simple love but piety, which along with hatred of other nations, was so nourished and inflamed by daily worship that it must have become second nature . . . all these things served to harden the minds of the Hebrews in bearing all things with singular constancy and courage on behalf of their country."

It is obvious, however, that Spinoza's praise of Jewish law is at best partial and that it implies two adverse judgments. First, because the law does not express God's eternal desires for the Jewish people, but was simply a political constitution for a specific time and place, it follows that after the destruction of the Jewish commonwealth the Torah ceased to have any power to compel obedience. "Now that their state is dissolved," Spinoza writes, "there is no doubt that the Jews are no more bound by the Law of Moses than they were before the commencement of their community and state." All the rituals of Judaism, which Spinoza dismisses as mere "ceremonies," are obsolete. What's more, because chosenness is only another name for collective good fortune, the dissolution of the collective also annuls the idea that the Jews have any special claim on or relationship with God. "No individual Jew," Spinoza says firmly, "considered apart from his society and state possesses any gift from God beyond what other men have, nor is there any difference between him and a Gentile."

Except, Spinoza implies, there is a difference, and it operates in the Christian's favor. This is the second implication of Spinoza's description of Judaism. For he follows Saint Paul in seeing Judaism as a religion of mere laws—meaningless rituals that were imposed on a stubborn people because they lacked the grace to know God directly. The one prophet who did teach an authentic knowledge of God, Spinoza writes, is none other than Jesus Christ. Where the Jewish prophets saw God indirectly, through visions and images, "Christ perceived or understood real things truly." Again, this does not mean exactly what a Christian might think it means. Spinoza is not saying that Jesus was God or the son of God, only that he was one of the rare human beings who could intuit God's nature, understanding that "in reality, God acts and governs all things from the necessity of his own nature and perfection alone." For this reason, Jesus's teachings did not take the form of commandments but of "eternal truths." In this sense, if not an orthodox one, Spinoza can write that "God sent his Christ to all nations, to free all men equally from the servitude of the law, so that they would no longer live good lives because the law so commanded, but from a fixed conviction of the mind."

Spinoza's disdain for Judaism and respect for Christianity could not, of course, have been displeasing to his Christian audience. But his views also leave him with a difficult question. If the Jewish commonwealth is long gone, the Jewish law annulled, and the individual Jew essentially no different from a non-Jew, how is it that Judaism still exists? For a believing Jew of any description, this question did not arise because the answer was obvious: God's covenant with the Jewish people was eternal, and he remained with them even if he punished them with exile and dispersion. One day, the Messiah would come and the Jews would be restored to their land. But how can Spinoza account, in rational and historical terms, for the survival of the Jews?

His answer reveals that his experience with the Jewish community in Amsterdam had not left him with warm feelings about Jews in general. Jewish survival, he argues, is a product of Jewish stubbornness and Gentile hostility. The latter he sees as a natural reaction to the former: "As for their being dispersed and stateless for so many years, it is not at all surprising that, after separating themselves from all the nations in this way, they brought the resentment of all men upon themselves." The classic symbol of this Jewish difference is circumcision, which presents a problem for Spinoza as it had for his predecessors since Philo. In Spinoza's view, however, there is no inherent meaning or value in circumcision. Instead, it functions only as an effective form of self-segregation: "I think that the sign of circumcision has such great importance as almost to persuade me that this thing alone will preserve their nation forever."

The pronoun, "their" and not "our," speaks to Spinoza's principled removal of himself from the community that had expelled him. And it is clear from this passage that Spinoza sees no inherent value in the preservation of Judaism, which to him is no more in possession of the truth about God than any other religion is. Indeed, he suggests that if the non-Jewish world took the first step and let the Jews in, they would quickly assimilate and disappear. This, he claims, is what happened in Spain when the Jews were forced to convert: "they immediately integrated with the Spanish, so that in a short time there were no remnants of them left and no memory of them." Of course, this is a drastic misreading of what happened in Spain, where the conversion of the Jews led not to happy assimilation but to generations of suspicion and persecution. But it is, perhaps, Spinoza's vision of what would happen to the Jews in an ideally rational, secular society.

Yet Spinoza also offers a glimpse of another possible Jewish future. As a Diaspora people, the Jews had no reason for being; but as a sovereign nation, their laws had served a purpose. Could it be possible for the Jews to become a nation once again? "In fact," Spinoza writes, "were it not that the principles of their religion weaken their courage, I would believe unreservedly that at some time, given an opportunity, since all things are changeable, they might reestablish their state, and God will choose them again." Since God's "choice" is nothing more than worldly success, it is not something that has to be passively awaited in a messianic future, but a political possibility that the Jews could actually seize. In this brief remark, Spinoza signals the possibility of another Jewish modernity, one whose name would be not assimilation but Zionism.

THE LARGER PART of the *Theological-Political Treatise* is devoted to theological questions. But in the last few chapters of the book, it becomes clear that all these reflections are just the preliminaries to Spinoza's main purpose, which is to argue for absolute freedom of thought and worship. Amsterdam, he writes, comes close to this ideal: "In this flourishing republic, this superb city, people of every sect and nation live together in the greatest harmony." But, in fact, as Spinoza well knew, Dutch politics were constantly embroiled in religious disputes, and the Koerbagh case showed that there were limits to Amsterdam's famed tolerance. The *Treatise*, one might say, is Spinoza's way of urging the city to live up to its best self—to become the secular, democratic republic he wanted it to be.

To explain why this form of government is the best, Spinoza offers a compressed account of his own theory of the social contract. Like Thomas Hobbes—whose pioneering work of political philosophy, *Leviathan*, was translated into Dutch just a few years before the *Treatise* was published—Spinoza imagines that humanity started out in a state of nature, with each individual free to do anything he liked. But this meant that life was a constant struggle, as each man exercised his natural right to achieve his own desires at the expense of others. To escape this anxious condition, human beings agreed to transfer their individual rights to a sovereign, which would exercise collective authority over the whole society, making and enforcing laws for the benefit of all. For Hobbes, the sovereign was an all-powerful monarch; but Spinoza argues that the ideal form of government is a democracy: "Democracy therefore is properly defined as a united gathering of people which collectively has the sovereign right to do all that it has the power to do."

This definition seems to grant the government virtually unlimited control over its subjects' lives, including their spiritual lives. And indeed, Spinoza argues that since there can be only one sovereign in a state, it must have control over religion. "Sacred matters remain under the sole jurisdiction of sovereigns," and any other body—such as a church—that claims authority over religion "is attempting to divide the government." Initially, this sounds strange coming from Spinoza, who has consistently championed freedom of thought. Yet he immediately emphasizes that the sovereign's power applies only to the public and official forms of religion: "I speak expressly of pious conduct and formal religious worship and not piety itself or private worship of God."

For Spinoza, of course, the rituals and ceremonies of religion are inconsequential. As he showed in his analysis of the Bible, he does not believe that scripture commands us to worship God in any particular way, so long as we practice "justice and charity." He is happy, then, to submit to any given formula for public worship, be it Jewish, Christian, or anything else, since he does not believe God cares what words and symbols we use to worship him. Indeed, after a century of wars between Catholics and Protestants, and living in a country where a conservative church frequently challenged the liberal state, Spinoza must have seen state control of religion as a key to peaceful coexistence.

When it comes to private belief, however, Spinoza is an absolutist: "internal veneration of God, and piety as such, are under everyone's individual jurisdiction." You can tell people how to behave, but not what to believe. One man might think of God as a judge sitting on a throne in the sky, while another—like Spinoza—might think of God as another name for everything that exists; but as long as both profess to worship God, the state has no right to interfere. This is because, as Spinoza has already established, the government has the right to do only what it has the power to do, and no government is able to reach into people's souls and ensure that they think only "correct" thoughts. "It is impossible," he writes in the *Treatise*'s last chapter, "for one person's mind to be absolutely under another's control. For no one can transfer to another person his natural right or ability to think freely and make his own judgments about any matter whatsoever, and cannot be compelled to do so."

Here Spinoza's argument about rights merges into an argument about public policy. Any government that was so foolhardy as to attempt to control its subjects' thoughts, he predicts, would only encourage hypocrisy and provoke sedition. For "what greater ill can be devised for any commonwealth," he asks, "than for honest men to be banished like outlaws because they think differently from the rest and do not know how to hide this?" The autobiographical bearing of the question is obvious. Spinoza himself was such a banished man, and the effect of being thrown out of the Jewish community was not to change his convictions, but to reinforce them. His own battle with religious dogmatism convinced him that the only way for people to live in harmony, especially in an urban, diverse, commercial society like the Dutch Republic, was to extend to every individual the maximum freedom to live as he sees fit: "the true purpose of the state is in fact freedom."

In this way, the theological and the political arguments in the *Treatise* end up pointing in the same direction. Neither scripture nor the state, in Spinoza's view, has the power to control our minds. Reason is always free, and the pursuit of reason is the best way of achieving wisdom and happiness, no matter how many ambitious priests or wild-eyed prophets might try to tell us otherwise. True piety and good citizenship demand nothing more than ethical behavior, and as long as we treat one another with justice and charity, we are free to think whatever we like about God. These ideas, which would become the bedrock of modern liberal democracy, find their earliest champion in Spinoza.

Considered as a Jewish book, too, the *Theological-Political Treatise* marks the beginning of a new era. As we have seen, the questions Spinoza asked about Judaism and the Bible are similar to the ones Maimonides had asked five hundred years earlier, and Philo a thousand years before that. How to reconcile reason and faith, how to give Jewish law meaning, how to read the Bible—these are not modern questions, but ones that recur whenever Jews confront the philosophical tradition. What made Spinoza's answer modern was that unlike all his predecessors, he did not finally believe that reason and Judaism could be reconciled—and he decided in favor of reason. Judaism as a religion, and Jewishness as an identity, appear for the first time in

Spinoza as unnecessary relics of the past, which the enlightened individual must discard on the road to the secular and universal society of the future. The great questions for Jews in the modern world would be whether such a society could really exist and whether discarding Judaism was too high a price to pay for admission.

BIBLIOGRAPHY

Nadler, Steven. *A Book Forged in Hell: Spinoza's Scandalous Treatise and the Birth of the Secular Age*. Princeton: Princeton University Press, 2011.

Nadler, Steven. *Spinoza: A Life*. New York: Cambridge University Press, 1999.

Schwartz, Daniel B. *The First Modern Jew: Spinoza and the History of an Image*. Princeton: Princeton University Press, 2012.

Spinoza, Benedict. *Theological-Political Treatise*. Edited by Jonathan Israel. New York: Cambridge University Press, 2007.

11

BETWEEN
TWO WORLDS

The *Autobiography* of
Solomon Maimon and *Jerusalem*
by Moses Mendelssohn

In Germany in the eighteenth century, the doors of
Gentile society began to open to Jews for the first time.
But gaining admission to the European Enlightenment
proved to be a difficult process for those rare Jews who
were socially and intellectually "advanced" enough to
attempt it. Solomon Maimon, born in a poor village in
Lithuania and raised as a Talmudic prodigy, spent his life
trying to reinvent himself as a secular philosopher—a
quest whose mixed results, and high personal cost, he
records in his moving and revealing *Autobiography*.
Moses Mendelssohn, the Jewish thinker who achieved
greatest success in Germany, worked hard to balance
his Jewish beliefs with his philosophical convictions. In
his influential treatise *Jerusalem*, he outlined a hopeful
vision of modern Judaism as an individual commitment
rather than a communal obligation. In combining an

argument for religious freedom with a plea for Jewish orthodoxy, Mendelssohn highlighted a tension that continues to define Jewish life to this day.

LATE ONE PURIM NIGHT in the early 1780s, Shlomo ben Yehoshua found himself leaning over a canal in the Hague, trying to work up the courage to commit suicide. Shlomo, as he was called by his Jewish friends and family—though he became known to his Gentile readers, and to posterity, by his pen name, Solomon Maimon—had begun to believe that the world had no place for someone like him. Born in Lithuania and educated to become a Talmudic scholar, he had rebelled against his Jewish upbringing and made his way to Berlin, the capital of Germany and of the German Enlightenment, hoping to remake himself as a philosopher. He took the name "Maimon" in honor of his intellectual idol, Maimonides, the great Jewish rationalist. But while he forged connections with some of the leading Jewish figures in the Enlightenment—above all, Moses Mendelssohn, known in his time as "the German Socrates"—the poor, village-born Maimon found himself unable to fit in with the city's highly sophisticated and assimilated Jews. He couldn't even make a living, since he would commit himself to nothing in life except study and writing.

Finally, that holiday night—when Maimon was seriously intoxicated, having "banqueted very heartily" in accordance with the Purim custom—he decided that he couldn't go on any longer. "My life is a burden," he recalled thinking, when he came to write his *Autobiography* ten years later. "At present, indeed, I have no wants; but how will it be with me in the future, and by what means shall I preserve my life, since I am of no use for anything in the world? I have already resolved, on cool reflection at different times, to put an end to my life, and nothing but my cowardice has restrained me hitherto. Now, when I am pretty drunk, on the brink of a deep canal, the thing may be done in a moment without any difficulty." Yet he couldn't quite resolve to make the plunge, and he describes himself stuck in a ludicrous posture:

> Already I had bent my body over the canal, in order to plunge in; but only the upper part of the body obeyed the command of the mind, trusting that the lower part would certainly refuse its services for such a purpose. So I stood for a good while with half the body bent over the water, and propped myself carefully with my legs planted firmly on the ground, so that a spectator might have fancied I was merely making my bow to the water. . . . I felt like a man who is going to take medicine, but, wanting the resolution required, raises the cup time after time to his mouth, and sets it down again.

Finally, Maimon recalled, he began to laugh at his own indecisiveness, climbed down, and went home to bed.

The way he writes about this episode in his *Autobiography* makes it seem comic, an example of the healthy will triumphing over the distressed intellect. Yet the image of Maimon bent over the canal, half on land and half over the water, offers an irresistible emblem of a predicament that was by no means laughable. For in a sense, he spent his entire life caught between two elements, unable to make himself at home in either. As a Jew, he was rooted in tradition, custom, poverty, and what he portrayed as the incurable backwardness of a superstitious people. As an enlightened thinker, however—an autodidact who ended up winning the respect of no less a figure than Immanuel Kant, the leading philosopher of the age—Maimon found himself unable to live among Jews, since he had come to scorn their beliefs and practices. At one point during his sojourn in the Hague, he writes, he caused a major scandal at a Jewish house by refusing to offer the customary prayer over wine: "It was merely, I explained further, the love of truth and the reluctance to do anything inconsistent, that made it impossible for me, without manifest aversion, to say prayers which I regarded as a result of an anthropomorphic system of theology." Whereupon the Jews of the city, predictably, turned against him, declaring "it would be a deadly sin to tolerate me in a Jewish house."

Yet unlike Spinoza, whom he deeply admired, Maimon was not in a position to create a secular life for himself, detached from both Jewish and Christian orthodoxy. Partly this was because Berlin in the late eighteenth century was no oasis of tolerance, like Amsterdam in the seventeenth. The Jews of the city were subjected to strict quotas, and the people and government extended them at best a grudging welcome. But it was also because unlike Spinoza the lens-grinder, Maimon lacked the self-discipline to take up an uncongenial trade. Urged by his friends, he studied pharmacy and even took a degree, but he refused to practice. His friends were disturbed by his personal slovenliness and fondness for drink (even when it wasn't Purim): "It was said of the *Autobiography* itself that it had been written on an alehouse bench."

And unlike the middle-class, urban, cosmopolitan Spinoza, who mixed easily with Dutch Gentiles, Maimon retained too much of the stamp of his provincial Jewish upbringing to join polite German society. The first time he called on Moses Mendelssohn, he writes, he saw "him and other gentlefolks who were there, as well as the beautiful rooms and elegant furniture, [and] I shrank back, closed the door again, and had a mind not to go in." While the elite Berlin Jews spoke excellent German, Maimon never lost his accent and had a tendency, in the heat of argument, to burst into Yiddish. While studying mathematics or other secular subjects, his friends noticed, "he would fall into the Talmudic sing-song and rhythmical swing of the body," unable to shake the habits of his early youth.

For all these reasons, Maimon found himself caught between two worlds. Indeed, the image of Maimon bending over the bridge recalls the disturbing metaphor that the twentieth-century writer Franz Kafka would use, in a letter to a friend, to describe his own generation of Germanized Jews almost 150 years later: "their hind legs were still mired in their fathers' Jewishness and their thrashing forelegs found no new ground." As this suggests, the dilemmas that Maimon faced were never to be entirely solved. His *Autobiography* is a classic Jewish document, not just because it is one of the first real memoirs by a Jewish writer—a literary and introspective work, unlike the chronicle-diary of Glückel of Hameln—but also because Maimon was one of the first of countless Jews to knock at the doors of European high culture and find himself only partly admitted.

WHEN SOLOMON MAIMON published his *Autobiography*, in 1792–93, he was only about forty years old. But even though most of his life had been passed in obscurity, he was certain that his story was worth telling—if not for its own sake, then as a parable. Writing in German for an advanced, intellectual public, Maimon cast himself as a kind of hero of the spirit, overcoming tremendous obstacles to lift himself up from ignorance to knowledge. This journey was also, not coincidentally, a geographical one—from the backward villages of Lithuania to the salons of Berlin—and a social-religious one—from obscurantist Judaism to the secular public sphere of the republic of letters. In showing how much he overcame, Maimon simultaneously paid homage to the values of the Enlightenment and reminded his readers how much of the world still lay in darkness.

The darkness of eastern European Jewish society is, in fact, Maimon's major subject in the *Autobiography*, even more than the events of his own life. He begins his book not with his own birth—in fact, he never actually mentions the year he was born, which other sources place sometime in 1752–54—but with a sociological sketch of Poland, in which he emphasizes the ignorance and poverty of nearly the whole population, from the nobility to the peasantry. Against this background, he writes, the Jews stand out as "almost the only useful inhabitants of the country," since they at least practice professions and trades—they are brewers, bakers, managers of estates.

Yet Maimon immediately goes on to show that Jewish life, too, is full of the "moral ignorance and stupor" that he decries. His examples are drawn from his own family's history, starting with his grandfather, a farmer who leased an estate from the local magnate, Prince Radziwill. On this estate, Maimon writes, there was a dilapidated bridge that the Prince, as landlord, was legally obligated to repair. But he never got around to it, and Maimon's grandfather stood on his rights and also refused to pay. The result was that whenever a nobleman drove over the bridge with his carriage it would collapse, and the infuriated passenger would come looking for the local farmer in order to give him a flogging. To escape these beatings, Maimon's grandfather would station a lookout at the bridge, and whenever a carriage approached, the whole family would flee into the woods and hide: "Everyone thereupon ran in terror out of the house, and not infrequently they were all obliged to remain the whole night in the open air, till one after another ventured to approach the house." On one occasion, an angry nobleman managed to catch hold of Maimon's father, then an eight-year-old boy, and forced him with lashes to drink an entire bucket full of water—an ordeal that, Maimon claims, permanently ruined his father's health.

"This sort of life," he writes with a combination of contempt and incredulity, "lasted for some generations." The story of the bridge encapsulates everything that infuriated Maimon about the way Jews lived: the passivity, the vulnerability, the sheer unreasonableness. If his grandfather had simply paid for a new bridge, these periodic humiliations would stop; but he was too stubborn to do it, and so the family went on suffering for generations. Even with all its disadvantages, Maimon claims, the farm was potentially profitable, had his grandfather only known how to make it pay. But he never did, and the family lived in poverty. They ate cornbread at every meal, wore clothing "made of poor linen and coarse stuff," and instead of wax candles burned strips of pinewood for light. Meanwhile, the barns were left unlocked, so they were regularly plundered, and even the cows were milked by thieves: "it was said in such cases that the milk had been taken from them by witchcraft—a misfortune against which it was supposed that nothing could be done."

The one exception from this general sloth, as Maimon portrays it—the one area of life in which talent and ambition were actually rewarded—was Talmud study. "Riches, bodily advantages, and talents of every kind have indeed in their eyes a certain worth, and are esteemed in proportion," Maimon writes—like Spinoza, using the third-person pronoun to describe the Jews, as if to emphasize his distance from them. "But nothing stands among them above the dignity of a good Talmudist. He has the first claim upon all offices and positions of honor in the community." In particular, Talmud scholars are desirable matches for eligible daughters: "A wealthy merchant, farmer, or professional man, who has a daughter, does everything in his power to get a good Talmudist for his son-in-law."

Yet this cultural ideal, which had remained at the center of Judaism since *Pirkei Avot* some fifteen hundred years earlier, appears in the *Autobiography* to have lost all its dignity. Maimon does not entirely begrudge the rabbinic elite its virtues. "Holiness with them extends even to the heart," he writes; "they do not come before you with courtesies, but their promise is sacred." Still, his treatment of Talmud study and Talmud scholars is deeply contemptuous, as he holds up to enlightened scorn what seems to him a tragic misuse of the intellect. For all the homage Jews pay to education, Maimon writes, the actual schooling of Jewish children is barbaric: "The school is commonly a small smoky hut, and the children are scattered, some on benches, some on the bare earth. The master, in a dirty blouse sitting on the table, holds between his knees a bowl, in which he grinds tobacco into snuff with a huge pestle like the club of Hercules, while at the same time he wields his authority. . . . Here the children are imprisoned from morning to night, and have not an hour to themselves."

Here again we see Maimon's instinctive recoil from what he saw as the ugliness and primitivism of eastern European Jewish life. (The only theft he ever committed as a child, he writes, was of a cheap decorated moneybox, which he took, not for the contents, but because it was the closest thing to a work of art he had ever seen.) But more than the bad manners and dirty surroundings, what troubles Maimon is the way all intellectual efforts are directed toward the study of Talmud, to the neglect of every other subject. Mathematics, science, and history—the core of a humanistic curriculum, as known in the West—are not just missing, but positively discouraged. As a child, he recalls, he once copied some designs from the title page of a Hebrew book, drawing leaves and foliage in chalk. A more sophisticated father might have seen the seeds of an artistic gift, but his own simply told him, "You want to become a painter? You are to study the Talmud, and become a rabbi. He who understands the Talmud, understands everything."

And what was the Talmud, Maimon asks, but a collection of useless trivia and hairsplitting? To illustrate what Talmud study actually entails, Maimon offers his readers a series of absurdities: "for example, how many white hairs may a red cow have, and yet remain a *red* cow; what sorts of scabs require this or that sort of purification; whether a louse or a flea may be killed on the Sabbath," and so on. Of course, these were among the same subjects that engaged the best Jewish minds for centuries—including Maimon's idol and namesake, Maimonides. But in the eighteenth century, seen in the light of scientific reason, they have become not just irrelevant but ridiculous. Once Jewish law is stripped of its divinity and its daily application, it becomes a mere burden, to be cast off in favor of subjects like "history, in which natural events are related in an instructive and agreeable manner."

Maimon was well placed to know the privileges and the limitations of the scholar's life, since he himself was a Talmudic prodigy, destined from an early age for the rabbinate. But even as a child, he writes, the roots of skepticism were growing in him. At age six, he recalls asking his father who created God; and when told that Esau chose the blessings of this world and Jacob the blessings of Heaven, he informed his father, "Jacob should not have been such a fool." Still, his intelligence, which later drove him away from Judaism, at first made him a master of it, and by the age of eleven he was sufficiently well known as a scholar to be in high demand as a bridegroom.

Maimon offers a much more jaded view of Jewish marriage customs than we find in other sources. Where Glückel of Hameln wrote straightforwardly about the bargaining that went along with matchmaking and saw successful marriages as strategic victories, Maimon makes out the whole process to be absurd and inhumane. Maimon's father refused one match, to a well-to-do and "amiable" girl, merely because she had a crooked leg. Another seemed promising until the bride-to-be died of smallpox; Maimon represents himself as utterly unmoved by the loss of a girl he never met, and his mother was sorry, he writes sarcastically, only on account of the cakes she had baked for the wedding. Then Maimon's father ended up promising him to two families at once, causing such conflict that one prospective father-in-law tried to kidnap the young groom. The whole process, he makes clear, was purely mercenary and, again, totally undignified. Sentiment and affection, which were in such vogue in eighteenth-century literature, were unknown commodities among poor Jews.

Once he was married off, things only got worse. A husband at age eleven, Maimon writes, he ended up being physically abused by his mother-in-law, and he gave as good as he got. In one scene, he describes smashing a dish of cream over her head; in another, he hides under her bed at night and pretends to be a ghost, warning her to treat her son-in-law better. Sexually, of course, he was totally ignorant, and when he proved unable to consummate the marriage he was taken to a "witch" to be "cured" of whatever black magic was afflicting him. Finally, he did manage to become a father—at the age of just fourteen.

Every item in Maimon's account is designed to underscore the barbarism of the world he knew and his own spiritual fortitude in having escaped it. From an early age, he makes clear, he was afflicted with a longing for more knowledge, and more amenity, than Jewish society could offer. At the age of seven, he discovered a Hebrew-language book on astronomy in his father's library and used it to construct an armillary sphere, a model of the stars. His father, though proud of his ingenuity, scolded him and once again told him to stick to the Talmud.

But Maimon's desire to learn only grew as he got older: "I burned with desire to acquire more knowledge, but how was this to be accomplished in the want of guidance, of scientific books, and of all other means for the purpose?" To really enter the world of science and philosophy, Maimon would have to learn Gentile languages like Latin and German; but the only possible teachers of such subjects were Catholics, who wouldn't accept him as a pupil. One day, however, he hit upon an ingenious, and unbelievably laborious, method of teaching himself. Reading some thick Hebrew books, he noticed that groups of pages were numbered with Latin and German letters. Seeing these letters in alphabetical order, he deduced that they must make the same sound as the analogous Hebrew letter—"I supposed that, for example, *a*, standing in the same place as *aleph*, must likewise be an aleph in sound." In this way, Maimon taught himself to read Latin and German, testing his knowledge on pages of an old German book that he happened to find. (Later, in Berlin, he would make his first acquaintance with modern philosophy when he entered a shop whose owner was tearing up a book on philosophy and using the pages to wrap butter.)

Maimon's curiosity and love of learning were clearly extraordinary. But what makes them historically significant is that unlike so many generations of learned Jews before him, he was unable to satisfy his intellectual appetites within the context of Judaism itself. Much of the *Autobiography* is devoted to explaining, for the benefit of Gentile readers, areas of the Jewish tradition that Maimon explored and found wanting. We have already seen that he considered Talmud study pointless. As an adolescent, he discovered Kabbalah and delved into the mysteries of the *Zohar* under the tutelage of a local rabbi. Yet as he studied the symbolic language of Kabbalah, he once again found himself confronting what appeared to be nonsense. The tree of *sefirot* and the image of God's beard, in particular, "gave me the greatest trouble. . . . With all my efforts I could not find in these representations any rational meaning." In retrospect, he was ashamed of believing that kabbalistic formulae could actually influence the Godhead: "I thought nothing else but that, when I uttered these words, and thought their occult meaning, an actual union of these divine spouses took place, from which the whole world could expect a blessing. Who can restrain the excesses of imagination, when it is not governed by reason?"

If nothing within Judaism could nourish his mind, Maimon's only option was to explore the world outside Judaism. This could only be done, however, by physically uprooting himself from the Lithuania of his youth and making the long pilgrimage to Berlin, the center of Enlightenment. At the age of twenty-five, then, Maimon left his family and took ship with a local merchant for Koenigsberg in East Prussia. Thus began what Maimon describes as an extended period of wandering in which he repeatedly tried, and failed, to find a home where his spiritual and material needs could be met. On the whole, Maimon's great gamble has to be accounted a success: he did manage to make a name for himself as a secular philosopher. Yet unlike Moses Mendelssohn, one of his most important sponsors, he never really found a place in German culture. Not until the last years of his life, when he took refuge on the estate of a sympathetic nobleman, did he find a permanent home.

His first attempt to enter Berlin was an ironic fiasco. The city's Jewish population was strictly limited by law, and at the entrance to the city there was a poorhouse where Jewish arrivals were detained until they proved that they could support themselves. Here Maimon met a rabbi and explained his dreams and plans—including his hope of publishing a commentary on the *Guide of the Perplexed*, the work of Jewish philosophy that had done the most to open his mind. Little did he suspect that the rabbi would turn out to be "a zealot in his orthodoxy," for whom a love of Maimonides was a dangerous sign of freethinking. There was nothing the Jews of Berlin needed less than a penniless intellectual who had just liberated himself from the chains of religion. Such figures were regarded like "a man who, after being famished for a long time, suddenly comes upon a well-spread table, who will attack the food with violent greed, and fill himself even to surfeiting." Maimon was given a few coins in charity and told to leave Berlin immediately.

This setback was a sign that even as Maimon struggled to escape what he felt to be the straitjacket of Judaism, his fate would remain completely bound up with his fellow Jews. Everywhere he went in Germany and Holland in the years that followed, he escaped penury only when a local Jewish community discovered that he was a learned rabbi and paid him the honor traditionally due to scholars. This is what happened in Posen, where Maimon arrived "quite debilitated, half naked, and barefoot," only to be taken up by the town's chief rabbi and assigned a place at the table of a local rich man. "All the scholars of the town, therefore, came to see me and discuss with me as a famous traveling rabbi; and the more intimately they came to know me, so much the higher rose their esteem," Maimon writes.

The irony is glaring: it was precisely the Jewish knowledge he found worthless and wanted to discard that enabled him to earn a living and a reputation. Yet Maimon's freethinking instincts were sure to reveal themselves eventually, bringing his comfortable position crashing down. After two years in Posen, he managed to antagonize the Jewish community by his relentless mockery of their superstitions. One such incident involved a carp that, when cut up for sabbath dinner, seemed to utter a sound as if it were talking. Everyone wondered what to do with the talking fish, and the local rabbi declared that since it was clearly possessed by a spirit, it should be given a dignified burial. Maimon, however, quipped that "if they had sent it to me, I should have tried how such an inspired carp would taste." The result, he writes, was that the town's "learned men fell into a passion about it, denounced me as a heretic, and sought to persecute me in every way." No matter where he went, the same old, objectionable Jewish culture surrounded him; he could neither live with it nor make a living without it.

Driven from the town, Maimon made a second assault on Berlin, and this time, since he arrived by carriage rather than on foot, he was allowed to enter the city. He made himself known to Moses Mendelssohn by sending him Hebrew treatises on metaphysics and theology, in which he demonstrated mastery of both the sacred Jewish language and the vocabulary of secular thought. Mendelssohn, impressed by this autodidact, recommended Maimon to "the most eminent, enlightened and wealthy Jews" of the city, who helped to support him. It was, in other words, an exact replay of what had happened in Posen; except that now, instead of impressing religious Jews with his Talmudic knowledge, he was impressing assimilated Jews with his philosophical knowledge. Even as the content of his expertise changed, the form remained the same; Maimon never stopped benefiting from the traditional Jewish reverence for scholarship.

Still, Maimon could not manage to settle down once and for all. His patrons in Berlin encouraged him to study a trade so that he could support himself, but he refused to do so: "in consequence of my peculiar training, I was indisposed for any kind of business, and adapted merely for a quiet speculative life." He was, perhaps, accustomed to the deference he had been receiving ever since he was a child prodigy expounding the Talmud. In any case, he ended up leaving Berlin for Hamburg, then Amsterdam, then the Hague, then back to Berlin, then Breslau, then Berlin again. Everywhere he went, he managed to burn bridges and alienate friends. There was, he reflected, no place where he really belonged:

I had received too much education to return to Poland, to spend my life in misery without rational occupation or society, and to sink back into the darkness of superstition and ignorance, from which I had hardly delivered myself with so much labor. On the other hand, to succeed in Germany was a result on which I could not calculate, owing to my ignorance of the language, as well as of the manners and customs of the people, to which I had never yet been able to adapt myself properly.

In desperation, Maimon even considered converting to Christianity, thinking that this would make his path easier. Typically, however, he informed the priest he consulted that he did not really believe in Christianity, but considered its mysteries merely "allegorical representations of the truths that are most important for man." He would convert, he said proudly, only if he could do so without making "a confession of faith which contradicts my reason." Unsurprisingly, the priest rejected this highly contingent offer: "You are too much of a philosopher to be able to become a Christian," he replied. "I must therefore remain what I am," Maimon concluded, "a stiffnecked Jew." For all his criticisms of Judaism and Jewish society, for all his longing to enter a brighter and better world, Maimon was never really anything else.

IF MAIMON COULD have put his thwarted ambition in a single sentence, he might have said that what he wanted was to be Moses Mendelssohn. Not for nothing did Maimon immediately seek out Mendelssohn when he came to Berlin. As he wrote in a chapter of the *Autobiography* devoted to Mendelssohn, he was the great benefactor for "Jews newly arrived from Poland, whose thoughts are for the most part confused, and whose language is an unintelligible jargon." Mendelssohn "could understand perfectly" both the speech of Jews like Maimon and their ambitions, for he himself had made a similar journey.

Born in 1729 in the town of Dessau, Mendelssohn—whose name was a Germanized version of his Jewish patronymic, Moshe ben Mendel—was another Talmudic prodigy destined for the rabbinate. At the age of fourteen he set off alone for Berlin, where, like Maimon decades later, he was detained at the city gate by the Jewish guards.

Mendelssohn initially came to the capital to study with his favorite rabbi, but—again like Maimon—his intellectual horizons were broadened by reading the *Guide of the Perplexed*. He devoted such effort to studying Maimonides that, Mendelssohn said, "I became feeble because of him, and yet I loved him greatly for he transformed many hours in my lifetime from sorrow into joy." Soon his focus shifted from Jewish subjects to secular philosophical ones, and he began to make a name for himself in German literary circles. In 1767, at the age of thirty-seven, Mendelssohn achieved widespread fame with the publication of *Phaidon*, a treatise arguing for the immortality of the soul.

The significance of Mendelssohn's achievement was not lost on either Jews or Christians. After many centuries of alienation and hostility between Jewish and Christian culture, here was a man who seemed to be able to bridge the two. He incarnated the *Haskalah*, the Jewish Enlightenment, whose hope was to emancipate Judaism from the kind of burdensome superstitions that so appalled Maimon. A Jew who formed close friendships with some of Germany's leading Christian thinkers and writers, without ever giving up his ancestral traditions, Mendelssohn seemed to incarnate in his own person the hopes of a happier future for European Jewry. Such a role demanded a high degree of patience and tact, and Maimon pays tribute to Mendelssohn's self-possession: "In his character, as he himself confessed, he was by nature a man of strong passions, but by long exercise in Stoical morality he had learned to keep them under control."

Maimon met Mendelssohn around the year 1780, and just a few years later the latter's self-control would meet its greatest public test. A passionate discussion was under way among German intellectuals about the possibility of ending legal discrimination against Jews and admitting them to full citizenship. Such a step would be a triumph for the Enlightenment, and in the view of some of its Christian supporters, it would help rid the Jews of the objectionable character traits—commercial dishonesty, bodily feebleness—that they had developed over centuries of persecution. Mendelssohn made his own case for the emancipation of the Jews in a preface published in 1782, in which he defended his people against the slurs of even their Gentile allies.

At the same time, Mendelssohn argued that true legal equality meant that the Jews should be judged by the same laws as all other Germans and no longer be subject to the jurisdiction of rabbinic authorities. Mendelssohn did not envision Jews leaving Judaism. Rather, he argued that Jewish communities should not have legal autonomy, and in particular that they should not employ the dreaded *cherem,* or excommunication, which he saw as a barbaric way of controlling individual conscience. "If you would be protected, tolerated, and indulged," he adjured his fellow Jews, "protect, tolerate, and indulge one another."

It was not long before this preface provoked a public response, in the form of an anonymous pamphlet titled "The Search for Light and Right." The author of this tract—one August Cranz, whose identity was not confirmed until after Mendelssohn's death—seized on Mendelssohn's opposition to coercion in religious matters. Wasn't Judaism itself, Cranz asked, based on the idea of compulsion through law? Wasn't Jewish law a long set of prohibitions and commandments whose violation was supposed to be punished, often by harsh measures such as whipping and stoning? And if Mendelssohn rejected this aspect of the law, wasn't he actually rejecting Judaism itself? Cranz asked Mendelssohn to say explicitly what his logic implied: that he was no longer really a Jew, because he denied the authority of Jewish law. Not for the first time in his career, Mendelssohn was called upon, in an ostensibly friendly spirit, to convert to Christianity: "You, good Mr. Mendelssohn, have renounced the religion of your fathers," Cranz wrote. "One step more, and you will become one of us."

This anonymous attack demanded a response, because it struck at the heart of Mendelssohn's identity. Unlike Spinoza, who happily relinquished Jewishness in the name of secular individualism, Mendelssohn cherished his role as a spokesman for the Jewish community and could not imagine a life without Judaism. In a sense, his whole life was an experiment testing whether it was possible to be at the same time a pious Jew and an enlightened individual—whether modernity and orthodoxy could go together. If they could not, then the future for German Jewry was grim: either the Jews would go on being excluded from the benefits of modernity, or they would have to give up their Jewishness in exchange for acceptance. (The third possibility, that they would assimilate and still end up being hated and eventually annihilated, was not yet thinkable.)

To meet this challenge, Mendelssohn would have to explain how he understood Judaism as a faith compatible with individual freedom. Ever since Deuteronomy, the emphasis in Judaism had fallen on the community, the Jewish people. The curses and blessings Moses outlines are collective, and the redemption that Jews had always prayed for was a restoration of the whole people to Zion. The symbol of that community, and the means of enforcing it, was Jewish law, which was binding on all Jews. If Jews were to cease living under their own legal authority and enter into full political and legal equality with other Germans, how could Jewishness be preserved? What became of Judaism when religion was defined as an individual commitment rather than a communal obligation? These questions would define Jewish experience in the modern world, and they continue to shape Jewish observance even now.

To answer them, Mendelssohn produced what is today his best-known work: *Jerusalem*, a long essay in two parts that appeared in 1783. Like Spinoza's *Theological-Political Treatise*, which deeply influenced it, *Jerusalem* is a plea for absolute freedom of conscience in religious matters; and like Spinoza, Mendelssohn accompanies this plea with an argument about the origins and principles of Judaism. (The book's subtitle, *On Religious Power and Judaism*, points to the fusion of the two subjects.) But the spirit of *Jerusalem* is quite different from that of its radically secular predecessor. As its title suggests, Mendelssohn's book remains within a Jewish horizon. Where Spinoza's ideal was cosmopolitan Amsterdam, Mendelssohn invokes Jerusalem, the city that has always functioned as a symbol of Jewish redemption. Yet this redemption, in Mendelssohn's eyes, does not take the form of a return to Zion, but rather envisions something Jews had never before even dreamed about: admission to European society on free and equal terms.

Clearly, Jews can find a place in a non-Jewish state only if religion ceases to be a qualification for citizenship and public office. The liberal ideal of the separation of church and state, which just a few years later would be enshrined in the American Constitution, is for Mendelssohn a sine qua non of genuine Jewish emancipation. And so Mendelssohn begins *Jerusalem* by trying to delimit the proper spheres of church and state, the responsibilities that each must bear in a just society. "State and religion—civil and ecclesiastical constitution—secular and churchly authority—how to oppose these pillars of social life to one another so that they are in balance and do not, instead, become burdens on social life . . . that is one of the most difficult tasks in politics," he observes in his opening paragraph.

The usual way of defining the difference between church and state, Mendelssohn writes, is that the former is concerned with man's spiritual good, the latter with his temporal welfare. The state cares for our bodies in this life, while the church concerns itself with our souls in the life to come. Mendelssohn argues, however, that this is a misleading and potentially dangerous distinction. In fact, there is no opposition between our current good and our future good: "it is . . . neither in keeping with the truth nor advantageous to man's welfare to sever the temporal so neatly from the eternal." To do so creates the illusion that we might win favor in heaven by committing crimes on earth, in the name of religion: "many a man has become a bad citizen on earth in the hope of thereby becoming a better citizen of heaven."

Properly understood, however, we do not have certain duties to our fellow men and other, possibly conflicting, duties to God. Rather, Mendelssohn writes, "all of men's duties are obligations toward God." It is precisely the practice of justice and benevolence toward one another that God demands of us. To think otherwise is to imagine that God might need something from human beings, some service or sacrifice or reassurance of our loyalty. And while it must be admitted that the biblical God often does seem to need these things, the God of the philosophers, which is Mendelssohn's God, does not, because he is too perfect to need any help from his creatures. "God does not need our assistance," Mendelssohn emphasizes. "His rights can never come into conflict and confusion with ours. He wants only what is best for us, what is best for every single individual."

It follows that church and state are both responsible for human welfare in this life, on this earth. The difference between them is that the church—or "the synagogue or the mosque," he pointedly writes, making no distinction between different faiths—concerns itself with the convictions and moral beliefs of human beings, while the state is concerned only with their actions. From a secular legal point of view, it doesn't matter if someone refrains from stealing because he knows stealing is wrong or because he's afraid of being punished if he gets caught. All that matters, in the state's eyes, is that he doesn't steal. But this external view of human actions, though necessary, is not sufficient for a good society. The ideal is for human beings to practice charity, benevolence, and justice, not simply to avoid wrongdoing. And for this higher morality to prevail, men need an institution that deals not with their actions, but with their understandings and motivations. This is the role of the church: not to reward and punish, either in this life or the next, but to persuade and instruct.

It follows from this division of labor not only that the church has no right to coerce belief, but that such coercion runs directly counter to its true purpose. "The state has *physical power* and uses it when necessary," Mendelssohn writes, but "the power of religion is *love* and *beneficence*." And love is not genuine if it is produced by threats and rewards; it must proceed spontaneously from the individual's heart. That is why "religious actions without religious thoughts are mere puppetry, not service of God." "The only rights possessed by the church," he emphasizes later on, "are to admonish, to instruct, to fortify, and to comfort."

Religious coercion can take various forms. In Prussia, as throughout Europe, public offices and honors were available only to Christians. Mendelssohn knew this from bitter experience, since his own nomination to the Royal Academy of Science had been blocked by the king, who refused to admit a Jew to that prestigious society. But by offering such incentives to make a public confession of Christian faith, Mendelssohn argued, society was effectively bribing its members in matters of conscience: "the smallest privilege which you publicly grant to those who share your religion and convictions is to be called an *indirect bribe*." This encouraged ambitious men to swear to creeds they did not wholly accept or even necessarily comprehend. In fact, Mendelssohn is skeptical of the whole notion of a creed, insisting that no two people understand the same words in the same way. Even the same person may find his beliefs changing over time. "Many things for which I would suffer martyrdom today," he writes, "may perhaps appear problematic to me tomorrow." To bind people to a fixed formula of faith is to encourage hypocrisy.

If positive incentives to faith are not acceptable to Mendelssohn, negative incentives—punishments and threats—are even less so. "Excommunication and the right to banish," he states firmly, "are diametrically opposed to the spirit of religion." A church is not, in his view, meant to enforce orthodoxy, but to help individual believers find their way to the truth. A person who has gone astray, who doubts the moral truths the church teaches, is for that reason all the more in need of its guidance; to shut him out would be counterproductive and cruel. "To exclude a dissident," Mendelssohn writes, quoting a "worthy clergyman of this city," "is like forbidding a sick person to enter a pharmacy." By definition, excommunication only injures a person who is sufficiently committed to religion to care about his membership in the church. Mendelssohn surely has Spinoza's *cherem* in mind when he writes, "See if you do not find more true religion among the host of the excommunicated than among the far greater host of those who banished them."

The first section of *Jerusalem*, then, establishes the moral and intellectual case for the separation of church and state. Mendelssohn's ideal

is freedom of conscience in religious matters, with church or synagogue open to everyone who wants to attend, and no benefit or punishment attached to professions of belief. Only in this way can religion
fulfill its purpose of instructing and elevating the individual believer.
For that purpose, indeed, Mendelssohn doubts whether a church, in
the sense of an organized body with financial resources and official
legal status, is even necessary. "The church," he writes, "has no right
to goods and property," and ministers of religion should work for free,
or at most be paid for their time: "The church does not remunerate,
religion buys nothing, pays nothing, and allots no wages."

So far, however, Mendelssohn has said nothing about the key issue
in Cranz's challenge. How does Judaism fit into this liberal, individ-
ualist, voluntarist idea of religion? It is easy to see how a Protestant
Christian church could be organized along Mendelssohnian lines,
caring only for individual professions of belief. But the synagogue had
never been an association of individuals. It was the legal authority of a
community, whose members obeyed Jewish law under threat of punishment, including excommunication. How, Cranz wondered, could
Mendelssohn abolish this communal power and still call his faith
Judaism? "As reasonable as everything you say on this subject may be,"
Cranz maintained in his anonymous pamphlet, "it directly contradicts
the faith of your fathers in the strict sense. . . . How then, can you, my
dear Mr. Mendelssohn, remain an adherent of the faith of your fathers
and shake the entire structure by removing its cornerstone . . .?"

"This objection," Mendelssohn writes in the second part of *Jerusalem*, "cuts me to the heart." If it were indeed true that Judaism was
a religion based on the coercion of conscience, then the two halves
of Mendelssohn's identity—German and Jew, enlightenment and
orthodoxy—would be in irreconcilable conflict. "Were it true that the
word of God so manifestly contradicted my reason, the most I could
do would be to impose silence on my reason," he admits. The core of
his rational faith is that the truths of reason and the truths of religion
both come from God, and so they cannot contradict each other.

It follows that Cranz's objection must be founded on a mistake about the nature of Judaism, which Mendelssohn sets out to correct. "It is true," he acknowledges, "that I recognize no eternal truths other than those that are not merely comprehensible to reason but can also be demonstrated and verified by human powers." Everything that a human being needs to know about God—that he is One, that he is our Creator, that he rewards and punishes our actions—can be figured out by any thoughtful person, at any place or time. To say otherwise, Mendelssohn argues, is to impute an injustice to God. For if a special revelation like the one on Sinai—or the one that Christians believe Jesus offered—were necessary to salvation, then the vast majority of human beings would be damned simply because they never knew about it. "Why must the two Indies wait until it pleases the Europeans to send them a few comforters to bring them a message without which they can, according to this opinion, live neither virtuously nor happily?" he asks polemically.

This presents a serious challenge to Christianity, which maintains that only those who confess Jesus Christ can be saved. But, Mendelssohn argues, natural religion is perfectly compatible with what he calls "true Judaism"—that is, Judaism as he believes it was delivered to Moses, shorn of all its later superstitions and accretions. For "according to the concepts of true Judaism, all the inhabitants of the earth are destined to felicity; and the means of attaining it are as widespread as mankind itself, as charitably dispensed as the means of warding off hunger and other natural needs." Judaism teaches nothing about the nature of God that reason alone couldn't find out; it offers "no *exclusive* revelation of eternal truths that are indispensable to salvation." The unity of God, for instance, is the subject of the Shema prayer, which Mendelssohn translates this way: "Hear, O Israel, the Eternal, our God, is a unique, eternal being!" But the uniqueness and eternity of God are qualities that even pagan philosophers knew, without ever hearing a word about Judaism.

Another way of putting this is to say that Judaism, unlike Christianity, never tells its adherents what they must believe. "Among all the prescriptions and ordinances of the Mosaic law, there is not a single one which says: *You shall believe or not believe*," Mendelssohn points out. There have been some attempts in the history of Judaism to invent a creed, such as Maimonides's list of thirteen articles that all Jews must accept. But this "merely accidental" idea, as Mendelssohn calls it, never became central to Jewish practice. "Thank God," he writes, "they have not yet been forged into shackles of faith." Indeed, Judaism properly understood does not demand any particular affirmations from its followers: "No one has to swear to symbols or subscribe, by oath, to certain articles of faith." A Jew only needs to believe about God those basic truths that all human beings believe.

Why, then, does a Jew need Judaism at all? What was the point of the revelation on Sinai, if not to teach articles of faith? Mendelssohn has a simple answer: the essence of Judaism is not belief, but law. "Revealed *religion* is one thing, revealed *legislation* another," he insists. Judaism is a matter of "commandments and ordinances, not eternal religious truths." A Jew demonstrates his Jewishness by keeping the sabbath, circumcising his sons, eating kosher food, and following all the other laws God commanded. Even though the Jewish God is the same God that the rest of humanity worships, he demands more of the Jews than he does of other nations.

In a sense, Mendelssohn's view of Judaism is no different from that of Spinoza, who also saw the Torah as a matter of legislation, a code for the regulation of life in the Jewish commonwealth. But for Spinoza, this implied that after the fall of the Jewish state, the laws became null and void. Mendelssohn escapes this conclusion because he believes that the rituals and ceremonies of Judaism have an innate moral purpose, one that survives even in Diaspora. God designed Jewish law as a continuous lesson, in which every practice taught the Jews something about the nature of God or their duties to one another. "Each of these prescribed actions, each practice, each ceremony," he writes, "had its meaning, its valid significance; each was closely related to the speculative knowledge of religion and the teachings of morality, and was an occasion for a man in search of truth to reflect on these sacred matters or to seek instruction from wise men."

Mendelssohn does not offer specifics, the way Maimonides does when he points out the ethical purpose behind many Jewish laws. But he dwells on the way the laws had to be transmitted in person, from teacher to student or parent to child, rather than being written down. Until the Mishnah was compiled in the second century CE, the Oral Law—all those interpretations and practices that supplemented the Written Law—was never reduced to a text; to learn it, a Jew needed "social intercourse . . . oral, living instruction." To live in a Jewish community was to be constantly exposed to laws and the meanings of laws:

> In everything a youth saw being done, in all public as well as private dealings, on all gates and on all doorposts, in whatever he turned his eyes or ears to, he found occasion for inquiring and reflecting, occasion to follow an older and wiser man at his every step, to observe his minutest actions with childlike attentiveness and to master them with childlike docility, to inquire after the spirit and the purpose of these doings and to seek the instruction which his master considered him capable of absorbing and prepared to receive.

For Mendelssohn, this was a particularly ingenious aspect of Judaism, because it helped avoid what he sees as the modern curse of dependence on texts. In the eighteenth century, he laments, "our whole being depends on letters; and we can scarcely comprehend how a mortal man can educate and perfect himself without a *book*." This focus on texts is, of course, especially characteristic of Judaism, and it is often taken to be one of Judaism's glories. But for Mendelssohn—as for Plato, from whom he may have taken the idea—textuality is a later and decayed stage of spiritual life. Pristine Judaism didn't need it, because it communicated through the living language of *mitzvot*.

The understanding of Judaism that Mendelssohn builds up in the second part of *Jerusalem* seems, however, to end in a paradox. Judaism was a matter of legislation, and we ordinarily think of laws as things that can be enforced through punishments. Indeed, Mendelssohn had argued in the first part of the book that precisely this is the province of state power. But Jewish law is no longer the law of a state, as Mendelssohn acknowledges. After the destruction of the Temple in the Jewish War (see Chapter 4), "the civil bonds of the nation were dissolved; religious offenses were no longer crimes against the state." It follows that Jewish law has become strictly religious, and religion, he has already argued, cannot use compulsion. The result is that Jewish law now "knows of no punishment, no other penalty than the one the remorseful sinner *voluntarily* imposes on himself." Judaism is a law code without enforcement, except by individual conscience. It has been transformed from a communal rule for all Jews into a voluntary commitment of each Jew.

The future of Judaism, then, is one in which Jews take on themselves a double obligation. In all public matters, they must obey the laws of the country in which they live; in all private ones, they must continue to obey Jewish law. For unlike Spinoza, Mendelssohn insists that Jewish law remains in force until God himself sees fit to revoke it "in as clear voice, in as public a manner" as when he first delivered the Torah on Sinai. "Bear both burdens as well as you can!" he advises the Jewish reader. "Remain unflinchingly at the post which Providence has assigned to you." He even, daringly, takes over one of Jesus's most famous sayings, applying it to the Jew in a modern society: "Give to Caesar, and give to God too!"

But as Mendelssohn's metaphors here make clear, Judaism conceived as a soldierly discipline or a load to be carried does not sound like a very attractive proposition. Once the decision to obey Jewish law is left up to every individual, it is inevitable that some—maybe most—Jews will decide that the burden is too great, that there is no way and no need to go on living under two sets of laws. And, in fact, that is just what happened with Mendelssohn's own family. All of his grandchildren were baptized Christians, including the composer Felix Mendelssohn-Bartholdy, who created masterpieces of church music.

On the large scale, too, Mendelssohn's vision of strict orthodoxy failed to compel German Jews, most of whom opted either for conversion or for the new Reform movement, which did away with all the legal requirements that Mendelssohn insisted were still in force. The Mendelssohnian ideal is not dead—there are still, in America and elsewhere, Jews who strive to combine modernism and orthodoxy— but it has proved too austere for most Jews. For that matter, neither would Christian Europe, for all its Enlightenment, manage to heed the urgent plea for acceptance with which *Jerusalem* ends: "If we render unto *Caesar* what is *Caesar's*, then do you yourselves render unto *God* what is *God's! Love truth! Love peace!*"

BIBLIOGRAPHY

Feiner, Shmuel. *Moses Mendelssohn: Sage of Modernity.* Translated by Anthony Berris. New Haven: Yale University Press, 2010.

Maimon, Solomon. *An Autobiography.* Translated by J. Clark Murray, introduction by Michael Shapiro. Champaign: University of Illinois Press, 2001.

Mendelssohn, Moses. *Jerusalem: or On Religious Power and Judaism.* Translated by Allan Arkush, introduction and commentary by Alexander Altmann. Waltham, MA: Brandeis University Press, 1983.

12

BROKENNESS AND REDEMPTION

The *Tales* of Nachman of Bratslav

The rise of Hasidism in the eighteenth century revolutionized the spiritual lives of eastern European Jews. The charismatic founder of the movement, the Baal Shem Tov, became known through popular folktales about his supernatural powers and extraordinary holiness. These stories taught that Hasidism elevated spontaneity and sincerity over traditional forms of Jewish piety. Of all the stories told by Hasidic masters, however, the *Tales* of Nachman of Bratslav are unique in their literary sophistication and spiritual intensity. Taking secular fairy tales as a model, Nachman wove complex kabbalistic parables that are at the same time strikingly modern stories of spiritual longing and dislocation. With their engaging plots, fantastic adventures, and deep layers of hidden meaning, Nachman's *Tales* created a profound new genre of Jewish literature.

IN THE SECOND HALF OF THE EIGHTEENTH CENTURY, Solomon Maimon was far from the only eastern European Jew to look around him and long for something different. But the poverty, oppression, and hidebound tradition that propelled Maimon out of Judaism altogether had a different effect on the vast majority of Jews. Instead of leaving Judaism behind, hundreds of thousands of them flocked to a new kind of Judaism, a charismatic revival movement that would change the way they lived and worshiped. In the course of his education, Maimon himself encountered this movement, and in his *Autobiography* he left one of the first accounts of it—what he called "a sect of my nation called the New Hasidim."

Maimon referred to them as "new" hasidim because the word *hasid*, as he points out, had long been used to refer to Jews "who distinguish themselves by practicing the strictest piety." The name is as old as the Talmud, and it was used in the Middle Ages to refer to a circle of devout German Jews. But Hasidism, as the new movement was called, was something different. Maimon struggles to explain to the non-Jewish reader exactly how to think about the phenomenon. He compares Hasidic beliefs to Greek Epicureanism and calls it "a secret society" bent on winning political control of the Jewish people. But his own account makes clear that this was something much larger than a conspiracy. It was a new way of living as a Jew, and Maimon describes its main features faithfully, if without much sympathy.

Hasidism, in contrast to the intellectually strenuous and morally puritanical rabbinic tradition, emphasized "cheerfulness of spirit": "They maintained that man must satisfy all his bodily needs, and seek to enjoy the pleasures of the senses, so far as may be necessary for the development of his feelings, since God has created all for His glory." Maimon himself, like many other opponents of the new movement, found the hilarity of Hasidic worship, with its emphasis on singing and dancing, to be undignified. He describes a prayer service that degenerated into a free-for-all, where one worshiper, a new father celebrating his daughter's birth, was "seized, thrown down on the floor, and whipped unmercifully." Such antics infuriated the traditionalists who became known as *mitnagdim*, or "opponents" of Hasidism, and they counted some important authorities on their side—including the Vilna Gaon, the great rabbinic sage from Lithuania.

But for every rabbi who looked down on Hasidism, there were many more Jews who found it liberating. As Maimon writes, Hasidism unlocked the secrets of Kabbalah and gave them practical application, teaching that every Jew could strive for "annihilation of self before God." Ordinary people were guided along this path by the *tzaddik*, the holy man, who combined exceptional piety with mystical power. By the end of the eighteenth century, there were a number of rival *tzaddikim* holding court in the major towns of Ukraine and Poland. Maimon made a pilgrimage to see one of the greatest, Dov Baer of Mezeritch, known simply as the Maggid, or "preacher." He was impressed by the Maggid's ability to extemporize a sermon based on selected Bible verses, and still more by the way he made each man present feel that he was being addressed personally: "every one of the newcomers believed that he discovered . . . [something] that had reference to the facts of his own spiritual life. At this we were of course greatly astonished."

The Maggid of Mezeritch was the chief disciple of the man who founded the Hasidic movement, Israel ben Eliezer, known as the Baal Shem Tov. The *baal shem*, or "master of the name," was a familiar figure in eastern European Jewish communities: he was a kind of benevolent magician who used his knowledge of secret kabbalistic formulas, including the name of God, to cure sickness and cast out demons. Maimon the rationalist writes dismissively about the Baal Shem Tov, saying that "he became very celebrated . . . on account of some lucky cures which he effected by means of his medical knowledge and his conjuring tricks." But to his followers, the Baal Shem Tov, "master of the Good Name"—or, as he is frequently known by his Hebrew initials, the Besht—was unique among these holy men. Born around the year 1700, the Besht emerged in the 1740s as the leader of the new Hasidic movement, attracting followers by the power of his preaching, his personality, and his stories.

For one of the most important characteristics of Hasidism was that it spread its doctrines, not through complex legal or mystical treatises, but primarily through storytelling. This was a crucial part of its democratic appeal. As one of the Besht's disciples put it, "A healthy person drinks water to slake his thirst; that is not so for a sick person, who needs wine and milk." Sermons and moral exhortations were like water—good for you, but unappetizing. The suffering soul of the average Jew needed stories to convey religious truths.

The stories about the Besht make no secret of the fact that he lacked the usual credentials of a Jewish leader. At a time when, as Maimon wrote sarcastically, "every Polish Jew is destined from birth to be a rabbi, and only the greatest incapacity can exclude him from the office," Israel ben Eliezer was known to be a poor student. After his father died, the boy was sent to school by concerned neighbors, but he refused to stick to his books: "Israel studied diligently enough, but always only for a few days running. Then he played truant and they found him somewhere in the woods and alone . . . over and over the boy escaped to the woods until the people despaired of ever making an honest and upright man of him."

This tale may or may not be biographically accurate, but it makes an unmistakable ideological point. Individual inspiration, not mastery of Talmud, would be the basis for the Besht's authority. His whole way of being was a challenge to the conventionally "upright," who equated sanctity with learning. Certainly, his first jobs were not prestigious ones: tales are told of his work as a teacher's assistant, a servant in the study house, a butcher. Yet even then, the force of the Besht's personality was unmistakable, so that great scholars deferred to him. A certain Rabbi Efraim agreed to submit a legal dispute to the Besht for resolution after seeing an illuminated sign on his forehead; he was so impressed by the young man's wisdom that he chose him for a son-in-law. Efraim's son, a famous scholar, could not understand this decision, especially when he tried to teach his new brother-in-law some Torah: "it was impossible to get him to remember a single word of the teachings." Finally he told his sister, "I am ashamed of your husband."

On the night before his thirty-sixth birthday, however, the unimpressive Israel ben Eliezer decided it was time to reveal himself as the mighty Baal Shem Tov. The story begins with yet another example of the Besht's seeming simplicity. He was keeping an inn when a learned guest arrived one Shabbat, and the Besht feigned ignorance of the week's Torah portion, asking the guest to say some "words of teaching" about it. The guest, thinking he was dealing with an ignoramus, gave as simple and brief an explanation as possible. Late that night, the guest was awakened by what he thought was the light of a fire burning in the hearth. When he went to investigate, however, he saw that it was actually a supernatural illumination, "a great white light" that filled the house. Overcome, the guest fainted, and awoke to find the Besht standing over him, saying, "A man should not look upon what is not granted to him." Clearly, Israel ben Eliezer's apparent lack of book learning concealed his great mystical powers, which he kept secret from the world. The tale ends with the Besht going on to give his own explanation of the Torah portion, revealing "secrets of the teachings which no one had ever heard before": his intuitive insight into the holy text is far superior to the knowledge of scholars.

This guest, it is said, went on to become the Besht's first disciple. As the word spread and visitors began to arrive from near and far, they took home stories of his intense piety. One story was told of how the Besht trembled so mightily during prayer that nearby barrels of water and grain shook. His prayers came from a place deeper, or higher, than the mind: "When I weld my spirit to God, I let my mouth say what it will, for then all my words are bound to their root in Heaven," he once said, preferring individual inspiration to the traditional formulas of prayer. To those who found the Hasidic style of prayer uncouth, the Besht responded with a parable: "Once a fiddler played so sweetly that all who heard him began to dance, and whoever came near enough to hear joined in the dance. Then a deaf man who knew nothing of music happened along, and to him all he saw seemed the action of madmen—senseless and in bad taste." Only those in tune with the Besht's joyful spirit understood the reason for his unconventional actions.

Some of the tales of the Baal Shem Tov tell of his miraculous powers. For instance, there was the time he was walking in the mountains and almost fell off a cliff, until "a neighboring mountain leaped to the spot" and saved him. More important than the substance of these tales, however, is what they tell us about the Besht's religious style. Here, as in other stories, we see him communing with God in the midst of nature, in a way that was novel in Judaism. Other tales deprecate the Besht's wonder-working, directing attention instead to his deep piety: "What is the sense of telling miracle tales! Tell one another of his love of God! Every week, on the day before the Sabbath, around the hour of noon, his heart began to beat so loudly that all who were with him could hear it." And many stories emphasize that, as Maimon observed, the founder of Hasidism discouraged asceticism and solemnity. One of his main disciples, Jacob Joseph, was in the habit of fasting one week every month, until the Baal Shem Tov stopped him, saying: "the Divine Presence does not hover over gloom but over joy in the commandments."

The unmistakable message of the stories about the Besht is the superiority of feeling over intellect and sincerity over sophistication. Since ancient times, the ideal Jewish life had been one dedicated to the study of Torah. Solomon Maimon testified to the fact that this ideal was still alive in eighteenth-century eastern Europe. But inevitably, only a small fraction of the Jewish people had the time, resources, and intellectual capacity to master Torah and Talmud. To the worker and the merchant—though not, yet, to women—Hasidism brought the welcome message that devotion was even better than knowledge. One famous tale has the Baal Shem Tov refusing to enter a synagogue because "it is crowded with teachings and prayers from wall to wall and from floor to ceiling. How could there be room for me?" Ordinary prayer, the Besht seems to be saying, does not ascend to Heaven, but gets trapped in the synagogue, leaving no room for the passionate, individual prayer of the *tzaddik*. He prefers characters like the shepherd whom he once discovered jumping and somersaulting over a ditch, crying: "I am jumping for the love of God!" "Then the Baal Shem realized," the story says, "that the service of this shepherd was greater than his own." Another tale concerns a "dull-witted" boy who could never learn to read Hebrew and who prayed on Yom Kippur by blowing a whistle; his father is ashamed, but the Besht praises the boy's fervor. Clearly, for the founder of Hasidism, God prefers the prayer of the inarticulate but sincere heart to rote formulas.

Indeed, Hasidic mysticism centers around the kabbalistic idea that prayer, especially the prayer of the *tzaddik*, actively works to repair the universe, restoring harmony to the Godhead and hastening the coming of the Messiah. To support such a *tzaddik* materially and spiritually, to be guided by his words and example, was to participate in this cosmic drama. And the Besht was convinced that his own teachings were helping to speed the redemption of the world. In a letter to his brother-in-law—the same one who was initially so skeptical of his mission—the Besht recorded a vision he experienced on Rosh Hashanah in the year 1746. "Words cannot properly describe what I beheld and learned," he wrote, but he describes visiting Paradise, seeing the souls of the dead, and conversing with Satan and the Messiah. He asked the Messiah how long it would take for him to arrive and got this response: "When your teaching will be widespread and known throughout the world . . . then all the *kelipot* will have been removed and the propitious hour for salvation will have come." The *kelipot*, the evil "shells" that the *Zohar* describes as concealing the world's goodness, can be banished only when every Jew receives the liberating message of Hasidism.

After the death of the Baal Shem Tov in 1760, it fell to his disciples to effect this redemption. A Hasidic movement that had once been dominated by the Besht's singular personality now fragmented as various *tzaddikim* set up courts in different Jewish communities, establishing dynasties in which authority passed down from teacher to student and from father to son. Each of these Hasidic courts developed its own traditions, with figures like the Maggid of Mezeritch and Pinchas of Koretz featuring in their own legendary tales. Despite intense opposition from the rabbinic establishment, the appeal of Hasidism was so great that by the early nineteenth century as much as half the Jewish population of Ukraine and Poland was Hasidic.

But as with all charismatic religious movements, there was a sense of loss as the younger generations moved ever further from the founder. A well-known Hasidic story retold by Gershom Scholem captures this dynamic of loss and the central importance of storytelling itself in preserving the Besht's legacy:

When the Baal Shem had a difficult task before him, he would go to a certain place in the woods, light a fire and meditate in prayer—and what he had set out to perform was done. When a generation later the Maggid of Mezeritch was faced with the same task he would say: We can no longer light the fire, but we can still speak the prayers—and what he wanted done became reality. Again a generation later Rabbi Moshe Leib of Sassov had to perform the task. And he too went into the woods and said: We can no longer light a fire, nor do we know the secret meditations belonging to the prayer, but we do know the place in the woods to which it all belongs—and that must be sufficient; and sufficient it was. But when another generation had passed and Rabbi Israel of Rishin was called upon to perform the task, he said: We cannot light the fire, we cannot speak the prayers, we do not know the place, but we can tell the story of how it was done. And . . . the story which he told had the same effect as the actions of the other three.

HASIDIC TALES, USUALLY focused on the power and holiness of the *tzaddik*, constituted a new genre of Jewish literature. In the twentieth century, thanks to western European Jewish scholars like Martin Buber, they would become known to the wider world as a treasure of folk literature. For the first Jews who told and retold them, however, in the poor villages of Ukraine in the mid-eighteenth century, they were more than literature; they were themselves religious acts. Repeating a story about the Besht was a way of testifying to his holiness and spreading the good news of his teachings. These stories circulated orally for decades after the Besht died and were collected in print for the first time in 1815 in a volume titled *Shivhei HaBesht,* "Praises of the Baal Shem Tov."

The next year, however, a very different kind of Hasidic tale made its appearance in print: the *Sippurey Maasiyot*—literally, "accounts of deeds," but translated simply as *Tales*—of Rabbi Nachman of Bratslav. Nachman was Hasidic royalty: his mother was the granddaughter of the Baal Shem Tov, and his uncle Baruch was an important *tzaddik* in his own right. From the moment he was born, in 1772, twelve years after the death of the Besht, he carried as heavy a burden of expectation and responsibility as any prince. Nothing could be more natural than that such a man would grow up to be a *tzaddik* himself, nor that he would turn to the telling of stories as a way of communicating his spiritual message. Indeed, Nachman instructed his chief disciple, Rabbi Nathan, that his stories should be published in a bilingual edition, in the original Yiddish and in Hebrew translation, so that they would reach the widest possible audience.

Yet the *Tales* of Rabbi Nachman were like nothing else in Hasidic literature. For these were not tales about Nachman, his holiness, or his miracle-working powers, passed down by his followers. Rather, they were stories invented by Nachman himself; and while they were first delivered orally to gatherings of his Hasidim, they bear every sign of having been written, or at least composed, in advance. Unlike the usual Hasidic tale with its pious, didactic message, Nachman's stories are full of paradoxes and esoteric symbolism; the more deeply these stories are studied, the more enigmatic they become. For this reason, they have often struck readers as distinctively modern, akin to the legends of Hans Christian Andersen or the dark parables of Franz Kafka. To read Nachman's tales is to enter a world of elusive meanings, where the only thing certain is that the world as we know it is deeply broken.

Outwardly, Nachman's stories often resemble fairy tales. They are populated by princesses and kings and talking animals, and they feature babies switched at birth and heroes who go on quests. Scholars have found that they employ themes and plots common to folktales around the world, some of which Nachman must have absorbed from the surrounding non-Jewish cultures of eastern Europe. Indeed, it is notable that the characters in these stories are seldom Jewish, and the world they live in is not the *shtetl* Nachman himself knew, but the wide world of royal courts and remote desert islands. His first listeners must have been startled, perhaps even shocked, by the way their holy *tzaddik* moved so easily in this imaginative realm. Perhaps that is why Nachman himself ironically deprecated his stories: "What can people find to complain about? After all, they are nice stories to tell," he is quoted as saying in the introduction to the first edition of the *Tales*.

If Nachman's stories were unconventional, even controversial, that only made them a faithful reflection of their author. For while Nachman was born into the Hasidic elite, his career as a teacher and leader was deeply embattled, and his inner life even more so. One result of his dark and difficult teaching was that he was never one of the more popular Hasidic rabbis. On the contrary, his Hasidim were a self-selected elite, willing to undergo rigorous disciplines. At the same time, they were so dedicated to Nachman's presence that after he died of tuberculosis in 1810 they did not select a relative or follower to replace him. Rather, to this day, the Bratslaver Hasidim continue to see Nachman as their *rebbe*, for which reason they have been given the grim name of "dead Hasidim." Every year on Rosh Hashanah, thousands of Bratslavers and other admirers of Nachman congregate in Uman, the Ukrainian city where he died, to celebrate his memory and worship at his grave.

The gaiety and simplicity reflected in the stories about the Baal Shem Tov are nowhere to be found in the anecdotes recorded by Rabbi Nathan about Nachman's life. "No act in the service of God came easily to him; everything came only as a result of great and oft-repeated struggle," Nathan observes. Nachman felt the absence of God as acutely as the Besht seemed to feel his presence. Even as a child, "he would often speak to God in heartfelt supplications and pleas . . . but nevertheless he felt he wasn't being noticed or heard at all. On the contrary, it seemed to him that he was being pushed away from the service of God in all kinds of ways, as though he were utterly unwanted."

In response, Nachman seems to have turned instinctively toward the kind of self-tormenting asceticism that the Besht preached against. As a child, he decided that he must overcome the pleasure he felt in eating, so he began to swallow food in large pieces without chewing, so as not to taste it. As a teenager, he would fast from sabbath to sabbath and roll naked in the snow in winter. Rabbi Nathan compares Nachman's repeated assaults on his own body—above all, on his sexual urge—to military conquests: "being a powerful warrior . . . he succeeded in overcoming his passions." Haunted by the sense that he was unworthy to inherit his great-grandfather's mantle, Nachman created a religious style that was the opposite of the Besht's: not a simple celebration of God, but a kind of existential striving for him.

The course of Nachman's adult life was correspondingly stormy. At the age of twenty-six, in 1798, he decided to undertake a pilgrimage to the Land of Israel. This was not an uncommon aspiration for Hasidic rabbis. The Besht had set out on such a journey, though he couldn't complete it, and Nachman's own grandfather, who was a disciple of the Besht, had settled permanently in the Galilee. Nachman made his trip at an especially dangerous time, just as Napoleon's armies were embarking on their campaign in Egypt and Palestine. For Nachman, however, the danger was not an obstacle but an attraction: "Know that I want to place myself in danger, even great and terrible danger," he is supposed to have said. Indeed, just hours after he stepped off the boat in Haifa he announced that he wanted to return home—as if it was the ordeal of the journey that had been its whole point. Only with difficulty was he persuaded to remain in the Holy Land for several months, visiting sacred sites and the small but growing Hasidic communities. On his return journey, Nachman ran into still more trouble: he sailed in a Turkish warship that was attacked by the French, narrowly avoided shipwreck, and had to be redeemed from captivity by the Jewish community of Rhodes.

Once he returned to Ukraine in 1799, Nachman set out on his public career as a *tzaddik*, which turned out to be nearly as turbulent as his time at sea. Almost immediately he got into a vicious territorial dispute with a rival rabbi known as the Shpoler Zeide, "the grandfather of Shpole," which permanently damaged Nachman's reputation. He resettled in Bratslav, where he began a messianic agitation whose message seemed to be that Nachman was either the Messiah himself or else the key to his arrival. But the Messiah failed to come, and the death of Nachman's only son, in 1806, put an end to his apocalyptic ambitions. In the four years that remained to him he was occupied mainly with his mortal illness—and with his newfound calling as a teller of stories.

It was in the summer of 1806, at a time of personal and religious crisis, that Nachman began to tell his stories, usually during the gatherings of his followers that took place on certain Jewish holidays. "When the Rebbe began telling stories," according to Rabbi Nathan's introduction to the first edition of the *Tales*, "he said 'I am now beginning to tell stories.' His intent was as if to say, '[I must tell stories] because my lessons and conversations are not having any effect in bringing you back to God.'" At several moments in his teaching, Nachman alluded to this redemptive function of storytelling: "people may be asleep all their lives, but through stories told by a true *tzaddik*, they can be awakened." He went so far as to teach that even Gentile folktales contained the seeds of religious truth, though in distorted and confused form: "Many hidden meanings and lofty concepts are contained in the stories that the world tells. These stories, however, are deficient; they contain many omissions. They are also confused, and people do not tell them in the right order."

The clear implication is that Nachman's own stories are going to rectify this confusion, to tell the world's tales as they are meant to be told. And so it is appropriate that rectification, or *tikkun*, is the main theme of Nachman's *Tales*. As early as the *Zohar*, *tikkun olam* had been central to Jewish mysticism: the idea that the prayers and deeds of the individual Jew can help to heal the breach in the Godhead. This concept had been extensively developed in the sixteenth century by the great kabbalist Isaac Luria, who elaborated a mythology about the sparks of holiness left over from the Creation, which are lost in our world of shells, *kelipot*. The task of the Jew is to liberate these sparks and return them to God, thus hastening the advent of the Messiah; prayers and *mitzvot* could literally save the world.

CAN A STORY save the world? Nachman suggested that like every-thing else a *tzaddik* did, telling tales had a redemptive purpose: the right story told in the right way could bring a person back to God. But it was necessary for the storyteller to proceed carefully, adapting his spiritual truths to the capacity of his audience. A blind man who has just been healed, Nachman once explained, must be protected from bright lights; even so, a person in a state of spiritual convalescence should not be exposed to the full glare of truth. A story is a therapeutic device, allowing the listener to uncover its meaning at his own pace.

The first edition of Nachman's *Tales* included thirteen canonical stories (later editions added others, of more dubious authenticity). The simplest of these can barely be said to hide their meaning at all. Consider "The Rabbi's Son," the shortest tale, which tells of a certain rabbi's son who spends all his time studying. A key Hasidic tenet, however, is that knowledge without passion and inspiration is meaningless; and that is the case with this young man, who complains that "he felt that something was lacking. . . . Somehow, he did not feel any inspiration in his study or prayer." The remedy, his friends suggest, is to visit a *tzaddik*: Hasidism can supply the fervor that his spiritual life is lacking. But his father, displaying an attitude typical of the rabbinic establishment, looks down on the Hasidim as low-born and ignorant: "Why should you go to [the *tzaddik*]? You are a more accomplished scholar than he is. Your family background is better than his. It is not at all fitting that you should go to him."

There is no question where the reader's sympathy is supposed to lie in this contest of wills: we are rooting for the son to defy his father and visit the *tzaddik*. The story consists of a series of attempts by the son to do just that, each of which is thwarted by what appears to be a sign from God. First, the father and son set out to visit the *tzaddik* and their carriage overturns, which the father takes as a warning that "the journey is not approved by Heaven." When the son still feels "something missing in himself" and insists they try again, the carriage's axles break. On the third attempt, the father and son stop at an inn and get into conversation with a merchant. When they reveal that they are on the way to the *tzaddik*, the merchant remarks, "But he is worthless! . . . I was there when he committed a sin." This is surely another clear sign, and they break off their journey.

Before he can visit the *tzaddik*, the son dies. Soon after, he appears to his father the rabbi in a dream, full of reproaches: "Go to the *tzad-*

dik and he will tell you why I am angry," he instructs. The father brushes it off, but when he has the same dream three times in a row, he finally decides to do as he was told. On the way to the *tzaddik*, he runs into the merchant who had dissuaded him. Only now, the merchant suddenly reveals himself as a demon, an incarnation of Satan, the Evil One. This demon, it turns out, is the one who wrecked the carriage and broke its axles; he was trying at any cost to prevent the young man from visiting the Hasidic teacher. As he explains, "Your son was an aspect of the Lesser Light. The *tzaddik* was an aspect of the Greater Light." In other words, they were like the sun and the moon, two common kabbalistic symbols, and they had the potential to complete one another: "If the two had come together, the Messiah would have come." But by playing on the rabbi's resistance, pride, and condescension, the demon prevented the meeting from taking place and ensured that the world would remain in its fallen state.

The polemical message of this story is not hard to understand; it would have been familiar to the Baal Shem Tov and his followers. One must trust in the *tzaddik* and not the rabbi. No matter how respectable the latter, no matter how many good reasons he can give for not enlisting the Hasidic ranks, he is still working against God's will. A Jew's relationship with his *tzaddik* is more important even than a son's with his father. Indeed, the *tzaddik* becomes a substitute father, displacing the old authority.

Yet this clear-cut message is accompanied by a more troubling, and more genuinely Nachman-like, implication. After all, the rabbi in the story continually asked God for signs about whether his son should visit the *tzaddik*, and he received them. His failure was in not realizing that those signs were not from God, but from Satan. But in a world where Satan can counterfeit God so effectively, how can anyone tell a true prophet from a false one? This problem is as old as Deuteronomy—and still just as subversive. If the supernatural is not the province of God alone, if there are evil powers in the universe who can shape our lives, then it becomes impossible to read the universe's language. The believer is adrift in a world of contradictory messages, with nothing but faith to guide him—in this case, the total faith in the *tzaddik* that Nachman demands.

In "The Bull and the Ram," Nachman again delivers a message designed to bolster the faith of the reader. This time, however, he moves from the familiar world of eastern European Jewry, with its rabbis and *tzaddiks*, onto the plane of parable, while blending in allusions to several key episodes in Jewish history. The story tells of a king who decreed that all his subjects would have to convert to the official religion or be exiled. Clearly, Nachman has in mind the situation of the Jews of Spain in 1492, where just the same choice of conversion or expulsion was offered. And in this kingdom, as in Spain, some Jews publicly converted while still following Judaism in private. The Hebrew translation of the *Tales* refers to them as *anusim*, the same word used to refer to Sephardic *conversos*.

One of these forced converts was a royal minister, who continued in office when the king died and his son took the throne. In a reprise of the story of Mordecai from the book of Esther, this minister overheard some courtiers plotting to overthrow the new king. The minister revealed the conspiracy and was offered anything he wished for as a reward. Naturally, what he requested was the right to "be a Jew openly. I want to be able to wear my tallith and my tefillin publicly." Grudgingly, the king granted this concession. But then the second king died and was followed on the throne by a third king, of whom Nachman says that he was "a very wise man." Wisely, then, he summoned his court astrologers and asked them "what could destroy his children, so that they would be able to safeguard themselves against it." The answer was that he should beware of "a bull and a ram": as long as he avoided them, his children would survive.

In time, however, the third king also died and was succeeded by a fourth, who was a conqueror and a tyrant. Knowing the prophecy about the bull and the ram, he ordered that all such animals be banned from his kingdom. At the same time, he took away the privilege his grandfather had granted to the royal minister—still on the scene after so many reigns—and forbade him to practice openly as a Jew. The reader can already guess that this act will prove his undoing, and his dreams confirm it: the king has a dream about the signs of the zodiac, in which Taurus and Aries, the signs of the bull and the ram, are laughing at him. Clearly, the danger of the prophecy had not been overcome.

"Terror-stricken," the king consults a wise man, who tells him about a certain iron rod that grows out of the ground: "If a person has any fear, he can come to this rod and have his fear dispelled." The king decides to seek out this rod, but to get there he has to go down a path filled with fire. When he sees the fire, the king observes that "walking through [it] were kings, along with Jews wearing the tallith and tefillin." The king assumes that if these people could survive the fire, so could he, and he rashly walks into it—only to be burned to ash. But how could this have happened, his courtiers wondered, when he had been so scrupulous about avoiding bulls and rams? Was the prophecy false after all?

Once again, Nachman suggests that the difficult thing is not receiving messages from God, but interpreting them correctly. The bull and the ram were indeed the king's undoing, the converted Jewish minister explained, but not in the way he had expected. Rather, the prophecy was referring to the insignia of Jewishness—the *tefillin*, whose leather boxes and straps are made from the skin of a bull, and the *tallith*, whose fringes are made from the wool of the ram. The kings who survived the fire did so because they had treated their subject Jews well, allowing them to practice their faith openly. "But this king did not allow the Jews in his land to wear the tallith and tefillin," the minister explains, "and therefore he was destroyed."

The moral of this story, for an audience of nineteenth-century Jews living under czarist rule, was not exactly an optimistic one. The book of Esther, on which "The Bull and the Ram" is partly based, shows Mordecai not just thwarting a plot against the Jews of Persia but turn-

ing the tables on Haman, leading the Jews to triumph over their enemies. Nachman's story offers no such happy ending, and no promise
of one. Nothing can stop a wicked king, like the first and the fourth
kings in the story, from persecuting their Jewish subjects. Sometimes,
Jews do have to go into hiding, as the royal minister did. The only
compensation for this vulnerability is the assurance that in the end
God will judge Gentile kings by the way they treat their Jews. The
humble *tallith* and *tefillin* turn out to be more important than the
king's armies and wise men.

This much of the story would be clear to any listener. But to read
the traditional commentary of the Bratslaver Hasidim is to realize
that even a seemingly straightforward story like "The Bull and the
Ram" can be read on several levels. Thus the four kings can be taken
as symbols of the four empires that conquered the Jewish people. The
first king, who deprives the Jews of their religion, represents Babylon,
which destroyed the first Temple and sent the Israelites into exile. The
second, who restores the minister's right to be a Jew, represents Persia,
which brought the Jews back from exile and allowed them to rebuild
the Temple. The third, who is "very wise," represents Greece, famous
for its science and philosophy. And the fourth king, who persecutes
the Jews and is punished for it, stands for Rome, which destroyed the
Second Temple but was destroyed in turn a few centuries later. In this
way, "The Bull and the Ram" serves as a parable about Jewish history,
as well as a fable about the importance of the Jews in history.

It is when Nachman turns from this world to the next, from the
Jews to their God, that the real uncanniness of his stories blossoms.
This is what happens in "The Humble King," another short tale that
is one of Nachman's most enigmatic and Kafka-like. This story, like
many of Nachman's, begins with a king; but this king is himself in
search of another, greater king, one who is known as "a mighty warrior, man of truth and humble person." This humble king has never
been seen, because he lives in a kingdom cut off from the world by
quicksand and oceans. The first king longs to get a portrait of the

humble king, but "no king had that king's portrait, since he kept himself hidden from all people." So he sends a wise man as an emissary,
charged with obtaining the humble king's likeness.

Now the story takes an unlikely turn, as Nachman focuses on a new
subject—the nature of jokes. The wise man, arriving in the land of the
humble king, decides that the best way to find out about the character
of that land is to learn its jokes: "in order to understand something,
one must know the jokes related to it." All the jokes in the country, he
discovers, are made up by one man; and when the wise man goes to see
him, he realizes that the jokes are actually keys to the country's vices
and sins: "He saw that jokes were being made about how people were
cheated and deceived in business, and how when people took a case to
court, it was all decided on the basis of falsehood and bribery."

This discovery presents a serious problem for the wise man. If the
humble king is "a man of truth," how is it that the country he rules is
so corrupt? Determined to find an answer, the wise man makes it to
the humble king's palace and lays out his indictment: "Over whom are
you king? The land is completely full of falsehood, from beginning to
end. There is no truth in it at all." During all of this, he still doesn't
see the king, who is hidden behind a curtain. But then the wise man
changes tactics. It must be, he decides, that the humble king does
know about the evil of his country, and that is why he hides—because
he "cannot tolerate the land's falsehood." His seeming absence is actually what proves that he is a good king.

At this point, the wise man begins to praise the king in hyperbolic
terms. But the king's humility is so great that the more praise he hears,
the more he shrinks in size, until finally, "he literally became nothing." At this point, the nothing-sized king pulls back the curtain,
eager to see the wise man who understands him so well. "In doing so,
however, the king revealed his face, and the sage saw him. The wise
man was then able to paint his portrait and bring it to his king." And
so the story ends.

In the original edition of the *Tales*, "The Humble King" is followed by a note from the editor, Rabbi Nathan, who explains that when Nachman first told this story, he "expressly said that he was revealing some hints and verses alluding to the mysteries in the stories. . . . However, the mysteries of these stories extend far beyond the grasp of our knowledge." A sense of hidden depths is nowhere stronger than in this tale, which is so replete with paradoxes. A good king rules an evil kingdom; a great king is so humble that he can't abide praise; the sage makes a portrait of the king only once he has disappeared. Presumably, the painting that the sage brings home is blank, yet this blankness is somehow a true likeness.

It is precisely because of these contradictions, however, that "The Humble King" is so evocative. For it is plain that the humble king—the one whose reputation fills the world, but whom no one has ever seen—is Nachman's way of talking about God. God is constantly referred to as a king, in the Bible and in Jewish liturgy, and whenever a king appears in Nachman's tales there is a good chance that he is a stand-in for God. But if the humble king is God, then he is a God who rules over a world in disarray. Instead of making everything fair and orderly, he has withdrawn from the scene, leaving people so hardened and cynical that they joke about their own crimes.

Explaining this absence is one of the chief purposes of Kabbalah, and "The Humble King," like most of Nachman's stories, deals in kabbalistic symbolism. The *Zohar* explained that the world goes awry when God's attributes are out of harmony, allowing the evil "other side" to take over and resulting in the exile of the Shekhinah, the divine presence who is also the spirit of Israel. In "The Humble King," accordingly, we find a world so evil that God has withdrawn from it: "you keep yourself at a distance from your subjects," the wise man observes, in a perfect summary of kabbalistic theodicy. In this situation, the only way to approach God is through his nothingness; for as Kabbalah also teaches, the ultimate reality of God is the *En Sof,* the limitless, which cannot be grasped in human language or concepts. It is only once God disappears, when he ceases to take any apprehensible form, that we encounter his essence, and so it is only as a portrait of nothing that we can see his likeness.

Stated baldly, this might sound like a mere paradox; in the garb of Nachman's story, it becomes more comprehensible and more credible. Just as Nachman explained, the truths of Torah are easier to grasp in the form of narrative than in the form of propositions. "The Humble King" also makes clear how central a role the *tzaddik* himself plays in bringing the world closer to God. For the wise man who embarks on the quest for God, and who is vouchsafed a glimpse of his nothingness, is none other than the *tzaddik*. The king at the beginning of the story who longs to see the humble king does not try to approach on his own; he sends the wise man as an emissary. Just so, the soul of the ordinary Jew does not reach God directly, but through the intermediary of the *tzaddik*.

And these are just the plainer levels of meaning in this tale. The Bratslaver commentaries on "The Humble King" delve much deeper into kabbalistic symbolism, explaining that the story's two kings—the first king and the humble king—represent two *sefirot*, Malkhut and Binah, while the wise man who connects them represents Yesod. Again, the land in which the humble king dwells can be understood as either the world, or the Land of Israel, or one of the kabbalistic planes of creation. The fertility of kabbalistic interpretation is such that there is virtually no element of Nachman's tales in which some mystical meaning cannot be discovered. Still, the power of these stories is that each of their levels of meaning—historical, moral, metaphysical, mystical—functions on its own, even if the others remain obscure.

~~~~

LIKE "THE HUMBLE KING," the longest and most ambitious of Nachman's *Tales* are allegories of a broken world. The particular myth that stands behind these stories is the one Nachman learned from the Kabbalah of Isaac Luria, who taught that the divine light was too powerful to be contained in the "vessels" of the *sefirot*. In the primal catastrophe of the universe, these vessels shattered, causing the sparks of divinity to be scattered and lost in our fallen world of "shells" or "husks." Lurianic Kabbalah offers a very intricate cosmology explaining the stages of this process, and many of its terms of art can be detected in Nachman's stories. But the emotional truth that this myth encodes is not dissimilar from the one expressed in the myth of the fall of man, in Genesis. Our world was once perfect, and now it is imperfect. Something has gone wrong in the very fabric of creation, which it is our duty to put right.

It is no coincidence that these myths of falling and scattering should have become so central to Jewish thought. After all, Jewish history presents itself as a series of losses, descents, and catastrophes. As early as Deuteronomy, Moses envisioned the Jewish people losing their homeland and being sent into exile. This duly came to pass in the sixth century BCE under the Babylonians, and again in the first century CE under the Romans. Most of Jewish history took place in a condition of *galut*, or exile from the homeland. And within this exile the Jews experienced repeated flights and exoduses, as well as outright massacres. To live as a Jew was to live in a broken world. Nachman's mystical Hasidism offered the assurance that this world could be healed—that the power of the *tzaddik* could repair the universe, end the exile, bring the Messiah.

That is the message and the plot of Nachman's greatest stories. Each of these tales begins with a catastrophe that has introduced chaos and division into the world. Nachman's innovation is to clothe this theme in the traditional garb of the fairy tale, so that the primal disaster takes on a familiar narrative shape. In "The Exchanged Children," things begin to go wrong when a midwife switches the child of the queen for the child of a servant; in "The Master of Prayer," a hurricane turns the world upside down and scatters the king's courtiers; in "The Seven Beggars," there is a mass flight of people from a kingdom, during which a boy and girl are lost in the forest. Most mysterious of all, there is the rupture that occurs at the beginning of "The Lost Princess," when the king, in a momentary fit of anger, banishes his beloved daughter from his presence, saying, "May the Evil One take you away!" In kabbalistic terms, this can be taken as the moment when one aspect of God turns against another, causing the exile of the Shekhinah, who is the female aspect of the divinity. But in human terms, it has an almost Lear-like quality—as if God the king is as impetuous and full of regret as Shakespeare's doomed patriarch.

This merging of the human and the supernatural is key to the disorienting power of Nachman's stories. "The Lost Princess," for instance, turns into a quest narrative, as the king sends a viceroy to search for his missing daughter. To rescue her, the viceroy undergoes a series of tests, which he initially fails. Told by the princess to fast for a year, he ends up eating an apple on the very last day; then, given another chance and told to abstain from wine for a year, he ends up drinking from an enchanted fountain on the last day. In each case, the rescue of the princess is aborted, and she ends up being taken far away to a pearl castle on a golden mountain. To locate this magic place, the viceroy consults with a series of giants, who summon the world's animals and birds to search for it, in vain. Finally, a third giant summons the winds, and one of them knows where the castle is to be found. When the viceroy arrives there, he enters the castle and is on the brink of finding the princess when the story suddenly breaks off: "The Rebbe did not tell how he freed her," it ends, "but in the end he did free her."

Here we have a number of elements familiar from folk literature: the questing hero, the tests of commitment, the summoning of the elements. As in many fairy tales, too, things happen in groups of three: there are three chances to rescue the princess and three giants. It would be possible to tell this tale to a child as a simple story of adventure. Yet the details of "The Lost Princess" encode a wealth of allusions to Jewish scripture, history, and mysticism. The banishing of the king's daughter, as we have seen, represents the primal exile of the Shekhinah, the guardian spirit of the Jewish people. To restore her, and therefore to restore God to himself, requires the efforts of a hero, the viceroy—who can represent either the Jewish people as a whole, in their quest for God, or else the particular heroism of the *tzaddik*, who performs spiritual tasks on his people's behalf.

In the first part of the story, the viceroy is given two chances to rescue the king's daughter with relative ease. First, all he has to do is abstain from food; but like Adam, who was also told not to eat, he fails the test and partakes of forbidden fruit. Then he is given a second chance, like Noah, who is given the opportunity to repopulate the world after the Flood; but also like Noah, he succumbs to the temptation of drunkenness. As Kabbalah teaches, the balance of the world could have been restored at the very beginning of Creation, if only the first men had been able to obey God. Their failure deepened the rift in the Godhead, so that now it can only be overcome through arduous disciplines—like the journey of the viceroy to the golden mountain. Other aspects of the story can be similarly decoded: the three giants, for instance, might represent the three patriarchs, Abraham, Isaac, and Jacob, or the three levels of the kabbalistic soul, *nefesh, ruach*, and *neshamah*. Number mysticism, which plays a major role in kabbalism, here meets the numerical formulas of the fairy tale, creating a hybrid form of endless interpretability.

The most moving element of this story, however, is its abrupt conclusion. Nachman is able to narrate the viceroy's journey up to the brink of his rescue of the princess. One more step and he will become the Messiah, reuniting all that history has sundered—the Jewish people and the Land of Israel, the human race and God, the lower *sefirot* with the higher *sefirot*. But it is precisely this redemption that Nachman is unable to imagine. He knows that it must take place, because his faith assures him that it will. But the form the Messiah will take, the strategies he will use to rescue the Shekhinah, are hidden in futurity. Here the literary problem, which is that perfection cannot be narrated, coincides with the theological problem, which is that redemption cannot be anticipated. Nachman's silence is an eloquent response to this predicament.

A similar silence or omission marks the end of "The Seven Beggars," the last story he told, in April 1810, a few months before his death. Nachman himself saw it as his masterpiece: "If I only told the world this one story, I would still be truly great," he commented immodestly. In terms of narrative structure, it is certainly the most elaborate of the *Tales*, consisting of a series of nested stories. It begins by describing a king who transferred his kingdom to his only son, celebrating with a great feast. Yet this happiness is shadowed by the king's warning to his son that "a time will come when you will step down from the throne." This downfall comes about because the new king becomes obsessed with secular learning—a repeated theme in Nachman's tales, which are deeply distrustful of worldly knowledge. Nachman, living at a time when the *Haskalah*, the Jewish Enlightenment, had only barely begun to penetrate eastern Europe, nevertheless foresaw a day when the forces of secularism would become the greatest challenge to traditional Jewish faith. The king's son, who grows so interested in "wisdom" that he becomes a heretic, represents the intellectuals whom Nachman feared would go astray. Still, the tale assures us that "the simple people in country were not harmed by the wisdom of the great sages and did not become heretics": simplicity, for Nachman, was the best protection against heresy.

Possibly as a result of the king's freethinking—though this is not made totally explicit—a disaster is visited on his land, and "the entire population of the country took flight." Nachman does not say exactly what caused this flight, and its very motivelessness increases its power as a symbol. It can be taken as an allegory of Adam's fall, or of the exile of the Jewish people, or of the shattering of the cosmic vessels. However we read it, this exodus sets the stage for the next part of the tale, which concerns two young children, a boy and a girl, who get lost in the chaos and end up alone in the forest. On the brink of starvation, they survive thanks to a series of seven beggars who pass by and give them bread. Each of these beggars is afflicted in a different way: the first is blind, the second is deaf, the third cannot speak, and so on. It is therefore an ambiguous blessing when each leaves the children with the words, "May you be as I am."

The two children survive, and when they grow up they decide to get married. The only thing missing to complete the happiness of the wedding feast, they say, is the presence of the seven beggars who long ago saved their lives. No sooner is this said than the beggars appear, one by one. The significance of the beggars becomes clear when each of them arrives and reveals that what the children initially took to be a handicap was, in fact, the disguise of a great virtue. The blind beggar explains that he is not really blind: he sees nothing because "to me the time of the whole world is not worth a moment's fleeting glance." Similarly, the deaf beggar is able to hear, but doesn't listen to "the cries of want" that fill the world because "to me the whole world is worth nothing." And so on for the next four beggars—the one with a speech defect, the one with a crooked neck, the hunchback, and the one with no hands. Allegorically, each of the seven beggars can be identified with one of the biblical leaders of Israel, from Abraham down to King David. Kabbalistically, they can be identified with the *sefirot* that form the body of *Adam Kadmon*, the cosmic man. But again, these levels of interpretation supplement without canceling out the plain meaning, which is moral and spiritual: in a fallen world, what looks like weakness is often really strength, and vice versa.

When each of the beggars arrives at the wedding to bestow a blessing, he also tells a story; and these stories-within-the-story form the heart of "The Seven Beggars." Each is a poetic fable that illuminates a spiritual truth. The second beggar, for example, tells a complex tale about a garden whose gardener disappeared, leaving its inhabitants vulnerable to the attack of a cruel king. This cruel king ruined their existence by spoiling their sense of taste and smell, so that "whenever anyone tasted anything, it had the taste of a rotten carcass." The beggar determines that the reason for this affliction is that the people have succumbed to sexual immorality, profanity, and greed, and he tells them that if they mend their behavior their senses will be restored. They do so, and the land is "rectified." Finally, the gardener reappears, and after initial confusion—"everyone thought he was crazy so they threw stones at him and drove him away"—he is recognized and the garden is restored. Here Nachman offers another legible parable about the fallen condition of the universe, mankind, and the Jewish people. The references to a garden, a missing gardener, and a cruel king map easily onto the story of the Garden of Eden, where God and Satan battled for the future of humanity.

Each of the beggars' tales is distinctive in genre and theme: one is a fantasy about a princess trapped in a castle made of water, another a riddle-telling contest. But the stories told by the third and fourth beggars are the most memorable, partly because they are so similar that they read like variations on the same idea. The fourth beggar tells about a pair of birds, a male and a female, who get separated and must make their nests in different lands. At night, these birds cry out so sadly for one another that sorrow infects the whole country and no one can sleep. The beggar promises that he can use ventriloquism to lead the birds to one another, ending their separation. Meanwhile, the third beggar tells of the Heart of the World, which stands at one end of the earth and yearns for a Spring, which stands atop a mountain at the opposite end. The Heart "longs and yearns so much that its soul goes out, and it cries out." Yet it doesn't dare to go to the Spring, since the first step would mean losing sight of the beloved object, and the Heart couldn't bear that loss.

These poignant images of longing and separation can be parsed kabbalistically, with the birds representing God and the Shekhinah or Heaven and Earth, and the beggar who unites them representing the *tzaddik*. The story abounds in allusions to the Bible and the *Zohar*, as Nachman himself hinted: "One who is versed in the sacred literature will be able to understand some of the allusions," he said after telling it. But the power of "The Seven Beggars" is such that, as Nachman intended, it can be felt even by a reader who misses these references. For Nachman is a master of the broken heart as much as of the broken world, and he shows how the two go together: in human existence, in Jewish existence, longing is the supremely religious emotion. His faith promises that this longing will be rewarded, but here as in "The Lost Princess" Nachman leaves out that happy ending. For the story of the seventh beggar goes untold, and Rabbi Nathan adds that "we will not be worthy of hearing it until the Messiah comes."

BIBLIOGRAPHY

Buber, Martin. *Tales of the Hasidim.* New York: Schocken, 1991.

Green, Arthur. *Tormented Master: The Life and Spiritual Quest of Rabbi Nahman of Bratslav.* Woodstock, VT: Jewish Lights, 1992.

Rabbi Nachman's Stories. Translated by Aryeh Kaplan. Jerusalem: Breslov Research Institute, 1983.

Steinsaltz, Adin. *The Tales of Rabbi Nachman of Bratslav.* Translated by Yehuda Hanegbi et al. New Milford, CT: Maggid Books, 2010.

13

IF YOU WILL IT

The Jewish State and *Old New Land* by Theodor Herzl

The tomb of Theodor Herzl in Jerusalem

In the 1890s, a minor Viennese writer named Theodor Herzl transformed himself, through the power of his imagination, into one of the most important figures in Jewish history. In two visionary books, Herzl ignited the hopes of Jews around the world and started the process that would lead, half a century later, to the creation of the State of Israel. *The Jewish State*, a nonfiction pamphlet, laid out a detailed plan for the relocation of Europe's Jews to Palestine, where they would create a free and prosperous Jewish country. In the novel *Old New Land*, Herzl imagined this "new society" from the vantage point of the near future, describing its techno- logical and social achievements, and predicting that it would completely transform the Jewish character. While Jews had always dreamed of returning to their Promised Land, it was Herzl who transformed that dream into a practical political program—the movement that would become known as Zionism.

In January 1893, Theodor Herzl received a let- ter asking for his help with a new magazine dedicated to fighting anti-Semitism. Herzl, then thirty-two years old, was the Paris cor- respondent for Vienna's leading newspaper, the *Neue Freie Presse,* and a playwright of minor renown. Though he was Jewish, he had not written much about Jewish causes before, and he responded to the invitation with a certain reserve. Publishing a new magazine, he wrote to the Austrian nobleman who led the Vienna Society to Combat Anti-Semitism, would do less to raise the social position of Austria's Jews than a few well-publicized duels fought against leading anti-Semites. As the correspondence developed, Herzl's ambivalence grew more pronounced. Perhaps there was a good side to anti-Semi- tism, he mused, since it would "educate the Jews" out of their more objectionable behaviors. It was too late for him to convert to Christi- anity himself, but perhaps he should have his son baptized, to lift the burden of Jewishness.

Finally, Herzl came up with a spectacular solution to what was then widely called "the Jewish question": the mass conversion of Austria's Jews to Christianity, under the auspices of the Pope. Every Sunday, he imagined, thousands of Jews would appear at Vienna's largest cathedral to be baptized. In this way, conversion would no longer be a shameful act by individual Jews hoping to erase a stigma, but a proud and public solution to a great social problem. Herzl was so enthusiastic about the plan that he urged the editors of his newspaper, who were also Jewish, to publicize it. He was disappointed when they refused, calling the idea impossible and irresponsible. For a moment, Herzl believed, the salvation of the Jewish people—not spiritual, but temporal—had been within his grasp.

The outlandishness of Herzl's idea was a good gauge of the desperation he felt as a modern, secular European Jew. Herzl grew up in Budapest, the only son of a prosperous and assimilated family. Many of his relatives had converted to Christianity; as an adult, Herzl was entirely non-observant, celebrating Christmas at home rather than Chanukah. And like so many educated, urban Jews of his generation—in places like Berlin, Paris, and Vienna—Herzl was born into a world that believed implicitly in progress. The Jews of the Austro-Hungarian empire won full civil and legal equality in 1867, and the Jews of Germany followed in 1871. Jew-hatred seemed to be a relic of the past that would surely disappear in the light of science and liberalism. The story that had begun with Moses Mendelssohn, of Jewish emancipation and enlightenment, was about to receive its triumphant final chapter.

Yet by the time Herzl dreamed of the conversion of the Jews, it was abundantly clear that something had gone wrong. Rather than ending Jew-hatred, the entry of the Jews into modern European society only gave it a new form: anti-Semitism, a word coined in 1879 by the German polemicist Wilhelm Marr. Anti-Semitism, in the late nineteenth century in Europe, was not the name of a rather disreputable private prejudice, but an openly proclaimed social movement with its own political parties and newspapers. In 1895, the city of Vienna elected a popular mayor, Karl Lueger, on an explicitly anti-Semitic platform. At the same time, the Dreyfus Affair in France exposed the violent anti-Semitism of a majority of the French population. As a reporter,

Herzl was present at the ceremony where Alfred Dreyfus, a French Jewish army officer falsely accused of treason, was publicly stripped of his military rank, to the accompaniment of the crowd's cries of "Death to the Jews." Far from being solved, "the Jewish question" was growing more acute every day.

Even as he made a name for himself as a writer of stage comedies and *feuilletons*—the light, observational newspaper essays so popular in Vienna—Theodor Herzl was deeply aware of these developments. As a university student, he resigned from his fraternity after one of its members delivered an anti-Semitic speech. By 1893, as we have seen, he was contemplating a grandly theatrical solution to the Jewish problem in mass conversion. The following year, he wrote a play, *The New Ghetto*, whose hero is killed in a duel with an anti-Semite, proclaiming with his dying breath the need to break out of the invisible, psychological ghetto where Jews still resided. "I must do something for the Jews," Herzl wrote in his diary after visiting a synagogue for the first time in years.

By the spring of 1895, Herzl's concern with the Jewish question had become an obsession. He spent days and nights thinking of nothing else, fortifying himself with visits to the opera to hear the music of Wagner. In this way, the nineteenth century's leading musical anti-Semite furnished the soundtrack for the birth of modern Zionism. For the idea that Herzl conceived in those days in Paris was nothing less than the creation of a Jewish state. After almost two thousand years in Diaspora, he believed, the time had come when it was both necessary and possible to re-establish Jewish sovereignty. Millions of oppressed Jews would launch a new Exodus and find safety in a new Promised Land. The idea was as wild and improbable as Herzl's earlier plan for mass conversion, and it was born out of the same conviction that the Jews had no future in Europe. And just as with that earlier fantasy, the first people to whom Herzl confided his vision dismissed it out of hand. He called on one of the age's leading Jewish philanthropists, Baron Edmond de Hirsch, who had spent a fortune establishing Jewish agricultural colonies in Argentina; Herzl came armed with a twenty-two-page speech but only got to page six before being dismissed. "You are an intelligent man," the Baron told Herzl, according to the latter's account of the meeting. "But you have such fantastic brain waves!"

Instead of being daunted, Herzl raised his sights. To resettle the world's poor and oppressed Jews would require a great deal of money. And who had more money to devote to Jewish causes than the Rothschild family, whose branches in the various countries of Europe were legendarily wealthy? The best thing to do, Herzl decided, would be to convene a meeting of all the Rothschilds and win them over to his ideas. By June 1895, he had written a sixty-eight-page memorandum titled "Speech to the Rothschilds," in which he laid out his plan down to the smallest details. Herzl asked a friend, a doctor, to listen as he read the manuscript aloud; at the end of the reading, Herzl noticed that his listener was in tears. The tears, however, were not a response to the grandeur of the Zionist idea, but a sign of his friend's certainty that Herzl had lost his mind. "This book is a product of sickness," he advised Herzl. "You must see a doctor."

Herzl never had a chance to read his speech to the Rothschilds. His letter to Albert Rothschild, the head of the Viennese branch of the family, went unanswered; so too did a letter to Bismarck, the retired German chancellor. But if he could not win over the elite, Herzl decided, he would set his ideas before the Jewish public. He spent the last weeks of the year turning his speech into a small pamphlet, which was published at the beginning of 1896 in an edition of three thousand copies. Its title was *The Jewish State*.

BEFORE THEODOR HERZL DIED, in 1904 at the age of just forty-four, he instructed that he was to be buried in a metal coffin rather than the wooden one customary in Judaism. The reason was

that he wanted his body preserved, so that one day it could be transferred from the cemetery in Vienna to the Jewish state he was certain
would come into being. It took forty-four more years, but in 1948 the
State of Israel was born; the next year, Herzl's remains were disinterred
and reburied in a tomb in Jerusalem, at the top of a hill named Mount
Herzl. *The Jewish State,* the book that came into the world as a freak
and a fantasy, led within the space of half a century to the creation of a
Jewish state. In the history of Judaism, other books have done more to
shape Jewish religion and the Jewish spirit, but none had the same kind
of practical, political impact. Not since Moses stood on the slopes of
Mount Nebo and prophesied the fate of the Israelites in the Promised
Land, in the book of Deuteronomy, had a single person done more to
direct the course of Jewish history.

To read *The Jewish State* today, however, knowing what we know
about the history that led up to the creation of Israel and the history
that followed, is to be struck by how bad a prophet Herzl turned
out to be. In the eighty-odd pages of the pamphlet, Herzl offers not
merely an ideal vision or a call to arms, but a detailed program for
how the masses of European Jewry could be transferred, peacefully
and efficiently, to their new home in the Jewish state. This state did
not absolutely have to be located in Palestine—Herzl briefly considers
the possibility that it would be created in Argentina, and a few years
later he would entertain the British offer of a colony in Uganda. But
Palestine, which he calls "our ever-memorable historic home," was the
most likely and desirable choice. Herzl envisioned the new exodus of
Jews beginning very soon, with the acquiescence of the Turkish government that controlled Palestine, and the active encouragement of
European governments eager to be rid of their Jewish populations. It
would involve the orderly liquidation of Jewish property in Europe
and the creation of new cities and infrastructure in Palestine, a process Herzl describes in great detail. For instance, he specifies not just
a seven-hour work day in the new society, but the maximum amount

of paid overtime (three hours, "only ... permitted on a doctor's certificate"). When he came to write his novel about the Jewish state, *Old New Land*, he envisioned the entire process taking no more than twenty years.

If Herzl had been told that a Jewish state would indeed be created in Palestine, but only after fifty years, two world wars, and the annihilation of six million European Jews in the Holocaust, he would have been incredulous and horrified. He would have found it equally hard to believe that the creation of Israel would take place in the teeth of fierce resistance from the Palestinian Arab population and the surrounding Arab countries, and that its existence would be defined by war and occupation. Nor did Herzl predict any of the salient features of Israeli culture, from the restoration of Hebrew as a spoken language to the sharp division between secular and religious Israelis. Finally, the persistence of anti-Semitism even after the creation of the Jewish state—indeed, the link between twenty-first-century anti-Semitism and Zionism itself—falsifies one of the chief predictions of *The Jewish State*, which is that "the Jews, once settled in their own State, would probably have no more enemies."

In short, what Herzl failed to account for in his historic pamphlet was history, with all its obstacles, struggles, and disappointments. This is ironic, since he begins *The Jewish State* by repeatedly insisting on his plan's realism. Herzl knew that the rebirth of the Jewish state, more than eighteen hundred years after the Romans conquered Jerusalem and burned the Temple, might sound like sheer utopianism. By an odd coincidence, a colleague of his on the *Neue Freie Presse* with a nearly identical name, Theodor Hertzka, had published a utopian novel a few years earlier, called *Free-Land*; and in his preface, Herzl goes out of his way to dissociate his own book from that one. Like most utopias going back to Thomas More's, he writes, Hertzka's Free-Land is "a complicated piece of mechanism with numerous cogged wheels fitting into each other; but there is nothing to prove that they can be set in motion." In *The Jewish State*, Herzl would introduce plenty of mechanisms of his own devising, but the key to his scheme is that it also provides for a source of power to drive them.

That "propelling force," Herzl declares, is "the misery of the Jews," which he compares to boiling water. Attempts to "check anti-Semitism"—such as the magazine he had been invited to join a few years earlier—are like lids placed on top of a boiling kettle, in a pointless effort to contain it. But if you generate steam on a massive basis, Herzl points out, you can use it to power a train engine that will "move passengers and goods." Zionism is that engine, anti-Semitism is its fuel, and the passengers it intends to move are the millions of Jews trapped in a dead-end existence in Europe. This mechanical metaphor underscores Herzl's deeply nineteenth-century faith in science and reason. Like Karl Marx, he sees himself not as a mere prophet but as a technician of history, discovering the hydraulic forces that move people and nations. "I shall therefore clearly and emphatically state," he writes, "that I believe in the practical outcome of my scheme. . . . The Jewish State is essential to the world; it will therefore be created."

What is notable about Herzl's vision of Zionism is that it holds the entire tradition of Jewish longing for Zion at arm's length. Since the moment the Temple was destroyed, the idea of redemption and restoration to the Land of Israel had played a central role in every aspect of Judaism. The Talmud is full of detailed speculations about how and when the Temple would be rebuilt; Yehuda Halevi and the *Zohar*, in their very different ways, highlighted the metaphysical superiority of the Land of Israel to every other country; generations of Hasidic rabbis like Nachman of Bratslav made pilgrimages to Palestine. Indeed, less than twenty years before Herzl wrote, the increasing pressure on Jews in the Russian Empire had led to the creation of a new movement called *Hovevei Zion*, "Lovers of Zion," which led hundreds of idealistic young Jews to move to the Holy Land and create new agricultural settlements.

When he set out on his career as a Zionist leader, Herzl was totally ignorant of that movement, just as he had never heard of the handful of Jewish writers who had anticipated his themes. By the same token, he had never read a page of the Talmud or the *Zohar*. Herzl knew, of course, of the centrality of the Land of Israel to Judaism. "The idea which I have developed in this pamphlet is a very old one," begins *The Jewish State*. But the messianic fervor of this longing, the sense that the redemption of the Jews would be a sign and symbol of the redemption of the universe, was foreign to him. And it was, ironically, this alienation from the sources of Jewish tradition that allowed Herzl to become the most effective advocate for one of the chief hopes of that tradition. He did not believe in the Messiah, so he did not expect the Messiah. A man of the nineteenth century, he believed instead in political action, economic planning, and technological progress—in human achievement, not divine assistance. The slogan of the Zionist movement, which began as Herzl's epigraph to *Old New Land*, was "If you will it, it is no dream"; and this emphasis on Jewish self-help is what sets modern political Zionism apart from its religious antecedents.

If Herzl did not know much about Judaism, however, he knew intimately what it meant to be Jewish in fin-de-siècle Europe. That is why anti-Semitism was the impetus for his Zionism: to be a Jew, for Herzl, was in the first place to be the target of oppobrium and persecution. It was in reaction to this experience that he insisted on reclaiming a positive Jewish identity. "We are a people—one people," Herzl asserts, in words that thrilled his first readers. But he goes on to say that this unity emerged only after the failure of the Jews to join the several European nations in which they lived. "We have honestly endeavored everywhere to merge ourselves in the social life of our surrounding communities and to preserve the faith of our fathers. We are not permitted to do so," he observes. Herzl does not have a problem with assimilation per se; indeed, his whole life as a German writer was predicated on the idea. But unlike most of his fellow western Jews,

Herzl implies, he is ready to admit that assimilation has been tried and proved a failure. "Prosperity," he writes a little later on, "weakens our Judaism and extinguishes our peculiarities. It is only pressure that forces us back to the parent stem . . . We are one people—our enemies have made us one without our consent."

This is a strikingly reactive definition of Jewish unity. No wonder that as the Zionist movement rapidly evolved over the following years, Herzl's political Zionism would be challenged by the cultural Zionism of many eastern European Jews, who retained a more vital connection with tradition and saw the regeneration of Judaism as more urgent than the acquisition of territory. But it would be wrong to think of Herzl's Zionism as a purely negative phenomenon. Part of the purpose of the Jewish state, and of the struggle for that state, is to restore Jewish self-confidence, battered by the constant assaults of anti-Semitism. "There are more mistaken notions abroad concerning Jews than any other people," Herzl writes in *The Jewish State*. "And we have become so depressed and discouraged by our historic sufferings, that we ourselves repeat and believe those mistakes." Zionism is a therapy for this wounded self-esteem: "They will awaken from gloomy brooding, for into their lives will come a new significance," he writes in the pamphlet's conclusion. "I believe that a wondrous generation of Jews will spring into existence."

In a sense, it was the creation of this "wondrous generation," this newly energized and hopeful Jewish people, that was the immediate aim of Herzl's Zionism, even before the creation of a Jewish state. "The people is the subjective, land the objective foundation of a State, and the subjective basis is the more important of the two," he observes. But a people usually speaks politically through its chosen representatives; and who, it might fairly be objected, chose Theodor Herzl? The great institutional accomplishment of Herzl was the creation of an annual Zionist Congress, which could speak on behalf of the Jews with the governments of the world. Herzl himself negotiated face-to-face with the sultan of Turkey and the emperor of Germany, among other potentates. Later Zionist leaders like Chaim Weizmann would be instrumental in winning British support for the creation of a Jewish home in Palestine. Yet the Congress was largely a self-selected group, and Herzl's leadership owed everything to the force of his personality and conviction. Was this a legitimate form of authority?

For Herzl, as *The Jewish State* shows, legitimacy was a crucial concept. Some Zionists and Jewish philanthropists believed that their efforts should be focused on creating facts on the ground, in the form of new Jewish settlements in Palestine. This population would then become the nucleus of a Jewish state. Herzl, in contrast, strongly condemned what he called "a gradual infiltration of Jews," which he believed would eventually create an anti-Semitic backlash. The only safe way for Jews to settle in Palestine or any other territory was en masse, with the legal protection of the responsible government.

To accomplish this, the Jews needed an official political representative. This was the first piece of the machinery Herzl invented in *The Jewish State*: the institution he calls the Society of Jews. This Society he envisions as something like the World Zionist Organization he went on to create—a voluntary organization that would gain enough popular support to be recognized as the official spokesman for the Jewish people. "The Society," he writes, "will thus be acknowledged in its relations with Governments as a State-creating power. This acknowledgment will practically create the State." The Society of Jews is a government in exile; create the government, Herzl promises, and the state will follow. Thus after the First Zionist Congress was held in Basel, Switzerland, in August 1897, Herzl wrote in his diary: "Were I to sum up the Basel congress in a few words—which I must guard against uttering publicly—it would be this: In Basel I founded the Jewish state. If I said this aloud today, I would be answered by universal laughter. Perhaps in five years, certainly in fifty, everyone will agree. The state is already founded, in essence, in the will of the people to be a state."

If anyone should object that the Society of Jews had no electoral mandate to represent the Jewish people, Herzl has a legal argument at the ready. In Roman law, he writes in *The Jewish State*, there is a concept called *negotiorum gestio*, which holds that "when the property of an oppressed person is in danger, any man may step forward to save it. This man is the *gestor*, the director of affairs not strictly his own." The Jewish people are in danger, and they need a *gestor*, an agency that although self-appointed will look after the affairs of the Jews as a whole. This is the role of the Society of Jews, Herzl writes; but beneath this statement lies the inevitable implication that in fact it is Herzl himself who is the *gestor*. It is significant that Herzl found his terminology not in any Jewish source, but in the Roman legal tradition he studied at the University of Vienna. Rather than seeing himself as a successor to the biblical judges, who arose to lead Israel in times of need, he turned to the respectable language of Roman law, which made his mission appear somewhat less messianic.

IF THE SOCIETY OF JEWS is the political representative of the Zionist movement, its practical and economic work will be done by another new organization, which Herzl calls in his pamphlet the Jewish Company. (In 1901, at the fifth Zionist Congress, it would take concrete form as the Jewish National Fund.) The Jewish Company is conceived of as a quasi-official body with a government charter, on the model of the East India Company, under whose auspices Britain took control of India. But since the Jewish Company will be supervising not just the acquisition of land but the mass migration of European Jews, it has a unique mission, which Herzl spends a chapter of *The Jewish State* elaborating in great detail.

The role of the Jewish Company in Herzl's scheme is twofold. First, "it will convert into cash all vested interests left by departing Jews." The mass migration of European Jewry, he recognized, would present a serious economic problem: if millions of Jews had to dispose of their property all at once, it would create a glut on the market, and Jewish real estate and businesses would lose their value. To avoid this situation, the Jewish Company would be a buyer of first resort for Jewish property, which it would continue to manage until it could be profitably sold to Christian buyers. A Jew planning to leave Europe would deed his property to the Company; in exchange, he would receive land in the Jewish state, which the Company would buy in large quantities. Because land in Palestine, especially at first, would be much cheaper than land in Europe, this transaction would be profitable for the Jewish Company.

This plan is premised on the idea that the Jewish Company is not a philanthropic organization, but "strictly a business undertaking." While Herzl entrusts the Company with a great deal of responsibility for the new state—in addition to acquiring land, it is to build housing, run labor exchanges, and generally create an economy from scratch—he does not believe any of this can be accomplished by mere goodwill. The whole enterprise can only get started, Herzl calculates, if the Jewish Company has a huge amount of operating capital—he offers an estimate of fifty million pounds—and the only way to raise it is to promise a return on investment. "The promoters and stock holders of the Jewish Company are . . . expected to do a good piece of business," he emphasizes. Capitalism will provide the motive force that turns the wheels of Herzl's utopian machinery.

The easiest way to raise such a large amount of capital, Herzl writes, would be to sell shares in the company to "great Jewish financiers," like Hirsch or the Rothschilds. But by the time he wrote *The Jewish State*, Herzl had already learned that it was precisely these Jewish magnates who had the least interest in Zionism. They themselves had succeeded in Gentile society on a grand scale, and they feared that Zionism would undermine that precarious acceptance. Thus Herzl offers a contingency plan: the money for the Jewish Company could also be raised by public subscription, selling shares to the Jewish masses. (With his characteristic realism, he adds that "not only poor Jews, but also Christians who wanted to get rid of them, would subscribe a small amount to this fund.")

But if he is ostentatiously practical about money matters, at the same time *The Jewish State* gives Herzl a chance to allow his dramaturgical imagination to run free. Though he denies that his plan is a utopia, he shares with all utopia-builders a certain glee in inventing a new society, down to its smallest details. Among the topics Herzl addresses in the pamphlet are the design of the dwellings in the new state ("detached houses in little gardens will be united into attractive groups"), the clothing to be worn by immigrants ("even the new clothing of the poor settlers will have the symbolic meaning, 'You are now entering on a new life'"), and the age of marriage ("we shall have no delicate offspring of late marriages").

When it comes to more important cultural issues, however, Herzl can be oddly casual. He is well aware of the importance of symbols— for instance, he offers a design for the new state's flag, since "if we desire to lead many men, we must raise a symbol above their heads." But it is remarkable that his design—a white field with seven golden stars, to represent the progressive seven-hour work day—has no Jewish reference whatever. (The flag actually adopted by the Zionist movement, of course, would feature a Star of David.) Similarly, he dismisses the idea that the language of the new Jewish state should be a Jewish language: "Who amongst us has a sufficient acquaintance with Hebrew to ask for a railway ticket in that language? Such a thing cannot be done." And though he is talking about founding a state on the basis of religion, he envisions no particular role for religion in the state: "Every man will be as free and undisturbed in his faith or his disbelief as he is in his nationality."

These elisions of what would turn out to be crucial issues in the actual development of the State of Israel can be taken as mere blind spots, resulting from Herzl's essentially secular point of view. Yet they are equally owed to his estimate of the scale and timeframe of the

Jewish emigration. Herzl did not envision a decades-long process of pioneering, fueled by intense ideological commitment, which would result in the creation of a distinctively new Jewish culture. Rather, he imagined a practically instantaneous transplantation of almost all of Europe's Jews into a ready-built new society. Any country created in this way would inevitably be polyglot in language and European in culture. And in any case, wasn't the nineteenth century the first age of globalization? After all, Herzl writes, "there are English hotels in Egypt... Viennese cafes in South Africa, French theaters in Russia, German operas in America, and the best Bavarian beer in Paris." Why shouldn't the Jewish state be just as happily multicultural? "Every man will find his customs again... but they will be better, more beautiful, and more agreeable than before," Herzl promises.

THE PUBLICATION OF *The Jewish State* in 1896 launched Herzl on a whirlwind career as a Zionist speaker, organizer, and diplomat. Even as he held down a full-time job as an editor at the *Neue Freie Presse*—which refused as a matter of policy even to mention the word Zionism, much less cover Herzl's activities—he crisscrossed Europe, trying to put his plan into action. Within a remarkably short period of time, he managed to gain access to the highest corridors of power, lobbying kings and prime ministers to support Zionism. It is a sign of how urgent the Jewish question had become that even a self-appointed figure like Herzl could be accepted as the recognized spokesman for the Jewish people, by Jews and non-Jews alike. In his travels in eastern Europe, in particular, emotional crowds hailed him as a messiah and a king. Herzl made Zionism a serious actor on the world stage—the greatest achievement of his career as a dramatist.

But for all of Herzl's successes, the actual creation of a Jewish state still seemed unlikely. Many of the European leaders he spoke with professed support of Zionism, seeing it as a possible solution to their own countries' Jewish problems. But only the sultan of the Ottoman Empire had the power to grant the Jews the legal right to settle in Palestine; and this he refused to do, despite prolonged wooing and the payment of numerous bribes to his underlings. None of the European powers, for all their talk, were prepared to commit their diplomatic influence to changing the sultan's mind. Indeed, if for some reason the sultan had suddenly agreed to Herzl's proposals, it would have put Herzl in an embarrassing position, since his plan required enormous funds that the Zionist movement did not possess and had no real prospect of securing. The Zionist Congress continued to meet every year, and the number of Zionist clubs and organizations worldwide skyrocketed, but Zion itself remained stubbornly out of reach. Not until 1917, when the British conquered Palestine from the Ottomans, would the Zionist movement achieve the official great-power support Herzl longed for, in the form of the Balfour Declaration.

By 1902, Herzl was in poor health and deeply discouraged, though still fully committed to the cause. Idealistically, if unreasonably, he had imagined that by this time the mass movement of Jews to Palestine would be well under way. It now began to seem as though he would not live to see his hopes fulfilled. But if he had to imagine the Jewish state, he could at least do so publicly, in a form that would itself be a contribution to the Zionist movement. Instead of a play, this time Herzl decided to write a novel, which would return to the outline sketched in *The Jewish State* and bring it to life. The title of the book, *Altneuland*, or *Old New Land*, captured the twin impulses behind Herzl's dream: the fulfillment of an ancient Jewish hope combined with the achievement of an unprecedentedly modern society.

In literary terms, *Old New Land* has never been rated very highly. Like Nachman of Bratslav, Herzl turned to fiction to communicate truth in a more palatable form—in this case, not truths of Torah but political truths. Unlike Nachman, however, he did not raise his didacticism to the level of art. The characters in Herzl's novel tend to have a single quality each, and the plot can be quickly summarized: a young Viennese Jew, tired of life, retires to a desert island for twenty years, and when he returns he finds that Palestine has been transformed from a desert into a thriving Jewish society. Much of the novel comprises speeches by various inhabitants of that society, explaining its history and inner workings, and it is these explanations that are clearly the book's reason for being.

Before he gets to the Palestine of the future, however, Herzl offers a knowingly acidic portrait of the European Jewish society of the present. The main character in *Old New Land*, Friedrich Loewenberg, is a young Jewish lawyer in Vienna who suffers from severe *Weltschmerz*. He is disgusted by his café companions, disappointed that his beloved has gotten engaged to a richer man, and frustrated in his career. Above all, Herzl makes clear, it is the false position of the Jews in Austrian society that is responsible for Loewenberg's unhappiness. Herzl describes Vienna's bourgeois Jews—the people he himself lived among—as cynical, materialistic, and filled with unacknowledged self-hatred. In an early scene at a dinner party, a rabbi happens to mention Zionism to a group of these assimilated Jews, and they respond with laughter and contempt. "Whom are you mocking, gentlemen?" the rabbi asks meekly. "Yourselves?" The Jews of his time are so demoralized, Herzl suggests, that the very idea of Jews leading a free and dignified existence sounds like a joke to them. In this scene we can surely hear the echo of all the insults and jokes directed against Herzl himself by anti-Zionist Jews.

"If you are a Jew, you might as well throw yourself into the Danube," says a starving Jewish peddler, Littwak, whom Loewenberg meets at his café. He is contemplating just that when he comes across an unusual want ad in the newspaper. A rich man, Kingscourt, is advertising for a companion to join him in permanent exile on a desert island. Kingscourt was born a Prussian nobleman, then emigrated to America and made a fortune there, but his misanthropy has made him yearn to leave the human race behind. Loewenberg gladly agrees to throw his life away in this manner, and the two men set sail for the

South Seas. Before he goes, Kingscourt gives Loewenberg a large sum of money, which he bestows on the Littwaks, hoping to rescue at least one Jewish family from despair.

En route to their island, Kingscourt and Loewenberg decide to stop over in Palestine. There is no real novelistic reason for this, except to give Herzl a chance to describe the poor state of the country in 1902. In writing these passages, he drew on his memories of his one and only trip to Palestine, a brief visit in 1898 when he went to meet the German emperor in Jerusalem. Like so many nineteenth-century travelers to the Holy Land, Herzl was appalled by the poverty, disease, and dirt that he found there. "Jerusalem by daylight was less alluring," he writes in *Old New Land*. "Shouting, odors, a flurry of dirty colors, crowds of ragged people in narrow, musty lanes, beggars, sick people, hungry children, screeching women, shouting tradesmen. The once royal city of Jerusalem could have sunk no lower."

The travelers quickly depart for the Pacific. When the next chapter begins, twenty years have passed and they are on their way back to Europe—again, less for any internal reason than because of the necessities of Herzl's scheme. Their first hint that something has changed in the interim is the sight of the Suez Canal practically empty of passenger ships. The reason, they learn, is that traffic between Europe and Asia now passes through the extensive, up-to-date railroad network in Palestine. Intrigued, they decide to visit the country and find out what has happened to transform it.

No sooner are they off the boat than Loewenberg is spotted by a stranger and tearfully embraced. It turns out to be David Littwak, the young son of the peddler to whom Loewenberg had given the money before leaving Vienna. The Littwaks used the funds to move to Palestine, where David is now a rich man and a leading citizen of what he calls the New Society. The rest of the book is largely made up of David leading Loewenberg and Kingscourt on a guided tour of Palestine, showing off wonder after wonder—beautiful cities, thriving farms, scientific research institutes, a canal connecting the Mediterranean and the Dead Sea. In the process, Herzl even proves a kind of technological prophet, describing inventions like radio and air conditioning before they had come into common use. Much of this part of the book anticipates socialist realism, with its idealized vision of workers and their tools, and can be summed up by saying that Palestine, under Jewish sovereignty, has changed from a third world country to a first world country.

"The Jewish settlers who streamed into the country," Herzl writes, "had brought with them the experience of the whole civilized world." Indeed, one of the key points he wants to make in *Old New Land* is that most of the technical innovations needed for an ideal society already exist in the world of 1902. The problem in Europe is that history—centuries of outmoded technology, bad city planning, and class conflict—prevents people from starting over with these new tools. Palestine, for Herzl, is a blank slate where a society can be built rationally, from scratch—for instance, by using clean electric railroads instead of the smoky old coal engines. "There was one of the advantages of having begun from the beginning," he writes. "Just because everything here had been in a primitive, neglected state, it had been possible to install the most up-to-date technical appliances at once." Herzl is never more a man of his age than in his virtually unlimited faith in technological progress: "The real founders of Old New Land . . . were the hydraulic engineers," David Littwak remarks.

But it is not only technology that is cutting-edge in Palestine. Economically, too, Herzl imagines a society that draws on the most up-to-date ideas. For him, this means a form of syndicalism, or what he calls "mutualism," in which business is organized in a series of producer and consumer cooperatives. Private land ownership is forbidden, and land is acquired only on a forty-nine-year lease; in the fiftieth year it reverts to the government, in Herzl's variation on the biblical institution of the Jubilee Year, which canceled all debts and land transfers every fifty years. This system, which to Herzl combines the best features of capitalism and socialism, leaves no room for small traders or peddlers: "We did not want to be a nation of shopkeepers," David explains. Journalism, too—Herzl's own profession—is organized on a cooperative basis, with newspaper subscribers as shareholders. As a result, the vices of that business are also stamped out, and newspapers "work unceasingly to broaden the education of the public." Notably, both peddling and journalism were occupations closely associated with Jews in Herzl's Vienna. Herzl goes out of his way to emphasize that in his new Jewish society these functions will be transformed and their stigma removed.

Old New Land speaks of a New Society, not a new state. In this, it is a pointed departure from Herzl's program in *The Jewish State* a few years earlier. His dealings with the Ottoman Turks and other great powers had left him convinced that an independent, sovereign state in Palestine might never come to be. The Jewish homeland might have to take the form of a protectorate or an autonomous province instead. In the novel, Herzl explains that the New Society was formed by a "colonization treaty" with the Turkish government, but he leaves the details vague (though he names the amount of tribute paid to the Turks—two million pounds—perhaps to pique the interest of the sultan). Likewise, he nowhere actually specifies the borders of the Jewish colony. The main cities are Haifa and Jerusalem, but there are references to Damascus and the east bank of the Jordan River as well.

These are not the only contentious issues Herzl manages to glide over. In *The Jewish State*, he had made practically no mention of the Arab population of Palestine. In *Old New Land*, they make an appearance in the form of Reschid Bey, who is one of David Littwak's closest friends. Reschid is in the novel primarily to show that the Arabs, far from resenting the Jews' presence, are deeply grateful to them for all the economic benefits they brought to Palestine. When Kingscourt asks whether the "Moslems" regard the Jews as "intruders," he replies: "Would you call a man a robber who takes nothing from you, but brings you something instead? The Jews have enriched us. Why should we be angry with them? They dwell among us like brothers. Why should we not love them?"

This amity is owed to the fact that the New Society, though it is obviously made up of Jews, is not a Jewish entity. Members of the New Society are not citizens of a state but paid subscribers, and it appears to be possible to live in Palestine without being part of the New Society. Herzl makes clear that people of any religion and ethnicity can join, and he envisions no tensions among the different communities—Jewish, Muslim, Christian. Indeed, the closest thing to actual politics that we are allowed to see in *Old New Land* is an election dispute between Littwak, who represents the party of multicultural tolerance, and one Geyer, who is a vague kind of Jewish nationalist. In a scene set in the village of Neudorf—the towns in this Jewish country have German names—Littwak debates a supporter of Geyer's who is motivated less by ethnic or religious chauvinism than by a desire to keep out new economic competitors: "What we made with our own hands must remain ours," he cries. However, Littwak easily trounces this opponent with a long speech in which he praises the economic and social benefits of tolerance: "Our slogan must be, now and always: 'Man, thou art my brother!'" At the end of the book, Geyer's party is totally defeated in the election, leaving the sense that it never posed much of a threat to Herzl's harmonious vision. It is the absence of conflict from Herzl's New Society that marks it as the utopia he had once sworn to avoid.

~~~

THE CHARACTERS IN *Old New Land* are each assigned a cosily happy ending. Kingscourt, the misanthrope, has his icy heart melted by David Littwak's infant son and becomes the boy's doting companion. Loewenberg, who lost the woman he loved in Vienna, wins David's sister Miriam as a wife in Palestine. And David himself, the starving pauper, ends up being elected president of the New Society—

news he shares with his mother on her deathbed. (In an inadvertently comic touch, David initially wants to refuse the office but is forced to accept because it will make his mother happy.)

These individual redemptions, however, are less significant than the redemption of the Jewish character, which once again Herzl sees as the great spiritual achievement of Zionism. Early in the book, Herzl shows the Jews of Vienna laughing at Zionism; it is only Kingscourt, a Gentile, who sees its heroic potential. When Loewenberg disavows any interest in Palestine, Kingscourt rebukes him: "If I were in your place, I'd do something bold, something big, something that would make my enemies gape. . . . The more I think of it, the more it seems to me that it must be quite interesting to be a Jew these days. Just because one has the whole world against him." By painting the future of Palestine in such glowing colors, Herzl hopes to inspire this spirit of defiant adventure in his Jewish readers. Building the New Society is just the antidote they need for their inferiority complex.

In the later part of the novel, then, the transformation of the landscape of Palestine mirrors the transformation of the spirit of its inhabitants. David Littwak, who goes from beggar to president, is the most obvious example. "So this was the Jewboy beggar!" Loewenberg reflects. "A free, healthy, cultured man who gazed steadfastly upon the world and seemed to stand firmly in his own shoes." Later, David observes that "Jewish children used to be pale, weak, timid. Now look at them! . . . We took our children out of damp cellars and hovels, and brought them into the sunlight." The curative sunlight of Palestine is not just physical, but spiritual. Liberated from demoralizing anti-Semitism, the Jews will flourish into proud, self-sufficient human beings.

Not every single Jew in the novel turns into a paragon, however. In a scene set at a Haifa opera house, Loewenberg reencounters the snobbish, cynical Jews he knew in Vienna, and he finds them not much improved. But they are the exceptions, and their presence in the New Society allows the reader to gauge how far the Jewish people as a whole have progressed. Crucially, too, these "bad" Jews no longer shape the

Gentile world's ideas of what Jews are like. "Fops, upstarts, bejeweled women used to be regarded as representative Jews," one character tells Kingscourt. "Now people realize that there are other types of Jews also." The acute self-consciousness of European Jews, always feeling that the eyes of the non-Jewish world are upon them, has dissolved now that the Jews are at home among themselves.

One symptom of this new confidence is that the Jews can return to their ancestral religion without fear or shame. "What a degraded era that was," Loewenberg reflects late in *Old New Land*, "when the Jews had been ashamed of everything Jewish, when they thought they made a better showing when they concealed their Jewishness." However, when it comes to religion itself—to Judaism, rather than Jews—Herzl's attitude can be described as at best a kind of dispassionate benevolence. Herzl knew little about Judaism when he began his career as a Zionist. During one visit to a synagogue, he wrote in his diary, he was asked to recite the Hebrew blessings before the Torah reading, and the prospect made him more nervous than delivering a speech at the Zionist Congress. By the time he wrote *Old New Land*, he had come to recognize that the Jewish religion was an essential part of Jewish unity. Accordingly, he imagines the New Society living on a Jewish calendar: the roads empty out on Shabbat, and the schools go on vacation for Passover. A key scene in the novel takes place at Littwak's Passover Seder, where Loewenberg, hearing the "ancient, melodramatic words" of the Haggadah, feels reconnected with his childhood: "At this Seder table he seemed to himself a prodigal son, returned to his own people."

Most momentously of all, Herzl envisions the rebuilding of the Temple in Jerusalem. Yet the way in which he writes about this Temple is suggestive of how little his understanding of Judaism had to do with the traditional one. Herzl's description of the Third Temple echoes Josephus's description of Herod's Temple: "that wonderful structure of white and gold, whose roof rested on a whole forest of marble columns with gilt capitals." But this structure has clearly not been erected on the same site as the earlier Temple, since Herzl also writes that "the Mosque of Omar" on the Temple Mount remains standing. And while the new Temple features a "mighty bronze altar," it does not seem as if animal sacrifices are taking place there. In short, Herzl's Temple bears no relationship to the one pious Jews believed would be restored in messianic times; and Herzl displays no awareness that such an ersatz Temple might be looked upon by true believers as blasphemous.

Tellingly, while Herzl says little about the Temple in *Old New Land*, he lavishes several paragraphs on another grand structure in the new Jerusalem, "the splendid Peace Palace." This is described as half Red Cross, half United Nations. "International congresses of peace-lovers and scientists" are held there, and it also serves as a clearinghouse for "emergency relief" for victims of disasters "anywhere in the world." Over the door of the Peace Palace a Latin motto is inscribed: *Nihil humani a me alienum puto*, "Let nothing human be alien to me." This tag from the Roman playwright Terence, not any Hebrew phrase from the Bible, captures Herzl's grand ambitions for the New Society. In redeeming themselves, he imagines, the Jews of Palestine will simultaneously demonstrate to the whole world a new way of living. The lessons of the New Society can be applied everywhere. In one striking passage, Herzl suggests that African Americans might follow the Jews in returning from Diaspora. "Now that I have lived to see the restoration of the Jews, I should like to pave the way for the restoration of the Negroes," one character announces. For it is only in their own nation that any people can achieve full humanity: "All human beings ought to have a home. Then they will be kinder to one another."

Three thousand years earlier, the book of Deuteronomy records, the Israelites had stood on the bank of the Jordan River and received God's promise of a homeland. Now, after all the vicissitudes and achievements of those millennia—after creating new forms of Judaism and new ways of life in every land from Babylonia to Spain to Poland—Herzl was renewing that promise. But his Zionism was no atavism, no return to the conditions and beliefs of the past. On the contrary, he believed that it was only by making the difficult passage to modernity that the Jews of Europe had gained the technical skills and political insight necessary to regain their state. The dialectic of history had brought the Jews back to the Land of Israel, but it had changed what the Land of Israel would mean to them: not spiritual redemption, not the coming of the Messiah, not even divine chosenness, but simply the chance to enjoy the rights due to every people. Religion would exist in the Jewish state, Herzl imagined, as a cross between a civic ritual and a historical inspiration; but the state itself was a secular achievement. "Only here," Herzl writes, "had the Jews built up a free commonwealth in which they could strive for the loftiest human aims."

Yet even Herzl finally finds it impossible to excise God completely from his vision of the Promised Land. At the end of *Old New Land*, Friedrich Loewenberg asks the various friends he has made in Palestine how they account for its success. "We see a new and happy form of human society here. What created it?" They respond with a chorus of answers, each of which, Herzl suggests, contains part of the truth. "Necessity," "knowledge," and "will power," say some; "the forces of nature" or "the new means of transportation," say others. But the rabbi among them gives a different answer: "God!" It is the novel's last word.

BIBLIOGRAPHY

Avineri, Shlomo. *Herzl's Vision: Theodor Herzl and the Foundation of the Jewish State*. Katonah, NY: BlueBridge, 2014.

Elon, Amos. *Herzl*. New York: Holt Rinehart and Winston, 1975.

Herzl, Theodor. *The Jewish State*. Translated by Sylvie d'Avigdor. New York: Dover Books, 1988.

Herzl, Theodor. *Old New Land*. Translated by Lotte Levensohn. New York: M. Wiener, 1997.

14

ON THE
BRINK

Tevye the Dairyman
by Sholem Aleichem

At the turn of the twentieth century, Sholem Aleichem was the most beloved Yiddish writer in the world. His most famous creation—thanks in large part to the musical *Fiddler on the Roof*—is Tevye, an everyman who, in his vivid speech and deep feeling, captured the spirit of Eastern European Jewry. In a series of stories written before the First World War, Sholem Aleichem used Tevye and his daughters to explore the profound challenges that modernity was bringing to the Jewish world—from individualism to revolutionary politics to official persecution. The Tevye stories offer a record of a Jewish world on the brink, about to undergo tragedies and transformations that would permanently change the shape of Jewish life.

SHOLEM RABINOVICH SPENT THE SUMMER OF 1894 IN his favorite vacation spot, a dacha in the small town of Boyarka, an hour's train ride from Kiev. He was thirty-five years old and not nearly as rich as he had once been: after marrying a wealthy businessman's daughter, he had inherited a fortune, and he lived the high life for several years before stock-market reverses nearly wiped him out. But summering in Boyarka showed that he was still a bourgeois in good standing—certainly much better off than the small tradesmen and farmers who made their homes there and who supplied the visitors with food and provisions. That fall, Rabinovich—who was better known to the Yiddish-speaking world under his nom de plume, Sholem Aleichem, a common Yiddish greeting—wrote to an editor that he was planning a new story. He insisted that he had not invented the story, simply written it down as he had heard it from a certain local dairy farmer: "I heard the story from Tevye himself as he stood in front of my dacha with his horse and cart, weighing out butter and cheese. The story is interesting, but Tevye himself is a thousand times more interesting!"

Early the next year, "The Great Windfall" appeared in a Yiddish anthology, and Sholem Aleichem's greatest character was born. Much of the charm of the tale comes from the way the author preserves the illusion that we are, in fact, hearing the voice of a real person. The story takes the form of an anecdote told by Tevye to Sholem Aleichem, and it is possible that it was inspired by something the real Tevye said. But, of course, it is Sholem Aleichem himself who has created the turns of phrase and quirks of character that bring Tevye so convincingly to life. The end of the tale insists on this paradox: "Don't write about me in any of your books, and if you do, don't mention my name," Tevye implores the writer, but it is only in and through the book that Tevye exists in the first place.

Over the next twenty years, Sholem Aleichem would produce eight more Tevye stories. Altogether, they take up no more than 120 pages; yet no work of Yiddish literature has been more influential or more widely loved. Thanks to a series of stage and film adaptations—most famously, the 1964 musical *Fiddler on the Roof*—Tevye has been transformed into an Askhenazi Everyman, a symbol of the life lived by generations of eastern European Jews. But the Tevye stories are not folk literature. Indeed, the closer one looks at these seemingly familiar tales, the clearer it becomes that they are strikingly modern works, products of a moment of acute crisis in Jewish history.

If there is one thing everybody remembers about Tevye, it is that he is the father of daughters. Exactly how many varies from one story to the next, but five of them feature as major characters in the cycle. In the first Tevye story, however, the children are an afterthought; they are mentioned only as an economic burden, since they are daughters who will one day need dowries. "If each child were worth, as my wife Golde tells me, a million, I'd be richer than the richest man in Yehupetz," Tevye complains, using Sholem Aleichem's comic pseudonym for the city of Kiev. Instead, when the story begins, Tevye is one of the poorest Jews in the area, hauling logs for a few pennies a day and struggling to feed his starving brood. Indeed, for Tevye, poverty and Jewishness are virtually synonymous: "A Jew must hope, must keep on hoping," he insists. "So what if he goes under in the meantime? What better reason is there for being a Jew?" The note of bitterness in this profession of hope is unmistakable and will become more pronounced as the Tevye stories evolve.

In his emphasis on rural poverty, Sholem Aleichem was drawing an accurate portrait of Jewish life in eastern Europe at the time. In 1881, the Russian czar Alexander II had been assassinated by a group of radical terrorists known as the People's Will. Though the assassins were not Jewish, government incitement led popular anger to take the form of anti-Jewish pogroms, hundreds of which took place across the region. They were followed in 1882 by the so-called May Laws, which barred Jews from purchasing land and restricted their residence to small towns. These laws resulted in mass overcrowding and impoverishment among Jews in the Pale of Settlement, the swath of czarist-ruled eastern Europe where they were permitted to live. (Major cities like Kiev were off-limits to all but a few lucky and wealthy Jews, like Sholem Aleichem himself.) One result was a historic surge of emigration of Jews out of eastern Europe: over the next forty years, some two million Jews from Russia, Romania, and Austria-Hungary would leave for America. Another was the first stirrings of Zionist activism and a small but significant movement of Jews to Palestine, where fifty thousand settled before World War I.

In "The Great Windfall," however, the target of Tevye's anger and Sholem Aleichem's polemic is not oppression from without, but class divisions within Jewish society. The irony of the title becomes clear when we learn about the nature of Tevye's windfall, the stroke of good luck that transforms him from a wretched woodcutter to a merely poor dairyman. Driving his wagon in the woods one day, he comes across a pair of women who are visiting Boiberik, as Sholem Aleichem calls Boyarke. The women have gone for a walk and gotten lost, and Tevye agrees to drive them back to their dacha. When he arrives, he realizes that they belong to a rich family from Yehupetz; and the way these wealthy city Jews treat the poor country Jew is simultaneously generous and galling. After bantering with him and laughing at him, the visitors take some money from their pockets and bestow it on Tevye. This amounts to thirty-seven rubles: literally spare change to them, it is for Tevye a life-altering fortune, enabling him to buy a cow and set up as a dairyman. The very casualness of this gift only drives home the huge disparity between rich and poor, as Tevye muses:

> The crumbs that fell off their table would have fed my children for a week, at least till Saturday. God Almighty, compassionate, faithful one, is a great God and a good God, a God of mercy and justice. Why did He grant this one everything and the other nothing? This one got butter rolls, the other the ten plagues. But then I thought I was a great fool. I was giving *Him* advice on how to run the world? Most likely, if He wanted it that way, that was how it should be. The proof was that if it were meant to be otherwise, it would be otherwise. . . . A Jew must exist on hope and faith. He has to believe, above all, that there is a God and he has to have faith in Him who lives forever and hope that someday, with His help, perhaps things will be better.

This passage reveals Sholem Aleichem as a master of tone and ambiguity. It might seem that Tevye is simply repeating the eternal, consoling pieties: trust in God, accept your lot. Yet he also seems conscious that this trust is the meager final resource of the desperate—that a Jew "must exist on hope and faith" because he has nothing better or more tangible to rely on. And like Job, whom Tevye will increasingly resemble as the cycle progresses, his complaint about God's justice is silenced but not really answered by the assertion of God's wisdom. On the brink of the twentieth century, there were other ways of responding to social injustice than pious resignation, as Sholem Aleichem and his readers well knew. With socialism and communism on the rise and Russia heading for revolution, Tevye's passivity was giving way to dangerous new forms of activism.

The second story in the Tevye series, "The Roof Falls In," followed four years later, in 1899. Here Sholem Aleichem has Tevye cross paths with another of his own popular characters, the hapless stock-market speculator Menachem-Mendl, with inevitable results: Tevye hands over his nest egg to be invested, and Menachem-Mendl loses it all. This episode gives Sholem Aleichem an opportunity to expand his indictment of capitalism, which infects even a down-to-earth person like Tevye with idle dreams of making a killing. But riches mean something different to Tevye than they do to the average speculator. While he does dream of buying pearls for his wife and giving his daughters impressive dowries— the kind of dreams shared by Glückel of Hameln two hundred years earlier—Tevye also values money because it would enable him to be a better Jew. For him, being rich would mean giving charity, buying a new roof for the study hall, and having time to study Torah—"to step into the synagogue once in a while and look into a Jewish book."

One thing that sets Tevye apart from just about every other character in these stories is that he preserves the old Jewish veneration for the life of scholarship. Sholem Aleichem suggests that this makes him old-fashioned and a little ridiculous, especially since he is prone to quoting Torah and Talmud at the drop of a hat, often incorrectly and with little connection to the matter at hand. But there is also something deeply admirable about the way Tevye, unlike most of the Jews he meets, still clings to the ideal set forth in *Pirkei Avot* many centuries earlier. In a later story, when Tevye meets with a rich Yehupetz contractor who wants to marry his daughter, he is disgusted when the man admits, "I have never studied the Gemara and don't even know what it looks like." "Can you imagine?" Tevye muses. "One would think that if God had so punished him and made him an ignoramus, he would at least be ashamed and not boast about it."

This encroaching ignorance is one of the key transformations of Jewish society reflected in the Tevye stories. In the modern world, fewer and fewer Jews still know, or care about, the traditional sources of wisdom, whether sacred texts or time-honored customs. This is, of course, the great theme of the five stories that deal with Tevye's daughters, which make up the heart of the cycle. In each of these tales, Sholem Aleichem weighs the traditional power of paternal authority against the modern demand for personal autonomy, and every time the latter wins out. With one exception, Tevye's daughters marry whom they want to marry. Yet none of these matches ends up bringing what Tevye, or the reader, recognizes as simple happiness. The power of the stories lies in Sholem Aleichem's embrace of this tragic paradox: the rebellion of the daughters against the father is necessary and even admirable, yet also destructive, and in one case fatal.

"Today's Children," from 1899, is the first story to pivot from Tevye's financial concerns to his daughters' marital prospects. It is also the funniest and most high-spirited of the tales. When Tevye agrees to give his daughter Tzeitl in marriage to the prosperous butcher Lazer-Wolf, he thinks he is scoring a great coup: the match will lift Tzeitl into a higher economic class, making her life easier than his own has been. Yet even before he hears about Tzeitl's objections—it turns out she has already pledged herself to a poor tailor, Motl Komzoil, against all the principles of feminine modesty—Tevye himself has reservations about Lazer-Wolf. "He had one fault—he was somewhat common. Oh well, could everyone be a scholar?" he asks himself. The same crudeness that alienates Tzeitl from the butcher is perceived by Tevye in traditionally Jewish intellectual terms. Indeed, Tevye's daughters all take after him in their insistence on a certain nobility of spirit—though they define this in their own, defiantly modern ways.

The strategy Tevye uses to get Tzeitl away from Lazer-Wolf is comical: he invents a dream omen in which the ghost of Lazer-Wolf's first wife warns against the match. (The story recalls a similar episode in the life of Solomon Maimon, who played on his mother-in-law's superstitious fear of ghosts.) But by the time Sholem Aleichem came to write the next story in the series, "Hodl," in 1904, the comic elements of Tevye's predicament had disappeared and the tragic ones come to the fore. It was a fraught moment in Russian and Jewish history: the czar's forces were facing defeat by the Japanese, revolutionary sentiment was building across the Empire, and just the year before a terrible pogrom had taken the lives of forty-seven Jews in the town of Kishinev, shocking the conscience of the world. Politics were inescapable, and in "Hodl" Sholem Aleichem shows them overturning Tevye's existence in ways he barely comprehends.

The young student Perchik, known affectionately in Yiddish as Fefferl, "little pepper," appeals to Tevye in all the ways Lazer-Wolf did not: he is brilliant and has a good Jewish education. This matters more to Tevye than the fact that Perchik has turned away from Jewish observance. When he visits the house and fails to wash his hands before the meal, a customary *mitzvah*, Tevye says indulgently, "You can wash your hands or not, it's up to you. I am not God's watchman and will not be punished in the next world for your sins." Perchik wins Tevye over on the strength of his love of high-flown talk, which the two men share: "As I talked with this young fellow, for some reason I felt drawn to him. Maybe it's because I like a person with whom I can talk, with whom I can discuss a biblical commentary, have a philosophical argument, speculate about life, on this, on that."

Once again, Tevye's affection is a good predictor of his daughter's feelings. Hodl, it turns out, has followed Tzeitl's example by pledging herself to Perchik without her father's permission. Worse, she insists on a hurried wedding, without any of the ceremonies or displays of status that a Jewish marriage traditionally involved. The reason for her haste is that Perchik must travel far away, for reasons Hodl will not disclose; and the next we hear of him, he has been arrested and sentenced to exile. It is easy for the reader to put two and two together and figure out what has really happened. We have heard Perchik hold forth on socialism, though without actually using that word, and we know he is a revolutionary involved in some plot against the government. But Sholem Aleichem, in a clever stroke, withholds this knowledge from Tevye, who can't figure it all out. He is ignorant of the political trends that Hodl's generation, and the reader, know so well; he is a man of tradition in an age of revolution. So it is all the more moving when Tevye, against all his inclinations, gives his blessing to Hodl when she declares she is leaving forever to join Perchik in his penal exile. "Those daughters of mine—when they fall in love, it's with body and soul and heart and life itself!" he declares, with mixed chagrin and pride.

It is with Chava, the third daughter and the subject of the next story, that Sholem Aleichem intensifies this irony to the breaking point. In "Chava," written in 1906, one of Tevye's daughters is once again in love with an idealistic intellectual. "Chvedka is a second Gorky," she tells her father, prompting him to ask, "Who then was the first Gorky?" Unlike Tevye, Sholem Aleichem's readers would have known that Maxim Gorky was a revolutionary writer, an associate of Lenin and a strong opponent of anti-Semitism. His name stood for a future in which divisions between Jews and Gentiles would be dissolved in socialist brotherhood. The problem is that Tevye and Chava still live in the real world of czarist Russia, where the fact that Chvedka is Christian presents an insurmountable social and legal obstacle. Neither Jews nor Christians would recognize a "mixed marriage"; for Chava and Chvedka to be united, one of them would have to convert. And this is just what Chava does, clandestinely, at the price of being cut off from her family forever.

Conversion, of course, is the ultimate challenge to both paternal authority and Jewish tradition. In sitting shiva for his daughter, performing the rites of mourning as if she were actually dead, Tevye affirms the boundaries of Jewishness, which must remain fixed even in an era of change. But the emotional power of the story comes from the way Tevye allows himself to question and test those boundaries even as he enforces them. In the first story, "The Great Windfall," Tevye had wondered why God divided the human race into rich and poor. Now we see Chava, who like her sisters is a true reflection of her father, expanding that question in explosive ways. "You have a quotation for everything," she tells Tevye. "Maybe you can find one about how people separated themselves into Jews and Gentiles, into masters and slaves, into landowners and beggars?" In these years of revolutionary flux, every kind of distinction is up for grabs, and the new generation is not satisfied with the old answers. When Tevye replies, "Because that's the way God created it," Chava retorts, "Why did he create it like that?" God himself is brought before the bar of human reason; the process of enlightenment that began with Spinoza in Amsterdam and Mendelssohn in Berlin has now penetrated even to the village of Boiberik.

Sholem Aleichem allows Chava's question to linger, coloring the reader's reaction to everything that follows. When Tevye confronts the priest who has facilitated his daughter's conversion, his impotent fury is that of generations of powerless Jews in Christian societies. But when Tevye, returning home in his wagon, sees Chava in the woods—in a mysterious scene that may be merely a vision born of his longing—he allows himself to wonder whether the division between Christian and Jew is really more important than the bond between father and child. This humanistic impulse is consistent with everything we know about Tevye—his family loyalty, his instinctive tolerance, his strong emotions (which he keeps in check with the catchphrase "Tevye is not a woman!"). "And all sorts of strange thoughts came to my mind," Sholem Aleichem writes. "What did it mean to be a Jew, and what did it mean to be a non-Jew? And why did God create Jews and non-Jews, and why were they so set apart from one another, unable to get along, as if one had been created by God and the other not? To my regret, not being as learned as others in books and religious texts, I could not find an answer to these questions."

Tevye remains touchingly certain that Jewish tradition has the answer, if only he knew enough about it. Here again, Sholem Aleichem wrings pathos from the way the reader understands more than Tevye does. For the real problem is that in the modern world, the tradition itself no longer has the authority to banish doubt. The very distinction between Jew and non-Jew, which has been at the core of Judaism from the moment Abraham received the covenant, can no longer defend itself in the mind and the heart of modern people. Chava's conversion, in her own eyes, is simply the choice of love and idealism over cruelty and hidebound tradition; and the pain Tevye suffers over their separation offers strong support for this view. *"God is compassionate and good and knows what He is doing!"* Tevye rages at Golde after Chava's disappearance. But the seed of doubt that was already planted in "The Great Windfall" has blossomed, and there is no going back.

This desperation drives the story to its bizarre, almost postmodern conclusion. Sometimes, Tevye confides in Sholem Aleichem, he is overcome by the desire to visit Chava, and he goes to the railway station and asks for a ticket. "He asks, 'Where to?' I tell him, 'Yehupetz.' He says, 'There's no such place.' I say, 'That's not my fault,' and I turn around and go home." Of course, there is no such place as Yehupetz in the real world, since it is Sholem Aleichem's own creation. But then, Tevye too is his creation. It is as if Tevye has an intuition of his own fictionality, as if he longs to cross the boundary between the real world and the invented one. But this border proves to be even more absolute than the one between Christian and Jew, and Tevye can no more abolish it by imploring his author than by questioning his God.

THE REMAINING THREE STORIES in the Tevye sequence are, inevitably, less powerful than "Chava." But they extend Sholem Aleichem's critical portrait of his Jewish society in significant ways. "Shprintze," the slightest and most melodramatic of the five daughter stories, seems to start out as a reprise of "Today's Children." Shprintze, like Tzeitl before her, falls in love on her own initiative, against the traditions of matchmaking. But while Tzeitl loved a modest tailor, Shprintze has the bad luck to fall for Ahronchik, a rich and feckless young man who first proposes to her and then abandons her under pressure from his relatives. Once again, Sholem Aleichem insists on the arrogance and cruelty of the rich toward their fellow Jews: the scene in which Ahronchik's uncle offers to bribe Tevye is a stinging portrait of this contempt. Heartbroken, Shprintze drowns herself, a victim of the new freedom just as Tzeitl was its beneficiary. This story shows Sholem Aleichem at his most conservative: surely the old ways were better than such wayward romanticism.

But Sholem Aleichem is too subtle a writer to be content with such a conclusion; and in the next story, "Tevye Is Going to Eretz Yisroel," written in 1909, he turns it on its head. Now, at last, it seems Tevye has found a dutiful daughter—Beilke, his fifth, who agrees to an arranged marriage. She is motivated strictly by the filial loyalty so lacking in her sisters. Podhotsur, the intended groom, is a rich contractor who will be able to ensure a comfortable old age for Tevye. Once again, Tevye and his daughter have the same judgment of the suitor: they both despise him as a vulgarian and a show-off. But when Tevye tries to convince Beilke not to go through with the marriage, she waves away his protests. The roles have been reversed: now Tevye is the spokesman for idealism and love, while Beilke, who has lived through the failure of the 1905 Revolution, belongs to a cynical generation. "Don't compare me to Hodl," she says. "Hodl lived at a time when the whole world was in chaos ... and people were worrying about that and forgetting themselves. But now that the world is calm again, everyone is worried about himself, and they've forgotten about the world."

Predictably, however, this tough-minded self-sacrifice turns out to backfire. When Beilke returns from her honeymoon, she is as miserable as she expected to be. But Tevye, too, ends up paying a price. Ashamed of having a lowly dairyman as his father-in-law, Podhotsur offers to pay Tevye to move to Palestine and disappear. "All old Jews go to Eretz Yisroel," he says brutally. Sholem Aleichem was a Zionist and an admirer of Theodor Herzl; but this is no Zionist pilgrimage, and Tevye is too old to be a pioneer of the Jewish state. If he goes to the Holy Land, it will be to die, in the same way generations of pious Jews hoped to see Israel before their deaths.

Yet even this melancholy exile is out of reach for Tevye, as we learn in the last two stories, which are also the most despairing. "Get Thee Gone" takes its title from the Torah portion that recounts God's initial command to Abraham: "Get thee gone from thy land and from thy father's house and go to the land which I will show thee." But writing in 1914, Sholem Aleichem sees no possibility of escape and renewal for the Jews of eastern Europe. Tevye, it turns out, has not gone to Palestine after all; he was forced to stay at home to help Tzeitl's family after her husband died of tuberculosis. (Sholem Aleichem himself had suffered from the same disease for years and would die in 1916, at the age of fifty-seven.)

And the condition of the Jews of Boiberik is worse than ever. The story makes repeated mention of Mendel Beiliss, a Jewish man who had been accused of ritually murdering a Christian child in Kiev in 1913. "And even if we had, God forbid, nothing," Tevye says, "we are still better off than Mendel Beiliss!" But Tevye isn't, really, since he turns out to be a victim of the same hatred. The Gentiles of the village—his longtime neighbors and acquaintances, people he knew and trusted—arrive en masse in front of Tevye's house with a message: "We have come here, Tevel, to beat you up." Tevye tries to dissuade them, but they insist: "Since everywhere else people are getting beaten up, why should we let you get away without it?" When he at least convinces them not to burn down his house—instead, the mob breaks all his windows—Tevye congratulates himself: "Is Tevye right when he says we have a powerful God?"

The question is dripping with sarcasm, and it marks the moment when Sholem Aleichem moves from melancholy questioning of God to outright bitterness against him. From the first story in the Tevye series, Sholem Aleichem had shown that Tevye's embrace of God was a last resort: the worse his fate, the more ardently he clung to the maker of that fate, because there was nothing else to cling to. But by the time of World War I, it had never been clearer that God was powerless, or at least that he refused to use his power on behalf of his people. With escape to America temporarily blocked and Palestine still a small colony under Turkish rule, the millions of Jews living in eastern Europe were stuck in the middle of a war zone. The "get thee gone" of the Bible had been God's promise, but the "get thee gone" facing the Jews of eastern Europe was a threat, and it led to a dead end.

"We will go wherever our eyes take us, wherever all Jews go!" Tevye tells Tzeitl. "What will be for all the children of Israel will be for us." This proved to be an all-too-accurate prophecy, in ways that Sholem Aleichem could never have imagined. For, in fact, the Tevye stories manage to survey all the possible futures for the Jews of his time. There is America: we learn that Podhotsur and Beilke move to New York after they lose all their money and are forced to start over as manual laborers. Clearly, for Sholem Aleichem, America was not yet the new Promised Land it would become in the Jewish imagination. (This jaded view was partly owing to the failure of his own attempts to become a successful playwright in New York.) Then there is Palestine, where Tevye almost went. Had he made it there, he would have joined the Second Aliyah, the wave of immigrants inspired by Herzlian Zionism who laid the foundations for the State of Israel. And there is also the path of Communism, represented by

Hodl and Perchik. For millions of Jews, Soviet Communism would be at once a destroyer of Jewish culture and religion, and a protector of Jewish lives.

But the fate that looms over most of Tevye's family and friends, over all the Jews of Boiberik and Yehupetz and beyond, is the Holocaust. Theodor Herzl had predicted that life in Europe would get worse for the Jews, and Sholem Aleichem showed how desperate the situation was becoming; but never in their worst nightmares could they have guessed what the future held. On September 29 and 30, 1941, the German forces occupying Kiev murdered the entire Jewish population of the city, more than thirty-three thousand people, by shooting them in the ravine of Babi Yar. If Tzeitl had been real—as real as Tevye was when he tried to buy a ticket to Yehupetz—she and her children would have been among them.

The Tevye stories, then, carry us to the very brink of the Jewish world we inhabit today. For the Holocaust, the State of Israel, and the emergence of American Jewry define the constellation of Judaism in the twenty-first century. They set the terms of our thinking about God and providence, peoplehood and sovereignty, assimilation and chosenness, catastrophe and redemption. These themes, however, are not creations of the modern world. On the contrary, to read the books that have defined Jewish history is to realize that all these issues have been part of Judaism since the very beginning. The Jews of Alexandria in Philo's time, as well as the Jews of Spain in Yehuda Halevi's time, knew the challenge of remaining distinctive while still participating in the culture that surrounded them. The Jews who lived through the fall of Jerusalem, with Josephus, knew what it meant to redefine the terms of their faith after an unimaginable disaster shattered the basis for that faith. And the Jews who stood with Moses on the banks of the Jordan, in the book of Deuteronomy—like the Jews who followed Theodor Herzl to Basel two thousand years later—struggled to define their relationship to a land they had never seen, yet believed was their home. In the long perspective of Jewish history, our own era—which appears so unique and in some ways really is unique—can be seen as offering a new formulation of these ancient questions. If the answers keep changing while the questions keep being asked, what is this but a sign that the story of Judaism has not yet reached its conclusion?

BIBLIOGRAPHY

Dauber, Jeremy. *The Worlds of Sholem Aleichem*. New York: Nextbook/Schocken, 2013.

Sholem Aleichem. *Tevye the Dairyman and Motl the Cantor's Son*. Translated by Aliza Shevrin. New York: Penguin, 2009.

Index

Page numbers in *italics* refer to maps and illustrations.